HEALTH, ILLNESS, AND SOCIETY

An Introduction to Medical Sociology

STEVEN E. BARKAN

University of Maine

ROWMAN & LITTLEFIELD

Lanham • Boulder • New York • London

Executive Editor: Nancy Roberts
Associate Editor: Molly White
Senior Marketing Manager: Karin Cholak
Marketing Manager: Deborah Hudson
Interior Designer: Ilze Lemesis
Cover Designer: Sally Rinehart

Credits and acknowledgments borrowed from other sources and reproduced, with permission, in this textbook appear on appropriate page within the text.

Published by Rowman & Littlefield
A wholly owned subsidiary of The Rowman & Littlefield Publishing Group, Inc.
4501 Forbes Boulevard, Suite 200, Lanham, Maryland 20706
www.rowman.com

Unit A, Whitacre Mews, 26-34 Stannary Street, London SE11 4AB, United Kingdom

British Library Cataloguing in Publication Information Available

Library of Congress Cataloging-in-Publication Data

Names: Barkan, Steven E., 1951– author.
Title: Health, illness, and society : an introduction to medical sociology / Steven E. Barkan.
Description: Lanham : Rowman & Littlefield, [2017] | Includes bibliographical references and index.
Identifiers: LCCN 2016017185 (print) | LCCN 2016018275 (ebook) | ISBN 9781442234994 (cloth :
    alk. paper) | ISBN 9781442235007 (pbk. : alk. paper) | ISBN 9781442235014 (electronic)
Subjects: | MESH: Delivery of Health Care | Sociological Factors
Classification: LCC RA418 (print) | LCC RA418 (ebook) | NLM W 84.1 | DDC 362.1—dc23
LC record available at https://lccn.loc.gov/2016017185

∞™ The paper used in this publication meets the minimum requirements of American National Standard for Information Sciences—Permanence of Paper for Printed Library Materials, ANSI/NISO Z39.48-1992.

Printed in the United States of America

Brief Contents

Contents

6   Global Disparities in Health and Disease   92

7   Medical School and the Training of Physicians   108

Preface

Welcome to this introduction to medical sociology! Health problems have biological causes, but medical sociologists emphasize that these problems also have social causes. In particular, disease reflects the fault lines of our society. People of lower socioeconomic status tend to be sicker than wealthier people; African Americans, Native Americans, and Latinos tend to be sicker than non-Latino whites; women tend to be less healthy than men in several ways even though they outlive men; and LGBT people tend to be less healthy than straight people.

This new text accordingly stresses the social causes of health and disease and highlights issues of social class, race and ethnicity, and gender from cover to cover. It also provides an overview of the exciting and important field of medical sociology. This overview includes such topics as health behaviors and illness behaviors; medicalization and the social construction of illness; medical school and the health professions; health and disease in poor nations; the health care systems of the United States and other democracies; and Obamacare and health care reform.

A wide range of readers should find this book of interest. Although the text is intended primarily for undergraduates in sociology of health and illness/medical sociology classes and public health classes, graduate students and instructors will also find it a useful reference tool. Premedical students must now answer a series of sociology and psychology questions on the medical school entrance exam, the Medical College Admission Test (MCAT), and are advised to take sociology and psychology classes to prepare for the exam. These students, too, will benefit from this book's treatment. So will practicing physicians, nurses, and other health care professionals, who all encounter social aspects of health and disease virtually every day of their careers. Even the general public might benefit from this book, since it discusses some of the most important medical issues of the day and will help them understand why they as individuals are relatively healthy or, instead, relatively unhealthy.

All these parties will benefit from this new text's pedagogical aids. These include: (1) Learning Questions that begin each chapter; (2) a Health and Illness in the News story that also begins every chapter; (3) a Summary that ends each chapter; (4) a Giving It Some Thought section at the end of each chapter that spells out a hypothetical situation involving an issue from that chapter; (5) and a list of Key Terms that also ends each chapter.

Instructor Resources

Instructor's Manual

For each chapter in *Health, Illness, and Society*, this valuable resource provides student learning objectives, key terms with definitions, discussion questions, and web resources. The Instructor's Manual is available to adopters for download on the text's catalog page at www.rowman.com.

Test Bank

The Test Bank includes a variety of test questions and is available in either Word or Respondus formats. In either format, the test bank can be fully edited and customized to best meet your needs. The Word version of the Test Bank is available to adopters for download on the text's catalog page at www.rowman.com.

Our test bank is most flexibly used in Respondus, test authoring software which is available in two forms. Check with your university to see if you have a site license to the full program, Respondus 3.5, which offers the option to upload your tests to any of the most popular course management systems such as Blackboard. If you don't have a Respondus license or do not care about having your tests in a course management system, you can use our test bank file in Respondus LE. The LE program is free and can be used to automate the process of creating tests in print format. Visit the Respondus Test Bank Network to download the *Health, Illness, and Society* test bank for either Respondus 3.5 or Respondus LE.

Acknowledgments

My writing of this book owes a great debt to many people. Norman Miller was my major professor and good friend during my undergraduate days, while Forrest Dill served the same roles during graduate school. Although both these magnificent professors are no longer with us, I will never forget what they taught me, and I hope and trust that they would have been proud of this new book. Over the years, my colleagues and students at the University of Maine have provided a wonderful teaching and learning environment, and I thank them all for doing so. I also wish to thank Rowman & Littlefield editors Sarah Stanton and Nancy Roberts for sharing my enthusiasm about a new medical sociology text; the entire production team at Rowman & Littlefield for helping to bring my efforts to print; and the many fine reviewers who helped improve the manuscript: Sarah L. Allred, Berry College; Carol Apt, South Carolina State University; Stacye A. Blount, Fayetteville State University; Angelique Harris, Marquette University; Wesley James, University of Memphis; and Liza L. Kuecker, Western New Mexico University. Any mistakes that remain, of course, are mine alone.

I save my final thanks for my family, Barbara Tennent, David Barkan, and Joel Barkan; for my late parents, Morry and Sylvia Barkan; and for my parents-in-law, Howard and Jean Tennent. For so many reasons, I owe them all a profound debt that can never be repaid.

Sociology and the Study of Health and Illness

1

LEARNING QUESTIONS

1. How are sociology and medical sociology mutually relevant?

2. What is the scope of medical sociology?

3. What is meant by medicalization?.

4. What is meant by upstream factors in medical sociology?

5. What are the major research methods in medical sociology?

6. What are the four criteria of causality?

Health and Illness in the News

Students, teachers, and staff at a middle school in Charlotte, North Carolina, were mourning the death of a beloved teacher and cheerleader coach from breast cancer at the age of 44. One student said, "I will miss her love and respect for me," while another student added, "I will miss her sense of humor and how she made everybody smile even though she wasn't feeling well." The teacher continued teaching through much of her illness, a fact that prompted her principal to call her "a fighter to the end." To commemorate the teacher's passing, the school held a ceremony at which everyone dressed in pink and pink balloons were released. (Marusak 2014)

This sad story of a beloved teacher's death reminds us that many people die far too soon from cancer and other health problems. Many other people have chronic health problems that make their everyday lives difficult. You probably know someone who has cancer, heart disease, or another serious health problem. Perhaps you even have a health condition yourself.

When someone does develop cancer or another health problem, we usually think of the problem as an individual phenomenon with individual roots, usually biological. When cancer develops, we often blame bad genes or bad luck, and each of these factors may certainly matter. Depending on the condition, we might even blame a person's own behavior: someone might smoke, eat too much of the wrong food, not get enough exercise, and so forth. But the field of **medical sociology**—the study of the social causes of health and illness and of the operation of the health care system— recognizes that health and illness also have *social* causes and thus are social phenomena and not just individual phenomena. Medical sociology also recognizes that the quality of health care is fundamentally important not only for the treatment of disease and illness but also for their very prevention. This textbook introduces you to this understanding of health, illness, and health care in the United States and other contemporary societies. We will not have space to discuss every single topic that medical sociologists examine, but the book will acquaint you with the major issues they study, which are among the most significant issues facing the United States and the rest of the world today. The viewpoint of medical sociology is essential for a full understanding of these issues and, more specifically, for a full understanding of why some people are healthier than others, of how and why the health care system operates the way it does, and of what can be done to improve health and access to quality health care.

Before moving on, it will be helpful to define **health**, a word we have already used several times. Many definitions of health exist, and they usually refer to the quality of a person's physical and mental well-being. A standard definition comes from the World Health Organization's 1948 constitution, which defines health as "a state of complete physical, mental and social well-being and not merely the absence of disease or infirmity." This definition's inclusion of "social well-being" has been criticized for over-broadening the concept of health to include social problems like war and poverty (Callahan 1973). However, it does call attention to an ideal state of health, and it rightly implies that social well-being is important for physical and mental well-being. Medical sociology certainly agrees with this implication. In studying health, medical sociology as a whole pays somewhat more attention to physical health than to mental health (Bird et al. 2010), as will this book. With health now defined for our purposes, we turn to the relationship between medical sociology and its parent field, the discipline of sociology.

Sociology and Medical Sociology

Medical sociology draws in several ways from the larger discipline of sociology for its understanding of health and health care. This section outlines medical sociology's roots in the larger discipline.

Sociology's Major Themes

Introduction to sociology courses commonly highlight three major themes as hallmarks of the discipline of sociology: (1) *the sociological perspective*; (2) *social inequality*; and (3) *social institutions*. These emphases, in turn, guide the field of medical sociology, whose many research findings both reflect and contribute to the larger discipline's body of knowledge. Another way of saying this is that sociology and medical sociology are *mutually relevant*. Let's review sociology's three major themes briefly and show their relevance for understanding health and illness.

The Sociological Perspective   The first theme involves the sociological perspective, which is the view that the social environment influences people's behaviors, attitudes, and life outcomes (e.g., their chances of achieving a college degree, of having a satisfying, good-paying job, etc.). The social environment includes our social backgrounds, including, but not limited to, our gender, social class, race and ethnicity, age, religion, and social networks; it also includes various aspects of our place of residence: the nation in which we live and our region of residence within that nation (e.g., the Northeast versus the South in the United States or urban versus rural residence). The social environment does not totally determine our behaviors, attitudes, and life outcomes, but it often still greatly influences them. This emphasis leads sociology to regard people more as social beings than as mere individuals.

To take an oft-cited example unrelated to medical sociology, gender and race influence voting preferences: women and African Americans have been much more likely than men and white Americans to vote for the Democratic candidate in recent presidential elections. This generalization does not mean that all women and all African Americans vote for the Democratic candidate, only that they are statistically more likely than their counterparts to do so, presumably because their various life experiences lead them to favor the political positions of the Democratic Party and of its presidential candidate.

As this textbook will make clear again and again, the social environment also greatly influences the quality of our health and also our access to high-quality health care. How and why this happens requires explanations that later chapters will present, but medical sociology certainly provides compelling evidence of the influence of the social environment on the quality of our health and on the quality of the health care we receive (Cockerham 2013b).

Social Inequality   The second major theme of sociology is social inequality, or the unequal distribution of wealth and other important resources valued by a society. Fundamental dimensions of social inequality in the United States and many other societies involve gender, social class, race and ethnicity, age, and sexual orientation and gender identity. Simply put, men enjoy many more social, political, and economic advantages than women; wealthy people enjoy more advantages than low-income people; whites enjoy more advantages than people of color; younger people enjoy more advantages than the elderly; and straight people enjoy more advantages than LGBT persons. Much sociological research documents the existence of social inequality and its negative effects on people disadvantaged because of their gender, social class, race and ethnicity, age, and/or sexual orientation and gender identity (Hurst 2015).

Medical sociology has long recognized the role that social inequality plays in the quality of health. Low-income people generally have worse health than wealthier people; people of color have worse health than whites; and women are less healthy than men in certain ways that reflect their status in a society filled with gender inequality. Age certainly affects health for biological reasons, but it is also true that age-related inequalities affect health as well. Sexual orientation and gender identity also affect aspects of physical and mental health because of inequalities in the larger society affecting LGBT individuals. Chapter 5 discusses all these differences, which are collectively termed health inequalities. Social inequalities also affect the quality of health care that people receive, and chapter 12 discusses inequalities in health care along these dimensions.

Social Institutions   Sociology's third major theme concerns social institutions, or socially organized systems of behavior that help a society satisfy its basic needs. The key social institutions in contemporary societies include the family, religion, education, the economy, the political system, and certainly medicine. In studying the health care system, then, medical sociology studies one of the major social institutions. Medical sociology's research on the practice of health care contributes to the more general understanding of social institutions in the larger discipline of sociology.

The Sociological Imagination

All these themes informed C. Wright Mills' (1959) important concept of the sociological imagination. Mills reasoned that people often have many individual problems, such as unemployment, divorce, and illness. He termed these problems *personal troubles* (also called *private troubles*) and said our society often attributes these troubles to a fault of the individual experiencing them. For example, someone who is unemployed may be considered rather lazy and not willing to look hard for a job. But Mills further reasoned that structural problems, or *public issues*, in a society often underlie the personal troubles that individuals experience. Thus, an individual may be unemployed not because he or she is lazy but because the economy lacks employment opportunities or because the individual was born into poverty and could not afford to go to college. The sociological imagination, said Mills, involves the ability to recognize that public issues often lie at the root of personal troubles.

When medical sociology (and thus this book) discusses how social backgrounds, social inequality, and the quality of health care affect health and illness, it applies Mills' concept of the sociological imagination (Pescosolido 2011). Although people are indeed sometimes partly to blame for the health problems they experience (e.g., they smoke), larger social forces beyond any one individual's control also often play a fundamental role.

Sociology's Theoretical Traditions

Several theoretical traditions have guided the development of sociology since the discipline originated during the nineteenth century and have also guided the development of medical sociology since this subfield began more than half a century ago (Cockerham 2013a). These traditions are commonly termed *functionalism* (or *functional theory*), *conflict theory*, and *symbolic interactionism*.

Functionalism   Derived from the pathbreaking work of French sociologist Émile Durkheim, functionalism assumes that society's social institutions all help society to survive and thrive, and that each social institution serves several functions in this regard. For example, the family ideally helps socialize and protect children, while the health care system helps keep people healthy. Medical sociology certainly emphasizes this latter fact, but it also emphasizes the ways in which the health care system falls short of achieving this goal and thus is *dysfunctional.* Several chapters in this book discuss these dysfunctions. The important sociological concept of the *sick role*, discussed in chapter 4, provides a functional analysis of patient behavior and of physician-patient interaction.

Conflict Theory   Conflict theory, derived from the monumental writings of Karl Marx, assumes that individuals and groups with wealth, power, and other advantages dominate society, and that many people lie at or near the bottom of society's social hierarchy. This theory's emphasis on social inequality lies at the heart of sociology's own emphasis on this phenomenon. Conflict theory further assumes that individuals and groups at different levels of this hierarchy have different *vested interests* that create conflict over public policy and other important issues. As already noted, medical sociology highlights health disparities arising from inequality in the larger society, as well as problems in health care arising from this inequality. It is also true that the health care system is filled with various groups with conflicting vested interests. For example, health insurance companies are interested in making as much profit as possible, and this interest often clashes with patients' interests in reducing their medical costs as much as possible.

Symbolic Interactionism   A third theoretical tradition is symbolic interactionism, which emphasizes how individuals act with other individuals and how they interpret this social interaction. This emphasis on social behavior at the *micro* level has informed numerous influential studies in sociology. Many medical sociologists also study social interaction. For example, they examine the interaction between physicians and patients and between physicians and nurses, and they analyze how people behave when they are ill. Several chapters of this book discuss these types of studies.

The Scope of Medical Sociology

So, what exactly does medical sociology study? The answer to this question will be found in the pages of this book, but the scope of medical sociology encompasses three very broad areas: (1) the influence of the social environment on health, illness, and behaviors related to health and illness; (2) the operation of the health care system; and (3) the social construction of illness.

The Influence of the Social Environment

First, medical sociology examines the influence of the social environment on individuals' health and illness and on their behaviors and attitudes related to health and illness. Many, many studies have provided voluminous evidence of this influence, and this evidence is perhaps the signature contribution of medical sociology. As noted medical sociologist William C. Cockerham (2013b:1) pithily summarizes this influence, "Society may indeed make you sick or conversely, promote your health." Evidence of this impact of the social environment will be found throughout this book but especially in chapter 3, "Health Behavior"; chapter 4, "Illness Behavior and the Illness Experience"; chapter 5, "Social Causes of Health and Health Problems"; and chapter 6, "Global Disparities in Health and Disease."

Because the social environment does affect health and illness, health problems are more common among some social groups than others and more common in some locations than in others. This means that health and illness are *socially patterned* and that medical sociologists study this form of social patterning. Social epidemiology refers to this study, and can be defined more formally as the study of the social causes and social distribution of disease, illness, and other health problems.

Medical sociology's emphasis on the social environment represents a significant departure from the understanding of illness held by the traditional biomedical model (also called the *medical model*) (Cockerham 2013b). This model assumes that illness, disease, and other health problems have one or more specific medical causes and can be treated with appropriate medications and/or other medical procedures. This model is certainly important: as chapter 2 on the social history of health and health care will discuss, advances in scientific medicine based on this model have saved untold lives and improved the health of countless people. At the same time, the biomedical model generally disregards the many social factors affecting health and illness despite the importance of these factors. Health problems do have medical causes, but social factors often affect the likelihood of the medical causes arising in the first place. As chapter 2 will also discuss, improvement in certain social conditions (e.g., better public sanitation) during the nineteenth and early twentieth centuries also saved untold lives and improved the health of countless people, and some scholars think changes in the social environment were more effective in this regard than advances in scientific medicine (Conrad and Leiter 2013).

The importance of the social environment is certainly a central theme of this book, and particularly of chapter 5 on the social causes of health and illness, but it will be helpful here to provide a brief illustration of this importance. Our illustration concerns a very significant health problem, low birth weight (Cockerham 2013b).

Low birth weight is defined as a weight less than 5.5 to 5.8 pounds at birth. It is common among premature babies, but it can also occur among newborns who reach full term. Newborns with low birth weight may have several immediate health problems, including respiratory distress and bleeding in the brain, and babies born with low birth weight are also more likely to develop various health problems as they grow older and to experience learning difficulties (March of Dimes 2014; Strully, Rehkopf, and Xuan 2010).

Low birth weight has specific medical causes, and sometimes it stems from problems in the placenta or from other aspects related to fetal development that are unpredictable and unpreventable. There is, therefore, a biological risk in all pregnancies for low birth weight. But social factors also matter, as low birth weight is more common among mothers: (1) who have inadequate nutrition during their pregnancy; (2) who have chronic health conditions such as diabetes; (3) who smoke or drink during their pregnancy; (4) who experience high amounts of stress; (5) who live in unhealthy physical environments; (6) and who receive inadequate prenatal medical care. Income is a fundamental factor that affects the likelihood of all these risk factors for low birth weight, as low-income women are more likely than higher-income women to have these risk factors (Conley, Strully, and Bennett 2003; Strully, Rehkopf, and Xuan 2010). Thus, while there is always a biological chance for low birth weight, social factors raise or lower the actual occurrence of low birth weight.

Upstream Factors

Medical sociology uses the term upstream factors to refer to the factors in the social environment that influence health and illness. This term is often attributed to a parable told by medical sociologist Irving Zola about a physician saving people from drowning in a river:

> There I am standing by the shore of a swiftly flowing river and I hear the cry of a drowning man. So I jump into the river, put my arms around him, pull him to shore and apply artificial respiration. Just when he begins to breathe, there is another cry for help. So I jump into the river, reach him, pull him to shore, apply artificial respiration, and then just as he begins to breathe, another cry for help. So back to the river again, reaching, pulling, applying, breathing and then another yell. Again and again, without end, goes the sequence. You know, I am so busy jumping in, pulling them to shore, applying artificial respiration, that I have *no* time to see who the hell is upstream pushing them all in. (McKinlay 2013:583)

Upstream factors include social class, race and ethnicity, gender, and other aspects of our social backgrounds; the social and physical aspects of the communities in which we live; and the practices of the food, alcohol, tobacco, pharmaceutical, and other industries in terms of their marketing efforts and the safety of their products. All these upstream factors affect the quality of our health in ways that later chapters examine.

Zola's parable implies that it makes more sense to stop the people from being pushed into the river in the first place than to wait to save their lives. Similarly, it makes more sense to change the upstream factors affecting people's health rather than waiting to help them once they become ill. By the same token, to the extent that upstream factors do affect health, "downstream" efforts that focus only on changing people's risky health behaviors may have only a limited impact because the upstream factors harming their health will still remain. All these upstream factors, says John B. McKinlay (2013:583), are "pushing people in" and must be addressed to achieve far-reaching improvement in people's health.

The Practice of Health Care

The second broad area that medical sociology studies is the practice of health care. Much research in this area focuses on the training and behavior of physicians and other health care professionals, and much research also focuses on the functioning of hospitals and the delivery of health care. Specific topics in this line of research include the socialization of medical school students, the relationship between physicians and patients, the experience of being a hospital patient, the impact of not having health insurance, and inequalities in the delivery of health care based on social class, race and ethnicity, gender, and other social factors.

There is much to cover in this broad area of medical sociology. Accordingly, many chapters in this book discuss what medical sociology and other scholarship tell us about health care professionals and the more general operation of the health care system. These chapters include: chapter 7, "Medical School and the Training of Physicians"; chapter 8, "Physicians and Their Interaction with Patients"; chapter 9, "Nurses and Other Health Care Professionals"; chapter 10, "Hospitals and Other Health Care Settings"; chapter 11, "Health and Health Care in the World's Wealthy Democracies"; chapter 12, "The U.S. Health Care System"; and chapter 13, "Health Care Reform: Obamacare and Beyond."

The Social Construction of Illness

A final broad area of medical sociology theory and research is social constructionism. In the larger field of sociology, social constructionism refers to the idea that social reality is often socially constructed (Berger and Luckmann 1963). This means that certain social realities exist only because people decide they exist, and that these realities, therefore, have no objective basis. A *social construction*, then, is a concept that does not have objective reality, but that exists because people decide it exists.

Social constructionism can be a difficult concept to comprehend, so some examples from sociology will help you grasp it before we discuss its use within medical sociology. As a first example, many sociologists think race has little or no objective biological reality, even though people do differ in skin tone, hair texture, and other physical attributes. They instead regard race as a social construction, something that is real only because we think it has real meaning (Schaefer 2015). One reason sociologists hold this view is that we call many people "African American" or "white" even though their genealogy includes ancestors of both races or even of more than two races. Our society considers President Barak Obama an African American, as he does himself, even though his parentage is half African and half white. There is no more logic in calling him an African American than there is in calling him white.

A second sociological example of social constructionism concerns the possibility that certain conditions or behaviors might be considered social problems that need to be addressed even though there is no objective basis for thinking so (Mooney, Knox, and Schacht 2015). To illustrate, prominent educators and medical researchers in the late nineteenth century thought that efforts by women to attend college were a social problem. Why did they think this? They feared that the stress of the college experience would disrupt women's menstrual cycles, and that women would not do well on exams while they were menstruating (Ehrenreich and English 2005)! There was certainly no objective evidence to support these sexist notions, but they were used nonetheless to justify limits on women's admission into colleges and universities.

With this understanding of social constructionism in mind, we can now discuss its use in medical sociology. Put most basically, social constructionism in medical sociology emphasizes that "the meaning and experience of illness is shaped by cultural and social systems" (Conrad and Barker 2010:S67). Another way of saying this is that illness is to some degree socially constructed: culture and society affect whether certain traits (symptoms and behaviors) are perceived as illness, and they also affect how people with these traits are then regarded and treated socially and medically. For example, some illnesses such as most forms of cancer arouse our compassion and concern, while other illnesses, such as leprosy and HIV/AIDS, were originally stigmatized and aroused fear and other negative reactions in the general population (Conrad and Barker 2010). The fundamental insight, then, of social constructionism is that society and culture shape what people think of health and illness and how individuals considered ill should be regarded and treated. Chapter 4 revisits this insight.

An additional insight of social constructionism is the concept of medicalization. Recall that certain conditions and behaviors can be considered social problems even without an objective basis for this belief. By drawing on this important insight of social constructionism, medical sociology discusses certain conditions and behaviors that become defined as medical problems, often without a sufficient objective basis for thinking that they, in fact, have medical (i.e., biological) causes (Conrad and Barker 2010). These particular medical problems are best regarded as social constructions. The process by which they become defined as medical problems is termed **medicalization**, which can be formally defined as "a process by which nonmedical problems become defined and treated as medical problems, usually in terms of illness and disorders," often, but not always, "despite dubious evidence of their medical nature" (Conrad 2008:3–4). Chapter 4 discusses medicalization in much more detail.

Research Methods in Medical Sociology

Medical sociologists study health, illness, and health care in various ways, but their research methods reflect those used in the larger discipline of sociology and in the social sciences more generally. Because this book will be discussing a good deal of research, it will be helpful for you to become familiar with the major research methods in medical sociology. Generally, a particular research investigation tries to determine whether and to what degree an **independent variable** is influencing a **dependent variable**. Thus, if we say that poverty affects health, in this example poverty is the independent variable and health is the dependent variable. An independent variable, then, is a variable that affects or influences another variable (the dependent variable), while a dependent variable is a variable that is affected or influenced by another variable (the independent variable).

Surveys

Surveys are very common in sociology and certainly in medical sociology. They are conducted via face-to-face interviews, over the telephone, or increasingly via the Internet and, decreasingly, via snail mail. However surveys are conducted, they enable researchers to gather much information on the many topics that are included in the typical questionnaire.

Many surveys are given to *random samples* of the population. A *random sample* is a subset of the population in which every member of the population has an equal chance of being included in the sample. The mechanics of how a random sample is achieved need not concern us here, but the value of a random sample lies in the fact that the responses can safely be generalized to the entire population, even if the sample comprises only a very small percentage of the population. Thus, if 30% of a national random sample of 400 American adults report being in excellent health, we can safely assume that about 30% of all American adults would also report being in excellent health. Because it is much easier and less expensive to interview 400 adults in a random sample than some 250 million adults in the entire population, random samples are commonly used in survey research. Nonrandom samples, such as a class of first-year college students, are also used because it is very convenient to give them a questionnaire to answer. Although the results of surveys given to nonrandom samples cannot necessarily be generalized to the larger population, these results can nonetheless be useful and add to the general body of knowledge in medical sociology and other fields.

Surveys are a common method for gathering information about people's health and illness and aspects of their involvement with health care. They are also very useful for gathering information about people's attitudes about these same topics. The federal and state governments conduct important surveys about these topics regularly; researchers employed by universities, research organizations, and nonprofit organizations also conduct such surveys.

Two surveys are perhaps especially important. At the federal level, the National Health Interview Survey (NHIS) is administered to about 35,000 to 40,000 households around the nation (Centers for Disease Control and Prevention 2014a). Trained interviewers visit these households, and an interview using the standard questionnaire takes about one hour to complete. The NHIS is a major source of data on the extent to which Americans are healthy or instead have various illnesses, diseases, and risk factors for these health problems. At the state level, and in coordination with the federal government, all fifty states also conduct interviews for the Behavioral Risk Factor Surveillance System (BRFSS). The typical BRFSS questionnaire asks respondents to report their involvement in risky behaviors for their health such as tobacco use, alcohol abuse, lack of seat belt use, and so forth. The primary method of administering this survey is via telephone, and some 500,000 interviews are conducted for the BRFSS every year (Centers for Disease Control and Prevention 2014b).

Qualitative Research

Survey research is often called *quantitative research* because answers to questionnaires are typically coded into numbers (e.g., a "yes" answer to a question may be assigned a score of 1, and a "no" may be assigned a 2) for computer use and then analyzed statistically. In contrast, *qualitative research* involves extended observation and/or in-depth interviewing. There are many insightful observational studies by medical sociologists and other researchers of such dynamics as the interaction between physicians and patients and of the experiences of hospital patients (Cassell 2008; Emerson 1970). There are also many fine studies that use in-depth interviews to shed light on such topics as how patients respond emotionally to their health problem, how family members and friends react to a patient's health problem, and how medical professionals are treating a patient (Nack 2008; Scott 2013). Many studies also combine observation and in-depth interviewing; a notable example is an early pathbreaking study of the experiences and socialization of medical students (Becker et al. 1961).

Qualitative studies like these provide a rich, detailed understanding of the lives and experiences of their subjects and thus shed much light on the nature of health, illness, and health care. Because they are usually not conducted with random samples of the population, their conclusions cannot necessarily be generalized to other people and other settings. Yet, they still have a ring of truth that renders their findings compelling and probably generalizable to other individuals and other places.

Experiments

In the social sciences, experiments are very common in the field of psychology, and they are certainly very common in biomedical research involving the effects of new medications. In the "gold standard" type of experiment, subjects (let's assume they are all heart patients) are randomly assigned to three groups; the experimental group, a placebo group, and a control group. Random assignment helps rule out the effects of preexisting differences among the subjects. The experimental group receives the medication; the placebo group receives a substance that looks identical to the real medication but one that has no medication in it (a "sugar pill"); and the control group receives nothing. In the classic "double-blind" experiment, neither the researchers nor the subjects know whether the actual medication or just the placebo is being administered. After some time goes by, the researchers measure all three groups' quality of health. If the experimental group shows improvement compared to the other two groups, it can reasonably be concluded that the medication produced this positive effect.

In medical sociology, experiments are much less common than surveys or qualitative research because experiments do not easily lend themselves to the kinds of topics medical sociologists study. For example, if a medical sociologist wants to study the effects of poverty on health, it would be both unethical and impractical, to say the least, to randomly assign some subjects to be poor and some subjects to be wealthier and then to monitor any changes in their health for the next several months or years.

Still, researchers in various fields have conducted some very interesting experiments on important topics in medical sociology. In one very influential study, physicians were shown a video of either an African American or a white patient of each sex complaining of heart-related symptoms and then asked whether they thought the patient should receive certain procedures to test for heart problems (Schulman et al. 1999). In reality, the video they saw was of a trained actor, and each actor was reporting identical symptoms and using identical gestures. However, physicians viewing the African American actor were less likely than those viewing the white actor to recommend the cardiac procedures, and those viewing the female actor were less likely than those viewing the male actor to recommend the procedures. These results suggested possible racial and gender bias in this particular aspect of health care.

Criteria of Causality

Because this book will be discussing the results of many studies in medical sociology, it will be helpful here to discuss the criteria that must be satisfied for researchers to be able to conclude that an independent variable is, in fact, affecting a dependent variable. These criteria are called **criteria of causality** (Babbie 2014). These are important criteria to keep in mind, so please follow along carefully.

1. Initial Relationship between the Independent and Dependent Variables The first criterion is that the independent variable and dependent variable must be statistically related initially. For example, let's hypothesize that education affects health. In this example, education is the independent variable and health is the dependent variable. To keep things simple, let's restrict the example to high-school graduates and college graduates. If survey evidence finds that 28% of high-school graduates report being in only fair or poor health compared to 11% of college graduates (an actual finding from the 2014 General Social Survey, given to a national random sample), then education and health are indeed statistically related, and it appears that lower education is related to being in worse health. (This assumes that the education difference is large enough to be statistically significant, but let's not worry about that for now.) If an equal percentage of both education categories had reported being in fair or poor health, there would have been no relationship, and criterion #1 would not have been satisfied.

2. Causal Order Even if an independent variable and dependent variable are related, that does not automatically mean the former variable is affecting the latter variable. We cannot draw that conclusion unless the remaining three criteria of causality are satisfied. The second criterion, then, is that the independent variable must precede the dependent variable in time and/or in logic. If this is not true, there can be a *causal-order* question, or, as it is often called, a *chicken-or-egg* question. A causal-order question arises when it is difficult to know, when two variables are related, which variable is affecting the other variable. Sometimes there is no such difficulty. For example, if we find a racial difference in physical health, with African Americans having poorer health than whites, physical health cannot affect race because race certainly precedes physical health in time and/or in logic. In this example, no causal-order question arises.

But in the education and health example with which we started, the situation is not so clear. Although it makes more sense to think that education affects health than to think that health affects education (see chapters 3 and 5), it is at least possible that health affects education for some people. For example, someone who grew up with a serious chronic illness may not have had the chance to go to college and so ended up with only a high-school degree. To take another example, married people are generally healthier than unmarried people (chapter 5). Being married probably does enhance health, at least in a happy marriage, but it is also possible that unhealthy people are less likely to get married.

3. Spuriousness The third criterion is that the relationship between the independent and dependent variables must not be spurious. A *spurious* relationship is a relationship that initially exists only because a third variable, called an *antecedent variable,* is affecting both the independent variable and the dependent variable. To use a silly example, there is probably a statistical relationship between ice-cream consumption and crime rates: the higher the ice-cream consumption, the higher the crime rate. Maybe eating ice cream causes a sugar high and after that a violent tendency! Of course, this is a spurious relationship: we have not taken into account the effects of an antecedent variable that affects both ice-cream consumption and crime rates. That variable, of course, is temperature: when it is warmer outside, ice-cream consumption is higher, and, for very different reasons, so are crime rates.

To return to our education and health example, it is possible that this relationship is at least partly spurious because of an antecedent variable like parents' income. When parental income is low, the chances of achieving only a high-school degree are higher, and so are the chances of being in worse health. Although there is good reason to believe that education in and of itself affects health, at least some of the relationship might be spurious because of the effects of parental income.

4. No Better Explanation The fourth criterion is that there should be no better explanation for the relationship between the independent and dependent variables. Sometimes a relationship might satisfy the first three criteria but still be a coincidence. For (a silly) example, the United States beat the Soviet Union in hockey in the February 1980 Olympics. Over the next few years, the U.S. crime rate declined. This relationship would seem to satisfy the first three criteria (think about it!), but that does not mean that the U.S. Olympic victory was the reason for the crime rate decline. This decline was instead due to other factors such as a reduced number of Americans in the crime-prone 15–30 age bracket (Travis and Waul 2002). In practice, scholars worry far less about this fourth criterion than they do about the first three criteria.

Conclusion

This chapter introduced the major themes of medical sociology and thus of this book. Medical sociology emphasizes the importance of the social environment for understanding health, illness, and health care. As part of this emphasis, it stresses that social inequalities in the larger society affect the quality of health and of health care, and it stresses that the society and culture affect what is or is not considered illness as well as the experience of illness. The next chapter sets the stage for the subsequent chapters, as it will discuss both the rise of scientific medicine, which uses the biomedical model, and the rise of social epidemiology, which is a fundamental component of medical sociology.

Summary

1. Medical sociology reflects and contributes to major themes in the larger discipline of sociology, including the sociological perspective, social inequality, and social institutions.
2. Medical sociology also reflects the major theoretical traditions in sociology: functionalism, conflict theory, and symbolic interactionism.
3. The scope of medical sociology encompasses: (1) the influence of the social environment on health, illness, and behaviors related to health and illness; (2) the operation of the health care system; and (3) the social construction of illness.
4. Medicalization involves the turning of nonmedical behaviors and experiences into medical problems for which medication is often an appropriate treatment.
5. The major research methods in medical sociology include surveys, qualitative research, and experiments. The results of surveys of random samples can be generalized to the population, while the results of qualitative research provide a rich understanding of many aspects of illness and other health-related topics.
6. To conclude that a relationship between an independent variable and dependent variable is indeed causal, questions of causal order and spuriousness must be ruled out.

Giving It Some Thought

You are a patient in a hospital and are recovering from minor surgery and staying overnight. Although you were expecting to be placed in a two-bed room, the hospital instead places you in a five-bed room. During the night, nurses and other personnel come into the room periodically to take blood and attend to other duties for all five patients, including you. As a result, the room is hardly ever quiet, and the patients only get about two or three hours of sleep all night. How might a medical sociologist interpret and explain this situation?

Key Terms

biomedical model, 5
conflict theory, 4
criteria of causality, 10
dependent variable, 8
functionalism, 4
health, 3
health inequalities, 3
independent variable, 8
medical sociology, 1
medicalization, 8

social institutions, 3
social constructionism, 7
social environment, 2
social epidemiology, 5
social inequality, 3
sociological imagination, 3
sociological perspective, 2
symbolic interactionism, 4
upstream factors, 6

A Social History of Health and Illness

2

LEARNING QUESTIONS

1. How did preliterate societies explain illness?

2. What was Hippocrates' humoral theory of disease?

3. Why did scientific medicine not advance during the Middle Ages?

4. Why was Pasteur's germ theory of disease so important?

5. Why was John Snow's research on water and cholera so important?

6. Why is public health controversial?

Health and Illness in the News

Polio was once a virulent, incurable disease that affected millions of people, most of them children, worldwide. It paralyzed many thousands of them, including President Franklin D. Roosevelt, and killed some of them. Polio vaccines developed during the 1950s were eventually administered to several billion people across the world, and the disease was virtually eradicated by the beginning of this decade. That is why a recent World Health Organization (WHO) report was so troubling. The report declared a world health emergency because polio was returning to nations like Afghanistan, Iraq, Pakistan, and Syria: war and other conflict in these nations had made it difficult to administer childhood vaccinations. Religious beliefs were also limiting vaccinations in some regions, and the polio virus was spreading as wartime refugees crossed national borders. The rise of polio in this part of the world threatened nations in nearby Africa, where vaccination rates are shockingly low, leaving children and adults vulnerable to the spread of the polio virus. A WHO spokesperson warned, "Things are going in the wrong direction and have to get back on track before something terrible happens." (McNeil 2014)

This chapter discusses the development of two dynamics represented in this unsettling news story about the return of polio. These dynamics are scientific medicine and social epidemiology. **Scientific medicine** refers to the use of science to understand the causes and treatment of, and possible cures for, disease and illness; its application is reflected in the biomedical model introduced in chapter 1. **Social epidemiology** was also introduced in chapter 1 and refers to the study of the social causes and social distribution of disease, illness, and other health problems. In the polio news story, scientific medicine manifests itself in the development and administration of the polio vaccine, while social epidemiology manifests itself in the discussion of the reasons for the recent rise in polio cases in a troubled part of the world.

People have always had health problems, but humanity's understanding of why these problems emerge and of how best to treat them has changed dramatically from ancient times to the present day. For most of human history, the understanding of health was *unscientific*. Scientific medicine and social epidemiology are relatively new developments, as they trace their roots primarily to the nineteenth century (the 1800s). Together they have saved countless lives and prevented much suffering, and a healthy (pun partly intended) debate exists today over which of these two developments has saved more lives over the last two centuries. Improvement in the world's health is popularly attributed to the rise of scientific medicine, but a case can be made that the rise of social epidemiology (along with its practical application, public health, discussed later in this chapter) had an even greater benefit (Link and Phelan 2002; McKinlay and McKinlay 2013). Regardless of which side of this debate is correct, assuming a correct side can even be determined, it is fair to say that scientific medicine and social epidemiology are still both enormously significant, both historically and today.

With this backdrop in mind, we now turn to the history of health and illness and of the treatment of illness. Whole volumes have been written on this history, and we have space here only to highlight the major events and developments. Further detail of this history can be found elsewhere (e.g., Bynum 2008; Duffin 2010; Kennedy 2004; Magner 2005; Nutton 2013; Waddington 2011). We first discuss the rise of scientific medicine before turning to the development of social epidemiology.

Health and Illness in the Preindustrial World

The term *preindustrial world* refers to human history before the dawn of the Industrial Age during the nineteenth century. At the risk of oversimplification, the major periods of the preindustrial world include: (1) the ancient world, including preliterate tribes and the great ancient civilizations of Egypt, Greece, Rome, and elsewhere; (2) the medieval world (Middle Ages), extending from the fall of Rome in 476 A.D. to the beginning of the Renaissance in the 1300s and early 1400s; and (3) the Renaissance, extending from the 1300s to the 1600s. The period between the 1600s and the early 1800s marked a transition between the preindustrial world and the industrial world and also the very early beginning of scientific medicine.

Before this transition, spanning many millennia and despite some exceptions, human understanding of health and illness was decidedly unscientific and primarily religious in nature. Preliterate tribes thought illness was the work of evil spirits or angry gods. Given this belief, these societies used magic and religious practices (which were rather synonymous in these societies), or, to use a single term, *supernatural practices*, to drive the evil spirits out of a sick person's body or to cure them of whatever an angry god had done to them. These practices included incantations and the use of amulets.

Many preliterate societies had an individual(s) whose special role was to perform these tasks, someone that today we call a *shaman* or, in two more terms that have lost popularity, medicine man or witch doctor. These ancient societies also used what today we call *folk medicine*, especially the use of herbs and other plants they thought had curative properties. An additional procedure that some of these societies used was **trepanning**, the drilling of holes in the skull of an ill individual to release the evil spirits who had taken over the person's body.

As literate societies developed, they, too, held a religious conception of illness. For example, although the ancient Hebrews believed in only one God, they commonly attributed illness to God's will: they thought God was punishing someone for not believing in Him or for violating His commands, or that God was testing the person's faith in Him. The ancient Babylonians similarly thought that illness was punishment for a sin or other infraction committed by the person who became ill.

The Ancient Civilizations

We mentioned just above that the preindustrial approach to health and illness was unscientific and religious despite some exceptions. These exceptions appeared in the great ancient civilizations and are worth recounting here, as they suggest the path that health and medicine could have taken if these civilizations' insights had not gone unrecognized during the reign of the Middle Ages, when the theology of the Catholic Church governed most of Europe and much of Asia.

Ancient Egypt   Considered to have begun about 3100 B.C., ancient Egypt lasted until 30 B.C., when the Roman Empire conquered it. Its reign included many notable developments beyond the scope of this book, but for our purposes the relevant development was a quasi-scientific approach to the understanding of health and illness. To be sure, ancient Egypt mainly held a religious understanding of health and illness, but the beginning of an approach that went beyond religion is evident from inspection of various papyrus writings and from archeological investigations (Nutton 2013). This research reveals that ancient Egyptians not only believed in the use of supernatural practices to cure illness, but they used certain herb-based substances to relieve pain and to treat burns, skin and stomach diseases, and wounds; they also used massage for muscular aches. Moreover, ancient Egyptians apparently recognized that worms and other parasites could cause serious intestinal disease, and that frequent washing could help prevent certain health problems. In another development, the ancient Egyptian practice of mummification involved removal of bodily organs of the dead. This process helped Egyptians learn about human anatomy.

Ancient Greece   During the last millennium B.C., ancient Greece made monumental contributions to philosophy, the arts, and mathematics and physics. Like ancient Egypt, ancient Greece continued to believe that their gods governed much of their daily lives, including illness, and many ill people went to religious temples to be cured by one or more gods. Still, we again begin to observe the rudiments of a scientific approach to health and illness.

This is perhaps most clearly seen in the life of the Greek physician Hippocrates (460–377 B.C.), after whom the Hippocratic Oath that new medical students take is named. Hippocrates' views on the causes of illness derived from the more general ancient Greek belief that the world consisted of four natural elements: air, earth, fire, and water. These elements had four natural properties or qualities: hot, cold, dry, and wet. In line with this general belief, Hippocrates reasoned that the human body has four fluids or *humors*: (1) *blood*, which was hot; (2) *phlegm*, which was cold; (3) *yellow bile*, which was dry; and (4) *black bile*, which was wet. All four humors, he thought, had to be in the proper balance for a person to be healthy. When they were not in the proper balance, a person could become ill: illness thus signaled an imbalance in the patient's humors. Hippocrates' view on this cause of illness is called the **humoral theory** of disease.

Ancient Greeks pursued a less religious and more scientific approach to health care in other ways. A great source of knowledge for their physicians was war (Salazar 2013). Because many Greek soldiers were wounded on the battlefields of the many wars in which Greece fought, physicians had ample opportunity to learn about human anatomy as they tried to heal the soldier's wounds and save their lives. Physicians learned (without having the modern scientific understanding of infection) of the need to remove arrowheads and other foreign objects from these soldiers' bodies and to clean their wounds. More generally, ancient Greek physicians thought that a proper diet was important for keeping people healthy and for helping ill people regain their health. In all these ways, we see the beginning of a scientific approach to health and healing.

Ancient Rome The heyday of the Roman Empire began around 27 B.C., when Augustus became the first Roman emperor, and ended 476 A.D. when Rome fell to Germanic barbarians. In that roughly 500-year span, ancient Rome was one of the world's great civilizations, with its politics, law, and many other aspects of its society still studied today.

Although the ancient Romans continued to believe in many gods, they were also familiar with Greek advances in medicine, thanks in part to Greek physicians who moved to Rome. Romans sought to build on these advances (Hanson 2010). As in Greece, the treatment of wartime wounded contributed to the Romans' knowledge of anatomy. Roman physicians wrote books and other publications on the use of herbs for certain medical problems and even made pills from various plants and herbs. Archeologists have found scalpels, needles, and other medical instruments from ancient Rome. As these instruments indicate, surgery was sometimes used in ancient Rome, albeit for minor problems.

Perhaps the greatest Roman physician was Galen (c.130 A.D–c.210 A.D.), who was born in Greece but moved to Rome in his early 30s and eventually became the personal physician to Emperor Marcus Aurelius. Galen believed in humoral theory and sought to restore the humoral imbalance of people who were ill. He advocated, for example, that people with fevers be treated with cold substances. He also dissected apes and pigs to learn about anatomy and wrote detailed reports about his results. These results included the discovery that the kidneys produce urine and that certain spinal nerves control certain muscles. Galen is also credited with discovering the pulse.

One of the ancient Romans' greatest medical contributions was their recognition of the need for clean water and adequate sanitation (the removal of human waste) to maintain good health. They had no actual biological understanding of why clean water and good sanitation were essential for good health, but they did sense that poor health often accompanied unclean water and poor sanitation. This knowledge prompted the Romans to develop a system of piping to bring clean water into cities and a sewage system to dispose of waste. The Romans also built large public baths to enable people from all ranks of life to clean themselves. The Romans' emphasis on clean water and adequate sanitation was a very early example of the public health approach that this chapter discusses later.

The Middle Ages

The Middle Ages (476 A.D–early 1400s A.D.) are often called the Dark Ages, and rightly so, for the many intellectual advances of the great ancient civilizations were lost and forgotten for the 900 years or so that the Middle Ages lasted. Religion, and specifically the Catholic Church's teachings, dominated the medieval understanding of health and illness. Because the church believed that illness was God's way of punishing people for their sins, most medieval people held this same belief. A major location for healing illness was the monastery. People with various health problems would go to a monastery to be cured by a mixture of prayer, other religious practices, and the administration of herbal remedies. Repentance for one's supposed sins was also emphasized as a way to cure an illness.

The medical insights of the ancient civilizations were not completely forgotten during this period (Bishop 2007; Glick, Livesey, and Wallis 2005). Medieval physicians did exist, even though some theologians thought that the practice of medicine was anti-religious because illness was God's will. Generally familiar with the work of Hippocrates in ancient Greece and Galen in ancient Rome, these physicians accepted humoral theory and thought that many diseases stemmed from having too much blood in the body. They thus thought that *bloodletting* (the removal of blood from the body), often with the aid of leeches, could cure these diseases. Several medical schools in Europe developed by the end of the medieval period. Although Europeans at that time knew precious little about the real causes of illness and disease and about how to treat these problems effectively, these schools at least enabled their students to learn the accepted medical wisdom of the day. The students also learned about anatomy by dissecting human bodies.

Accusations of witchcraft were rampant during much of the medieval period. The church attributed witchcraft to possession by the Devil and burned many "witches" at the stake and drowned many others (Demos 2009). Most of these witches were women. Many of these women were simply using folk medicine to heal family members, and others were what we now call religious heretics, people who challenged the teachings of the church. Some so-called witches were actually people with mental disorders who acted strangely. Today's scientific medicine certainly does not attribute mental illness to demonic possession, but this was a popular medieval belief thanks to the church's teachings.

One of the major medical events of the Middle Ages, and indeed of recorded human history, occurred at the end of the Middle Ages during the late 1340s. This event was the dreaded plague, or the so-called Black Death, which killed an estimated one-third of all Europeans, with some estimates putting the death toll at more than half of all Europeans (Byrne 2004). Although we now know that the plague was probably caused by bacteria spread by fleas on rats, medieval peoples attributed it to God's punishment for their sins or to air that had been contaminated by the movement of certain planets far away from Earth.

The Rise of Scientific Medicine

The rise of scientific medicine took more than 400 years, ranging from the beginning of the Renaissance in the 1300s to scientific medicine's quick advance and fruition during the second half of the nineteenth century (1800s).

The Renaissance

The Renaissance (mid-1300s–late-1600s) was a period in which Italians and other Europeans began to reject religion as the dominant mode of thinking in favor of reason and intellect. Renaissance intellectuals rediscovered the writings of the ancient Greeks and Romans and, for our purposes, rediscovered in particular various writings regarding health, illness, and medicine. Islamic scholars had translated many of these texts into Arabic, and Renaissance scholars then translated these Arabic texts into their own language. These scholars in effect picked up where the Greeks and Romans had left off and were able to make important advances in anatomy and other areas of medical understanding.

An important Renaissance thinker in this regard was Andreas Vesalius (1514–1564), a professor at Italy's University of Padua, who spent many hours dissecting human cadavers. This practice enabled him to learn much about human anatomy. In 1543 he published a detailed, illustrated anatomy book, *"De Humani Corporis Fabrica (On the Structure of the Human Body)."* Other Padua professors also made important advances: Girolamo Frabrizio (1537–1619) recognized the heart valves, while Gabriele Fallopio (1523–1562) identified the female reproductive organs. The name of the Fallopian tubes comes from his discovery.

Yet another Italian scholar, Girolamo Fracastoro (1478–1553), proposed the then-novel idea that epidemics stemmed from *pathogenic* (disease-causing) substances outside the body that were spread by human contact. Meanwhile, a Swiss scholar and alchemist, Paracelsus (1493–1541), advocated the use of certain chemicals and minerals to treat illness. Perhaps the most famous medical scholar of the Renaissance was the great Leonardo da Vinci (1452–1519). Better known for his paintings, da Vinci also dissected human cadavers and rendered many drawings of bones, muscles, and other parts of the human anatomy.

Toward the end of the Renaissance, the English physician William Harvey (1578–1657) made important discoveries about how blood circulates inside the human body and about the role played by the heart in blood circulation. The Roman physician, Galen, discussed earlier, had thought that blood formed in the liver and then proceeded into the heart, and this belief persisted into Harvey's era. Refuting this theory, Harvey discovered that blood instead continuously flows from the heart through arteries and back to the heart through veins. His 1628 book, *Exercitatio Anatomica de Motu Cordis et Sanguinis in Animalibus* (*An Anatomical Study of the Motion of the Heart and of the Blood in Animals*), presented his evidence, gleaned from many small animal dissections, for this discovery. Harvey's monumental contribution has been called as significant as Darwin's theory of evolution and Newton's theory of gravity (Wright 2013).

Another key development in this period involved the use of the microscope, which was invented by the early 1600s but remained a rather crude, unhelpful device for several decades. By the 1670s, however, improvements in the microscope enabled scientists to use it to discover and describe biological tissues, red blood cells, sperm cells, bacteria and other microorganisms, and plant cells. A key figure here was Dutch scientist Anton van Leeuwenhoek (1632–1723), who built a microscope with more than five times the magnifying power of existing microscopes and was the first person to observe bacteria and blood corpuscles.

All these advances in medicine during the Renaissance were ironically, and tragically, accompanied by the spread of infectious disease. This spread stemmed from the increased exploration and trade on the high seas that were a hallmark of the Renaissance economy. When Christopher Columbus and other explorers traveled to the New World, they brought with them certain infectious diseases against which New World residents had no natural immunity (Kotar and Gessler 2013). When Columbus reached the Caribbean in 1492, the island of Hispaniola, now known as the Dominican Republic and Haiti, had an estimated 250,000 people. Smallpox carried to the island by the Spanish explorers was so deadly that the island's population dropped to only about 6,000 within two decades. Smallpox eventually spread to Central and South America and killed millions of people by the end of the sixteenth century (the 1500s). The entry of the plague into Europe, already discussed, probably occurred because European traders brought the disease back with them from their trading trips to Asia.

If the explorers and traders helped spread disease to the lands to which they traveled, they also brought back with them substances from these lands that had medicinal properties. One of these substances was the bark of the Quina tree, which was used to produce quinine, a medicine effective against malaria. Another substance was an opiate derivative, laudanum, which proved to be an effective, popular painkiller for several centuries.

The Eighteenth Century

Scholars during the eighteenth century (1700s), or the Age of Enlightenment (which actually began in the latter 1600s), built upon the medical advances of the Renaissance in several important ways (Cunningham and French 2006; Spray 2013). A key figure of this period was Swiss scholar Albrecht von Haller (1708–1777), who discovered certain aspects of the operation of the nervous system and in particular of the effects of the brain cortex on peripheral nerves. Another scientist, Stephen Hales (1677–1761), identified the role of the capillary system in blood circulation. An Italian medical professor, Giovanni Battista Morgagni (1682–1771), gained fame with his 1761 book, *De Sedibus et Causis Morborum* (*On the Sites and Causes of Diseases*), in which he used the results of some 500 human autopsies he performed to describe the damage to bodily organs from several diseases, including syphilis and tuberculosis. His discovery of the link between disease and organic damage provided important insights about why the diseases he studied had caused the health symptoms that eventually killed the patients. These insights have since been called the *anatomical concept of disease*.

Other scholars made notable contributions in embryology and pathology. Regarding embryology, prior generations of scholars had embraced the theory of *preformation*, the idea that embryos were miniature replicas of the beings that appeared at birth. Countering this notion, Enlightenment scholars advocated the correct idea of *epigenesis*, the idea that embryos begin as a tiny, unformed mass (which we now know is an egg) and then grow into the bodily form with which they are born.

Despite these advances, physicians knew preciously little by the end of the eighteenth century about how to effectively treat and cure illness and disease, in large part because they still knew almost nothing about the actual causes of illness and disease. Following the practices of previous centuries, they continued to bleed patients and sometimes would purge them. They used mercury to treat syphilis and other venereal diseases, but the mercury often killed the patients with these diseases. At the very end of the century, though, English physician Edward Jenner (1749–1823) published a booklet in 1798 on the use of cowpox, a cattle disease, as a vaccination to prevent smallpox; the term *vaccination*, coined by Jenner, comes from the Latin word, *vacca*, for cow. Jenner's discovery paved the way for the widespread administration over the next two centuries of the smallpox vaccine, which saved countless lives and eventually eradicated smallpox around the world by 1980. According to the website for the Jenner Museum, the house where Jenner performed the work that led to his discovery, Jenner perhaps saved more lives with his vaccination than any other person in history (http://www.jennermuseum.com/).

The Nineteenth Century

This century (the 1800s) completed the rise of scientific medicine, and by the end of the century its biomedical model had thoroughly displaced religion and tradition as the dominant paradigm for understanding health, illness, and medicine. The success of the model in this regard stemmed from many significant medical discoveries, including the invention of certain medical devices and equipment, at various points in the nineteenth century. All these advances again saved many lives and set the stage for further advances during the next century.

One of the key developments in this century involved an increased knowledge of cells, thanks to improvements in the microscope. Several German scientists, but especially Rudolf Virchow (1821–1902), identified many properties of cells and formulated the **cell theory**, which says that cells are the basic functional and structural unit of all organisms.

But perhaps the most important discovery, and one of the most important discoveries in the history of scientific medicine, was the realization that germs cause disease. Before the nineteenth century, many scholars had, as we have seen, attributed disease to humoral imbalance, while theologians and lay citizens often attributed disease to religious and other supernatural forces. Many scholars also attributed disease to foul-smelling "bad air," or *miasma*, resulting from decaying organic matter or other sources. Some scholars realized that disease was spread by contagion, since they observed people becoming ill after being in contact with someone already ill, but they did not suspect that microorganisms were the source of this contagion.

We now know, of course, that bacteria and other microorganisms are the source of many diseases, and this realization has played a fundamental role in the development of medicines to treat and cure patients. Credit for this achievement goes to the great French chemist Louis Pasteur (1822–1895), who was the first scientist to demonstrate that microorganisms cause disease. His discovery in the late 1870s, called the **germ theory** of disease, ranks as one of the greatest medical achievements of all time, as it "transformed the way we think about disease," to cite the subtitle of a book on this theory (Waller 2002).

Another scientist, Robert Koch (1843–1910), built on Pasteur's work to discover the specific bacteria that cause anthrax, cholera, and tuberculosis (Goetz 2014). By 1890, scientists had also identified the microorganisms responsible for diseases such as diphtheria, gonorrhea, and typhoid fever. Pasteur's research also led other scientists to realize that microorganisms were causing serious infections during and after surgery. Thanks to the pioneering work of British surgeon Joseph Lister (1827–1912) during the 1860s, surgeons began using carbolic acid to wash their hands and medical instruments, a practice that helped prevent many infections and the problems they caused, including death (Gaynes 2011).

An additional medical advance during the nineteenth century is worth noting, and that is the use of anesthesia during surgery. Before this century, anesthesia was unknown, and patients undergoing surgery could certainly experience severe pain. This pain limited the extent of the surgery that could be done and made it difficult to perform surgery because of the patient's possible movements. American dentists began using nitrous oxide ("laughing gas") and ether in the 1840s for their patients, and ether was soon being used for general surgery. The development of surgical anesthesia, then, permitted more extensive surgeries and for this reason helped save lives.

Although scientific medicine and its biomedical model had ascended by the end of the nineteenth century, medical advances certainly continued in the twentieth century and the current century in ways unimaginable to nineteenth-century scientists. There are far too many advances to list here, but one of the most important developments was the discovery in 1928 of penicillin, which was recognized as the first antibiotic some two decades later. Other major developments occurred in surgery, diagnostic and other medical equipment, and, perhaps most important of all, genetics, after the discovery of DNA in the 1950s. This discovery led to the important advances in molecular biology and molecular medicine, and the more recent mapping of the human genome has taken scientific medicine into new frontiers.

Ethical Issues in Scientific Medicine

Although scientific medicine has been a godsend to humanity, to say the least, it has also brought with it some ethical issues, many of them involving pharmaceutical companies. Before we leave scientific medicine, it is worthwhile discussing some of these ethical issues here.

Medical Experimentation   One ethical problem concerns medical experimentation j typical experiment, one group of subjects is given the new drug; another group is given a placebo; and a third group is given nothing (see chapter 1). Neither the researchers and staff administering the drugs nor the subjects know whether the actual drug or just a placebo is being administered. Because many of these drugs have serious side effects, subjects must be fully informed of these side effects and sign informed consent forms before they can participate in the experiment. Although the subjects do give their consent, the seriousness of many of the side effects does raise questions of the ethical propriety of these experiments.

These experiments now have strict protocols that must be followed to protect subjects, but the earlier days of scientific medicine had no such protections, and several ethically questionable episodes occurred. Perhaps the most despicable experiment was conducted by the U.S. Public Health Service on about 400 illiterate African-American men in Tuskegee, Alabama, who had syphilis. Beginning in 1932, government doctors monitored these men's health to determine how syphilis was affecting their bodies. Although scientists discovered during the 1940s that penicillin could cure syphilis, government doctors decided not to tell the Tuskegee men about this cure so that the study could continue. After journalistic investigations revealed the experiment in 1972, the surviving men were finally given antibiotics, but for some thirty years government doctors had let syphilis ravage many of the men's bodies and kill some of them. During this period, the men's wives who contracted syphilis from them also went untreated, as did some of their children who were born with syphilis (Washington 2006).

The Tuskegee study was not the last one in which health and lives of human subjects in the United States were put at unconscionable risk. Beginning in the 1940s, the U.S. military and the Central Intelligence Agency (CIA) conducted a series of secret experiments to determine the effects of radiation and other dangerous substances. Between 1946 and 1963, the military conducted several radiation experiments involving hundreds of thousands of people. In some of these experiments, soldiers were ordered to stand near the sites of atomic bomb testing; in other experiments, military planes released radiation over towns in the Southwest. The affected soldiers and civilians developed various cancers, and the military destroyed evidence of the experiments (Kershaw 2004; Schneider 1993).

In other experiments, government doctors injected prisoners and developmentally disabled individuals with radioactive substances without telling them of the substances, and the government also put radioactive iodine into land and drinking water in Idaho (Lee 1995). And during the 1950s and 1960s, the CIA conducted a secret experiment involving LSD on hundreds of American civilians and military personnel. As a news report summarized this massive experiment, "So, incredibly, it (the CIA) decided to slip acid secretly to Americans—at the beach, in city bars, at restaurants. For a decade, the CIA conducted completely uncontrolled tests in which they drugged people unknowingly, then followed and watched them without intervening" (Szalavitz 2012). A military scientist who had his drink spiked with LSD committed suicide by jumping from a window, and the CIA hid the reasons for his death for more than twenty years (Thomas 1989).

Some highly unethical medical experiments have admittedly yielded important results (Boodman 2015). For example, in the 1960s, a physician decided to study hepatitis by giving intellectually disabled children milkshakes that contained human feces infected with a hepatitis virus. Although many of these children incurred hepatitis as a result, this physician's experiments revealed that different viruses cause Hepatitis A and Hepatitis B. This discovery in turn enabled the development of the Hepatitis B vaccine, which has since prevented an untold number of Hepatitis B cases from occurring. Did the ends justify the means in this example? The answer to this question is beyond the scope of this book and perhaps best left for a philosophy class, but this and other examples of unethical medical experiments still remind us that some terrible things have been done over the decades in the name of scientific medicine.

Conflict of Interest in Drug Testing New drugs in the United States must be tested before they can win approval from the Food and Drug Administration (FDA). This certainly makes sense, but it is also true that pharmaceutical companies pay for much of the drug testing research (called *clinical trials*) that occurs and often do their own research on their drugs. This situation creates a noticeable conflict of interest because the companies have a vested interest in the results of their drug testing. If the testing shows the drug is safe and effective, the company stands to make large sums of money, often billions of dollars; if the testing shows the drug is unsafe and/or ineffective, the company loses this money and also in effect loses all the money that the drug's development cost them.

This conflict of interest underlies at least two ethically questionable practices arising from drug testing. First, companies have hidden evidence that their drugs were unsafe. For example, during the 1980s the Eli Lilly company put a new arthritis drug, Oraflex, on the market despite knowing that its use could be fatal; the company kept this evidence hidden from the FDA. Many people died after the drug went on the market, and by the time the FDA forced Eli Lilly to take Oraflex off the market a few years later, Oraflex had killed more than five dozen people (Coleman 2006). In a more recent example, Purdue Pharma, the company that manufactures OxyContin, the well-known narcotic painkiller, pleaded guilty in 2007 to charges that it hid evidence that the drug was very addictive; the company had marketed OxyContin as a drug that was less addictive than other narcotic painkillers (Meier 2007).

The second ethically questionable practice surrounding drug testing involves the fact that pharmaceutical companies often fail to publish or otherwise disclose the results of clinical trials showing the drug is *ineffective*. For this reason, the results of published clinical trials financed by pharmaceutical companies are much more likely to be positive (in showing the drug is effective) than the results of trials financed by the federal government (Friedman 2016; Goldacre 2014).

The companies' failure to make their contrary results known robs the medical community of important scientific knowledge. It is also true that if a particular study's results are not positive from a company's perspective, it may then conduct another study. If that study yields positive results, the company then publishes that study but not the earlier one, even though the earlier one might cast some doubt on the positive results that were later found.

Payments to Physicians Pharmaceutical companies routinely engage in practices that critics say amount to bribery of physicians to prescribe the companies' drugs for their patients. Company representatives make frequent visits to doctors' office and leave them with free samples to give to their patients. They also give physicians free gifts such as boxed candy and computer accessories and treat them to lavish dinners. These practices may sound relatively innocent, but there is evidence that at least one group of physicians, dermatologists, who receive free samples are more likely to prescribe these drugs than less expensive generic alternatives (Conger 2014).

In addition, pharmaceutical companies routinely finance physicians' trips to medical conferences at ski resorts and other attractive locations (Clark 2016). At these conferences the physicians hear about the latest advances in scientific medicine, but the fact that a company is totally or partially paying for their trip troubles medical ethicists. Moreover, many of the speakers at these conferences are physicians who extol the benefits of a new or fairly new medication; the fact that many of these speakers receive a large fee from a pharmaceutical company to give their talks again troubles medical ethicists.

These concerns have led some companies to reduce their payments to physicians for promotional speeches at conferences and other venues. Eli Lilly, for example, reduced its payments from $47.9 million in 2011 to $21.6 million, still a considerable sum, in 2012. A news report noted that "the sharp declines coincide with increased attention from regulators, academic institutions, and the public to pharmaceutical company marketing practices" (Ornstein, Sagara, and Jones 2014). At least one company, GlaxoSmithKline, decided to stop paying any speaking fees. The Physician Payment Sunshine Act, part of the Affordable Care Act ("Obamacare"), now requires pharmaceutical and medical device companies to report their payments to physicians.

Other Ethical Issues   Many other ethical issues are found in today's scientific medicine, and perhaps your campus offers a course in biomedical ethics. Interested readers may wish to consult one of the many available biomedical ethics texts (e.g., Hammaker and Knadig 2017). Some of the most interesting and troubling ethical issues in today's scientific medicine include:

- Is it ever acceptable for a physician to help a gravely ill patient commit suicide?
- Should we screen newborns for genetic problems and, if so, what should happen if a problem is found?
- How forthcoming should a physician be with a patient who has a fatal illness?
- Should a frozen embryo be considered equivalent to a child if the parents divorce?
- Should patients awaiting an organ transplant be allowed to pay a potential donor or donor's family in order to ensure a suitable organ becomes available?
- If cloning technology ever becomes sufficiently advanced, would it then ever be acceptable to clone a human?

This is just a sampling of the ethical issues affecting scientific medicine today, but it does indicate that the biomedical model has brought with it some serious moral dilemmas even as it has improved our lives in ways that our ancestors, including those just a few decades ago, could never have imagined.

Social Epidemiology Yesterday and Today

Although scientific medicine has saved countless lives, so has social epidemiology, to which we now turn. This chapter's title promised a "social history," but our discussion of the rise of scientific medicine was rather *nonsocial*: it said little about changes in society that were occurring as nineteenth-century scientists worked in their laboratories and offices to develop the insights that secured scientific medicine's dominance. Social epidemiology's rise traces its roots precisely to these societal changes, which involved problems in the social and physical environments that caused disease and illness.

The Industrial Revolution

What were these changes? The answer to this question lies in one of the most momentous events in human history, the Industrial Revolution of the nineteenth century. As medical scientists in that century worked in their laboratories and offices, the world was swiftly transforming around them. First in Europe and then in the United States, factories sprang up as the agricultural and mercantile economies of those continents began changing to industrial economies. As factories were built, people had to move to live near the factories. This meant that cities grew rapidly during the nineteenth century and reached numbers greatly exceeding their populations a century earlier. People crowded into these cities in some of the worst living conditions imaginable, as Charles Dickens so movingly depicted in some of his great novels. Cleanliness might be next to godliness, but nineteenth-century urban residents did not live in clean conditions. Because modern plumbing did not yet exist, public sanitation was substandard. Clean water was often unavailable. The sheer crowding of tens and hundreds of thousands of people into small areas meant that infectious diseases were easily spread.

Unfortunately, scientific medicine before Pasteur's discoveries in the last third of the nineteenth century did not realize that microbes caused these diseases. A few scientists did suspect microbes in this regard, but most scientists dismissed this view. And even though some scholars did suspect microbes, cures for the infectious diseases still had not been discovered. Scientists and public officials also did not realize that horrific living conditions in cities were generating the microbes causing these diseases. This general unawareness meant that thousands and thousands of people became sick and died in European and American cities from these diseases (Whooley 2013).

The Beginning of Epidemiology: John Snow and Cholera

Against this backdrop, history honors English physician John Snow (1813–1858) for being the first scientist to empirically trace an infectious disease to living conditions. He did this after an epidemic of cholera (a highly infectious, often fatal disease marked by severe diarrhea and vomiting) hit parts of London in 1854. To try to determine what was causing the cholera, Snow gathered data on which London areas had higher and lower rates of the disease, and he interviewed people with cholera (or people who had known someone who died of cholera) about where they had traveled and what they had been eating and drinking. He determined that many of the people with cholera had been drinking water supplied by a particular public water pump in London's water system.

This fact led London officials to shut down the tainted pump and to take other measures to ensure clean water, and the cholera epidemic then receded. It was later found that the pump's water had been contaminated by a nearby house's cesspool. In other outbreaks of cholera, Snow also determined that households receiving water from sections of the Thames River that had been contaminated by human waste (which was routinely dumped into the river) were more likely to be stricken with cholera than households receiving water from uncontaminated sections of the Thames. This finding again led to changes in the provision of water. Although Snow suspected that microbes in contaminated water were the immediate cause of cholera, most scientists, as just mentioned, thought otherwise until germ theory was accepted about two decades later. In the meantime, Snow's discovery about contaminated water and cholera had prevented much suffering and saved many lives. This great English physician died in 1858, just four years after his pathbreaking research, from a stroke at the tender age of 45.

Snow's work is credited today with beginning the field of **epidemiology**, the study of the causes and the distribution of disease and illness. Within two decades, the work of Pasteur and other scientists established the role played by bacteria in disease and cemented biomedical epidemiology as one of the most important areas of scientific medicine.

However, Snow's discovery about contaminated water and cholera was not, strictly speaking, a *biomedical* discovery. Instead, it was a discovery that emphasized two related *social* factors: first, tainted water, and second, the human activities that caused the water to become tainted. For this reason, Snow's work may be considered an early example of *social* epidemiology, as was the work of a few scientists of his era who linked poverty and substandard working conditions to poor health (Berkman and Kawachi 2014). Although epidemiology began as a biomedical approach favoring biological factors, then, it eventually expanded to include social factors as well, as researchers in the late nineteenth and early twentieth centuries began highlighting the pathogenic (disease-causing) effects of contaminated water, poor sanitation, dilapidated housing, overcrowding, and malnutrition. Their research led to improvements in these conditions that saved untold lives. Social epidemiology accelerated during the last half of the twentieth century and has "grown exponentially" since the late 1990s (Berkman and Kawachi 2014:1). Much of this growth has involved research on the effects of social class (education and income), race and ethnicity, gender, and neighborhood conditions on health and illness (see chapter 5). Medical sociologists have made perhaps the most significant contributions to our understanding of these effects.

The Epidemiological Transition

The nature of disease and illness has changed significantly from centuries ago to the present day, thanks to basic changes in society and to advances in scientific medicine and social epidemiology. Diseases that were rampant in an earlier century are less common or absent today, while diseases that were less common earlier are now more common today. Scholars refer to this shift as the **epidemiological transition** (Gaziano 2010; Olshansky and Ault 1986; Omran 2005). This transition, which involves several stages or phases, is worth discussing, as it reinforces the idea that health problems are not fixed in time and space but rather depend on a constellation of social and scientific forces. This transition's stages also alert us to what kinds of biomedical and social strategies are needed to combat the most common and serious health problems appearing in a specific stage.

The first stage was the *Age of Pestilence and Famine*. This stage characterized human history until the late nineteenth century and still characterizes many poor nations today to some degree (see chapter 6). As its name implies, infectious diseases (including cholera, pneumonia, smallpox, and tuberculosis) and starvation characterized this stage. Infectious disease became rampant during the nineteenth century because of the growth of cities and their horrific living conditions, as described earlier. Average life expectancy was as low as 30 years in many parts of the world for the many millennia that comprised this first stage, as children routinely died during infancy or childhood and adults died from disease or starvation.

The second stage, which characterized Europe and the United States in the late nineteenth and early twentieth centuries, was the *Age of Receding Pandemics*.

Pandemics (very widespread epidemics) grew less common and severe during this stage. This improvement resulted from the public health efforts described earlier: sanitation improved, water became cleaner, and nutrition improved. Infant and childhood mortality declined, and adult life expectancy increased. People in these continents still did not live nearly as long as they do now (their life expectancy was only 45–50 years), but they lived longer than in the first stage because pandemics had became less frequent and deadly.

The third stage was the *Age of Degenerative and Human-made Diseases*. This stage characterized Europe and the United States during the middle of the twentieth century. By this time, people here were now living long enough, with an average life expectancy of about 70, that they could incur chronic illnesses like cancer, cardiovascular disease, and diabetes. These problems also became more common because of increased levels of smoking, eating of high-fat and processed foods, and sedentary lifestyles.

The fourth stage was the *Age of Delayed Degenerative Diseases* and arrived during the 1960s. This era was marked by fewer deaths from cardiovascular disease and from certain cancers, thanks to the beginning of lower smoking rates and medical advances such as better blood pressure control and bypass surgery for heart disease.

The fifth and final stage is the *Age of Obesity and Inactivity*, which has held reign for the half century since the 1960s. As its name implies, obesity levels have increased greatly because of even more sedentary lifestyles and greater intake of high-caloric foods. In the early 1960s, about 32% of adult Americans were overweight and another 13% were obese; by the end of first decade of this century, 34% of adults were overweight and another 34% were obese. Obesity thus almost tripled during the past half century. This increase in overweight and obesity has led to higher risks of hypertension (high blood pressure), heart disease, type 2 diabetes, and many other health problems (Harvard T.H. Chan School of Public Health 2016).

Another type of health problem has emerged in this latest, current stage, and that is the rise of strains of infectious diseases that are resistant to antibiotics because of the overuse of antibiotics in humans and animals (Consumer Reports 2015). These strains are particularly affecting the developing world (poor nations), but resistant strains of meningitis, bacterial pneumonia, tuberculosis, and other diseases are also increasingly appearing in the United States, where they kill more than 23,000 people annually (Centers for Disease Control and Prevention 2013; Price 2014).

Another new health problem, indicated by the polio news story that began this chapter, is the return of some virulent diseases that had been virtually eradicated. This return stems from the lack of vaccination. In the polio news story, this lack stemmed from war and conflict in a troubled part of the world. In the United States, however, measles and whooping cough have returned because some parents have refused to have their children vaccinated for religious reasons or for (unfounded) fear that vaccination can cause autism. Although these diseases are still rare, their return puts some people who were vaccinated at risk for incurring them, as a small proportion of all vaccinations do not provide immunity (Haelle 2014; Lopez 2014). An outbreak of measles occurred across the United States in early 2015 thanks to an infected child who visited Disneyland in California (Freyer 2015).

Public Health

When medical researchers first discovered and developed penicillin and other antibiotics, they were applying the basic knowledge that Pasteur and the early epidemiologists had gained about the role played by bacteria in disease. Another way of saying this is that Pasteur and the early epidemiologists engaged in *basic research*, while medical researchers then engaged in *applied research*. Similarly, while social epidemiology provides basic knowledge of the role of social factors in health problems, the basic knowledge gained from both social epidemiology and biomedical epidemiology then has to be applied to reduce and prevent the occurrence of these health problems. The field of **public health**, which may be defined as "all organized measures (whether public or private) to prevent disease, promote health, and prolong life among the population as a whole" (World Health Organization 2014), performs this application.

The mass immunization program during the 1950s to eliminate polio, mentioned at this chapter's outset, is just one of many notable achievements in the field of public health. In more recent decades, public health researchers and advocates have played important roles in increasing motor vehicle safety, in reducing the spread of the AIDS virus, in calling attention to violence and handguns as public health problems, and in many other areas. Public health represents an exciting career option for anyone wanting to put social epidemiology specifically, and medical sociology more broadly, into action. Public health programs exist at colleges and universities around the United States, and the field represents an exciting career option for anyone interested in the social aspects of health and illness.

Levels of Prevention   Public health operates at three levels (Schneider 2017). The first level is **primary prevention**. This level involves a focus on aspects of the social and physical environments that increase the risk for health problems (disease, illness, and/or injury). The aim of public health efforts at this level of prevention is to minimize or prevent exposure to these risk factors, which include poverty and environmental pollution.

The second level is **secondary prevention**. At this level, the goal is to distinguish behaviors and situations that put specific individuals at risk for a health problem. The idea here is that many people may live amid primary risk factors such as poverty or pollution, but some of these people are still more likely than others in similar conditions to develop health problems. Similarly, many people are fortunate enough not to live amid primary risk factors, but some of these are again more likely than others in this fortunate situation to develop health problems. Examples of the behaviors and situations addressed by secondary prevention include parental abuse and smoking.

The final level is **tertiary prevention**. This type of prevention occurs after a health problem has emerged and aims to minimize or prevent short- and long-term consequences of the problem. Physicians who treat patients are engaging in tertiary prevention, as are pharmaceutical companies that develop new drugs to treat people with cancer or other health conditions.

Public Health and Controversy   Although these public health efforts seem quite sensible and have surely saved many lives, it is also true that public health is often controversial. According to public health professor Mary-Jane Schneider (2017), several reasons account for this controversy.

First, many public health efforts have focused on problems caused by the behavior of corporations. These problems include pollution, smoking, tainted meat, and motor vehicle safety. A common response of the corporations involved in these problems is that it would cost them millions of dollars to address the problems, prompt the layoffs of many employees, and increase prices and other expenses for consumers. These possible economic consequences prompt many parties to criticize public health efforts.

Second, many public health efforts aim to minimize the chance that people will put themselves at risk for a health problem by, to be blunt, acting stupidly. For example, the public health community was a strong early advocate for seat belt laws and continues to advocate for motorcycle helmet laws. A common response to such efforts to prevent people from harming themselves is that people should be allowed in a free society to engage in behavior that puts themselves at risk, and that these public health efforts thus endanger individual liberty.

A final source of controversy lies in morality and religious belief. Certain public health efforts advocate practices that trouble people with traditional moral and/or religious views. These practices include, but are not limited to: (1) providing contraceptive education and devices to young people; (2) providing clean needles to heroin addicts; (3) providing condoms to people with HIV or AIDS and contraceptives to students in high school and middle school; (4) maintaining access to legal abortion; and (5) legalizing prostitution. When the public health community advocates such measures, the response from individuals and groups with traditional views can be, and has been, very negative.

A Word about Rates

Social epidemiologists and many medical sociologists and public health scholars rely heavily on data that take the form of rates of health, of illness, of risky behaviors, and of involvement in aspects of the health care system. It will help here to explain what is meant by a *rate*. A **rate** is just another way of expressing a percentage. For example, if 5 people in a town of 20,000 have a particular health problem, then 0.025% [= (5/20,000) × 100] of this town's population has this health problem, and we would say the rate of this problem is 0.025 for every 100 people (or 0.025 per 100 population). But the number 0.025 looks a bit clumsy because of all the numerals to the right of the decimal point. To make the number a bit easier to understand, it would make more sense to multiply 5/20,000 by at least 10,000, which would yield a rate of 2.5 per 10,000 (which is the same result as 0.025 per 100). Depending on how common the illness is and the size of the population, sometimes we multiply instead by 1,000 or by 100,000, which yields rates per 1,000 or 100,000, respectively. Because the United States and the various states have so many people, rates per 100,000 are often used in measuring health and illness and other relevant variables.

The term **prevalence** (or *prevalence rate*) refers to a rate of the number of people in a given location with a particular health problem and is obtained by dividing that number of people by the population of that location and then multiplying that ratio by 100,000 (assuming we are measuring prevalence at the national or state level). Finally, the term **incidence** (or *incidence rate*) refers to a rate of the number of cases of illness in a given location, and is obtained by dividing that number by the population of the location and then multiplying by 100,000. Thus, if one person has three common colds in a year, that person's experience would count once in the numerator for prevalence rate for the common cold but three times in the numerator for incidence rate for the common cold. Because medical sociologists are primarily concerned with how many people have a particular health problem, this book will report prevalence rates (percentages or otherwise) more often than incidence rates.

Before we leave the subject of rates, we should indicate why rates are particularly important in medical sociology (and the related fields of social epidemiology and public health). When medical sociologists and other scholars investigate the effects of the social environment, they do not try to understand why any one person

TABLE 2.1	John Snow's Findings on Cholera Deaths		
Water Company	**Number of Households**	**Number of Cholera Deaths**	**Number of Deaths per 10,000 Households**
Lambeth	26,107	98	37
Southwark	40,046	1,263	315

Source: Snow, John. 1855. *On the Mode of Communication of Cholera*. London: John Churchill.

becomes ill. Rather, they examine *rates* of illness to explain why people from certain social backgrounds and locations are more likely than others to become ill. If we find, for example, that the rate of a certain immune disease is higher in women than in men, this gender difference alerts medical sociologists and other researchers to the distinct possibility that social and/or biological factors account for this difference. Similarly, if urban residents have a higher rate of severe anxiety than rural people with similar incomes, this suggests (but does not prove) that there may be something about urban life that leads urban residents to experience more anxiety. The use of rates allows researchers to compare the health problems of various groups, and this comparison can then help point to possible causes of these problems.

John Snow's research on cholera provides a very early example of the usefulness of calculating and comparing rates. Recall that he linked cholera deaths to water that had come from a contaminated section of the Thames. The way Snow did this was rather ingenious for his time. He began by gathering data for a particular area of South London. Some households in this area had their water supplied by the Lambreth company, which obtained its water from a clean section of the Thames, and other households in the area had their water supplied by the Southwark company, which obtained its water from the contaminated section. Snow gathered data on the number of cholera deaths in July and August, 1854, in the South London neighborhood and also on the number of households in the neighborhood served by each of the two water companies. He then calculated the cholera death rate per 10,000 households. Table 2.1 reports his findings.

Note that the death rate for the households supplied by the Southwark company was almost nine times higher than the death rate for the households supplied by the Lambeth company. This startling difference led Snow to conclude that the contaminated water supplied by Southwark was accounting for the much higher death rate in its households. (Suggestion: For practice in computing rates, use the numbers in the middle two columns of Table 2.1 to compute the rates shown in the last column. Allowing for rounding error, your computation should yield rates very similar to the rates in the last column.)

Conclusion

This chapter traced the social history of health and medicine. We saw that changes in society over the centuries and millennia affected conceptions of disease and illness and the types of health problems most confronting a society. Until the late nineteenth century, humanity had virtually no conception of the true causes of disease and illness and of how to treat patients with these health problems. As a result, life spans were short, as infant and childhood mortality was high and adults were very vulnerable to fatal diseases. The development of scientific medicine and social epidemiology during the nineteenth century changed humanity forever. Medical sociology today owes a considerable debt to the early pioneers in social epidemiology.

Summary

1. The understanding of health and medicine in the ancient world was unscientific and primarily religious. Preliterate tribes thought illness was the work of evil spirits or angry gods.

2. The great ancient civilizations continued to attribute illness to their gods, but some scholars in these civilizations also had views of illness and medicine that were somewhat more scientific.

3. During the Middle Ages, the work of ancient scholars on health and medicine was generally lost and forgotten. Medieval people attributed illness to the work of God and evil spirits and engaged in religious rituals to cure illness.

4. The Renaissance saw the beginning of a scientific approach to health and medicine, as reason and intellect began to replace religion as the dominant mode of thinking. Advances during the Renaissance and the eighteenth century set the stage for the rapid development of scientific medicine during the nineteenth century.

5. The development of germ theory and other advances during the nineteenth century led to scientific medicine as the dominant paradigm for understanding health and illness. Meanwhile, rapid city growth during this century led to horrid living conditions that generated serious infectious diseases. John Snow and other researchers began to link these conditions to these diseases, and their work led to the emergence of social epidemiology and of the public health approach to preventing disease and illness.

6. The epidemiological transition identifies five stages of health and illness throughout human history. During the current stage, the Age of Obesity and Inactivity, overweight and obesity have increased rates of cardiovascular disease, hypertension, type 2 diabetes, and other health problems. Infectious diseases are also returning because of bacteria resistance to antibiotics and because of the lack of vaccinations.

Giving It Some Thought

You are an elementary school principal who recognizes the importance of timely childhood vaccinations for the health of your students, faculty, and staff. A family moves into your school district and wants to enroll their first-grade child. The child's parents tell you that the child has never been vaccinated for measles, mumps, and whooping cough because they believe vaccinations are dangerous for children. They are very sincere in their belief and admit that it is not related to their religious beliefs. Your state provides a religious exception for vaccination, but it does not allow parents to refuse vaccination because they think it could pose risks to their children. What do you do?

Key Terms

cell theory, 20

epidemiological transition, 25

epidemiology, 25

germ theory, 20

humoral theory, 15

incidence, 28

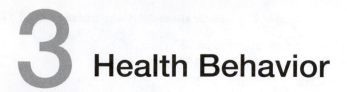

3 Health Behavior

Health and Illness in the News

Wayne Curry, the first African American executive of Prince George's County outside of Washington, DC, died from lung cancer at the relatively young age of 63. Beloved by his friends and colleagues, Curry had smoked cigarettes for many years and was diagnosed with his cancer a year earlier. In his last months, he often spoke of the dangers of smoking. Just weeks before he died, he told a reporter, "You get to talk to people you love and you say, 'Man, I love you,' which you would never say if you were not dealing with something potentially fatal." (Wood 2014)

Wayne Curry died before his time, as do many smokers, and did not get the chance to live peacefully into his twilight years. Smoking is only one of the many behaviors that potentially harm our health. We can enhance our chances of living a full, healthy life if we avoid these behaviors and instead engage in behaviors like exercise that promote good health. This chapter discusses medical sociology's perspective on health behavior. We often regard people's behaviors related to health as personal choices, but medical sociology emphasizes the influence of the social environment on these choices. We will see much evidence of this insight throughout the chapter.

What Is Health Behavior?

Health behavior refers to the activities people do that either maintain or improve their health or potentially harm their health. The full set of health behaviors, then, consists of activities that promote good health (*promotive, positive, protective,* or *preventive behaviors*) and of activities that may harm their health (*risky, negative,* or *dangerous behaviors*). These two types of behaviors are generally the opposite of each other. Important promotive health behaviors include everyday activities such as getting enough exercise and eating a good diet, drinking moderately or not at all, refraining from smoking, and getting enough sleep. Risky behaviors are the opposite of these: not getting enough exercise, eating too much processed and sugary and fatty food, excessive drinking, smoking, and not getting enough sleep. Health behavior also includes the periodic activities we do to screen for various health problems: an annual physical exam that involves monitoring blood pressure, cholesterol levels, and other data; screening for colorectal and other cancers; regular dentist visits; and occasional eye exams.

Because of their importance, everyday health activities have probably received more attention from medical sociologists than periodic health activities, but the latter activities are also important for good health. For example, regular screening via colonoscopy could probably prevent 40% of all colorectal cancers, the nation's second-leading cause of cancer death (Dwyer 2013).

In discussing the epidemiological transition, chapter 2 mentioned the rise of chronic disease by the middle of the last century as people began living long enough to be able to incur these diseases. Chronic disease also became more common because of increases in smoking, the consumption of fatty, sugary, and processed foods, and a decline in physical activity. These two trends alerted health scholars to the role that health behavior was playing in the rise of chronic disease. As the importance of health behavior became recognized, so, too, did the realization that individuals need to pay attention to the good and bad choices they make regarding their health.

On the face of it, these choices are easy to identify. The Centers for Disease Control and Prevention (CDC) (2011) tells us that four risky behaviors underlie chronic diseases such as cancer and heart disease that account for 70% of all U.S. deaths annually. These four risky behaviors are (1) smoking; (2) poor nutrition; (3) physical inactivity; and (4) excessive alcohol use. These and other risky health behaviors (such as using illegal drugs, not taking prescriptions as directed, and not getting enough sleep) combine to account for nearly half of all premature deaths in the United States annually (Umberson, Crosnoe, and Reczek 2010).

Americans would thus prolong their lives if they practiced one or more, and preferably all, of these promotive health behaviors:

- Limiting alcohol use
- Exercising regularly
- Eating a healthy diet
- Not smoking or otherwise using tobacco

Compared to people who practice all four of the risky behaviors, people who practice all four promotive health behaviors are 63% less likely to die prematurely from a chronic illness (Ford et al. 2011). Some research suggests that people who practice all four promotive behaviors live an average of 14 years longer than people who practice the opposite risky behaviors (Khaw et al. 2008).

Understanding Health Behavior

Sociologically speaking, our health behaviors are like many behaviors: they are the complex result of the twin processes of **socialization**, or the learning of norms and values, and **social control**, or the regulation of behavior by society's various components. We learn many behaviors, including health behaviors (positive and risky behaviors alike) from our parents, friends, and other people. We also behave in ways these people prefer us to behave lest we disappoint or anger them. As children we brush our teeth, or at least pretend to brush our teeth, to avoid parental wrath. At later life stages, a major motivation for our particular health behaviors lies in the expectations of friends, partners and spouses, and other people important to us.

This basic understanding of health behavior raises a provocative question: to what degree are people responsible for their health behaviors? A popular view is that people freely choose whether to engage in risky health behaviors: they can decide how much to drink and whether to smoke, and they can decide how much to exercise and what kind of diet to enjoy. When they make bad choices, as many Americans do, it is tempting to blame them for these choices. To some degree, they do bear responsibility for deciding to engage in risky behaviors. As medical sociologist William C. Cockerham (2013b:58) summarizes this popular view, "The responsibility for one's health ultimately falls on oneself through healthy living. Greater personal responsibility means that achieving and maintaining a healthy lifestyle has become more of a life or (time of) death option."

Yet, risky health behaviors do not occur in a social vacuum. As CDC emphasizes, "The majority of these risk factors do not occur randomly in populations; they are closely aligned with the social, demographic, environmental, economic, and geographic attributes of the neighborhoods in which people live and work" (Yoon et al. 2014:372). Medical sociologist Lee F. Monaghan (2013:56) adds that choices regarding health behaviors "are shaped and constrained by the inequitable material conditions of existence" and that decisions regarding these behaviors "are always indebted to social structures such as class, gender, and ethnicity."

Macro Factors

This general sociological understanding of the importance of *macro* factors for health behavior derives from the work of one of the great founders of sociology, Max Weber (1864–1920), who among his many other writings discussed life chances and lifestyles (Weber 1978[1921]). **Life chances** refer to people's ability to live a happy, fulfilling life and to improve their position in life, while **lifestyles** refer to how people live their lives, including the choices they make about what products to purchase and about which activities to pursue. Weber emphasized that people's life chances, which stem largely from their socioeconomic status, affect their lifestyles and in particular make it either easier or more difficult to pursue certain lifestyles. Life chances, then, affect choices to engage in positive health behaviors or, instead, risky health behaviors.

Drawing on this particular insight of Weber, medical sociologists use the term **health lifestyle** to refer to a general pattern of high or low involvement in promotive health behaviors. In line with Weber, they further emphasize that the ability to practice a promotive health lifestyle is often constrained by socioeconomic status (SES) and other macro aspects of our social backgrounds, including race and ethnicity and where we live (Bourdieu 1984; Cockerham 2010). As William C. Cockerham (2013b:63) observes, "Assuming people have the freedom to make health choices is out of line with what many people experience as real possibilities in their everyday lives." Much research indeed finds that SES and other structural factors affect health behaviors. Later sections of this chapter summarize how and why these factors exert their effects. These factors' collective impact indicates that health lifestyle is not just the result of purely individual choices but instead also reflects the strong influence of our social location in society.

Micro Factors

Among people living in the same macro circumstances, some people are still more likely to practice positive health behaviors, and others are more likely to engage in risky behaviors (Yap and Lee 2013). *Micro* factors focusing on individuals help understand why this is so.

One such factor is *personality*. Psychologists have found both direct and indirect associations between certain personality traits and health behavior (Umberson, Crosnoe, and Reczek 2010). *Direct association* here means that a personality trait itself influences choices about health behaviors. In particular, people who are more impulsive or hostile are more likely to engage in risky behaviors such as drinking or violence. *Indirect association* means that a personality trait influences the development and maintenance of good social relationships, with these relationships, in turn, affecting health behavior. Personality's effect thus occurs through the pathway of social relationships. For example, people who are extroverted may have more social ties and thus be less likely to engage in risky behavior.

What psychologists call *locus of control* also may matter for health behavior. **Locus of control** refers to the extent to which individuals feel they have control over their own lives. Low internal locus of control often coincides with low self-esteem and characterizes individuals who feel they cannot control their own lives. These individuals may then engage in risky health behaviors in an unfortunate attempt to regain control over their lives. A notable example here involves eating disorders. Many people, mostly women, fail to eat enough (*anorexia*) or force themselves to throw up after eating (*bulimia*). They feel that this behavior at least lets them control their own bodies even if they have little or no control over what else happens to them (Arthur-Cameselle and Quatromoni 2014). Conversely, when individuals have high internal locus of control, they may be more likely to practice positive health behaviors, although evidence on this point is mixed (Janowski et al. 2013).

The Health Belief Model   To explain individual choices regarding health behavior, some social psychologists developed the **health belief model** (HBM) several decades ago (Becker 1974; Rosenstock 1966). Drawing on other behavioral models in social psychology, the HBM assumes that promotive health behavior, including visiting a physician, is more likely among individuals who satisfy five conditions:

- They perceive they are susceptible to incurring a health problem
- They perceive the health problem could be serious
- They perceive that a potential health behavior will prove beneficial
- They have a high level of self-efficacy (the belief that one's actions make a difference)
- They lack *barriers* (such as unavailable transportation to see a doctor) to undertaking a health behavior.

Thus, individuals who feel susceptible to a health problem that they also regard as potentially serious are more likely to engage in promotive health behaviors than individuals who hold neither perception. By the same token, individuals who feel that a potential health behavior will not help them or who have some barriers to health behaviors are less likely to practice the behavior than individuals in neither circumstance. Structural variables such as SES and race and ethnicity and social-psychological variables such as personality influence an individual's likelihood of satisfying all five of the HBM conditions.

Even if a person satisfies all these conditions, the person may not undertake a health behavior unless galvanized to do so by what the HBM calls *cues to action*.

These cues are events, people, or conditions that stimulate or "trigger," to use an HBM term, someone to engage in promotive health behaviors. For example, a person may hear a media report of the dangers of an illness or of the need to wash one's hands for personal health, or a family member may tell the person in no uncertain terms to see a doctor. These and other cues for action are often necessary, or at least helpful, to spur someone to undertake a promotive health behavior.

The HBM implies that people's *perceptions* about their health may matter more than *objective evidence* of potential health problems for their decisions to engage in health behaviors. Physicians, other health care providers, and public health officials often lament the fact that so many people with symptoms or risk factors for disease and illness fail to practice the various health behaviors that would probably help them. The HBM helps us to understand why these people fail to do so. At the same time, the HBM has been criticized for applying mostly to individuals who already have a specific health problem or great potential for developing the health problem; it is less clear whether the model applies to preventive health behavior among the public more generally. Questions also remain about the relative importance of each of the model's conditions for health behavior decisions (Champion and Skinner 2008).

The Social Context of Health Behavior: Social Class, Race and Ethnicity, and Gender

Social class, race and ethnicity, and gender are three important dimensions of social inequality in the United States and other societies. All three dimensions shape health behavior. To some extent, and perhaps to a large extent, the degree to which we practice promotive health behavior versus risky behavior reflects these three fundamental aspects of our social backgrounds.

Social Class

Of the three dimensions, health behavior scholars have paid the most attention to social class and its components of education and income. Social class makes the largest and clearest difference for health behavior, while the effects of race and ethnicity and gender are somewhat smaller, though still important, and also more complex.

Social class and health behavior are related as follows: higher SES is linked to promotive health behaviors, while lower SES is linked to risky health behaviors (Pampel, Krueger, and Denney 2010). As discussed later in this chapter, people with higher levels of education and income are less likely to smoke, more likely to be physically active, less likely to be obese, and less likely to drink excessively.

It is easier to document these differences than to explain them. Some of the reasons scholars advance seem to make sense but are difficult to determine precisely. A particular problem is that education and income are so closely correlated, which makes it difficult to know whether the reasons for social class's effects stem more from education or more from income. Involvement in one health behavior (promotive or risky) may have more to do with education, while involvement in another health behavior may have more to do with income, although scholars think education matters overall more than income (Ross and Mirowsky 2010). With these caveats in mind, let's examine the reasons for social class's relationship with health behavior (Elo 2009; Pampel, Krueger, and Denney 2010; Ross and Mirowsky 2010). Some of these reasons apply to certain health behaviors more than to other health behaviors, but together they help explain the link between social class and promotive versus risky health behavior.

First, a lack of education leads people to be either unaware of or unconcerned about the effects of risky behaviors for their health, increasing their involvement in these behaviors. This problem apparently stems from a fatalistic attitude and sense of powerlessness that less educated and poorer people have about their lives. Because they think they will die from something sooner or later, they are less apt to be concerned about maintaining good health. Evidence for this reasoning comes from a study of middle-aged smokers who had heart attacks. Although all their physicians presumably advised them to stop smoking after their heart attack, only half of these patients with a high-school degree did so, compared to almost 90% of those with a college degree (Wray et al. 1998). The lower-educated patients apparently chose to disbelieve their doctor's warning, were not sufficiently concerned with smoking's risk to stop smoking, or else felt the need to continue smoking to help relieve stress in their lives.

A second and related reason for the social class-health behavior link involves the cognitive abilities that accompany a college education. As Catherine E. Ross and John Mirowsky (2010:34) observe, "Higher education teaches people to think logically and rationally, see many sides of an issue, and analyze problems and solve them. Education also develops broadly effective habits and attitudes such as dependability, judgment, motivation, effort, trust and confidence, as well as skills and abilities." All these traits presumably help college-educated people to better understand the importance of health behavior and to appreciate the consequences of health behaviors for their own lives and for members of their families. These traits also promote confidence in one's ability to address problems (*self-efficacy*) and the motivation to do so, along with a sense of control over one's life. Self-efficacy and a sense of control in turn help promote the willingness to practice positive health behaviors.

Third, people with more education usually have more money are thus better able to "buy the things that maintain health" (Ross and Mirowsky 2010:34). For example, nutritious food such as fruits and vegetables, fish, whole grains, and organic food cost more than the fatty and processed foods that most Americans eat. People with higher SES have better diets partly because they are better able to afford healthy foods; conversely, people with lower SES have poorer nutrition partly because they are less able to pay for these foods.

Although this discussion has concerned everyday preventive health behavior, income also affects the ability to undertake periodic health behavior as defined earlier, that is, preventive health screening and other health measures such as an annual visit to a physician. Simply put, low-income people practice periodic health behavior less often because they cannot afford the expense of this behavior. In addition to their lack of money, another reason for their lack of periodic behavior is that they are less likely to have health insurance. In 2012, before Obamacare took full effect, only 25% of uninsured adults aged 50–64 were up-to-date on health screenings and other periodic preventive services like an annual doctor visit, compared to 58% of their insured counterparts (Schoen et al. 2014). Although more low-income people have health insurance now than in 2012, their rates of insurance still remain lower (see chapter 12), and thus, too, their use of periodic health services.

A fourth reason for the SES difference in promotive health behavior involves childhood experiences. People's SES often reflects their family's SES when they were children. Family SES has a large impact on children's health behaviors. For example, children from lower SES families are more likely to have unhealthy diets and lack sufficient exercise (Faienza et al. 2016). These health behaviors often continue into adolescence and adulthood. To some extent, then, the relationship between adults' social class and health behavior reflects their socioeconomic circumstances and socialization during childhood.

Fifth, SES is related to stress, with low-SES individuals and households experiencing much more severe and constant stress in their lives (Thoits 2010) (see chapter 5). Stress, in turn, can promote bad eating habits, lead people to smoke and use other harmful drugs, and promote other risky health behaviors such as sleeplessness.

A sixth reason concerns social relationships. We shall see later in this chapter that social relationships affect health behavior, as our family and friends influence our health behavior choices to some extent. When our family and friends practice good health behaviors themselves and encourage or prod us to do the same, we are more likely to follow their example. The reverse is also true. Social relationships conform to the principle of **homophily**, the tendency of people to have relationships with other people with similar backgrounds, beliefs, interests, and other traits: our family and friends usually share our SES. This means that high-SES people have social relationships with other high-SES people, and low-SES people have social relationships with other low-SES people. Some of the social class difference in health behavior, then, stems from the fact that we learn and conform to different health behaviors because of our SES-related social relationships.

Next, SES greatly affects where we live and the living conditions of the areas in which we live, as we shall also see later in this chapter. Consider two families: an upper-middle class family living in a wealthy suburb, and a poor family living in a dense, dilapidated urban area. The first family probably lives fairly near some very nice supermarkets stocked with fruits, vegetables, and other healthy foods, while the poor family probably lives near convenience stores. Even if the poor family could afford to buy healthy food, it would have to travel longer distances to a supermarket selling such food and have to drive through city streets or take public transportation to do so. In short, the urban family lacks the access to healthy food that the suburban family enjoys because the urban family lives amid a so-called food desert (Kelli et al. 2016).

A similar health behavior difference exists for exercise. People in suburbs probably think nothing of going for a long walk or run around their neighborhoods; people in dense urban areas may well be reluctant to do so because of crime, traffic, or other concerns (Ross 2000). The greater physical activity of higher-SES people stems to some degree, then, from the fact that it is easier for them to safely exercise. More generally, SES affects the physical and social attributes of the areas in which we live, and these attributes in turn affect our ability and likelihood of practicing certain promotive health behaviors versus risky behaviors.

Race and Ethnicity

Racial/ethnic differences in health behavior are rather difficult to document and to explain. One reason for this difficulty is that these differences are more complex than they are for social class. Whereas the social class "split" in health behavior is consistent across the gamut of health behaviors, racial/ethnic differences are somewhat inconsistent: for complex reasons, some racial/ethnic groups are more likely than others both to practice a particular positive health behavior and a particular risky health behavior. We will see evidence of this inconsistency later in this chapter.

A second reason for this difficulty concerns the concept of race. Most sociologists and anthropologists view race as a *social construction* (see chapter 1) rather than a real biological category (Schaefer 2015; Williams and Sternthal 2010). For example, many people call themselves, and are assumed to be, one specific race, even though their ancestry comes from two or more races. Because race is a slippery concept, any measure of race is best a rough measure rather a highly valid measure. For example, people we call "white" or "black" might not be as "white" or "black" as we think they are. Moreover, many people we call *African American* and *white* have Latino origins, making it difficult to separate the effects of race from those of ethnicity. For this reason, our discussion here of African Americans and whites will focus on people from these races who describe themselves as non-Latinos. A further complication is the fact that the terms *Asian* and *Latino* combine peoples from many different national origins, making it difficult to generalize for Asians and Latinos as a whole. Finally, as with social class, some possible reasons for racial/ethnic differences in health behavior might make more sense for certain behaviors than for other behaviors.

Setting aside all these concerns for the moment, race and ethnicity do appear to affect health behavior: African Americans, Latinos, and Native Americans are more likely than Asians and whites to engage in many, but not all, risky health behaviors (Dubowitz et al. 2011; Krueger et al. 2011). For example, African Americans are more likely than whites to be obese but also less likely to drink excessively; Latinos are also more likely than whites to be obese but less likely to smoke. Native Americans tend to have the worst health behavior overall, while Asians tend to have the best health behavior. These generalizations have many exceptions, but they do provide a helpful summary of the relationship between race and ethnicity and health behavior.

The overall pattern of worse health behaviors among African Americans, Latinos, and Native Americans is thought to stem in large part from their lower SES (Cubbins and Buchanan 2009; Krueger, Saint Onge, and Chang 2011). These three groups are much poorer and less educated than Asians and whites. Because Asians and whites have higher SES on average, their health behaviors are generally better. The previous section discussed why low SES promotes risky health behaviors and reduces promotive health behaviors, and why higher SES has the opposite effects. The reasons discussed in that section help explain why African Americans, Latinos, and Native American exhibit worse health behavior than Asians and whites and, conversely, why Asians and whites exhibit better health behavior.

A second reason for the racial/ethnic patterning in some health behavior concerns where racial/ethnic groups tend to live. For example, the previous section noted that residence in poor urban areas promotes bad nutrition and obesity because these areas lack access to healthy foods and inhibit walking and other exercise. One reason, then, for the greater obesity of African Americans is that they are especially likely to live in poor urban areas (Krueger et al. 2011). Although heavy drinking by African Americans is somewhat lower than that by whites, their drinking is still promoted by the common presence of liquor stores and other alcohol outlets in urban neighborhoods (Boardman et al. 2005).

A third reason concerns the influence of norms and values on health behavior via socialization and social control. Recalling our discussion of homophily in regard to social class, we tend to practice our health behaviors because of the influence of our family and friends. As Boardman et al. (2005) summarize this view, "Neighborhoods provide a social context in which otherwise subcultural values regarding health-related behaviors become normative. Neighborhood context can influence behavior directly via imitation processes, or indirectly through the internalization of norms and values within the collective lifestyles of the neighborhood." Because the United States still has a racially segregated society, people of a certain race and/or ethnicity tend to live among people of the same race and/or ethnicity; African Americans are especially likely to live in segregated circumstances. Racial/ethnic homophily thus fosters the spread of health behaviors. If, for example, African Americans in an urban area are surrounded entirely by other African Americans, many of whom are overweight or obese, any one person in that area is therefore more likely to be obese.

A fourth reason concerns possible racial/ethnic differences in norms and values regarding certain health behaviors. We must be careful not to stereotype here, but African Americans do appear to "prefer large body sizes" (Boardman et al. 2005:231). To the extent this is true, African Americans are less likely than members of other racial and ethnic groups to be discouraged from overeating by their family and friends. This cultural value helps produce a higher rate of obesity. By the same token, African Americans tend to be more religious than whites and thus more likely to view drinking negatively. This fact helps explain African Americans' lower level of heavy drinking compared to that of whites (Stevens-Watkins and Rostosky 2010).

Gender

Gender, too, affects health behavior. Although gender differences are often modest, women are generally more likely than men to engage in positive health behaviors, while men are more likely to engage in risky behaviors (Read and Gorman 2010). For example, women are more likely than men to visit a physician for an annual checkup. Meanwhile, men are more likely than women to smoke, to drink heavily, and to use illegal drugs. They are also more likely to drive drunk and/or recklessly, to be involved in violent encounters, and to have multiple sex partners (which raises the risk of STDs). In all these ways, men are more likely than women to put themselves at risk for disease and/or injury. However, men are also more likely than women to exercise (Rogers et al. 2010) and slightly less likely to be obese (Ogden et al. 2014).

It is worth noting that women have better health behavior than men overall even though women are more likely than men to have lower SES (which, as we have seen, is associated with worse health behavior). This bit of contradiction reinforces the influence that gender exerts over health behavior.

An important question is why men are indeed more likely than women to engage in risky health behaviors. Some scholars, mostly in the fields of biology and evolutionary psychology, say that risk taking and risk aversion are wired into the genes of men and women, respectively (Buss 2015). According to this way of thinking, eons ago men were more attractive to (female) mates and thus more likely to reproduce if they engaged in risky behavior. Conversely, women who were *averse* to risky behavior were more likely to stay alive and thus to be able to reproduce or to protect children they already had. For these reasons, natural selection favored risk-prone males and risk-averse females. Other biologically oriented scholars attribute men's riskier behavior to their higher levels of testosterone (Booth et al. 2006). Although these evolutionary explanations might sound appealing, critics say that methodological and other problems cast doubt on their credibility (Begley 2009; Gould 1981).

Sociologists instead attribute gender differences in health behavior largely to gender socialization during childhood and adolescence that shapes behavior into adulthood (Courtenay 2000; Lindsey 2015; Waldron 1997). According to this way of thinking, boys are raised from infancy to be assertive and to take risks, while girls are raised to be less assertive and not to take risks. Girls are also raised more than boys to think about the needs of others. This "caring" orientation leads girls and then women to shun risky behavior for two reasons: their risky behavior might harm others, and their risky behavior might harm themselves and thus make it difficult for them to care for others. Gender differences in health behavior, then, reflect the fact that women and men are acting out notions of femininity and masculinity, respectively, that they learned as children and adolescents.

Another reason for gender differences in health behavior relates to religion. Women overall are more religious than men (Collett and Lizardo 2009). As we discuss later in this chapter, people who are more religious are less likely to engage in risky health behavior. One reason, then, that women practice healthier behavior than men may be that they are more religious than men, although questions remain whether women are more risk averse because they are more religious, or more religious because they are more risk averse (Collett and Lizardo 2009).

Illustrating the Effects of Social Class, Race and Ethnicity, and Gender

Ample evidence, much of it from national survey data, illustrates the social class, racial/ethnic, and gender differences in health behavior just summarized. This section presents a bit of this evidence for four very important health behaviors: smoking, aerobic activity, obesity, and excessive drinking. Unless otherwise noted, all data come from an annual publication, *Health, United States* (National Center for Health Statistics 2015), that compiles data from many sources to provide a detailed picture of the nation's health and use of health care.

Smoking   We begin with smoking because it leads all risky health behaviors in the number of preventable deaths it causes annually. Almost one-fifth (17.9%) of all adults 18 and older smoke cigarettes regularly (2013 data). CDC calls smoking the major cause of preventable death and disease in the nation (Garrett et al. 2013): if no one smoked, all the health problems caused by smoking would simply not occur. It is no exaggeration to say tobacco's harmful ingredients are a slow poison. Smoking and other tobacco use cause cancer, heart disease, lung disease and other health problems and account for more than 480,000 premature deaths annually in the United States, including 41,000 deaths from exposure to second-hand smoke. The average smoker dies 10 years earlier than the average non-smoker. Smoking costs the United States $133 billion annually in medical costs and $156 billion in lost productivity, for total economic cost near $300 billion (Centers for Disease Control and Prevention 2014b). By any measure, smoking and other tobacco use are a serious public health problem.

Starting with social class, smoking rates vary dramatically by education and income. As Figure 3.1 shows, adults without a high-school degree are much more likely than those with a college degree to smoke. Similarly, adults below 100% poverty are much more likely than wealthier adults to smoke.

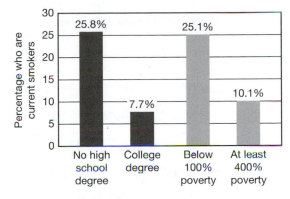

FIG. 3.1 Education, Income, and Smoking (% of adults 25 and over who are current smokers).

Notes: Adults 25 and older for education; adults 18 and older for income.
Source: National Center for Health Statistics. 2015. *Health, United States, 2014.* Hyattsville, MD: Centers for Disease Control and Prevention.

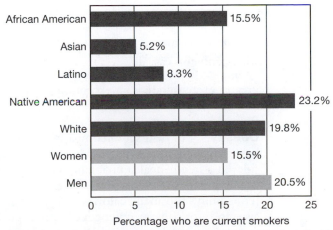

FIG. 3.2 Race and Ethnicity, Gender, and Smoking (% of adults 18 and older who are current smokers).

Source: National Center for Health Statistics. 2015. *Health, United States, 2014.* Hyattsville, MD: Centers for Disease Control and Prevention.

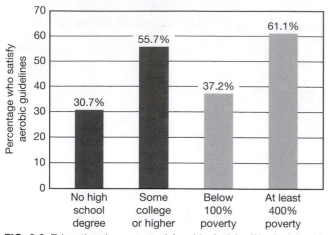

FIG. 3.3 Education, Income, and Aerobic Activity (% of adults 18 and older who satisfy aerobic guidelines).

Source: National Center for Health Statistics. 2015. *Health, United States, 2014.* Hyattsville, MD: Centers for Disease Control and Prevention.

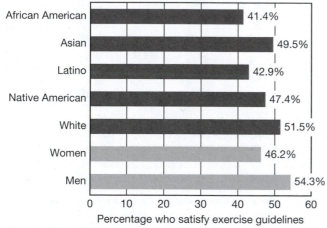

FIG. 3.4 Race and Ethnicity, Gender, and Aerobic Activity (% of adults 18 and older who satisfy aerobic guidelines).

Source: National Center for Health Statistics. 2015. *Health, United States, 2014.* Hyattsville, MD: Centers for Disease Control and Prevention.

Race and ethnicity (Latino or non-Latino), and gender also matter for smoking rates. As Figure 3.2 shows, Asians and Latinos are much less likely to smoke than African Americans, Native Americans, or whites. Meanwhile, men are somewhat more likely than women to smoke.

Aerobic Activity As noted earlier, CDC considers regular exercise important for good health. It and other government agencies have developed guidelines for adequate aerobic activity. Based on responses to questions included in the National Health Interview Survey, CDC determines the percentage of Americans who satisfy these guidelines. Our illustration presents these percentages.

We begin once more with education and income and again see some strong relationships (see Figure 3.3). Adults with some college education are much more likely than those without a high-school degree to satisfy the aerobic guidelines. Wealthier adults are also much more likely than those living in poverty to satisfy them.

Racial/ethnic and gender differences in aerobic activity also exist but are not as large (see Figure 3.4). Whites are somewhat more likely than the other racial/ethnic groups to satisfy the aerobic guidelines, while African Americans are least likely. Meanwhile, men are somewhat more likely than women to satisfy the guidelines, as indicated earlier. Men's greater exercise rate is an exception to their overall worse health behavior compared to women.

Obesity Our next set of comparisons involves obesity. As chapter 2 noted, obesity has risen dramatically in the United States during the last few decades and is considered a major health problem, with more than one-third of adults being obese. At the purely individual level, obesity is the complex consequence of bad nutrition (consuming too many calories and the "wrong kinds" of foods), insufficient exercise, and, for some people, genetic predisposition (Centers for Disease Control and Prevention 2013; Datz and Dwyer 2014). In line with CDC (Schoenborn, Adams, and Peregoy 2013), we use obesity here as an indicator of the first two reasons, bad nutrition and insufficient exercise, both of which are, of course, risky health behaviors.

TABLE 3.1	Sociodemographic Comparisons for Obesity, Adults 20 and older (years vary)

	% Obese
No high-school degree	38.6
College degree	26.9
Below 100% poverty	35.0
At least 400% poverty	28.9
African American	47.8
Asian	10.8
Latino	42.5
White	32.6
Men	34.6
Women	35.9
African American men	38.1
African American women	57.5
Mexican origin men	40.2
Mexican origin women	46.3
White men	34.4
White women	32.3

Note: education data are for adults 25 and older

Sources: Befort, Christie A., Niaman Nazir, and Michael G. Perri. 2012. "Prevalence of Obesity Among Adults From Rural and Urban Areas of the United States: Findings From NHANES (2005–2008)." *The Journal of Rural Health* 28:392–397; Centers for Disease Control and Prevention. 2014. "Overweight and Obesity: Adult Obesity Facts." *http://www.cdc. gov/obesity/data/adult.html;* National Center for Health Statistics. 2015. *Health, United States, 2014.* Hyattsville, MD: Centers for Disease Control and Prevention.

Table 3.1 presents several sociodemographic comparisons for obesity. Lower levels of education and income are both linked to somewhat higher rates of obesity. However, in data not shown in the table, this linkage exists only among women, as men's obesity rates are generally similar across education and income levels. Meanwhile, some 42% of women without a high-school degree are obese compared to 23% of women with a college degree, while 42% of low-income women are obese compared to 29% of wealthier women (Ogden et al. 2010).

Returning to Table 3.1, African Americans and Latinos have the highest rates of obesity, while Asians have noticeably lower rates. On the surface, gender hardly matters for obesity, as women are just slightly more likely than men to be obese. However, gender does make a much larger difference if we take race into account, as obesity is much higher among African American women than African American men and somewhat higher among Mexican-origin women than Mexican-origin men.

Excessive Drinking   Excessive alcohol use causes about 88,000 deaths in the United States annually and accounts for about one-tenth of the deaths of adults in the 18–64 age range. People in this age range who die from drinking lose an average of thirty years from their lives. Their deaths occur from the long-term health effects of alcohol abuse, including liver and heart disease and certain cancers, and from alcohol poisoning, motor vehicle accidents, violence, and other dangers stemming from drinking too

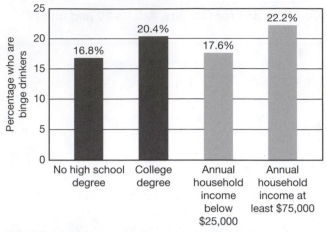

FIG. 3.5 Education, Income, and Binge Drinking (% of adults 18 and over who report binge drinking).

Source: Kanny, Dafna, Yong Liu, Robert D. Brewer, and Hua Lu. 2013. "Binge Drinking—United States, 2011." *Morbidity and Mortality Weekly Report* 62:77–80.

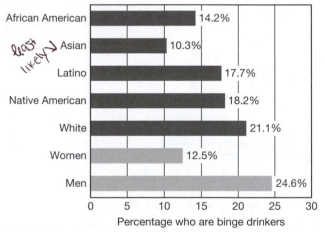

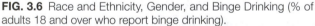

FIG. 3.6 Race and Ethnicity, Gender, and Binge Drinking (% of adults 18 and over who report binge drinking).

Source: Kanny, Dafna, Yong Liu, Robert D. Brewer, and Hua Lu. 2013. "Binge Drinking—United States, 2011." *Morbidity and Mortality Weekly Report* 62:77–80.

much in too short a time period (Centers for Disease Control and Prevention 2014a). Excessive drinking also destroys many lives and families even if it does not lead to death. It costs the United States and estimated $224 billion annually in reduced earnings and other lost productivity. By any standard, excessive drinking is a very risky behavior and a major health problem.

Two common measures of excessive drinking are *binge drinking* and *heavy drinking*. The National Center for Health Statistics (2014) defines **binge drinking** as having "five or more drinks on the same occasion on at least 1 day in the past 30 days" and **binge drinking** as having "five or more drinks on the same occasion on each of 5 or more days in the past 30 days." Binge drinking will be used for our comparisons.

Figure 3.5 reports binge drinking prevalence rates by education and income. In contrast to the usual pattern of riskier behavior among people with less education and income, binge drinking is actually slightly *lower* among people from these backgrounds.

Figure 3.6 presents the racial/ethnic and gender comparisons for binge drinking. Whites have the highest binge drinking rate and Asians the lowest, while the rates for Latinos and Native Americans are slightly higher than that for African Americans. Meanwhile, men are twice as likely as women to be binge drinkers.

The comparisons you have just seen are a bit complex but still tell an important tale: social class, race and ethnicity, and gender as key aspects of our social backgrounds matter, often greatly, for our involvement in promotive versus risky health behaviors. The patterns are not perfectly consistent but are more consistent for social class (education and income) and gender than for race and ethnicity. Taken together, the comparisons show that social class, race and ethnicity, and gender all affect our likelihood of engaging in positive health behaviors versus risky health behaviors. This general social patterning suggests that health behavior is not just an individual choice but is instead shaped by who we are in a sociological sense.

The Social Context of Health Behavior: Other Factors

Although social class, race and ethnicity, and gender shape health behavior, other social factors do so as well. This section discusses some of these factors, which again show how our social backgrounds and other social aspects affect our choices to practice positive versus risky health behaviors.

Social Relationships

Earlier we noted that health behaviors are an outcome of socialization and social control. This dynamic points to the significance for health behaviors of our **social relationships**, or our social ties to other individuals such as spouses, romantic partners, family, and friends. These are the types of social relationships we probably think about most often, but social relationships also stem from our involvement in *voluntary associations* such as religious institutions and civic groups and from workplace friendships we may form from our jobs. Whatever their source, the extent and quality of social relationships are important for our health and for our health behavior (Umberson and Montez 2010).

Recognition of this importance derives from a classic study by the great French sociologist Émile Durkheim (1858–1917), a founder of sociology. Durkheim considered **social integration**, which he conceptualized as strong, extensive social bonds and the shared norms and values stemming from social bonds, as important for personal well-being and for society as a whole. He therefore hypothesized that weak social integration should be linked to higher suicide rates. Durkheim (1952 [1897]) then studied suicide rates in regions of several European nations, along with marriage rates and other indicators of social integration. As he hypothesized, suicide rates were higher in areas with lower social integration. Durkhiem's research on this topic highlighted the importance of social relationships for well-being and set the stage for contemporary research on this connection.

This research underscores the importance of social relationships for health behavior: many studies find that our various social relationships influence our health behavior, just as they affect many other aspects of our lives (Qualls 2014). This influence occurs because we learn health behaviors from our social relationships and also because we want to both please and avoid angering or disappointing the people we like and love. The regard we hold for them thus exercises *social control* over our health behaviors.

The social relationships affecting health behaviors change over the life course. During early childhood, the dominant social relationship involves parents; during adolescence, peer relationships loom very large; and during young adulthood, romantic partners and spouses often become the primary social relationship. All these very different types of relationships affect our health behavior.

The impact of social relationships during childhood and adolescence is especially important. The health behaviors children learn from their parents regarding diet, exercise, and other matters often carry into adolescence and adulthood and can have a lifelong impact on health. During adolescence, peer relationships begin to exert more influence than the parental relationship. As a recent review emphasized, "Substantial evidence shows that peers are the biggest social factor in predicting adolescent health behavior" (Umberson, Crosnoe, and Reczek 2010:142).

Whatever the stage of life, social relationships are usually thought to promote positive health behaviors. Many parents teach their children good eating habits and the value of exercise, and friends provide us opportunities for outdoor activities such as hiking and sports. During adulthood, romantic partners and spouses encourage or even demand that we practice good health behaviors. Marriage often reduces risky behaviors like smoking and heavy drinking (Umberson, Crosnoe, and Reczek 2010).

At the same time, however, social relationships can also promote risky health behaviors. Many parents let their children eat junk food and watch too much TV (thus not getting enough exercise). Many children and adults live in families filled with conflict, abuse, and stress; their living situation can make it very difficult to practice good health behaviors and may promote risky health behaviors such as drinking, smoking, and overeating or undereating. Friendships with delinquent peers often lead adolescents to engage in delinquency and to use alcohol and other drugs. Friendships can even be a source of obesity, as having obese friends seem to make it more likely that we ourselves will be obese (Jalali et al. 2016; Smith and Christakis 2008). However, *selectivity* issues (the possibility that obese people choose obese friends and partners) preclude clear conclusions about this particular influence (Fletcher 2011).

Marriage's effects on health behaviors are somewhat complicated. Although, as just mentioned, marriage generally reduces drinking, smoking, and some other risky health behaviors, it also generally raises the risk of obesity. Parenthood is similar to marriage in these respects. Although parenthood often reduces risky behaviors, it also can raise the risk of obesity, as parents tend to exercise less than nonparents (Umberson, Crosnoe, and Reczek 2010).

This brief summary suggests two general conclusions about social relationships and health behaviors. First, social relationships can lead to both positive health behaviors and to risky health behaviors. Second, both the quantity and quality of our social relationships affect our health behaviors. In general, a lack of social ties can generate unhealthy behaviors, in part because loneliness produces physical inactivity and sleep problems, while a greater number of social ties help promote healthy behaviors (Cacioppo and Cacioppo 2014). Meanwhile, good social relationships tend to promote positive health behaviors, while bad social relationships tend to promote risky health behaviors. This complexity aside, the impact of social relationships on health behaviors is one of the signature findings of medical sociologists and health psychologists.

Neighborhood Living Conditions

As noted earlier regarding SES and race and ethnicity, where we live can affect our ability to engage in at least two health behaviors, practicing good nutrition and getting enough exercise (Cockerham 2013b; MacIntyre and Ellaway 2003). For example, many people who live in poor, urban neighborhoods have to buy most of their food at convenience stores, which lack fresh fruits and vegetables and other types of healthy foods and instead feature processed and fatty foods. These residents thus face a "grocery gap" (Treuhaft and Karpyn 2010). This urban fact of life makes it more difficult, all things equal, for residents in these neighborhoods to have a healthy diet. Similarly, living in these same neighborhoods may make it difficult to get enough exercise, and people may be afraid (of crime and/or of traffic) just to go for a long walk or in a high-crime area. Many people like to exercise in well-equipped gyms or attractive parks, but these exercise venues and general "walkability" are also lacking in many urban neighborhoods (Creatore et al. 2016). For these reasons, many urban residents are unable to get enough physical activity (Boone-Heinonen and Gordon-Larsen 2011).

Sexual Orientation and Gender Identity

About 3–4% of the U.S. population is estimated to be LGBT, although the exact number is difficult to know. Despite many advances, LGBT Americans still live in a homophobic society. They face everyday slights and discrimination and sometimes bullying and violence that straight people avoid because of their **heterosexual**

privilege. LGBT status therefore leads to stress and other problems, which in turn promote greater involvement in risky health behaviors such as unprotected sex, smoking, poor nutrition, and drinking and other drug use (Bränström et al. 2016; Institute of Medicine 2011; Melnick 2011; Ward et al. 2014). In an interesting finding, gay and bisexual men have lower rates of obesity than straight men, while lesbians and bisexual women have higher rates of obesity than straight women. Despite this one inconsistency, sexual orientation and gender identity, as other dimensions of social inequality, are also other factors affecting health behavior.

Religious Involvement

Religious involvement promotes positive health behavior. This view again derives from Durkheim (1947 [1915]), who considered religion a potent force for social integration and social control that promotes positive behaviors and personal well-being. In this way of thinking, religious individuals should tend to behave better for at least two reasons. First, traditional religious beliefs generally frown on such "sinful" behaviors as drinking and using other drugs, sex outside marriage, and gambling. Second, and recalling the power of social relationships, religious individuals tend to have family, friends, and members of their congregations who hold these traditional beliefs. These persons' expectations help orient religious individuals toward healthy behaviors and away from risky behaviors.

Testing these assumptions, contemporary research finds that religious involvement—attendance at religious services, praying, and strong religious beliefs—deters risky health behaviors (Idler 2010; Koenig, King, and Carson 2012). In particular, it finds that religious adolescents are less likely than nonreligious adolescents to use legal or illegal drugs, to engage in premarital sex, and to commit delinquency. As this summary suggests, much research on religion and health behavior focuses on adolescents, but some research finds religious involvement promoting healthy behavior among adults as well, with religious adults more likely to be physically active, to practice good nutrition, and to avoid smoking and drinking (Hill et al. 2007; Kirk and Lewis 2013). One study using national data on adults aged 18–89 found that *never-married* adults who are more religious have fewer (premarital) sex partners than never-married adults who are less religious (Barkan 2006). Because having multiple sex partners is a risky health behavior, this study reinforced the findings on religion from the adolescent research.

Corporate Practices

Corporations do many good things, including publishing this textbook, and modern societies would be impossible without them. At the same time, corporations also engage in certain practices that affect health behavior (Cohen, Scribner, and Farley 2000). We specifically have in mind here the fact that corporations readily provide products such as alcohol, fatty/sugary/processed food, and tobacco. They also spend billions of dollars annually on advertising and other marketing to increase consumption of these products. As we have emphasized, people who drink too much alcohol, eat too much fatty/sugary/processed food, or smoke or otherwise use tobacco are engaging in a risky health behavior. Although their decision to do so is certainly their choice, there would be much less risky behavior if these products did not exist or at least were marketed less vigorously. Corporate practices therefore help promote these risky health behaviors and must share the blame for these behaviors.

Tobacco and alcohol companies spend billions of dollars annually on marketing their products, a practice that has been called "deadly persuasion" (Kilbourne 2011).

According to federal data, tobacco companies spend more than $8 billion annually on cigarette advertising and other promotional efforts, or some $23 million per day (Centers for Disease Control and Prevention 2014c). Alcohol companies spend about $3.5 billion annually on advertising and other promotional efforts, including sponsorship of sporting and entertainment events (Federal Trade Commission 2014).

Critics say that much of the marketing of tobacco and alcohol is aimed at teenagers in an effort to get them to start using these products early in life, and that this targeted marketing does achieve its goal (Centers for Disease Control and Prevention 2012; Ross et al. 2014). To the extent that public policy efforts to reduce teenage smoking and drinking focus on urging teenagers to change their behaviors, these efforts deflect attention from the role that tobacco and alcohol companies play in these behaviors. As two scholars explain this problem for tobacco, "Morbidity and mortality due to tobacco is attributed to an individually-based bad habit [smoking] rather than to a heavily advertised, government-subsidized, highly profitable killer industry" (Link and Phelan 1995:90).

Public Policy

Public policy does not always affect individual behavior as much as policymakers might wish, but certain policies may influence health behavior (Cohen, Scribner, and Farley 2000). For example, most smokers begin smoking during adolescence, when they have little money even though cigarettes can be expensive. Raising taxes on cigarettes has been shown to reduce smoking by teenagers and also low-income people because of the extra expense in purchasing cigarettes (Marr and Huang 2014). Similarly, consistent enforcement of laws against selling alcohol to minors may help reduce underage drinking. To some degree, then, public policy influences health behavior.

Conclusion

Health behavior contributes mightily to good health or bad health depending on the health lifestyle a person has adopted. This chapter's discussion underscores the significance of social factors for the choices we make regarding health behavior. Although we are all ultimately responsible for these choices, a sociological perspective reminds us how much our choices may be influenced by our social backgrounds and by other social forces. The same type of influence occurs for illness behavior, the subject of the next chapter.

Summary

1. Consistent practicing of health behaviors improves the quality of health and prolongs lifespans. The four most important health behaviors are not smoking, eating a healthy diet, getting sufficient exercise, and limiting alcohol use.
2. The sociological emphasis on macro factors and health lifestyles derives from the work of Max Weber on social class and general lifestyle. At the same time, personality and other micro factors help explain why some people are more likely than others in similar structural circumstances to practice healthy versus risky behaviors.
3. Social class exhibits the clearest macro patterning of health behavior, with people with less education and lower income more likely to engage in risky behaviors

and less likely to engage in positive behaviors. Racial/ethnic differences in health behavior are less consistent, but generally Asians exhibit the most positive behaviors and Native Americans the most risky behaviors. Racial/ethnic differences in health behavior reflect to a large degree racial/ethnic differences in socioeconomic status.

4. Women are generally more likely than men to practice positive health behaviors and less likely to engage in risky behavior. A notable exception is exercise, which men practice more than women.

5. Another social factor affecting health behavior is the extent and quality of social relationships. Individuals are more likely to practice positive health behavior if they have a greater number of high-quality social relationships. This effect results from processes of socialization and social control associated with social relationships.

6. Sexual orientation and gender identity, religiosity, and neighborhood living conditions are some additional social factors that affect health behavior. LGBT people are more likely to practice risky behavior, while religious people are more likely to practice positive behavior. Several social and physical characteristics of urban life contribute to risky health behavior.

7. Corporate practices also bear responsibility for risky health behavior. The alcohol, food, and tobacco industries spend billions of dollars annually marketing unhealthy products.

Giving It Some Thought

You are a social worker who specializes in children's welfare. One of the new families in your caseload consists of two parents and two children, aged 3 and 5. When you first visit this family, you notice both parents smoking throughout your visit. Although you didn't ask them to stop, you recognize that their smoke could be very harmful to their children both in the short run and in the long run. What, if anything, do you do?

Key Terms

binge drinking, 44

health behavior, 32

health belief model, 35

health lifestyle, 34

heavy drinking, 44

heterosexual privilege, 46

homophily, 38

life chances, 34

lifestyles, 34

locus of control, 35

social control, 33

social integration, 45

social relationships, 45

socialization, 33

4 Illness Behavior and the Illness Experience

LEARNING QUESTIONS

1. How do medical sociologists distinguish illness from disease?

2. What are examples of how illness is a social construction?

3. Why are some medical sociologists critical of medicalization?

4. What are the stages of the illness experience?

5. How and why does social class affect help-seeking behavior?

6. How and why does chronic illness often create biographical disruption?

Health and Health Care in the News

Society's reaction to José Ramirez Jr. changed forever when he was diagnosed with leprosy at age 20 in 1969. He had to live the next seven years at the National Leprosarium in Louisiana, the only such institution in the United States and 750 miles from his Texas home, from where he was taken in a hearse to the leprosarium. When interviewed some 45 years later, Ramirez said he was totally cured with no remaining scars or other traces of the disease. "I'm very fortunate that the experimental medications they gave me prevented a lot of that," he explained. Still, he had suffered emotionally since he first developed leprosy due to the "stigma, guilt and shame," as he termed it, associated with this disease. He has since written a memoir and news articles about his experience with leprosy and given many talks about it. (Angier 2014; Ramirez 2009)

Leprosy is a disfiguring disease that has long been stigmatized. It is mentioned many times in the Bible, and the Bible's references to it are hardly flattering. Leviticus 13:45–46 declares, "The leprous person who has the disease shall wear torn clothes and let the hair of his head hang loose, and he shall cover his upper lip and cry out, 'Unclean, unclean.' He shall remain unclean as long as he has the disease. He is unclean. He shall live alone. His dwelling shall be outside the camp." José Ramirez Jr., the subject of our opening news story, learned all too well how it felt to live "outside the camp." His poignant story reminds us that illness is not just a personal experience but also a social experience, as people designated as ill must come to terms with their illness, which often means dealing with society's reaction to it. This is certainly true of leprosy but also of other health problems. The way in which ill people respond to their illness is part of their illness experience.

This chapter discusses medical sociology's perspective on illness, illness behavior, and the illness experience. As with health behavior in the previous chapter, we will again see that many aspects of the social environment affect illness behavior and experience.

Understanding Illness

The terms *disease* and *illness* are often used interchangeably to refer to a health problem that is not an injury, although "disease" probably sounds more serious than "illness." However, medical sociology considers disease a *biological* concept and illness a *social* concept (Charmaz and Rosenfeld 2010; Eisenberg 1977). In this way of thinking, **disease** refers to the actual medical symptoms affecting an individual, and more generally to a biological problem affecting the structure or functioning of some part of the body. In contrast, **illness** refers to a person's perceptions of and reactions to these medical symptoms and their underlying biological problem, and to similar perceptions and reactions by other people about that person's symptoms.

This social conception of illness involves three elements: (1) the designation of medical symptoms as illness; (2) the reaction of the ill person and other people to this designation, including the meaning they all attach to the symptoms and how they attempt to deal with the symptoms; and (3) the social, psychological, physiological, and economic consequences of the illness designation and of any medical symptoms underlying the designation. The basic idea here is that illness is more than just medical symptoms. Instead it involves people's perceptions and reactions.

These perceptions and reactions (or responses) form the **illness experience**, which may be defined more formally as the ways in which people perceive and react to medical symptoms. An important component of the illness experience is **illness behavior**, or the health care activities that people with perceived medical symptoms choose to practice or not to practice. People with perceived symptoms must decide what, if anything, to do regarding health care for these symptoms (*illness behavior*), but they must also grapple emotionally and in other ways with what their disease means for their lives. Depending on the particular disease, they may have to deal with the seriousness of their symptoms, and/or they may have to deal with people's reactions to those symptoms. Illness behavior, then, is a subset, however important, of the more general illness experience.

The illness experience varies in several ways. First, people can respond to similar symptoms very differently, with their responses often shaped by the same social factors that shape health behavior (see chapter 3). Second, some people have minor symptoms while others have serious symptoms, with different consequences for their illness experience. Third, some people have symptoms of diseases like cancer that arouse our sympathy, and others have symptoms of diseases that arouse our disapproval, as the leprosy story that began this chapter reminds us: these different social reactions also affect the illness experience. Fourth, some individuals may have symptoms for which medical professionals can find no known medical cause, and these individuals then find that their claims of illness may not be taken seriously. Finally, people diagnosed with disabilities face their own set of practical and emotional difficulties. These many scenarios show that the illness experience is far from a simple dynamic. As we see throughout this chapter, this complexity of the illness experience is a key topic in medical sociology.

Illness as a Social Construction

The basic sociological understanding of illness just presented reflects the social constructionist approach to illness introduced in chapter 1. To recall, a social construction is a concept that does not have objective reality but that exists because people decide it exists. In medical sociology, illness is considered a social construction (Conrad and Barker 2010). Medical symptoms and thus disease may have objective reality, but illness does not. Instead illness is a social designation resulting from the meaning that people attach to medical symptoms. Because illness is a social construction, society and culture affect both whether medical symptoms are perceived as illness and how individuals considered ill should be regarded and treated. Illness, then, is far more than just medical symptoms.

Cross-cultural studies provide fascinating evidence of the role that culture plays in shaping views about aspects of health and illness as well as the social responses to illness (Quah 2010; Wiley and Allen 2013). Some of the most remarkable evidence comes from anthropological studies of traditional societies. In some of these societies, men whose wives are pregnant experience morning sickness even though the men are obviously not pregnant (Doja 2005). The morning sickness these men experience has no biological basis, but they experience it nonetheless. The reason they experience it is that their society expects them to experience it through a process of socialization, making their morning sickness a social construction. In some traditional societies, men whose pregnant wives are giving birth also experience labor pain. The men's labor pain again has no biological basis (they are not the ones giving birth!), but they feel labor pain nonetheless. The reason for this is again society's expectation, and the labor pain they feel is again a social construction. Anthropologists use the term *couvade* to refer to the morning sickness and labor pain that men feel in these societies.

Another example of culture's influence comes from Japan and concerns organ donations. In the United States and many other nations, medical advances have enabled organ donations to save people's lives. The organs come from people who are living donors but more often from people who have just died. Organ donation is not a pleasant topic to think about, but a national survey found that 95% of Americans support organ donation and that 60% have indicated on their driver's license their willingness to be an organ donor (U.S. Department of Health and Human Services 2013). (Perhaps you are one of the people who have designated yourself in this way.)

In Japan the situation is very different, as Japanese citizens generally oppose organ transplantation (Asai, Kadooka, and Aizawa 2012). This opposition stems from their cultural and religious aversion to disfiguring bodies of the dead, even for autopsies. Most Japanese decline to identify themselves as organ donors, and families typically refuse permission for organ donation after a family member dies. Because of all these factors, organ transplants are much less common in Japan than in other industrial nations.

Medicalization The concept of *medicalization*, also introduced in chapter 1, reinforces the idea that illness is a social construction. Recall that **medicalization** refers to the process by which nonmedical problems become defined and treated as medical problems, often without good evidence of their medical nature (Conrad and Barker 2010). This process exemplifies the idea that illness is a social designation stemming from meanings and perceptions attached to symptoms, and that various social and cultural factors influence this designation. The nonmedical problems that are medicalized may be behaviors or life events such as menopause, baldness, and sexual decline due to aging that were previously thought to be a normal part of the human experience, or they may be social problems such as alcoholism and child abuse that were previously considered to have nonmedical causes and to need nonmedical solutions.

Medicalization results from efforts by the medical profession and the pharmaceutical industry, and it also can result from efforts by patient advocacy groups and social movements. Alcoholics Anonymous, for example, was instrumental in defining alcoholism as a disease, whereas alcoholism had previously been considered a behavioral problem stemming from moral weaknesses (Conrad 2008).

Consequences of Medicalization   Medicalization has several consequences, both negative and positive. First, once medicalization occurs, persons with the new medical problem are now regarded as medical patients, the problem they have is now thought to be appropriately treated with medication, and these patients then have to see a physician to obtain a prescription for the medication they are now advised to take. As this brief description implies, medicalization can be very profitable for physicians, pharmacies, and especially pharmaceutical companies. Medical sociologists attribute much medicalization to these companies' desire to increase their profits and suggest that the companies sometimes give a greater priority to their bottom line than to what is best for the public (Bell and Figert 2015; Conrad 2008).

Second, medicalization takes attention away from the underlying social causes of the condition or behavior that has been medicalized. For example, defining alcoholism as a disease emphasizes the need to treat the individual alcoholic while diverting attention away from the role that the alcohol industry's advertising and other marketing plays in the extent of drinking. Similarly, defining behavioral and attention problems in schoolchildren as attention-deficit hyperactivity disorder (ADHD; formerly called attention-deficit disorder, or ADD) diverts attention from inadequate parenting and aspects of the school experience such as overcrowded classrooms that promote these problems (Conrad and Barker 2010).

Two additional consequences of medicalization are more positive (Gabe 2013). When medicalization occurs, society's view of the persons with the new medical problem may improve because they are now seen as patients whose problems have medical causes beyond their control. To illustrate, whereas alcoholism was seen as a sign of moral weakness a century ago, the fact that it is now seen as a disease means that we are less likely to blame someone for becoming an alcoholic. Similarly, when parents have a child who is diagnosed with ADHD, we become more likely to attribute the child's problems to a medical cause and less likely to blame the parents for these problems (Malacrida 2003).

In another positive consequence, medicalization can help devote the attention of the medical community to health problems that previously went untreated even though they were affecting many people. Considering alcoholism as a disease, for example, has opened the door for certain medical treatments to help alcoholics that are often covered by medical insurance. Similarly, chronic fatigue syndrome, which has no known cause, has increasingly become recognized, thanks in large part to the efforts of patient advocacy groups, as an actual disease and not just something the people experiencing it were imagining. This new designation has led to medical efforts, again often covered by insurance, to help people with this condition (Barker 2010).

Examples of Medicalization   Many accounts document efforts by pharmaceutical companies and other interested parties to define as medical problems certain behaviors or life events that were previously considered to be normal occurrences in the wide range of human experiences (Conrad 2013). Most of these accounts emphasize the negative aspects of medicalization.

ADHD   A much-discussed example is ADHD, mentioned just earlier. Before the 1960s, there were always children, mostly boys, who were more active, restless, and less attentive than other children during school, at home, and elsewhere. Most of their "extra" activity, restlessness, and inattention were well within the wide range of childhood behaviors and were tolerated as such. Boys whose behavior exceeded these boundaries faced possible discipline by school professionals and by their parents. Relatively few experts thought their behavior was, in fact, a medical problem needing to be treated with medication. By the 1960s, this situation had changed, as medical experts now said that these children suffered from *hyperkinesis* (now called ADHD, a term that was coined during the 1980s) and that they needed to be treated with Ritalin and other stimulant medications (Conrad 1975).

This diagnosis and use of medications have since been extended to adults who also report problems with restlessness and inattention. Today some 6.4 million American children are said to have ADHD, or about 11% of all school-age children and 15% of high-school-aged children, and more than 4 million adults. Many of these individuals, including two-thirds of these children, take Ritalin, Adderall, or other medications, which can have severe side effects, to help control their symptoms. The number of children taking these medications has risen from 600,000 in 1990 to about 3.5 million today (Conrad 2008; Schwarz 2013; Visser et al. 2014).

Although some individuals do have serious problems of hyperactivity and inattention, critics say that ADHD has nonetheless been greatly overdiagnosed in both children and adults, with "too many people with scant symptoms receiving the diagnosis and medication," according to a recent news report (Schwarz 2013:A1). A psychologist who played a lead role decades ago in winning recognition for ADHD agreed with this view, saying the overdiagnosing was "a national disaster of dangerous proportions" and adding, "The numbers make it look like an epidemic. Well, it's not. It's preposterous. This is a concoction to justify the giving out of medication at unprecedented and unjustifiable levels" (Schwarz 2013:A1). The news report noted that the rise of ADHD diagnoses and medication stemmed from a marketing campaign by pharmaceutical companies aimed at parents, physicians, and school officials. This marketing, said the report, "has stretched the image of classic A.D.H.D. to include relatively normal behavior like carelessness and impatience, and has often overstated the pills' benefits" (Schwarz 2013:A1).

Women's Bodies In another example, feminist scholars highlight the medicalization of women's bodies and body-related experiences (Barker 2010; Bell and Figert 2010; Lorber and Moore 2002). Women have experienced menstruation, pregnancy, childbirth, and menopause for millennia, and these experiences are therefore normal life events and natural aspects of the reproductive process. Even so, the medical community has long medicalized these experiences. An early example, discussed in chapter 1, was the view of medical experts in the late nineteenth century that women should not attend college lest they disrupt their menstrual cycles.

A more recent example involves menopause, which is a natural stage of the life cycle that women begin to experience during their middle-aged years. The symptoms of entering menopause, which include hot flashes and night sweats, are entirely normal, however uncomfortable, and not a medical problem in and of themselves. Some women have unusually severe symptoms for which medical treatment is appropriate. However, millions of women with just the normal symptoms began a few decades ago to take long-term estrogen or estrogen-progestin supplements. They did so not only to minimize these symptoms, but also because advertising by pharmaceutical companies and promotional efforts directed at physicians emphasized that hormone therapy would also reduce their risk of heart disease, osteoporosis, and Alzheimer's and more generally help keep them looking youthful (Meyer 2001; Singer and Wilson 2009). However, these supplements were later found to greatly increase the risk of breast cancer, blood clots, and other serious health problems, especially among older women. Responding to this evidence, many women stopped using these supplements or decided not to use them in the first place, and sales of the drugs sharply declined (Grady 2013; U.S. Department of Health & Human Services 2005).

Men's Bodies Medicalization has involved men's bodies as well. Two facts of life for many men as they age are baldness and sexual decline (in particular, the ability to sustain an erection). In the past, these experiences were both considered normal aspects of male aging, no matter how much they dismayed men, and not medical issues. Now, however, "aging men's lives and bodies are increasingly coming under medical jurisdiction" (Conrad 2008:23). Countless TV commercials and magazine ads since the 1990s tell men to visit their physician for medication to cure their baldness or erectile dysfunction.

Moreover, the scope of erectile dysfunction medications has expanded beyond their original purpose (Conrad 2013). When Viagra was first marketed in 1998, it was initially recommended for men with erectile dysfunction caused by old age or medical conditions such as prostate cancer. Over time, however, the companies producing Viagra and other such medications have increasingly aimed their marketing at younger, healthy men who merely want to perform better in the bedroom. The result is annual sales of about $5 billion worldwide for erectile dysfunction drugs (Friedman 2014).

Obesity A final example of medicalization, obesity, illustrates both the positive and negative consequences of medicalization. Obesity in the United States has traditionally been regarded as a moral fault of the obese individual, who is blamed for overeating. When children are fat, their parents have been blamed for letting them get that way. As a study of news coverage of obesity summarized this depiction, "News reports also draw upon and reproduce stereotypes of fat people as gluttonous, slothful, and ignorant, and of parents of fat children as neglectful and irresponsible" (Saguy and Gruys 2013:139). However, in June 2013 the American Medical Association (AMA) labeled obesity a disease, specifically "a multi-metabolic and hormonal disease state." Two psychology professors wryly noted that "in June 2013, millions of Americans contracted a disease" only because of this new designation (Hoyt and Burnette 2014:SR12).

What will be the effects of this new way of thinking of obesity? At least two consequences should be positive, and both these benefits motivated the AMA's decision to label obesity a disease (Pollack 2013). First, defining obesity as a disease calls attention to its risks for health and should spur physicians to enhance their efforts to help obese patients lose weight and medical insurance companies to decide to cover these efforts. Second, now that obesity has been called a disease, it is less likely to be regarded as evidence of moral failure, ignorance, or neglect. The social treatment of obese individuals may well improve now that they are considered to have a disease, and so should their self-image.

But some negative consequences of obesity's medicalization are also likely. Now that obese individuals "officially" have a disease, the use of medical measures, including diet pills, other obesity medication, and gastric bypass surgery, to "cure" this disease is likely to increase, along with profits for the medical and pharmaceutical industries. Moreover, defining obesity as a disease diverts attention from efforts by the food industry to encourage Americans to eat unhealthy products, from the role that poverty plays in producing obesity, and from the need to change eating habits. And there is evidence that obese individuals may decide there is not much sense in trying to change their eating habits since their obesity is due to a disease rather than what they eat. As the researchers who reported this evidence concluded, "Calling obesity a disease may make people feel better about their bodies, but may also contribute to the maintenance, rather than reduction, of obesity" (Hoyt and Burnette 2014:SR12).

Illness Behavior

When people perceive that they are experiencing medical symptoms, they can initially do one of three things regarding their health care options: (1) they may do nothing and either live with the symptom(s) or wait until the symptoms go away; (2) they may engage in **self-care** by taking medications or using other measures in attempt to relieve the symptoms; or (3) they may engage in **help-seeking behavior** (also called *health care utilization*) by visiting a physician or other medical professional. These choices, which represent choices of illness behavior, are not mutually exclusive as time goes by. People may initially do nothing, then engage in self-care if the symptoms persist or become worse, and then visit a physician if self-care is not effective. Patients also typically practice self-care after seeing a physician by following the physician's instructions regarding medication and/or measures designed to improve their health.

Stages of the Illness Experience

To help explain illness behavior, scholars find it useful to conceive of illness as a multi-stage process that begins with symptoms and ends with treatment and, hopefully, recovery. Edward A. Suchman (1966) penned one of the most useful discussions of these stages.

Stage 1 is the *symptom experience*. Here a person perceives symptoms of a possible health problem and must decide what, if anything, to do about these symptoms. If the person decides that the symptoms are indeed those of illness and thus need attention, she or he enters Stage 2, the *assumption of the sick role*. We will have more to say about the sick role in a later section, but at this stage the person begins to engage in behavior expected of people designated as being ill. If the person further decides to seek professional care, the person enters Stage 3, *medical care contact*. This, of course, is a stage with which many of us are all too familiar. A major goal of the patient here is to get an accurate diagnosis of the symptoms and achieve the understanding that she or he is, in fact, legitimately sick.

If some form of medical treatment begins, Stage 4, the *dependent-patient role*, follows. Here the patient undergoes whatever medical tests might be necessary and takes any medications that might be recommended. As physicians know very well, some patients comply more than others with their physician's directives at this stage. Stage 5, the final stage, is the *recovery and rehabilitation* stage. Here the patient continues to perform the sick role until recovery occurs and then gives up this role. If a patient has a chronic illness, however, or does not comply with the physician's directives, full recovery cannot occur and the sick role may continue.

Self-Care

As noted just earlier, self-care (also called *self-management* or *self-treatment*) is a common and time-honored way of treating medical symptoms. It is used for both minor symptoms, as when we take aspirin for a headache, as well as for more serious symptoms, as when someone with diabetes self-injects insulin.

Several developments in recent decades have increased the practice of self-care (Tausig 2013; Ziguras 2004). First, the rise of chronic illness (see chapter 2) meant that many more people began living for many years with ongoing medical symptoms. To maintain their health or to prevent their symptoms from worsening, many chronically ill people engage in various types of self-care, including watching their diets and managing their weight. Second, the rise of the Internet enabled people to learn almost anything they wanted to know about disease and its remedies. The Internet also enabled people to engage in virtual chat rooms and support groups that shared medical information. Third, dissatisfaction with physicians and the health care system has grown in recent decades (see chapter 9). This dissatisfaction has spurred people to treat at least some of their symptoms themselves.

The rise of self-care has spurred a flurry of articles in health and medical journals about its use and effectiveness (Ludman et al. 2013; Wilde et al. 2014). Scholars have also studied social aspects of self-care. For example, a recent study interviewed almost three dozen older adults with chronic illnesses about their self-care (Clarke and Bennett 2013). Although all the adults considered self-care important, their reasons for feeling this way differed by gender. Women said that self-care enabled them to remain able to help other people in their lives and sensitive to their needs, while men said self-care enabled them to remain strong and in control of their lives.

Help-Seeking Behavior

Medical sociologists and health psychologists have identified several factors that affect what people do when they perceive they are ill and in particular their decision to seek professional medical care. At the micro level, an important factor is certainly the *severity of the symptoms*. If our symptom is a slight sniffle, we may just ignore it; if our symptom is a sharp pain in our abdomen that persists for several weeks, we are much more likely to see a physician.

Yet, people with similar symptoms, even fairly serious symptoms, do not always respond to these symptoms in the same way. Some are more likely to do nothing; some are more likely to practice self-care; and some are more likely to seek medical help. As we will soon be discussing, a constellation of personal and social factors affects these decisions and in particular the decision to seek professional care. While the severity of symptoms definitely matters, it is far from the only factor affecting what people do after perceiving symptoms. Other factors both related and unrelated to symptoms also matter, and sometimes may matter more than symptom severity.

A Theory of Help-Seeking Behavior   David Mechanic's (1978) influential theory of help-seeking behavior points to several of these factors:

They all interact & emphasize with their social Backround

- *The visibility and recognizability of symptoms.* This is perhaps the most basic factor; the more a symptom seems to a person to be a "real" symptom to be taken seriously, the more likely the person will seek professional help.
- *The perceived danger of the symptoms.* This factor is closely related to the first factor: when persons think their symptoms are very serious, they are more likely to seek professional help.
- *The extent to which symptoms disrupt normal social activities.* When symptoms interfere with a person's family life, work responsibilities, and other everyday activities, the person is more likely to seek professional help.

- *The frequency and persistence of symptoms.* When symptoms often occur and last for many days or week rather than just a day or two, we are more likely to seek professional help.
- *Tolerance for pain and discomfort.* Some people are better able or more willing than others to "have a stiff upper lip" and deal with their pain or discomfort. Those who have less such tolerance are more likely to seek professional care.
- *Information and knowledge about the symptoms.* Some people have more knowledge than others about symptoms, and this level of information affects their likelihood of seeking professional care.
- *Level of anxiety and fear.* Some people are more anxious than others about similar symptoms. This anxiety may lead some people to head to the doctor and others to avoid a doctor for fear of hearing the worst news.
- *Other competing needs.* It takes time to seek professional medical care, and some people have other demands, such as childcare or college classes, that compete for their time and energy. Those with more burdensome competing needs are less likely, all things equal, to seek professional care.
- *Competing interpretations of symptoms.* Many conditions cause similar symptoms. If we are always tired, we may attribute this problem simply to a lack of sleep rather than to anemia, diabetes, or another problem. If our back hurts, we may attribute the pain to heavy lifting we do in our job rather than to cancer. People who interpret their symptoms as not reflecting a real health problem are less likely to seek professional medical help.
- *Availability of medical treatment based on cost and proximity.* If we cannot afford medical treatment, or if treatment facilities, including a physician's office, are too far from our residence or too difficult to travel to, we are less likely to seek professional care.

Several of Mechanic's factors reflect the influence of a person's cultural and social background. For example, low-income people often find it difficult to afford medical services and thus do not seek professional care, a point to which we return below. Rural residents may live so far from the nearest physician's office that they, too, do not seek professional care. Cultural backgrounds also affect decisions to seek professional help (Quah 2010). This is partly because culture affects our perceptions of, and reactions to, pain and other symptoms of physical or mental illness. For example, the traditional Vietnamese culture tends to tolerate aberrant behavior that Americans might be quick to label mental illness. Such behavior is thus less likely to prompt help-seeking behavior among the Vietnamese than among Americans (Quah 2010).

The Social Context of Help-Seeking Behavior

These examples point to the importance of a wide range of social and cultural factors for decisions to seek professional medical care (Young 2004). The social patterning of help-seeking behavior is similar to that we saw in the previous chapter for preventive health behavior.

To illustrate this patterning, we will examine some data for one of the many types of help-seeking behavior. This measure, one that may not immediately come to mind when you think about health care use, is whether people with tooth decay (*dental caries*, or cavities) go to a dentist for treatment. National survey evidence tells us that more than one-fourth of adults aged 25–64 have *untreated* tooth decay, meaning they have not been to a dentist for treatment. This percentage is high, but it also varies by social class and other sociodemographic factors, as we shall now see.

Social Class: Education and Income Chapter 3 showed that preventive health behavior varies greatly by education and income. The same is true for health care utilization: people with lower levels of education and income are *less* likely than those with more education and higher income to visit a physician or otherwise seek needed professional care (Mirowsky and Ross 2003; Young 2004). This is true even though people with lower SES are more likely to have health problems.

Social class probably matters more for health care utilization than any other sociodemographic factor. It affects help-seeking behavior for reasons similar to those for preventive health behavior (see chapter 3). For example, people of low SES may simply find help-seeking behavior to be too expensive, especially because so many lacked health insurance before Obamacare and many still do today (Schoen et al. 2014). In addition, they may lack convenient access to professional care or have beliefs that deter them from seeking such care.

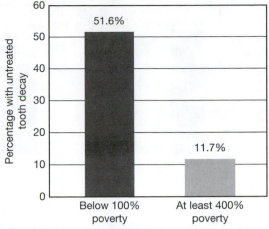

FIG. 4.1 Annual Household Income and Percentage with Untreated Tooth Decay, Ages 45–64.

Source: National Center for Health Statistics. 2015. *Health, United States*, 2014. Hyattsville, MD: Centers for Disease Control and Prevention.

The social class difference exists for untreated tooth decay as it does for other measures of health care utilization. Figure 4.1 shows that that people aged 45–64 whose incomes are below 100% poverty are almost five times more likely than those with incomes at least 400% poverty to have *untreated* tooth decay.

Race and Ethnicity Race and ethnicity matter to some degree for help-seeking behavior: although African Americans and whites make about the same number of needed visits to health care facilities each year, Asians, Latinos, and Native Americans make fewer such visits (Agency for Healthcare Research and Quality 2014; Young 2004), partly because they may lack health insurance and partly for the other reasons discussed in chapter 3 for preventive health behavior. An African American/white

difference does appear in our measure of untreated tooth decay, however. As Figure 4.2 shows for people aged 20–44, African Americans and people of Mexican origin are almost twice as likely as whites to have tooth decay go untreated.

Social class and race and ethnicity may combine to produce a greater effect on health care use than either category produces by itself. To illustrate, among people aged 20–44, 40.2% of poor people have untreated tooth decay, and 41.4% of African Americans have untreated tooth decay (see Figure 4.2). If we combine these two variables by considering people aged 20–44 who are both poor *and* African American, the percentage

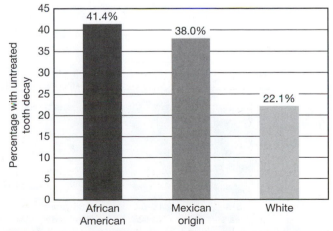

FIG. 4.2 Race and Ethnicity, and Percentage with Untreated Tooth Decay, Ages 20–44.

Source: National Center for Health Statistics. 2015. *Health, United States*, 2014. Hyattsville, MD: Centers for Disease Control and Prevention.

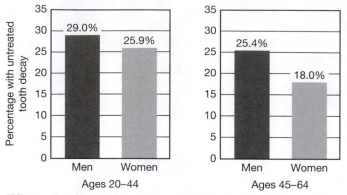

FIG. 4.3 Gender and Percentage with Untreated Tooth Decay, Ages 20–44 and 45–64.

Source: National Center for Health Statistics. 2015. *Health, United States,* 2014. Hyattsville, MD: Centers for Disease Control and Prevention.

with untreated tooth decay rises to 48.0% (National Center for Health Statistics 2014).

Gender Gender is yet another sociodemographic variable that affects help-seeking behavior, with men less likely than women to seek medical care (Young 2004). Women do have more health problems overall than men (see chapter 5), and this difference helps explain why they use health care more often than men, even though they find medical costs especially burdensome because of their lower incomes (Rustgi, Doty, and Collins 2009). In fact, if women had more money, they probably would visit a doctor even more often. But among people who exhibit medical symptoms, men are still somewhat less likely than women to seek professional care. Scholars attribute this gender difference to male socialization. Boys are brought up not to cry and not to complain about pain, and to appear strong at all times. These traits, sometimes called the "John Wayne image" in recognition of the famous twentieth century actor's stoic persona, all help deter men from seeking professional care when needed (Addis and Mahalik 2003; Sierra Hernandez et al. 2014).

We see an example of this gender difference in Figure 4.3 for untreated tooth decay. Men are indeed more likely than women to leave their tooth decay untreated.

Age As people age past their middle years and into their 60s and 70s, they are much more likely to experience many types of health problems. Engaging in preventive health behaviors greatly increases their chances of remaining very healthy, but age does take its toll. Accordingly, older people use health care services much more often than younger adults. Figure 4.4 depicts the percentage of adults who make at least four health care visits annually to a physician office or emergency room. The age difference here is noticeable.

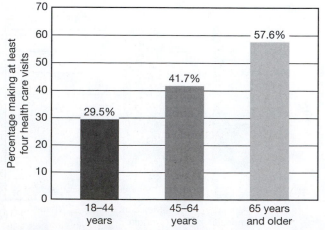

FIG. 4.4 Age and Health Care Visits (% making at least four health care visits annually).

Source: National Center for Health Statistics. 2015. *Health, United States,* 2014. Hyattsville, MD: Centers for Disease Control and Prevention.

Social Relationships We saw in chapter 3 that people with more extensive, high-quality social relationships are more likely to practice promotive health behavior. They are also more likely to seek medical help when they perceive symptoms of a health problem (Umberson, Crosnoe, and Reczek 2010). The people in their social networks encourage or prod them to seek medical help, and they may also practically help them to do so by, for example, providing transportation or childcare.

Some ill people may happen to have friends or acquaintances who are health care providers themselves. This particular type of social tie may promote health care use. For example, if a friend is a physician, that friend's judgment that a symptomatic person should see professional care may be especially persuasive. The friend may also help the ill person to make a medical appointment and help the person in other ways to get appropriate care.

Proximity and Transportation to Health Care   Sometimes help-seeking behavior is just a matter of practicality. Two such practical factors are: (1) how closely we live near physicians or other health care professionals, and (2) whether we have transportation to visit the health care facility. For example, rural residents often live very far from the nearest physician or from a hospital. This fact makes it more difficult for them to seek professional care when they have illness symptoms. Even if they live near a hospital, many rural hospitals are small and unable to provide medical services such as chemotherapy for certain cancers. Someone who needs that type of chemotherapy must then potentially travel dozens or hundreds of miles to an appropriate hospital. This difficulty may force them to forgo chemotherapy or at least to miss some of their treatments.

Transportation may also be a problem. Someone who is too ill or otherwise unable to drive must have family, friends, neighbors, or a taxi (or Lyft or Uber) transport them to a health care provider. The same is true for someone without a car. Because many urban residents do not own a car, they often take public transportation to receive health care, but public transportation can be expensive and time-consuming, deterring them from seeking health care. Public transportation is often lacking in rural areas, adding to the problems that many rural residents face in seeking health care. For evident reasons, low-income people face more transportation problems to obtain needed health care than wealthier people, just as they do for periodic preventive health behavior (chapter 3).

Health Insurance   A final factor affecting the use of needed health care is whether someone has health insurance, as mentioned earlier. A major reason given for the passage and implementation of the Affordable Care Act (Obamacare) was that the many Americans without health insurance were much less likely to use health care when they had health problems (see chapter 12). Survey data in 2012, before the full implementation of Obamacare, show the dramatic difference that health insurance makes (Figure 4.5). Uninsured people were much less likely than insured people to make at least one health care visit during the year. This was true even though uninsured individuals tend to be in worse health, partly because they are poorer on average and partly because they are not insured. Not surprisingly, the cost of health care is a major reason the insured do not get needed health care. One-third (32.4%) of the uninsured say they had to forgo or delay needed medical care for cost reasons, compared to only 7.4% of the insured (National Center for Health Statistics 2015). The uninsured are thus about four times more likely than the insured to have financial problems in receiving needed medical care.

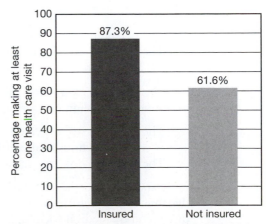

FIG. 4.5 Health Insurance and Health Care Visits, Adults 18–64 years (% making at least one health care visit annually).

Source: National Center for Health Statistics. 2014. *Health, United States,* 2013. Hyattsville, MD: Centers for Disease Control and Prevention.

The Experience of Illness

We now turn to the broader experience of illness: how people are expected to behave when they are ill, and how they react to the physiological, social, psychological, and financial implications of their illness. We begin with the sick role, which was mentioned earlier in this chapter and is one of the most famous concepts in medical sociology history.

The Sick Role

Medical sociology's understanding of the illness experience owes a considerable debt to sociologist Talcott Parsons' (1951) classic discussion of the *sick role*. Parsons' conception of this role was pathbreaking for its time but also limited in several respects, especially in view of the many changes in society and medicine that have occurred since he wrote about the sick role more than six decades ago (Monaghan 2013).

Parsons was a prime proponent of functional theory in sociology (see chapter 1). As such, he emphasized the need for social institutions and individuals to function properly to help ensure society's ongoing functionality and stability. When someone is deemed ill, he wrote, this person's illness is potentially dysfunctional not only for the individual but also for society as a whole. The reason for this is that the person is unable to contribute as productively, if at all, to society during the course of the illness; for chronic illness, this period of productivity is likely to be very long. For this reason, the ill person may be viewed by society as at least somewhat deviant unless and until the person successfully performs the sick role.

By **sick role** Parsons meant the expectations for behavior of someone designated as ill by society, usually by a medical practitioner. This concept derives from the important sociological concept of the *role*, which refers to the learned expectations for behavior of someone who occupies a certain position, or status, in society. The role of a professor, for example, includes coming to class prepared and doing the best job possible to ensure students' learning. The role of a college student also includes coming to class prepared and trying to learn as much as possible from the course. Not all persons satisfy their role expectations successfully, of course: some professors are simply bad professors, and (dare we say it?) some students are bad students. But the field of sociology emphasizes that our roles do affect our behavior in many ways, whether or not we realize the influence of our roles.

For successful fulfillment of the sick role, Parsons wrote, an ill person must meet two obligations:

- The person must want to become healthy and must try to become healthy
- The person should seek help from one or more medical professionals and follow the advice and instructions of these professionals

Once an ill person meets these obligations, society then provides the person two exemptions regarding the person's behavior. These exemptions are:

- The person is not expected while ill to perform the behaviors normally expected of someone who is healthy (the person is exempt from normal social roles)
- The person is not blamed or otherwise held responsible for the illness

Parsons' conception of the sick role brought attention to an important social dynamic in the illness experience. At the same time, it stimulated much criticism and discussion by medical sociologists that increased the understanding of illness behavior. As society has changed over the past six decades, so has illness behavior in ways that medical sociologists have documented, often in the form of qualitative research (see chapter 1) relying on in-depth interviews and/or observation of people with various illnesses. We now turn to some criticisms of the sick role before discussing contemporary findings on illness behavior.

Criticisms of the Sick Role   When a new social concept stimulates much criticism, this is often a sign that the concept is breaking new ground by prompting social scientists to think of things they did not consider before. The criticism that Parsons' sick role concept received is thus not necessarily a sign of the concept's weakness, though it did have its limitations; instead it is a sign of the concept's strength. With that stipulation in mind, let's review some of the major criticisms of Parsons' sick role concept (Freidson 1988; Levine and Kozoloff 1978; Young 2004).

A first criticism is that Parsons overly favored the traditional, hierarchical physician-patient model in which the physician is the expert and the patient is a medically uninformed layperson who should rather meekly believe everything the physician says and follow all the physician's instructions. Developments since Parsons' era have made the physician-patient model less hierarchical. Medical sociologist J.T. Young (2004:6) summarizes this criticism as follows: "Parsons' configuration assumes that the power to manage an illness resides with the caregiver. The rise of medical information systems and the Internet, self-help groups and the expansion of over-the-counter remedies, as well as the control of physician decisionmaking by corporate interests, place this power relationship in doubt." As chapter 7 will discuss, contemporary views of the physician-patient relationship stress a patient's need to take a knowledgeable, proactive role in trying to get healthy; this role includes questioning doctors when necessary. For these reasons, Parsons' favored hierarchical model may not, in fact, be the best from a patient's perspective.

A second criticism is that Parsons exaggerated the degree to which patients and physicians agree on the diagnosis of the patient's health problem and the steps needed to improve the patient's health. Patients and physicians in fact often disagree on these matters, and this disagreement may lead the patient to ignore the physician's directions or seek care from another physician.

Third, Parsons (1951:298) wrote that the sick role requires the patient to do everything possible to achieve a "complete recovery." This goal implies that the patient could indeed achieve a complete recovery, something that is often not possible in chronic illness such as heart disease and cancer. Critics say that Parsons' concept of the sick role thus was more applicable to acute (short-term) illness than to chronic illness. In a related point, they add that chronic illness often causes difficulties in the physician-patient relationship precisely because chronic illness is by definition long-lasting. This basic fact can prompt patients to become frustrated with their doctors and to not trust them. Parsons (1975) later conceded his neglect of chronic illness and said that managing chronic illness fulfills the sick role's obligation to become well.

Fourth, Parsons' sick role model implicitly assumes that a patient visits a physician with clear symptoms of a health problem that can be diagnosed fairly easily. In contrast, many patients have symptoms that do not clearly signify a specific health problem. The term contested illness refers to illnesses such as chronic fatigue syndrome and Gulf War syndrome that physicians cannot identify as medically caused (Barker 2010). People with contested illnesses face difficulties in having their symptoms accepted as something other than what "is just in their heads." A major goal of patient advocacy groups for chronic fatigue syndrome and other contested illnesses is to convince the medical community that contested illnesses are, in fact, real illnesses with real medical causes. Once contested illnesses become accepted as real rather than imagined, the patients' illness experience is legitimized, and they are better able to fill a key obligation of the sick role.

Another criticism of Parsons' model is that it failed to recognize that patients with certain health problems might not receive society's "blessing" even if they fulfill their sick role obligations. These health problems include stigmatized diseases such as leprosy, HIV and AIDs during the decade after they originated in the early 1980s, and some sexually transmitted diseases (STDs). Depending on the disease, much of society may react to it with some horror or disgust or at least blame patients for engaging in the behavior that led them to contract the disease. In today's society, a smoker who incurs lung cancer is probably viewed less favorably than someone who gets cancer randomly. But Parsons' model overlooked these types of differences in society's reaction based on the nature of the health problem patients have.

Finally, Parsons' sick role model failed to appreciate the fact that the social environment, broadly defined, affects patients' perceptions and behaviors. If corporate executives have persistent significant leg pain, for example, they may well seek medical help. In contrast, if construction workers have the same type of pain, they might be much less likely to seek medical help: they may lack medical insurance or cannot afford the deductible, or they may have already used up their sick leave (or might not even have sick leave) and cannot afford to take time off from work without pay. This social class difference indicates that Parsons' model may be more applicable to middle- and upper-class patients than to low-income patients.

As noted earlier, gender and cultural differences also exist in the reaction to similar medical symptoms. It might sound like a stereotype, but men are indeed more likely than women to remain stoic, or relatively quiet, about their medical symptoms. Conversely, women, as discussed earlier, are more likely than men to seek medical help for similar symptoms (Young 2004). Regarding culture, many studies document how different cultural backgrounds affect illness behavior. An early study found that men in a New York City veterans' hospital reacted to similar levels of pain in different ways depending on their ethnic background (Zborowski 1952). Irish-American veterans tended to be stoic and not to complain about their pain; Italian-American veterans were much less stoic and more likely to complain about their pain; and Jewish veterans worried more openly about what their pain and condition meant for their futures. DIFF Culture → DIFF response to PAIN

Coping with Illness

One of the most important aspects of the illness experience is coping with its physiological effects, including pain or other discomfort, and with its effects on our social lives. When an illness is especially serious, we also have concerns and even fear about our future and possible death. How patients deal with illness is a critical aspect of being ill. Medical sociology has contributed greatly to the understanding of how people cope with their illnesses.

Medical sociology's focus on coping is commonly accredited to a classic book by Anselm L. Strauss and Barney G. Glaser (1975), *Chronic Illness and the Quality of Life*, which was a collection of their students' studies of patients' coping with chronic illness (Conrad and Bury 1997). Before this time, scholars had paid little or no attention to how patients dealt with their illness's repercussions. Thus Strauss and Glaser (1975:viii) emphasized that their book was focused on how chronically ill patients "manage to live as normal a life as possible" and how they deal with "the social and psychological aspects (not the medical) of *living with chronic illness*" (emphasis in original). Their book inspired a wave of studies in the four decades since on how patients experience and manage their illness. Many of these studies are poignant accounts based on interviews with and/or observations of patients with various conditions. Most of these accounts concern people with chronic illnesses such as rheumatoid arthritis and heart disease, stigmatized illness such as HIV/AIDS and STDs (which can also be chronic), impairment (e.g., the loss of a leg), or a physical or mental disability. This deep literature paints a moving picture of the many difficulties these patients face but also of their quiet courage in coping with their health problem (Pierret 2003).

Biographical Disruption   These studies of the illness experience address several related themes (Charmaz and Rosenfeld 2010; Pierret 2003; Rier 2010). A major theme is that chronic illness often disrupts a person's normal life activities and social relationships and forces patients to question their quality of life for the foreseeable future. As Mike Bury (1982:169) first presented this thesis of **biographical disruption**, "Chronic illness involves a recognition of the worlds of pain and suffering, possibly eve of death, which are normally only seen as distant possibilities or the plight of others. In addition, it brings individuals, their families, and wider social networks face to face with the character of their relationships in stark form, disrupting normal rules of reciprocity and mutual support."

This disruption takes many forms. First, chronically ill persons can no longer take for granted behaviors, abilities, and even appearance to which they never before gave a second thought. Depending on the specific chronic illness, they may have trouble walking, climbing steps, or sitting into a chair and rising from it; they may need to rely on family members and friends for help with bathing, dressing, and other daily activities; or they may exhibit facial or other disfigurement. Any of these situations can be embarrassing and humiliating and may affect the patients' self-concept, self-esteem, and self-confidence.

Second, chronically ill people also worry about what lies ahead, since chronic illness by definition can be a lifelong condition. Accordingly, Bury (1982:173) found that many of the rheumatoid arthritis patients he interviewed were "beset with anxiety and fear, especially about the future" when first told they had their disease. People with life-threatening chronic illness such as heart disease or cancer also worry about possible early death.

Third, chronic illness can make it difficult to spend time with family members and friends and thus disrupt social relationships. It can also strain social relationships because of the effects of a disease itself and the demands that patients make on family members and friends for assistance. As Kathy Charmaz and Dana Rosenfeld (2010:316) observe, "Family strains increase when the illness results in sexual dysfunction, confusion, or uncontrolled anger . . . . Illness means adjusting to reduced activities, handling fatigue, learning to juggle and pace previously taken-for-granted tasks, and asking for help. All pose difficulties when relationships are strained or when expectations persist for the ill person to carry on as before."

Fourth, chronic illness can also make it difficult for some employed individuals to perform their jobs and even force some of them to go part-time or even retire. This consequence has obvious implications for their financial well-being, and it also involves a major change in their daily activities.

The extent of biographical disruption varies for individuals (Pierret 2003). The extent and severity of medical symptoms certainly matter greatly in this regard. Yet even for patients with similar symptoms, some experience more disruption (i.e., the consequences just outlined) than others. Many factors affect the degree of disruption. For example, the consequences of chronic illness tend to be more troublesome for people who live by themselves and have few friends, who live with an unsupportive spouse or partner, or who have low incomes or are less educated. As with many things in life, good social relationships, good financial resources, and a college education help mightily in dealing with the repercussions of chronic illness. Consequences also tend to be more troublesome for rural patients and other people who live far from medical facilities and social service agencies, or who lack convenient transportation to these venues.

Social factors such as age, gender, and social class also affect the subjective meaning that chronic illness has for patients. For example, people in their 70s who develop severe arthritis may regard it as a normal stage of life, but people in their 40s who develop this disease will be more likely to regard it as unfair and debilitating (Pierret 2003). Illness that involves disfigurement may also be more difficult for younger people than older people to accept as somehow normal or "not that bad." And because women have more caretaking responsibilities than men for other family members such as children, they may be especially concerned about their illness's repercussions for their ability to care for these other people (Pierret 2003).

For all these reasons, then, some individuals are better able than others to deal with the biographical consequences of illness. These relatively fortunate individuals are said to experience biographical *flow* more than biographical *disruption* (Charmaz and Rosenfeld 2010).

The "Why Me? Why Now?" Response   A second theme in studies of the illness experience is that chronically ill patients are often shocked to learn they have a chronic illness and struggle to understand why they developed it. This reaction is called the "Why me? Why now?" response (Bury 1982). They try to make some sense of why they incurred their disease by looking at their personal history and wondering if it was biologically inherited (depending on the illness) or occurred due to other reasons beyond their control. This effort to make sense of their disease's onset is called *narrative reconstruction*. For many people, one goal of this effort is to deflect blame for their illness from themselves, both to help them feel somewhat better about their illness and to deter other people from blaming them for developing it. This goal may especially be important for stigmatized illnesses: the stigma is difficult enough to experience, but even more so if someone could be said to have brought the illness on herself/himself. Some patients with embarrassing or otherwise stigmatized illnesses practice a policy of *selective disclosure*, meaning that they reveal their illness only to close family and friends and not to employers, coworkers, or other members of their social networks (Pierret 2003). They also act in other ways, for example, by trying to conceal evidence of their disease, to reduce the shame and embarrassment they would otherwise feel if their symptoms were very obvious (Charmaz and Rosenfeld 2010).

Uncertainty   A third theme concerns general *uncertainty* about the illness and about how it will be affecting one's life. This uncertainty can be unsettling and have many consequences (Charmaz and Rosenfeld 2010). As Janine Pierret (2003:11) observes, "By upsetting everyday routines, becoming ill and being ill are causes of uncertainty for patients and those close to them. This uncertainty affects various activities or even the person's whole existence. Patients work out strategies for coping with this upheaval and use various resources to reorganize their lives." Some medical conditions are difficult to diagnose, adding to patients' uncertainty and complicating their relationship with their physicians and other medical professionals.

The Internet   A fourth theme is that the Internet has helped patients to cope better with their disease. Before the the Internet, it was difficult to learn about various diseases (and almost anything else), and any one person with a specific disease often lived a lonely existence, knowing few or no people with the same disease. The Internet changed these aspects of the illness experience because it now provides detailed information about almost any disease imaginable and because it enables patients to communicate virtually with people having the same medical symptoms and problems (Conrad and Stults 2010). This body of information and these electronic support groups benefit patients both practically and emotionally and make them more knowledgeable about their condition and its possible treatments when they visit their physicians.

Contested Illness   A final theme is that people with *contested illnesses*, described earlier, fare better if and when they finally receive a definitive medical diagnosis and when the medical profession officially designates the symptoms they and other people are experiencing as a "real" disease (Barker 2010; Rier 2010). If and when both events occur, these patients are now seen as having credible diseases and less likely to be considered malingerers.

A Representative Study of the Illness Experience: Women with STDs

One or more of these themes emerge in many studies of people with chronic illness. A representative study is medical sociologist Adina Nack's (2008) insightful discussion of women with STDs, published under the telling title, *Damaged Goods: Women Living with Incurable Sexually Transmitted Diseases.* Nack conducted in-depth interviews of 43 women with one or both of two chronic, incurable STDs: genital herpes and/or human papillomavirus (HPV). HPV is the most common STD and can cause genital warts and cervical or other cancers.

Although STDs infect more than 15 million Americans annually, they remain highly stigmatized. As Nack observed, when people are diagnosed with STDs, it is common for them to feel both "dirty" and violated. But "these negative feelings," she wrote,

> are compounded by the social acceptability of blaming infected individuals for their illnesses. Often the blame comes with judgments, such as *irresponsible*, *naïve*, or *stupid*. Others will likely view this illness as a sign of immorality and label the person a promiscuous *slut*, having low character and bad values. . . . It is easy to understand why many Americans with STDs are left wondering whether they are, in fact, *damaged goods*—their bodies and reputations so spoiled that they may never again feel healthy, whole, and valuable (Nack 2008:2, emphasis in original).

The women in Nack's study thus had to deal not only with their disease's *health* consequences, but also with its many *social* consequences. They had generally never imagined they could incur an STD and were both shocked and troubled when they did so. An immediate worry was that they would find it very difficult to have romantic relationships or get married and might never be able to bear a healthy child. As one woman recalled, "When I found out about the STD, it was really a slam. I was just like, 'I'm so screwed!' The rest of my life is totally dead" (Nack 2008:67).

But beyond these practical concerns, the women also had to struggle with what STDs' stigma meant for how they would be regarded and for their own self-concept. Because many had previously viewed women with STDs as dirty, stupid, and/or immoral, they now had to struggle with thinking of themselves in this way, and they also worried that their family, friends, lovers, and physicians would view them that way. Because of this fear, many of the women in the study had kept quiet about their new health status, even when with a new sex partner, and cringed in silence when they heard friends ridiculing women with STDs. When some did have surgery and other treatment for their STD, they told family and friends the treatment was for another health problem. Ironically, this series of deceptions made them feel guilty, and their guilt only added to the shame many them were already feeling for having contracted an STD.

Over time, the women were generally able to come to terms with what their illness meant for their sexuality and sexual self-identity. In what Nack (2008:13) calls the "reintegration stage," most of the women who had incurred their disease some years earlier had "reached a point where they felt they had reclaimed their sexual selves from illness" and even felt that they had grown and matured because of everything that happened to them after being diagnosed with their STD. A few, however, did not reach this stage, as their way of dealing with their illness was celibacy, a practice they were still continuing when interviewed years after they contracted their STD.

Conclusion

Many people become ill, and many people become chronically ill. How people respond to illness is the essence of the illness experience. This response includes the decision to seek professional medical care and the ways in which people deal with the emotional, social, and other consequences of illness. Many social and individual factors affect this response, with social class having perhaps the strongest impact of all the relevant social factors. The study of illness behavior and the illness experience reminds us that illness as a social concept is far more than the medical symptoms and problems that prompt an illness designation. The next chapter's focus on the social causes of health and illness underscores this central insight of medical sociology.

Summary

1. Illness refers to people's perceptions of and reactions to medical symptoms. The illness experience consists of their general emotional and practical responses to the illness designation and their decisions to seek or not seek professional medical care.
2. Because illness is a social construction, the perception and experience of illness are shaped by a variety of social and cultural factors. The impact of these factors underscores the idea that illness is best regarded as a social concept rather than a medical concept.
3. Medicalization occurs when nonmedical behaviors or conditions come to be understood and treated as medical problems. Medicalization is profitable for the medical community and industry and has several negative consequences, but it also has some benefits in certain circumstances.
4. Many social factors affect whether people with a perceived illness seek professional medical care. These factors include social class, race and ethnicity, and gender.
5. Parsons' concept of the sick role alerted sociologists to the patient's experience. Criticisms of this concept have added to medical sociology's understanding of this experience.
6. One of the major themes in studies of the illness experience is biological disruption. When people develop a chronic illness, their lives change in many ways, and they must deal with the emotional and practical consequences of their illness.

Giving It Some Thought

You have reached your 50th birthday. Having been married for more than twenty years, you are generally happy with your marriage, family, and life in general. Your spouse, Logan, has been in good health over the years, but lately Logan has been experiencing severe joint pain. After many medical tests, Logan is diagnosed with rheumatoid arthritis, a serious chronic autoimmune disease for which there is no cure. Logan's disease will probably become progressively worse over the next several years, although it can be managed somewhat with appropriate medication and exercise. How, if at all, do you think Logan's diagnosis will affect your marriage?

Key Terms

biographical disruption, 65

contested illness, 63

disease, 51

help-seeking behavior, 56

illness, 51

illness behavior, 51

illness experience, 51

medicalization, 52

self-care, 56

sick role, 62

social construction, 52

theory of help-seeking behavior, 57

5 Social Causes of Health and Health Problems

LEARNING QUESTIONS

1. What is a fundamental cause of disease?

2. What is meant by health disparities?

3. How and why does social class influence health and disease?

4. How and why do race and ethnicity influence health and disease?

5. Why do women have worse health overall than men?

6. Why does religiosity promote better health?

Health and Illness in the News

The headline said it all: "Old Housing May Have Rampant Lead Violations." These violations were suspected in San Francisco's Sunnydale housing projects, built in the 1940s when paint still contained lead, a toxic substance for children. Lead exposure increases children's risk of anemia, hearing problems, and slow growth, and it also increases their risk of behavioral and learning problems. After one mother in the Sunnydale projects discovered that her three-year-old daughter had elevated blood levels, she had their home tested for lead. The testing found lead dust levels in her bathroom to be 15 times higher than acceptable levels. In the prior five years, only 9 of the 767 housing units in the Sunnydale projects had been inspected for lead or other hazards. (Roberts 2014)

This news story reminds us that health and disease are not just the results of biological problems. Lead paint's effects on children are certainly biologically driven, but poverty and official neglect in San Francisco combined to make a mother's three-year-old daughter have elevated levels of lead in the first place. Although it is true that every disease has a biological cause, it is also true that social conditions affect our likelihood of being healthy or unhealthy. As chapter 1 emphasized, disease is often a matter of bad biology or bad luck, but society can also help make us sick. This chapter discusses the many social factors that help make us sick or instead be healthy. To say that another way, this chapter discusses social differences in **morbidity** (the incidence of disease).

Social Conditions as Fundamental Causes of Disease

This section's title is borrowed from a classic article by medical sociologists Bruce G. Link and Jo Phelan (1995). In that article, Link and Phelan (1995:80) argued for greater attention to "basic social conditions" as causes of disease. Although individual-level risk factors such as smoking, poor nutrition, and lack of exercise help cause disease, they wrote, it is important to "understand how people come to be exposed" to these risk factors in the first place (p. 81). Underlying social conditions, they wrote, "put people at risk" for experiencing these more immediate, individual-level risk factors.

Link and Phelan conceded that the common emphasis on individual risk factors is understandable in view of the American value of individual responsibility for one's fate. But they argued that this emphasis leads to neglect of the social conditions producing these risk factors. These social conditions must be identified and addressed, they said, for real progress in improving the nation's health to occur. For example, it does little good to advise people to eat a healthier diet when they cannot afford it or when healthy foods are difficult to find in their neighborhoods; it also does little good to advise women to exercise more when they have childcare or elder care needs that prevent them from getting out of the house.

Smoking and heart disease further illustrate the importance of addressing underlying social conditions to improve the nation's health. As chapter 3 emphasized, smoking is a known risk factor for lung cancer, heart disease, respiratory disease, and other serious health problems. Guided by the biomedical model (see chapter 1), medical researchers uncovered and now understand the biological mechanisms through which smoking causes these problems. Although these biological mechanisms are crucial, William C. Cockerham (2013b:3) reminds us that the dangerous substances in tobacco have to first "enter the human body to have any effect." This fact in turn calls attention not only to smoking as an immediate risk factor, but also to the social reasons that people smoke in the first place. These reasons are social conditions or social factors. As Cockerham (2013b:3) observes, "There is a social pattern to smoking that indicates tobacco use is not a random, individual decision completely independent of social structural influences." As chapter 3 discussed, these social influences include low socioeconomic status (SES), social networks (especially teenagers' peer groups) that encourage smoking, and advertising and other marketing by the tobacco industry.

Heart disease also illustrates the importance of social conditions. Every heart attack has a specific medical cause, usually a blocked artery from a blood clot, with the clot itself stemming from a buildup of plaque within an artery. Once the heart attack occurs, medical personnel will try to help the patient with appropriate medication and medical procedures.

This description provides a very simple biomedical understanding of what a heart attack involves. Medical students thankfully acquire a much more detailed understanding in their classes, where they also learn how and why individual risk factors such as high blood pressure high cholesterol, poor nutrition, and lack of exercise lead to heart attacks. These factors are indeed important, but social conditions such as poverty and stress make it much more likely that some people will have these risk factors. As chapter 3 noted, we could also add the marketing efforts of the tobacco and food industries to this list of social factors: without such marketing, fewer Americans would start smoking, and fewer Americans would eat the many products like doughnuts and ice cream that contribute to arterial plaque buildup. We could even add air pollution to this list of factors because it, too, raises the risk of heart attacks (American Heart Association 2014). Although air pollution is part of the physical environment, it is higher than it needs to be because of human activity and lack of regulation and thus can also be considered a social condition.

The lesson of these smoking and heart attack examples is this: a full understanding of the causes and also the prevention of many diseases requires that we understand not only the biomedical factors that trigger these health problems and the individual risk factors that help trigger these biomedical factors, but also the underlying social conditions for both kinds of factors.

Applying this lesson, Link and Phelan (1995) argued that some social conditions are *fundamental causes* of disease. In their framework, a **fundamental cause** has four features: *"Social Decisions Are Causes Of Funda-*

mental illness."

1. *It influences the likelihood of many diseases and other health problems, not just a few diseases or health problems.* This feature underscores the idea that fundamental causes are indeed *fundamental* in nature because they affect the chances of incurring so many diseases.

2. *It affects disease via many types of risk factors (intervening mechanisms), such as smoking and poor nutrition.* A fundamental cause affects susceptibility to disease for many reasons, and it will continue to affect susceptibility if only one of these reasons is addressed. Thus even if the nutrition of low-income people could somehow be improved, their other risk factors would still lead them to have worse health.

3. *It involves access to resources that help people avoid health risks and/or limit the effects of disease after they become sick.* These resources include "knowledge, money, power, prestige, and beneficial social connections" (Phelan, Link, and Tehranifar 2010:S29).

4. *Its effects on health persist over time even though intervening mechanisms may change.* For example, poor people in the nineteenth century were more at risk for cholera and other infectious diseases because of poor sanitation and other problems. Even though these diseases were eradicated a century later by improved living conditions and medical advances, poor people continue to be more at risk for chronic illness and other health problems because of "new" intervening mechanisms such as poor nutrition.

These four features and their explanation combine to form Link and Phelan's (2010) **theory of fundamental causes**. The heart of the theory is the idea that a social condition as a fundamental cause underlies multiple diseases for multiple reasons. Addressing any one reason for disease still permits a fundamental cause to bring about many other diseases for many other reasons. Moreover, when a new disease arises or returns after being eradicated, a fundamental cause will make vulnerable the same kinds of people it makes vulnerable for other diseases. For example, when AIDS arose during the 1980s or tuberculosis reemerged more recently, poor people were more susceptible to incurring these diseases, just as they are, and have been for centuries, for other diseases. To reduce the health effects of a fundamental cause, then, society must change the fundamental cause itself.

In their original article and subsequent work, Link and Phelan (1995) considered SES as the most important fundamental cause of disease, but they also emphasized that race and ethnicity, gender, stress, and other social conditions can be considered additional fundamental causes. We examine these and other conditions in the remainder of this chapter.

Social Conditions as Fundamental Causes of Health Inequalities

Because imitation is the sincerest form of flattery, this section's title comes from another essay by Link and Phelan (2010). Social conditions are not just fundamental causes of disease; they are also fundamental causes of *health inequalities*. As chapter 1 noted, a major theme of sociology is that society is filled with social inequality based on social class, race and ethnicity, gender, sexual orientation and gender identity, age, and even geographic location. These social inequalities have many negative consequences for people who rank lower on these dimensions, including the poor, people of color, women, and the LGBT community. One of these consequences involves health, as people are more or less likely to be healthy or sick depending on where they rank. In short, society's many social inequalities reproduce and manifest themselves in the areas of health and disease.

Fundamental causes, as conceived by Link and Phelan, reflect inequalities in the larger society and thus lead to inequality in who gets sick (or, to use a more scholarly phrase, inequality in the social distribution of health and disease). This inequality is called **health inequalities** or **health disparities** (Barr 2014). These terms do not simply mean that some people are healthier or sicker than others. Instead they mean that some people are more or less likely to be healthy because they are unequal in terms of social class, race and ethnicity, and other social inequalities. The documentation and explanation of health inequalities are one of the signature findings of medical sociology and the related fields of social epidemiology and public health.

This body of research has gained the attention of policymakers. In 2011, the Centers for Disease Control and Prevention (CDC) began publishing its periodic *Health Disparities and Inequalities Report—United States*. This report draws on national survey and other data to show how social inequalities are related to the quality of health and the likelihood of illness. Meanwhile, the federal Agency for Healthcare Research and Quality has been publishing its annual *National Healthcare Disparities Report* since the early 2000s. These reports and other federal publications underscore the importance of social inequalities for the quality of health and health care.

Health inequalities stem from a complex of factors. Two of the most important factors are differences in health behavior (chapter 3) and in illness behavior (chapter 4). Another important factor is health *care* disparities: people who receive poor health care are more likely to have poorer health (see chapter 12). Although these three factors are indeed very important, other factors such as stress and discrimination matter as well. The remainder of this section presents evidence of the fundamental causes of health inequalities and examines the major reasons for their effects.

Social Class

Social class probably produces the greatest disparities in health and disease and is a fundamental cause of health inequalities (Link and Phelan 2010). Study after study has shown that people with low income and low education are much more likely to experience virtually every health problem, including chronic disease, communicable disease, and injury (Kaplan 2009). They have higher rates of arthritis, diabetes, heart disease, and some forms of cancer, and they also have higher rates of mental health problems (McLeod 2013). At birth, poor Americans can expect to live about 6.5 fewer years on average than Americans with annual household incomes more than four times the poverty level (Kaplan 2009). At age 25, people without a high-school degree can expect to live about 8.5 fewer additional years on average than

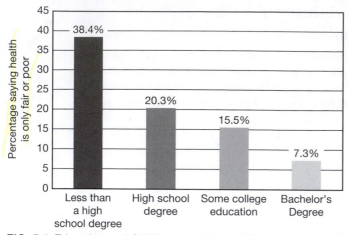

FIG. 5.1 Education and Self-Reported Health (% of adults 18 and older saying their health is only fair or poor).

Source: Centers for Disease Control and Prevention. 2013. CDC Health Disparities and Inequalities Report—United Sates, 2013. Atlanta, GA: Centers for Disease Control and Prevention.

people with at least a bachelor's degree (National Center for Health Statistics 2012). Given these figures, it is no exaggeration to say that social class is a matter of life and death.

Social class affects our chances of becoming sick, and it also affects what happens after people do become sick. When low-income people are initially diagnosed with cancer, diabetes, and other health problems, the severity of their disease is often worse than that for higher-income people when they are first diagnosed. Partly for this reason and partly for other reasons, such as differences in access to quality health care and in patients' compliance with medical instructions, disease outcomes are often worse for low-income patients than for wealthier patients. Low-income cancer patients tend to die sooner than wealthier cancer patients, and low-income diabetes patients are more likely to need a lower limb amputated than wealthier diabetes patients (Stevens et al. 2014; Woods, Rachet, and Coleman 2006).

One way to illustrate social class's impact on health is to examine responses to a national survey question that asks people to indicate the quality of their health, for example, excellent, good, fair, or poor. Because federal health officials think responses of only "fair" or "poor" are a red flag for health problems, the percentage of people who provide either response is a common measure of the quality of the nation's health. About 16% of adults 18 years and older say their health is only fair or poor, but this percentage depends heavily on SES (Figure 5.1). People with less education are much more likely than those with more education to say their health is only fair or poor.

Explaining the Impact of Social Class   The fundamental social class disparity in physical and mental health stems from a complex of factors that have been called a "massive multiplicity of mechanisms" (Lutfey and Freese 2005:1328). Although much remains unknown about how and why SES affects health, medical sociologists and other scholars identify several factors that help account for SES's effects (Barr 2014; Elo 2009; Pampel, Krueger, and Denney 2010).

First, low SES people lack the resources for better health identified by the theory of fundamental causes as discussed earlier in this chapter. Lacking these resources, they are less likely to practice positive health behavior and more likely to practice risky health behavior (see chapter 3), and they are also less likely to seek needed professional medical care (chapter 4) and more likely to have low-quality care when they do seek it (chapter 12). As chapter 3 indicated, education is thought to play a greater role than income in producing these problems (Ross and Mirowsky 2010).

Second, there is growing recognition that chronic stress produces disease (Thoits 2010). Low SES people are much more likely to experience stressful life events, a problem called *social stress* (Hatch and Dohrenwend 2007). They experience stress from trying to pay for the necessities of life, including medical bills; from their greater degree of unemployment; from their greater levels of violence in their households and neighborhoods; from their higher rates of illness, disease, and early death; and from their belief that they have little control over what happens in their lives. We discuss social stress in greater detail below, but for now point out that the higher stress levels of low SES people are a significant source of their poorer health (Elo 2009).

Third, low SES people are more likely than wealthier people to work in jobs that are highly stressful and alienating and that provide them little autonomy and control over their workplace duties and conditions. These circumstances are thought to impair these employees' health (Elo 2009).

Fourth, low SES people are more likely to live amid neighborhood physical and social conditions that impair their health, including overcrowding, dilapidated housing, and air pollution. The news story that began this chapter discussed this situation with regard to lead paint. We again discuss these conditions in greater detail below, but some of the poorer health of poor people stems simply from where they live, through no fault of their own.

Fifth, some and perhaps much of the SES difference in health in adulthood originates in childhood. Children in low-income families experience many risk factors including poor nutrition, physical inactivity, family conflict, stress, secondhand smoke, and high levels of lead and pollution. All these risks impair poor children's health (Cabieses, Pickett, and Wilkinson 2016; Haas, Glymour and Berkman 2011; Kaplan 2009). They exhibit more health problems by the age of 9 months, and later on they are much more likely than wealthier children to have asthma and to be obese. Based on their parents' self-reports, one-third of poor American children have less than very good health, compared to only 7 percent of wealthier children.

The relevance for adult SES differences in health is that poor children's health problems often persist into adulthood or at least set the stage for adult health problems. Low-income adults thus have poorer health in part because they had poor health as children. This consequence has been called "the long arm of childhood" (Hayward and Gorman 2004:87). This dynamic has important implications for how to improve the nation's health. As Mark D. Hayward and Bridget K. Gorman (2004:87) explain, "Economic and educational policies that are targeted at children's well-being are implicitly health policies with effects that reach far into the adult life course."

Low SES and Early Mortality   For all these reasons, social class impairs health and leads to early death. A provocative study recently estimated the number of annual deaths stemming from all the effects of poverty and low education just discussed: 133,000 deaths from individual-level poverty, 33,000 deaths from area-level poverty, and 245,000 deaths from low education (Galea et al. 2011). As the study's lead author commented, "In some ways, the question is not 'Why should we think of poverty as a cause of death' but rather 'Why should we not think of poverty as a cause of death?'" (Bakalar 2011:D5).

Race and Ethnicity

Keeping in mind the problems in measuring race (chapter 3), another fundamental cause of health and disease and of health inequalities is race and ethnicity (Phelan and Link 2015). The social patterning here is not as clear-cut as it is for social class, but African Americans, Latinos, and Native Americans generally have worse health than Asians or whites; they also tend to develop disease earlier in life and have more serious symptoms when they do develop disease (National Center for Health Statistics 2014; Takeuchi, Walton, and Leung 2010; Williams and Sternthal 2010).

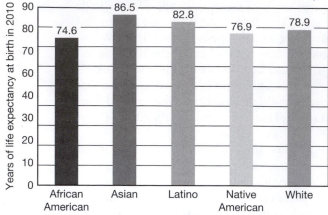

FIG. 5.2 Race and Ethnicity, and Life Expectancy at Birth (years).

Source: Kaiser Family Foundation. 2016. Life Expectancy at Birth (in Years), by Race/Ethnicity. http://kff.org/other/state-indicator/life-expectancy-by-re/.

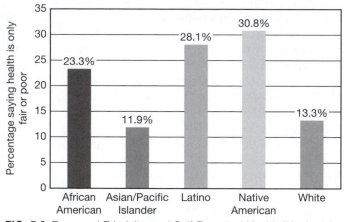

FIG. 5.3 Race and Ethnicity, and Self-Reported Health (% of adults 18 and older saying their health is only fair or poor).

Source: Centers for Disease Control and Prevention. 2013. *CDC Health Disparities and Inequalities Report—United Sates, 2013.* Atlanta, GA: Centers for Disease Control and Prevention.

African Americans have particularly high rates of asthma, diabetes, heart disease, high blood pressure, overweight and obesity, and several types of cancer. Latinos and Native Americans also have higher rates of several health problems, including diabetes and liver cirrhosis, although Latinos have lower rates of heart disease and some other health problems. Meanwhile, Asians are generally healthier than whites but have higher rates of hepatitis B, liver cancer, and tuberculosis.

Reflecting these patterns, life expectancy at birth is shortest for African Americans and Native Americans and highest for Asian Americans and Latinos (see Figure 5.2). African Americans have the shortest life expectancy and live about two years fewer on average than Native Americans, four years fewer than whites, and eight and twelve years fewer than Latinos and Asian Americans, respectively.

It is again illustrative to examine differences in the percentage of people who say their health is only fair or poor. As Figure 5.3 shows, African Americans, Latinos and Native Americans are more likely than Asians or whites to say that their health is only fair or poor.

More than a decade ago, the secretary of the U.S. Department of Health and Human Services said of the racial/ethnic health disparity, "We have been, and remain, two nations: one majority, one minority—separated by the quality of our health" (Penn et al. 2000:102). The body of evidence just presented indicates that little has changed since this statement. If racial/ethnic disparities in health did not exist, the nation would save an estimated $309 billion annually in medical expenditures and lost earnings and economic productivity (LaVeist, Gaskin, and Richard 2009).

Explaining the Impact of Race and Ethnicity It is somewhat difficult to explain the impact of race and ethnicity on health and disease because the racial/ethnic patterning for health is not always consistent. For example, Asians and Latinos are healthier in some ways but less healthy in other ways. Most explanations focus on the worse health of African Americans, Latinos, and Native Americans compared to that of Asians or whites. Because most studies have compared African Americans and whites, these explanations further tend to have this particular comparison in mind. Keeping in mind these issues, scholars say several factors do explain racial/ethnic differences in health and disease (Barr 2014; Bradby and Nazroo 2010; Phelan and Link 2015; Williams 2012; Williams and Sternthal 2010).

The most important factor is probably social class. African Americans, Latinos, and Native Americans are much poorer than Asians and whites and have less formal education. All the reasons discussed in the previous section on social class thus help explain why these three racial/ethnic groups have worse health. Compared to Asians and whites, they tend to lack the important resources for good health identified by the theory of fundamental causes; they experience higher levels of chronic stress because of their lower SES; they are more likely to work in stressful and alienating jobs with little autonomy; they tend to live in areas that lack access to healthy foods and that make people less willing to go outside to exercise; they tend to live in areas with social and physical conditions such as pollution and overcrowding that impair their health; and they are more likely to have had health problems during childhood (Umberson et al. 2014). To a large degree, then, the racial/ethnic difference in health reflects the racial/ethnic difference in SES.

However, racial/ethnic differences in health persist even when comparisons are made for people with similar SES. For example, middle-class African Americans have worse health than middle-class whites, and African Americans with college degrees have four fewer years of life expectancy at age 25 than whites with college degrees (Williams and Sternthal 2010). Although social class matters greatly, then, it is not the only reason for racial/ethnic differences in health. Because people of color have worse health from their lower social class and also from their race and ethnicity, their health suffers from a "double jeopardy" (Williams and Sternthal 2010). This fact leads scholars to identify reasons for the racial/ethnic gap in health beyond those relating to social class (Phelan and Link 2015; Williams 2012).

One reason is that people of color receive less adequate medical care because they are more likely to lack health insurance and also because of unconscious racial/ethnic bias among health care professionals (see chapter 12). For example, African Americans are less likely than whites to receive certain medical tests and procedures when they seek professional care (Samal, Lipsitz, and Hicks 2012; Smedley, Stith, and Nelson 2003).

Another reason is diet, at least for African Americans. Although African Americans have poorer nutrition because of their lower incomes, they also have poorer nutrition because they have a cultural preference for several foods high in fat (Figaro, BeLue, and Beech 2010; Kulkarni 2004). Their diets thus contribute to their higher levels of overweight and obesity (see chapter 3) and to the many diseases resulting from these levels.

Yet another reason is that people of color face extra stress because of racial/ethnic discrimination and slights in their daily lives (Bratter and Gorman 2011; Lewis, Cogburn, and Williams 2015; Phelan and Link 2015). This extra stress induces long-lasting high blood pressure and overweight (Anderson 2013; Brody et al. 2014). In an interesting finding, African Americans and Latinos who experience more discrimination on a daily basis have worse health on average than those who experience less such discrimination (Lee and Ferraro 2009). In another interesting finding, African Americans with darker skin tone experience more discrimination than those with lighter skin tone and thus have worse mental and physical health than their lighter-skin-tone counterparts (Monk 2015). The impact of racial/ethnic discrimination on stress and hence on health is again one of the signature findings of medical sociologists and other health scholars.

An additional reason for the poor health of people of color, even when controlling for SES, is racial segregation (Phelan and Link 2015; Takeuchi, Walton, and

Leung 2010; Williams and Collins 2001). African Americans and, to a smaller extent, Latinos and Native Americans tend to live in racially segregated neighborhoods throughout the United States. Research finds that racial segregation impairs African Americans' health, as it is associated with higher infant mortality and lower birth weight among African American families, lower quality of self-reported health, and a higher rate of being overweight. Reflecting these patterns, African Americans living in highly segregated neighborhoods have a higher mortality rate than those living in less segregated areas.

Racial segregation impairs health because it "shapes access to important structural and social resources" (Takeuchi, Walton, and Leung 2010:99). In this way of thinking, racial segregation results in *concentrated poverty* and raises crime rates, unemployment, air pollution and lead paint exposure, and traffic noise while reducing the quality of schooling and social services (Moody, Darden, and Pigozzi 2016). All these problems harm health because they engender much stress, lead to physical inactivity and other risky health behaviors, and weaken supportive social networks (Ross and Mirowsky 2001l; Takeuchi, Walton, and Leung 2010). The estimated deaths study mentioned earlier attributed 176,000 annual deaths to racial segregation (Galea et al. 2011).

A final reason for racial/ethnic differences in health might be biology. Here we must first emphasize that sociologists are very wary and even critical of any explanation that highlights alleged biological differences among the races (Frank 2007; Williams and Sternthal 2010). Their criticism stems from their belief that race is best considered a social construction, not a real biological category, and from many historical examples of treating African Americans, Native Americans, and other racial/ethnic groups appallingly because it was thought that they were biologically inferior. Nonetheless, some scientists say that certain genetic differences exist among the races that help account for the racial/ethnic gap in health. Some research also points to other biological differences that may make African American women more susceptible to fatal breast cancer, African American men more susceptible to prostate cancer, and African Americans of both sexes more vulnerable to hypertension and heart disease (Batina et al. 2013; Ricker and Bird 2005).

Still, history and sociology tell us that our society should be very careful in emphasizing biological differences for the racial/ethnic gap in health. Stressing the need to take a sociological approach, David R. Williams and Michelle Sternthal (2010:S23) say that efforts to improve the health of racial/ethnic groups should be "those that are targeted not at internal biological processes, but those that seek to improve the quality of life in the places where Americans spend most of their time: their homes, schools, workplaces, neighborhoods, and places of worship."

The Latino Paradox We noted earlier that racial/ethnic differences in health are not clear-cut. An interesting example of this inconsistency concerns the health of Latinos. Simply put, Latinos overall tend to be healthier than their low SES would suggest they should be and even have lower rates of some diseases than other racial/ethnic groups. For example, older Latinos tend to have lower rates of heart disease and stroke than older people in other racial/ethnic groups (Zhang, Hayward, and Lu 2012), and as we saw earlier, Latinos have a longer life expectancy than whites. As Williams and Sternthal (2010:S21) observe, "Hispanic immigrants, especially those of Mexican background, have high rates of poverty and low levels of access to health insurance in the United States. However, their levels of health are equivalent and sometimes superior to that of the white population."

Researchers call this anomaly the **Latino** (or **Hispanic**) **paradox** (Markides and Eschbach 2005; Scommegna 2013). They note that the overall quality of U.S. health would be worse if Latinos' health were as poor as would be expected from their low SES and other life experiences (for instance, working as farmworkers and doing other taxing physical labor) (Dubowitz, Bates, and Acevedo-Garcia 2010). To the extent the Latino paradox is found, it is found more often for people of Mexican origin than for other Latinos. For example, the health of people of Puerto Rican origin tends to be worse than that for people of Mexican origin or for non-Latino whites (Dubowitz, Bates, and Acevedo-Garcia 2010).

Researchers offer many reasons for the Latino paradox (Dubowitz, Bates, and Acevedo-Garcia 2010). First, Latinos practice several types of healthy behavior more often than African Americans, Native Americans, and non-Latino whites. They tend to have diets based on beans and other low-fat foods, and these diets help minimize the health problems that otherwise result from their greater poverty (Escarce, Morales, and Rumbaut 2006). They also have lower smoking rates than most other racial/ethnic groups (see chapter 3), which greatly helps them avoid heart disease, lung cancer, and other diseases (Blue and Fenelon 2011).

Second, Latino families are very religious and especially close-knit and supportive. These attributes help them deal with stress and other problems of everyday living that are usually risk factors for health (Yasmin 2014).

Third, the Latino paradox might partly reflect **selectivity** factors. In this way of thinking, and again applying mostly to Mexicans, people who immigrate to the United States might be healthier on average than those who stay in Mexico. Similarly, when Mexican immigrants become ill, many return to Mexico. Either dynamic results in healthier Mexicans living in the United States, helping to account for the data showing them to be in better health than might be expected (Riosmena, Wong, and Palloni 2013). Despite some evidence for these processes, this selectivity hypothesis continues to be debated.

Some telling evidence related to the Latino paradox is that Latinos' health behavior and quality of health tend to worsen as they live longer in the United States (Tavernise 2013). Their smoking rates rise, and they also begin eating much more of the typical American high-fat diet (Escarce, Morales, and Rumbaut 2006). In turn, their rates of overweight and obesity also rise, and so do their rates of diabetes, heart disease, and other diseases resulting from overweight and obesity (Pérez-Escamilla 2009). Moreover, the children of first-generation Latinos (those who immigrate to the United States) tend to have worse health than their parents as they grow up, and their children's children tend to have worse health yet (Dubowitz, Bates, and Acevedo-Garcia 2010). Thus, the longer Latinos of any generation have lived in the United States, the worse their health becomes, and the more their health conforms to what would be expected from their low SES. These trends suggest that **acculturation**—adopting the American culture and lifestyle—tends to be bad for their health (Escarce, Morales, and Rumbaut 2006).

Gender and Sex

Sociologists and other scholars distinguish *sex* from *gender*. *Sex* is a biological category and refers to the biological differences between females and males, while *gender* is a social construction and refers to the different expectations society has of females and males and to the two sexes' different experiences based on their biological sex. The title of this section refers to both gender and sex because female/male differences in health and disease result from complex factors that are both social (gender) and biological (sex) in origin.

With that bit of explanation behind us, a central fact of gender and sex differences in health becomes very interesting: women outlive men even though they also tend to have worse health than men. Another way of saying this is that women have better *mortality* than men but worse *morbidity*. Females born in 2010 in the United States could expect to live 81.0 years on average, compared to only 76.2 years for men, a difference of almost five years (National Center for Health Statistics 2014). Even so, women are much more likely than men to have chronic illnesses such as migraine headaches, osteoporosis, lupus, rheumatoid arthritis, and other immune disorders. The term **gender paradox** refers to this combination of better mortality and worse morbidity for women (or worse mortality and better morbidity for men) (Rieker, Bird, and Lang 2010).

Explaining the Gender Paradox   If we ask why women do outlive men (or conversely, why men die sooner than women), a quick answer is that men have more life-threatening diseases, such as heart disease and lung cancer, than women do, and also more life-threatening injuries. In fact, they have a higher risk of death from almost every cause of death (Rogers et al. 2010). But this quick answer then raises the question of why men indeed are more likely to have life-threatening disease and to die from other reasons such as injury and violence. A more complete explanation of the gender paradox takes into account biological differences between the sexes and sociological differences between the genders that help women to live longer but also render them more susceptible to chronic illnesses.

The mortality difference is thought to exist for both biological and sociological reasons (Read and Gorman 2010; Rogers et al. 2010). Women's greater estrogen levels and certain other biological differences probably protect them from heart disease and other life-threatening health problems. Women are also more religious than men and more likely to socialize with friends and relatives; both these factors are also thought to help them live longer (Rogers et al. 2010). Meanwhile, and as chapter 3 explained, men's gender socialization leads them to practice more risky health behaviors such as smoking, heavy drinking, reckless driving, and violence that raise their risk of death, and also to be more reluctant to practice periodic preventive care like an annual checkup. As one physician has commented, "I've often said men don't come in for checkups because they have a big S tattooed on their chests; they think they're Superman" (Guttman 1999:10). Men's socialization also makes them reluctant to seek professional care when they do have a health problem (see chapter 4). A final reason for men's greater mortality is that they are more likely than women to labor in workplaces with environmental and/or safety hazards that kill thousands of workers every year.

The morbidity difference also exists for both biological and sociological reasons (Read and Gorman 2010; Rieker, Bird, and Lang 2010). Women's higher levels of estrogen and other biological traits may protect them from life-threatening diseases, but they also render them more susceptible to many chronic illnesses. Meanwhile, they experience certain problems because of their subordinate status in a sexist society that create stress and other difficulties that impair their health. For example, women have lower SES than men overall and thus are less healthy, all things equal, for at least some of the SES reasons discussed earlier. Women are also less healthy than men because they have more caretaking responsibilities for children and older adults (an infirmed parent or other relative) (Terrill et al. 2012); these responsibilities limit their ability to exercise and also subject them to high levels of stress (Hatch and Dohrenwend 2007). This stress, in turn, weakens their immune systems, aggravates their blood pressure, and causes them to experience higher rates of depression, anxiety, and mood disorders than men.

A final reason for women's worse health is similar to one discussed earlier for people of color: discrimination and slights. Because women live in a sexist society, they experience discrimination, slights, and other problems (e.g., fear of sexual assault and actual sexual assault) that men do not experience as often because they enjoy **male privilege** (McIntosh 2007). This situation adds to women's stress and, in turn, weakens their physical and mental health (Landry and Mercurio 2009). In addition to gender-related stress, African American women also experience stress from racial discrimination and slights. This combination of stressors is thought to have particular effects on their physical and mental health (Perry, Harp, and Oser 2013).

Reproductive Health   In addition to experiencing higher morbidity, women's health is disadvantaged compared to men in one other area, and that is reproductive health. Because women can become pregnant and bear children, this basic fact of their biology renders them more vulnerable to many types of reproductive health issues, including infertility, pregnancy and childbirth complications, postpartum depression, and unintended and unwanted pregnancy. Women are also vulnerable to certain diseases related to their complex reproductive systems, including endometriosis, uterine fibroids, and several types of cancer (cervical, ovarian, uterine, vaginal, vulvar). Moreover, women experience much higher rates of breast cancer than men do: about 120 of every 1,000 women will develop breast cancer during their lifetime, compared to 1 of every 1,000 men (Centers for Disease Control and Prevention 2013). Men, of course, may incur prostate and testicular cancer, which women cannot; about 150 of every 1,000 men will develop prostate cancer during their lifetime, and about 4 of every 1,000 men will develop testicular cancer (National Cancer Institute 2014).

Reproductive health problems for many women are worsened by their lack of access to contraception and adequate gynecological care and by inadequate reproductive and sexual health education during adolescence. The women who are most likely to suffer from these problems are those who are poor and African American, Latino, or Asian American. For African American women, these problems result in much higher rates of maternal and infant mortality. Their average annual rate of infant mortality, for example, is 12.2 deaths before age 1 per 1,000 live births, compared to less than half that for white women. Native American women also have a higher infant mortality rate at 8.4 (National Center for Health Statistics 2014). This general situation for poor women and those of color is termed **reproductive injustice** (Center for Reproductive Rights 2014).

Violence Against Women   A final area of concern for women's health is violence against women. Although men are much more likely than women to be victims of violence, adding to their higher mortality, women are much more likely than men to be targets of violence because of their gender (Barkan 2015). This type of violence takes four forms: sexual assault, domestic violence, stalking, and sexual harassment. Based on national survey data, CDC estimates that more than one-fourth (27.2%) of U.S. women have been raped or sexually assaulted; that one-third of women have been physically assaulted by an intimate partner (husband, ex-husband, boyfriend, ex-boyfriend); and that 16% of women have been stalked (Black et al. 2011). Meanwhile, some evidence suggests that up to 70% of women employees are sexually harassed in the workplace and that almost one-third of women undergraduates are sexually harassed by a faculty member (Blackstone 2012; Clodfelter et al. 2010). Many studies find that all these experiences may cause anxiety, sleeplessness, severe stress, and psychological trauma and depression, and for these and other reasons also impair physical health (Garcia et al. 2014).

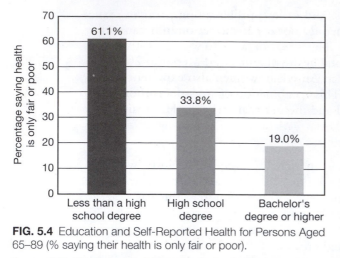

FIG. 5.4 Education and Self-Reported Health for Persons Aged 65–89 (% saying their health is only fair or poor).

Source: 2008–2014 General Social Survey (author's calculation).

Age

Like gender, age affects physical health for both biological and social reasons. The major reason is biological. One of the facts of life is that as our bodies age, our health tends to worsen (Hillier and Barrow 2015). Older people, those 65 and older and even those in their middle ages, tend to have worse health along many dimensions than younger adults. Accordingly, almost 23% of adults 65 and older say their health is only fair or poor, compared to less than 4% of those ages 18–24. Similarly, 56% of adults 65 and older report at least one "basic actions difficulty" (e.g., walking, standing, hearing, remembering) compared to only 24% of adults under 65 (National Center for Health Statistics 2014).

If aging has such strong biological effects, how does it also affect health for social reasons? The answer is that sociodemographic and other social aspects of people's lives affect their chances of experiencing **successful aging**, that is, living a long and healthy life free or relatively free of health problems. It should go without saying that practicing good health behaviors enhances successful aging. But we have seen in this and previous chapters that SES, race and ethnicity, and other social factors affect the likelihood of practicing these behaviors and otherwise of maintaining one's health. For example, among people aged 65–89 interviewed by the national General Social Survey from 2008 to 2014, 61% of those without a high-school degree reported being in fair or poor health, compared to only 19% of those with a bachelor's or graduate degree (see Figure 5.4). A social factor that is often very important for successful aging is a person's social network of family, friends, and neighbors: older people with a strong network tend to have better health because they can rely on their social network for both emotional and practical support (Binstock and George 2011).

Older people have worse health because of their age, and their age also makes it more difficult for them to deal with their worse health. For example, because many older people think pain is a normal part of aging, they may decline to seek medical care when they do experience pain and instead become more inactive because of the pain. Unfortunately, their activity often worsens the pain or makes it less likely that it will subside. Their untreated pain may then worsen their health in other ways, for example, by making it difficult for them to eat or sleep or spend time with people (Brody 2014b).

Sexual Orientation and Gender Identity

LGBT individuals tend to have worse physical and mental health overall than straight people (Institute of Medicine 2011; Ward et al. 2014). A major reason for this difference is health behavior. As chapter 3 noted, LGBT individuals are more likely to engage in risky health behavior such as smoking and drinking because of the stress and other problems of living in a homophobic society. These behaviors contribute to their worse health. Because stress is a significant risk factor itself for worse health (to be discussed later in this chapter), the stress of being LGBT is another major reason for the worse health of the LGBT population. Certain problems in the health care of LGBT individuals, to be examined further in chapter 12, also account for their worse health status (Harvey and Housel 2014).

Studies of LGBT health disparities are less numerous than one might think, in part because the major national surveys of health and disease did not ask about sexual orientation and gender identity until very recently. For example, the National Health Interview Survey (NHIS) first asked about sexual orientation and gender identity in 2013. Still, the available evidence shows that the LGBT population has higher rates than the straight population of asthma, heart disease, diabetes, and other health problems (Ward et al. 2014). Although it is difficult to measure LGBT status accurately, the new national measures of sexual orientation and gender identity should spur additional data on, and studies of, LGBT status and health and health behavior.

Other Social Causes of Health and Health Problems

Several other social causes of health and disease exist. They all interact with social class, race and ethnicity, gender, and age in complex ways, and this chapter has already mentioned some of these causes in passing. This final part of the chapter examines these additional social causes. Some of them may be *fundamental* causes depending on how "fundamental" is defined, but regardless of this conceptual issue, they all contribute to the extent of health and disease and to their social distribution.

Social Stress

A first social cause is **stress**, or emotional and mental tension resulting from very adverse circumstances or situations. Stress results from three sources: (1) *negative life events,* such as divorce, sudden unemployment, or death of a family member; (2) *chronic strains,* such as poverty, overcrowding, or alcoholism in one's family; and (3) *traumas,* such as violent victimization or a serious accident. Each such reason for stress is termed a *stressor*. Sociologists, psychologists, and biologists are increasingly recognizing that extreme, chronic stress impairs physical and mental health and in particular can lead to high blood pressure, chronic pain, and cardiovascular disease among other problems (Avison and Thomas 2010; Carr 2014; Velasquez-Manoff 2013). Summarizing the literature, medical sociologist Peggy A. Thoits (2010:541) says that stressors' "damaging impacts on physical and mental health are substantial." Stress has these effects in part because it affects the functioning of the immune system and the hypothalamic-pituitary-adrenal (HPA) axis, a major component of the neuroendocrine system (Garcia et al. 2014).

We have already commented that stress helps account for the associations of social class, race and ethnicity, gender, and sexual orientation and gender identity with health outcomes. The higher levels of stress experienced by people with low SES, by people of color, by women, and by LGBT persons help greatly to explain why these groups have worse health overall than their more advantaged counterparts. As medical sociologist Leonard Pearlin (1999;398–399) once commented, "People's standing in the stratified orders of social and economic class, gender, race, and ethnicity have the potential to pervade the structure of their daily existence . . . shaping the contexts of people's lives, the stressors to which they are exposed, and the moderating resources they possess." The role that stress plays in health inequalities is a key finding of work in medical sociology during the past few decades.

Factors Affecting the Stress-Health Dynamic   Several factors affecting the stressPhealth dynamic are worth noting (Avison and Thomas 2010; Thoits 2010).

The first factor is how stressful any stressors are. The death of a spouse is very stressful, but a minor injury is less stressful. The second factor is the number of stressors an individual experiences: all things equal, the greater the number of stressors, the greater the impact on health. Another factor is the time frame in which stressors occur; several stressors occurring within, say, a six-month period will likely have a greater impact than the same number of stressors occurring over a ten-year period. In addition, chronic strains have more impact than negative life events or traumas on mental health and likely on physical health. Next, and as we noted earlier, people of color experience stress not only from their lower SES but also from discrimination and slights stemming from racial/ethnic prejudice. The combined stress from these two sources can be a particular risk factor for their physical and mental health.

Buffering the Impact of Stress   Although stress can harm health, it is also true that certain factors can reduce the impact of stress (Carr 2014). These factors are called **stress buffers**. Two personal buffers are a se*nse of control ov*er one's life and hig*h self-esteem. P*eople with one or both of these traits are better able to deal with stressors than those with neither trait. A third buffer is soc*ial support fr*om one's social network of family, friends, and other people, including coworkers and members of a person's religious congregation. All these people can provide emotional and/or practical support to help deal with whatever stressors someone might be experiencing. Unfortunately, all these stress buffers are less likely to be found among people from the types of social class, racial/ethnic, and gender backgrounds that produce greater stress, adding to the impact that stress has on their health.

Childhood Toxic Stress and Stress Proliferation   Toxic stress is childhood stress that is frequent, severe, and prolonged (Bornstein 2013). Experienced by many children growing up in poverty, as noted earlier, toxic stress stems from such adv*erse childhood experiences (A*CEs) as child abuse and neglect, family conflict and violence, and neighborhood violence (Monnat and Chandler 2015; Turner et al. 2013). Children's toxic stress harms their physical and mental health, cognitive development and learning potential, and behavior not only in the short run, but also well into adolescence and adulthood (Friedman et al. 2015; Umberson et al. 2014). A key reason for these effects is that children's brains are rapidly developing, and toxic stress can change how their brains develop. It also causes children to experience overly high levels of stress hormones such as cortisol and norepinephrine, induces high blood pressure, weakens the immune system, and leads to eating problems in childhood and drug and alcohol problems by adolescence (Evans, Brooks-Gunn, and Klebanov 2011). As one pediatrician has written, "When this level of stress is experienced at an early age, and without sufficient protection, it may actually reset the neurological and hormonal systems, permanently affecting children's brains and even, we are learning, their genes" (Klass 2013).

Poor children's toxic stress concerns social scientists, educators, and health officials. As two poverty scholars observe, "It's not just that poverty-induced stress is mentally tasking. If it's experienced early enough in childhood, it can in fact get 'under the skin' and change the way in which the body copes with the environment and the way in which the brain develops. These deep, enduring, and sometimes irreversible physiological changes are the very human price of running a high-poverty society" (Grusky and Wimer 2011:2).

Childhood stress is one of the bases for **stress proliferation**, which refers to the fact that one stressor may lead to additional stressors (Pearlin et al. 2005). Three forms of stress proliferation may occur. The first form involves a stressor in one sphere of life that leads to stress in other aspects of one's life. For example, the stress from unemployment may lead to family conflict, which then causes additional stress; this new source of stress aggravates the initial source's impact on health. To return to childhood stress, the second form involves stress proliferation over the life course, as childhood problems lead to stressful events during adolescence (such as alcohol abuse or being arrested), and these events in turn generate additional stressors in young adulthood and beyond. The third form also concerns childhood stress and involves stress proliferation from one generation to the next. Stressors such as poverty and divorce experienced by parents can impair their child-rearing skills and for this and other reasons generate stressors in their children.

The differences between more stressed children and less stressed children often become larger as they age into adolescence and adulthood, just as two lines with the same beginning point (picture two sides of a triangle) widen from each other by the time they reach their endpoints. Stressed children's disadvantages during their young years lead to more disadvantages during adolescence and then to more disadvantages yet during adulthood. This dynamic is called **cumulative disadvantage** and refers to the idea that the impact of stress and other problems experienced during childhood accumulates over the life course. As medical sociologist Peggy Thoits (2010:S47) observes "Structural disadvantages and abundant adversities in childhood ripple forward into adolescence, adulthood, and old age, as difficulties cascade and compound over the life course." For example, SES differences in health are smaller during childhood, become larger during adolescence, and larger yet during adulthood. Partly for this reason, low SES people not only have worse health, but also begin to have worse health earlier in life (Thoits 2010).

Social Relationships and Social Support

The extent and quality of social relationships affects people's health: those with more extensive and higher-quality social relationships have better physical and mental health overall than those with fewer and lower-quality social ties (Qualls 2014; Yanga et al. 2016). Partly as a result, people with better social relationships are also more likely to die later in life. The promotive effect of social relationships on health is found for many health problems, including heart disease, high blood pressure, and certain types of cancers. It is also found for biological markers for inflammation and immune dysfunction that indicate a higher risk of disease. People with serious health problems are also more likely to recover faster if they have good social relationships (Umberson and Montez 2010).

These health benefits exist for good social relationships generally, but much of the research in this area has focused on one social relationship, marriage (Hill, Reid, and Reczek 2013; Hughes and Waite 2009). Many studies find that marriage is associated with lower rates of a wide range of health problems, including heart disease, other chronic illness, and depression. Spouses with cancer are more likely than unmarried people to be diagnosed at an earlier stage of their cancer and to be appropriately treated for it, and less likely to die from it (Aizer et al. 2013). Spouses are also more likely than unmarried people to have better self-reported health; among people aged 40–59 interviewed in the 2008–2014 General Social Surveys, married individuals were less likely than unmarried individuals to report being in only fair or poor health (see Figure 5.5). In an interesting finding, marriage appears to be more beneficial for men's health than for women's health, in part because women are more likely than men to have stressful caregiving responsibilities for children and aging parents (Umberson and Montez 2010).

In a selectivity issue, it is possible that less healthy individuals are less likely to be married because of their health, but scholars do think that the marriage-health

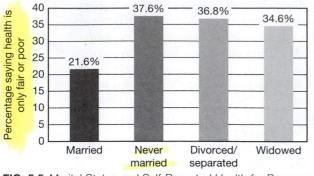

FIG. 5.5 Marital Status and Self-Reported Health for Persons Aged 40–59 (% saying their health is only fair or poor).

Source: 2008–2014 General Social Survey (author's calculation).

relationship reflects the effects of marriage on health more than the effects of health on marriage (Horn et al. 2013). Note that marriage enhances health only if the marriage is relatively strong and stable. Marriages filled with anger, conflict, and violence certainly have the opposite effect by damaging physical and mental health.

Major reasons for the many health benefits of social relationships generally and marriage specifically involve health behavior and help-seeking behavior (Umberson and Montez 2010). As chapters 3 and 4 noted, positive health behavior and help-seeking behavior are both more likely among people with good social relationships. People with such relationships, then, are healthier in part because they practice better health behavior and are more likely to seek professional care when needed.

Extensive and high-quality social relationships enhance health in other ways (Umberson and Montez 2010). As the discussion of social stress indicated, good social relationships provide emotional support that helps to reduce the impact of stress. This emotional support has certain physiological effects, including reduced blood pressure and lower levels of stress hormones, that enhance physical and mental health. Good social relationships also augment a person's sense of control, which again helps to reduce stress and improve health for other reasons. Certain types of social relationships, such as an adult raising a child, may prompt someone to feel responsible for maintaining good health since they are taking care of someone else.

If extensive and high-quality social relationships are important for good health, a lack these relationships contributes to poor health and early death. The estimated deaths study mentioned earlier attributed 162,000 annual deaths to a lack of social relationships and social support (Galea et al. 2011).

We have already mentioned that bad marriages damage physical and mental health. Other types of social relationships may also impair health (Umberson and Montez 2010). For example, someone raising a child with developmental disabilities may experience exhaustion and high levels of stress because this type of parenting is very difficult; the same problems may occur for someone taking care of an elderly parent with serious physical and/or cognitive limitations (Brody 2014a). Adolescent friendships can impair health if one's friends engage in risky health behaviors like alcohol and other drug use, and, as chapter 3 mentioned, some evidence suggests that social relationships may even promote obesity, which is more commonly found among individuals with an obese spouse or obese friends (Christakis and Fowler 2007; Cunningham et al. 2012).

Religion

Religion is another social factor affecting the quality of health. People who are more religious exhibit greater levels of physical and psychological health and die later in life (Doane and Elliott 2016; Ellison and Hummer 2010; Idler 2010; Koenig, King, and Carson 2012). A major reason for these benefits is that religious people are more likely to practice promotive health behaviors and to avoid risky behaviors (see chapter 3), partly because of the influence of their own religious beliefs, and partly because of the influence of the other religious people (in their families, friendships, and/or congregations) with whom they interact. Reflecting this dynamic, two religious groups with strict standards of behavior, Mormons and Seventh-Day Adventists, tend to live much longer than other religious groups (Enstrom and Breslow 2008; Heuch, Jacobsen, and Fraser 2005).

Another reason for religion's health benefits is that religious people receive social support, both emotional and practical, from the members of their religious congregations. We have already discussed the significance of social relationships for health, and religious people's congregant networks are an important type of social relationship that helps improve their health. These networks might be particularly important for the health of older people, as they are not only less healthy than younger people and in need of social support, but also more religious than younger people (Barkan and Greenwood 2003).

A third reason for religion's promotion of health might be that people with strong religious beliefs rely on their faith to help them cope with stress and health problems. Although evidence on this point is not conclusive, many scholars feel that religious belief does help people cope with the many problems that life often brings with it (Holt et al. 2014; Park, Sacco, and Edmondson 2012).

Neighborhood Living Conditions

People are often more or less healthy because of the neighborhoods in which they live (MacIntyre and Ellaway 2003; Robert, Cagney, and Weden 2010). This was certainly true during the nineteenth century, when poor public sanitation and overcrowding in urban neighborhoods helped spread cholera and other infectious diseases (see chapter 2). Many urban neighborhoods today also harm their residents' health. These neighborhoods are marked by several problems that together are called **concentrated disadvantage**. These problems include extreme poverty, high unemployment, high crime rates, dilapidated housing, substandard schools, abandoned buildings, inadequate public funding, environmental hazards, weak social ties and mutual trust among neighbors, and much graffiti and vandalism. These problems in a sense reproduce themselves, as concentrated disadvantage in turn produces lower high-school graduation rates, higher crime rates, higher unemployment, and other problems (Rodriguez 2013; Wodtke, Harding, and Elwert 2011). For our purposes, concentrated disadvantage in urban neighborhoods also harms health, as many studies have found (Diez Roux 2016; Finch et al. 2010; Robert, Cagney, and Weden 2010).

An important reason for this consequence is health behavior (Halonen et al. 2014). As chapter 3 explained, neighborhood conditions affect our likelihood of engaging in positive health behaviors as well as risky health behaviors. Healthy diets and sufficient exercise are more difficult to achieve in many urban neighborhoods, for example, because these neighborhoods lack outlets for healthy food and their crime rates may inhibit people from going outside for a jog or long walk. Many of these neighborhoods also have many fast food outlets that induce the consumption of unhealthy foods.

Another reason for the impact of neighborhoods on health is stress (Hill, Ross, and Angel 2005). Many urban neighborhoods feature conditions such as overcrowding, crime, and illegal drug use that are highly stressful for their residents. These neighborhoods' high stress levels in turn impair the residents' physical and mental health. As this chapter noted earlier, children who live in such neighborhoods are particularly vulnerable to the health effects of stress, and these effects may continue into their adolescence and adulthood.

Intervening mechanisms in addition to stress also help explain the neighborhood-health effect. By definition, disadvantaged urban neighborhoods are characterized by such features as poverty, unemployment, and substandard schools. These features may impair the socioeconomic status of families living in these neighborhoods. For example, adults may find it more difficult to find a job nearby, and the poor schooling that children receive may have a lifelong impact on their SES. These types of effects can in turn impair the physical and mental health of the residents of disadvantaged neighborhoods.

Another reason for the neighborhood effect on health concerns environmental pollution and hazards. Many urban neighborhoods have high levels of air and noise pollution from traffic and other sources (Kheirbek et al. 2014). As noted earlier in this chapter, some neighborhoods still have high levels of lead paint that can harm children's health (Moody et al. 2016). Living in all these neighborhoods may be hazardous to health because of these neighborhoods' environmental problems.

Although this discussion of neighborhoods has focused on urban areas, rural areas also have features that may impair health (Hartley 2004; Lavelle, Lorenz, and Wickrama 2012). As chapter 4 noted, many rural people live far from health care providers and facilities. This basic fact of rural life makes it difficult to practice periodic preventive health behavior (i.e., an annual checkup) and to seek needed professional medical care. Both these difficulties may harm rural residents' health.

The combination of extreme poverty and rural residence can be especially unhealthy. In the United States, we see this combination in Appalachia (the sweeping rural area along the Appalachian Mountains in the southeastern states) and in rural areas of Louisiana and Mississippi, among other regions. In Appalachia, which has been called "one of the nation's unhealthiest regions" (Ungar 2014), extreme poverty and low education, physician shortages and other health care access problems, proximity to convenience stores and distance from grocery stores, and unhealthy lifestyles join to produce very high rates of chronic illness and early death. Rural Kentucky has the nation's highest cancer death rate, and its diabetes and heart disease rates are also much higher than the national average. As one Kentucky health expert summarizes the situation, "We're in the stroke belt, the diabetes belt, the coronary valley. We get all those labels. We're in a sad state here" (Ungar 2014).

Environmental Pollution and Hazards

Although the previous section said that many urban residents are at risk of contracting health problems because of pollution, pollution is a still general health hazard for people everywhere and should be considered a *social* cause because it arises from human activity. Over time, air pollution, much of which is preventable, causes heart disease, stroke, respiratory disease, lung cancer, and other problems (American Lung Association 2014; Hart et al. 2015). A study by the American Cancer Society concluded that air pollution harms health as much as secondhand smoke, overweight, or being a former smoker (Pope et al. 2004). The number of annual premature deaths, mostly from heart disease and stroke, caused by outdoor air pollution is estimated at 200,000 in the United States and 3.7 million worldwide (Caiazzo et al. 2013; World Health Organization 2014). These figures led the World Health Organization (2014) to observe, "Outdoor air pollution is a major environmental health problem affecting everyone in developed and developing countries alike."

Hazardous waste is another environmental health hazard. Many companies have dumped toxic chemicals and other materials into the ground, lakes, and rivers: the resulting hazardous waste sites have harmed the health of many people. In the United States, the most notorious site is probably Love Canal in Niagara Falls, New

York. A chemical company dumped 20,000 tons of toxic chemicals into the canal during the 1940s and 1950s, filled it with dirt, and sold the new land for development. More than 800 homes and a school were built on top of the toxic chemicals, which eventually leached into the groundwater and people's homes and caused birth defects and other health problems (Gibbs 2011).

In the United States and around the world, environmental pollution and hazardous waste sites are more likely to be found in areas populated by low SES people and by people of color (Pais, Crowder, and Downey 2014). Environmental problems thus have a disproportionate impact on the health of these two disadvantaged groups (King and Auriffeille 2014). This impact is referred to as **environmental inequality** or, if just people of color are considered, **environmental racism**.

Toxic chemicals end up as hazardous waste, but they also end up in commonplace products that millions of Americans consume. These products include cosmetics, pesticides, plastics, and even shampoo. The chemicals in these products may lead to health problems such as diabetes, infertility, and many types of cancer (Kristof 2015).

Climate change is yet another environmental cause of health problems. As the Earth warms, mosquitos, ticks, and other insects that carry deadly diseases are increasingly spreading to locations where they were previously unknown or rare. As they do so, they are also spreading the diseases they carry. An example of this problem is the Zika virus, which is spread by mosquitos (McNeil 2016). Zika causes babies to be born with *microcephaly*, a condition involving babies born with tiny heads and brains. Before 2015, Zika was virtually unknown in the Western Hemisphere. Then an outbreak occurred in Brazil in May 2015 that affected thousands of newborns. By 2016, Zika had spread to many more nations in Central and South America, and some experts worried it would spread to the southern United States (Sifferlin 2016).

Unsafe Products and Workplaces

Many people die or become ill or injured because of unsafe products and workplaces. These problems, termed corporate violence, stem from the fact that corporations routinely violate standards and laws governing product and workplace safety. This is a strong charge, to be sure, but the evidence bears it out (Rosoff, Pontell, and Tillman 2014). An oft-cited example is a car called the Pinto, which Ford manufactured and sold during the 1970s even though it knew that the car was very vulnerable to fire and explosion if hit from behind in a minor accident (Cullen, Maakestad, and Cavender 2006). While the car was being manufactured, Ford realized it needed to shield the gas tank and that it would cost $11 per car to do so. After doing a cost-benefit analysis, Ford determined that it would cost more to repair all the Pintos than to pay money out in lawsuits and compensation after people died or were injured and burned after being hit from behind. Knowing that people would indeed die or otherwise be harmed, Ford then let the car go to market. An estimated 500 Pinto drivers and passengers eventually died because of Ford's inaction, and many more were burned or injured.

In a more recent example, seventeen manufacturers of cribs and other infant products have let their products go to market despite knowing their products could kill or maim infants. Several babies suffered amputated fingers, broken bones, or skull fractures. A news report concluded that the companies "kept quiet about products that were seriously injuring children until the government stepped in" (O'Donnell 2000:1A).

Unsafe workplaces also damage health and kill people. Some occupations such as coal mining and construction work are inevitably dangerous, but many workplace conditions are unnecessarily dangerous because they violate federal and state laws. It is estimated that almost 55,000 Americans die annually from workplace-caused disease and injury and that up to about 11 million workers are injured or become sick from workplace conditions (AFL-CIO 2014). In a recent example, an explosion in April 2013 at a fertilizer plant in Texas killed more than a dozen people and seriously injured about 200 others. The company that owned the plant had earlier been cited for several safety violations that were thought to have contributed to the explosion (Dreier and Cohen 2013).

Interpersonal Violence and Handgun Violence

An additional social cause of health problems, in this case injury, death, and poorer mental health, is interpersonal violence. We discussed violence against women earlier as a significant health problem for women. Public health scholars consider interpersonal violence more generally to be a significant public health problem for the entire nation, and they also consider a subset of this violence, handgun violence, to be a serious public health problem (Rivara et al. 2013; Welsh, Braga, and Sullivan 2014). In 2014, the United States experienced 14,249 homicides and almost 5.4 million other acts of violence (rape and sexual assault, aggravated and simple assault, and robbery), equal to 20 violent victimizations for every 1,000 people aged 12 or older (Federal Bureau of Investigation 2015; Truman and Langton 2015).

The United States experiences many more handgun deaths per capita (from violence, suicide and accidents) than any other developed nation (Leshner et al. 2013). Scholars debate whether the wide supply of handguns in the United States leads to more or less death and crime (Cook and Goss 2014). Although there is evidence on either side of this debate, a fair conclusion is that handguns sometimes promote crime and sometimes deter it, but that on the whole, they do much more harm than good. As evidence, households with guns experience more deaths than households without guns (Kellerman et al. 1998), states with higher rates of firearm ownership have higher homicide rates than states with lower rates (with no relationship between firearm ownership and non-firearm homicides) (Miller, Hemenway, and Azrael 2007), and the United States has a much higher homicide rate than other developed nations even though its overall violence rate is only about average (Zimring and Hawkins 1997).

Conclusion

This chapter's discussion emphasized that a person's quality of health depends to a large extent on social causes. Our chances of being healthy, sick, or injured are affected greatly by our socioeconomic status, race and ethnicity, gender, physical location, and the other social causes examined in this chapter. To achieve real improvements in Americans' health, it is critical for our nation to reduce poverty, improve neighborhood conditions, and otherwise address the underlying social factors that affect our likelihood of being healthy, sick, or injured. This chapter's emphasis on the social causation of health and health problems continues in the next chapter's examination of health and health problems across the world.

Summary

1. Some social conditions are fundamental causes of disease by affecting the likelihood of disease for multiple reasons.
2. Health disparities reflect the impact of various social inequalities, including those based on social class, race and ethnicity, gender, and neighborhood conditions. Social class is probably the most important reason for health disparities.

3. People of color generally have worse health than whites not only because of their lower socioeconomic status but also because of their experience of racial and ethnic discrimination.
4. Women live longer than men but are also generally less healthy than men. Social and biological reasons help explain this pattern.
5. Social stress is a critical intervening mechanism for explaining the impact of several fundamental courses on health and health problems. Childhood stress can have lifelong consequences for physical and mental health.
6. Neighborhood conditions, environmental problems, and unsafe products and workplaces are additional social causes of health and disease. These and other social causes must be addressed in order to make real improvements in the nation's health.

Giving It Some Thought

You are living in a large city with your spouse and two young children. You enjoy your urban living, but you also recognize that all the traffic in your neighborhood and throughout the city must be polluting the air and causing a health hazard. You're becoming increasingly worried about the possible health effects for your family and especially for your children. Your spouse is much less concerned and thinks you are worrying too much. Do you try to persuade your spouse to move out of the city, or do you decide not to press the issue?

Key Terms

acculturation, 79

concentrated disadvantage, 87

cumulative disadvantage, 85

environmental inequality, 89

environmental racism, 89

fundamental cause, 72

gender paradox, 80

health disparities, 73

health inequalities, 73

hispanic paradox, 78

latino paradox, 78

male privilege, 81

morbidity, 70

reproductive injustice, 81

selectivity, 79

stress, 83

stress buffers, 84

stress proliferation, 84

successful aging, 82

theory of fundamental causes, 72

toxic stress, 84

6 Global Disparities in Health and Disease

Health and Illness in the News

Earlier this decade, the dreaded Ebola virus broke out in several nations in West Africa. Before it came under control many months later, it had killed more than 11,000 people and infected more than 27,000 others. At the height of the epidemic, the director-general of the World Health Organization warned, "If the situation continues to deteriorate, the consequences can be catastrophic in terms of lost lives but also severe socioeconomic disruption and a high risk of spread to other countries." (DiBlasio 2014; Nossiter and Cowell 2014; UN News Centre 2015)

The previous chapter discussed health disparities in the United States stemming from social inequalities based on socioeconomic status and other fundamental causes of disease. We saw then that society's many inequalities reproduce and manifest themselves in disease and other health problems: for many reasons, people who have a low SES and are less equal in other ways have worse health and often die far too soon.

When we look around the world, the global society is even more unequal than American society, and health disparities are even more extreme than those found in the United States. Global inequality is a fundamental cause of disease and death for millions of people annually, with the deadly Ebola virus discussed in the opening news story just one of the many diseases and health problems the world's poor face. This chapter's discussion of global health disparities once again illustrates and reinforces medical sociology's emphasis on the social causation of health and disease. We begin with a brief discussion of global inequality before turning to these disparities.

Understanding Global Inequality

Imagine you are playing the classic Monopoly game with four other players. But now let's assume your Monopoly game is being played on the global level, so that each of the five players represents one-fifth of the world's population: Player A represents the richest one-fifth, Player B represents the second-richest fifth, and so on down to Player E, who represents the poorest fifth. Normally, every Monopoly player gets the same amount of money, $1,500, to begin the game, which would be $7,500 total for your game. But to make your game more realistic, the five players will split this total according to each player's share of the world's income.

Because the richest fifth of the world's population enjoys about 83% of the world's entire income, Player A starts the game with $6,225

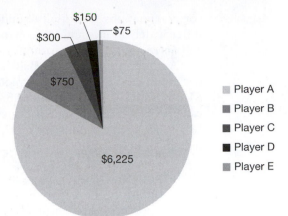

FIG. 6.1 Starting Cash if Monopoly Represented Global Inequality in Income.

Source: Author's calculation based on global distribution of income data from Oritz, Isabel and Matthew Cummins. 2011. *Global Inequality: Beyond the Bottom Billion—A Rapid Review of Income Distribution in 141 Countries.* New York, NY: United Nations Children's Fund (UNICEF).

(=83% of $7,500). Player B has 10% of world income, so that player begins with $750. Player C has 4% of world income and begins with $300. Player D has 2% of world income and begins with $150. Finally, Player E has just 1% of world income and begins with $75 (see Figure 6.1.)

Take a moment to look at these starting amounts of money. Who will almost certainly win the game? Does Player E or for that matter Players D, C, and probably B have any hope of winning? Could Players E and D even get around the board once before going bankrupt?

Although Monopoly and most similar games pretend everyone is equal at the start of the game, the real world is very different and marked by shocking inequality. As our fanciful Monopoly game illustrates, one-fifth of the world's population is very, very wealthy in terms of their share of the world's income, and the remaining four-fifths are poor, with the bottom fifth abjectly poor. The unequal distribution of nations in terms of wealth, power and influence, and resources is called **global stratification**, or **global inequality**. Global stratification has significant consequences for the life and welfare of the world population. Not the least of these consequences is health. As we will soon see, people in poor nations are at a much, much greater risk of disease and early death than those in wealthier nations.

Categorizing Global Inequality

To help understand global stratification before examining global disparities in health and disease, it is useful to combine the world's nations into three or four groups based on their wealth. To do so, it is common to use one of these two related measures as the criterion: (1) *gross national product* (GDP) per capita, the value of a nation's goods and services divided by its population size, or (2) *gross national income* (GNI) per capita, equal to a nation's GDP plus its income from foreign sources, divided by its population size. Using either of these measures, the nations are then sorted into three or four groups ranging from wealthiest to poorest.

Some typologies use the term *developed* to refer to the wealthiest nations and *developing* or *less-developed* to refer to poorer nations. Several international bodies use these terms: *high-income* (or *wealthy*) nations, *middle-income* nations, and *low-income* (or *poor*) nations. Because the middle-income nations include many countries that differ widely in income, some classifications divide them into *upper-middle-income* and *lower-middle-income* nations.

According to the World Bank's classification, high-income nations all have GNI per capita of at least $12,746; middle-income nations have GNI per capita between $1,046 and $12,746 (with $4.125 separating the *lower* and *upper* nations within this category); and low-income nations have GNI per capita less than $1,045. With this bit of measurement information behind us, let's take a brief look at these groups of nations.

High-Income Nations   As their name implies, these nations are the wealthiest in the world. Most of them are very industrialized, and they enjoy most of the world's entire income, control most of its resources, and wield most of its economic and other influence. These nations include Canada and the United States in North America; the nations of Western Europe, including Scandinavia; and Australia and New Zealand. They also include Israel, Kuwait, and some other nations in the Middle East; Croatia and some other nations of the former Soviet Union; and Japan and Singapore in Asia. There is great wealth variation (and also great variation in health and disease) across this large group of high-income nations; for example, the U.S. GNI per capita is almost $54,000, while Croatia's is about $13,300. There is also a high degree of stratification *within* each of many of these nations, along with great variation in health and disease within each nation. Still, their relatively great wealth justifies grouping them and distinguishing them from the other groups of nations with less wealth.

Middle-Income Nations   These nations tend to be somewhat industrialized, and many are rich in natural resources. They are largely found in Central and South America, Eastern Europe, and Africa and Asia. Specific nations in this group include Brazil, China, Lebanon, and Peru, which are all upper-middle-income nations, and Egypt, Guatemala, India, and Nigeria, which are all lower-middle-income nations. Some of the dozens of nations in this group, including China and India, have been experiencing great improvement in their economies in recent decades, although tens of millions of their citizens are still desperately poor.

Low-Income Nations   These nations include about half the world's population and are largely found in Africa and Asia. They have primarily agricultural economies and are characterized by abject poverty and deplorable living conditions almost beyond imagination. Specific low-income nations include Afghanistan, Cambodia, Ethiopia, Rwanda, and Uganda. We will soon see that people in these nations are at incredible risk for disease and have the world's highest rates of many diseases and the lowest life expectancy.

Measuring World Poverty

It is difficult to define and measure poverty at the international level. The United States has many poor people, about 15% of the nation, who experience a range of problems because of their poverty, including health problems as emphasized in chapter 5. Their standard of living, however unfortunate, is still not as deplorable as that of most people in low-income nations and many people in middle-income nations.

According to the World Bank, 900 million people live in extreme poverty, defined as an income under $1.90 per person per day, or the equivalent of a yearly income of $694 for one person or $2,774 for a family of four. Several billion other people are very poor (because their income exceeds $1.90 per day) but not extremely poor under this definition. About one-third of the world's extremely poor are children under age 13; doing some simple math, 300 million young children live in extreme poverty (Olinto et al. 2013). Almost 45% of people in Sub-Saharan Africa live in extreme poverty, compared to 22% in South Asia, 9% in East Asia and the Pacific, 6% in Latin America and the Caribbean, 3% in the Middle East and North Africa, and less than 3% in Europe (Cruz et al. 2015).

Sub-Saharan Africa and South Asia, then, have the largest concentrations of extreme poverty, and most of the world's poor live in these two regions. Because India, China, and some other middle-income nations are so large, most of the world's extremely poor also live in these nations. Whatever the region, most extremely poor people live in rural areas and earn what little money they have from agriculture.

Explaining Global Inequality

Why are low-income nations so poor and why are high-income nations so wealthy? Why do so many residents of low- and middle-income nations live in extreme poverty or less extreme poverty? To what extent, if any, does it make sense to hold poor people around the world responsible for the health problems and other problems they routinely suffer? These questions go to the heart of various explanations of global stratification, as these explanations imply different answers to these questions.

One explanation, called **modernization theory**, assumes that the wealthy nations of Western Europe became wealthy because several centuries ago they developed certain beliefs and values that helped them become wealthy (Rostow 1990). These beliefs included a desire to work hard and a willingness to break with the past in trying new ways of accomplishing various goals. These beliefs and values enabled these nations to move from an agricultural and mercantile (trade) economy to an industrial economy, which brought them great wealth and power. By implication, today's poor nations never developed the "correct" beliefs and values to enable them to move along the same path. Modernization theory thus implies that the world's poor today are poor because they lack the beliefs and values they need to lift themselves out of poverty. A further implication is that they are at least partly to blame for the health and other problems they routinely experience.

In contrast, **dependency theory** assumes that wealthy nations of Western Europe became wealthy because they colonized nations in Africa, South America, and other parts of the world centuries ago, took their natural resources, and enslaved many of their citizens or exploited their labor (Peet and Hartwick 2015). The nations that were colonized remained poor because they were unable to control their own resources and were often prevented by the colonial powers from becoming educated. When industrialization began during the nineteenth century, these nations were for these and other reasons unable to industrialize and become wealthier. According to dependency theorists, multinational corporations in today's world run sweatshops in many poor nations and in this and other ways continue the exploitation of the resources and labor of poor nations. As should be clear, dependency theory implies that poor nations are not poor through any fault of their own, and that the world's poor people should not be held responsible for the health and other problems they experience.

Although both modernization and dependency theories are worth considering, most sociologists probably favor dependency theory over modernization theory. As you read about global health disparities over the next several pages, keep in mind that there is little the world's poor can do about their fate unless they receive significant help from international bodies and the world's wealthy nations.

Dimensions of Global Health Disparities

To understand global disparities in health and disease today, we must first turn the clock back to the nineteenth century in the United States and Western Europe. As chapter 2 explained, that was a very dangerous era in terms of health because of deadly infectious diseases arising from poor sanitation, unclean water, overcrowding, the lack of today's scientific medicine and health care procedures, and other problems, all of these exacerbated by the deep poverty in which many people lived. As all these conditions improved and as scientific medicine developed, the epidemiological transition occurred, and infectious disease gradually became eradicated in the developed world, saving much suffering and millions of lives.

Low-income nations today have much disease and death because the epidemiological transition never occurred for them. In a sense, they are still living in the conditions that characterized the nineteenth century for today's developed nations, or are even living in far worse conditions. About half of the extremely poor in these nations lack electricity, three-fourths lack access to clean water, and four-fifths lack adequate sanitation (disposal of human waste) (Olinto et al. 2013). These three conditions greatly increase their chances of contracting many serious diseases. In particular, lack of sanitation and clean water set the stage for severe diarrhea; for infectious diseases such as cholera, malaria, and typhoid; and for several parasitic diseases such as schistosomiasis and worm infestations.

Malnutrition and Hunger

The world's poor also lack food and experience high rates of hunger. This hunger causes severe malnutrition that shortens their lives and makes them vulnerable to a host of serious and often fatal diseases. Diseases like diarrhea and parasitic infections that sap the body's nutrients also contribute to the poor's severe malnutrition.

Hunger does *not* exist because there is too little food in developing nations to feed too many people. According to sociologist Stephen J. Scanlan and colleagues (2010:35), the idea of food scarcity in the developing world "is largely a myth. On a per capita basis, food is more plentiful today than any other time in human history . . . Even in times of localized production shortfalls or regional famines there has long been a food surplus." Instead, they say, social inequality prevents food from reaching the world's poor. For example, ethnic minorities in poor nations are more likely than ethnic majority groups to go hungry. Similarly, women in developing nations are generally less educated and even poorer than men and therefore more likely to go hungry. Poor nations also lack the money to purchase food, and their political leaders often use government funds and international aid their nations receive to enhance their own power and lifestyles rather than to help their nations' poor (Basheka 2011).

Children's Health

Have you ever seen the poignant photos or documentaries of African children with swollen stomachs from malnutrition? As these images make clear, all the problems just outlined strike the world's poor children especially harshly. An estimated 19 million children under age 5 worldwide are severely malnourished (World Health Organization 2014e). Diarrhea afflicts children in poor nations 4–5 times every year on the average and kills almost 1.5 million children worldwide annually. Even when diarrhea is not fatal, the malnutrition it induces can cause permanent physical and mental health problems and open the door for fatal respiratory infections (UNICEF 2009). Meanwhile, respiratory infections kill 1.6 million children under age 5 every year, and malaria kills almost 1 million children (World Health Organization 2014a).

Because of malnutrition and related health problems, almost 150 million children under age 5 worldwide are underweight.

The global child death toll from all preventable causes due to poverty and related conditions is shocking: almost 9 million children under age 5 worldwide die every year from these causes, or more than 20,000 every day (You et al. 2010). This figure includes 4 million infants who die before age one month. In Sub-Saharan Africa, about 14% of children die before age 5, and in South Asia, the second-poorest region, more than 7% die before age 5.

Children in India face special risks from inadequate sanitation, which is more of a problem in India than in other low-income nations because half of that nation's population, or more than 600 million people, routinely defecate outside. This practice fosters the spread of harmful bacteria and intestinal and other infectious diseases. These particularly affect children, who become victims of malnutrition and stunting. As a recent news report summarized the situation, "A long economic boom has done little to reduce the vast number of children who are malnourished and stunted, leaving them with mental and physical deficits that will haunt them their entire lives" (Harris 2014:A1).

Although the health of the world's poor children remains shockingly bad, this fact should not obscure the great advances that have been made in combating childhood disease, thanks largely to the efforts of UNICEF, the World Health Organization, and other international agencies. Although almost 9 million children died annually in recent years, that number still represented a sharp decline from the 16.7 million children's deaths in 1970. This decline represents considerable progress, even if millions of children are still dying annually simply because they are poor.

Women's Health

Women in the developing world have worse health overall than men even though they outlive men. This gender patterning resembles the gender paradox discussed in chapter 5 for the United States, but certain aspects of women's lives in the developing world add to the health burden they face.

A major problem is that women in the developing world are generally poorer and less educated than men. This fact renders them more vulnerable to a range of health problems, including HIV/AIDS, as we discuss later.

A second problem is that the developing world is extremely patriarchal, much more so than the United States and other wealthy nations. Women have few or no rights and are often regarded as the property of their husbands or fathers, and they experience high rates of rape and sexual assault and of domestic violence (The World Bank 2014b). When caught in abusive relationships, they are more trapped than abused women in the wealthy world. The sexual control that their husbands, boyfriends, and other men exert over them increases their rates of HIV and AIDS and makes their children at risk for being born with HIV. In India and Pakistan, many women are killed annually because their families fail to render sufficient dowry after they marry. When families experience a sudden loss in access to food (as during drought or joblessness), women often have to reduce their food intake, but not their husbands. When drought, famine, or other problems occur, domestic violence against women often increases. In at least one region, rural Tanzania, family members during drought conditions have murdered elderly women relatives they suspect of witchcraft and blame for the drought (The World Bank 2014b).

A third problem involves reproductive health. Women in low-income nations often lack access to contraception or are too uneducated to realize the need for contraception or to use contraception correctly. Moreover, just as women in wealthy nations have reproductive health issues that men cannot have, so do women in low-income nations. Their situation, however, is far worse because of the substandard health care in their nations.

In a related issue, a recent report found that health workers in these nations often abuse women during childbirth by yelling at and slapping them, refusing to give them pain medication, and by making them share beds with other women who have just had a baby (Grady 2015). An author of the report said, "To imagine that women are mistreated during this very special time is truly devastating" (Grady 2015:A12). This mistreatment is thought to contribute to the high maternal mortality rate in poor nations, in part because it leads some women to have their babies outside of hospitals.

Environmental Pollution and Hazards

Adding to the world poor's health problems are environmental pollution and hazards (World Health Organization 2014b). Chapter 5 emphasized that poor people in the United States have health problems because they are more likely to be exposed to environmental pollution and hazards, a consequence called *environmental inequality*. This type of inequality also exists at the global level, as the world's poor are also more likely to suffer the consequences of environmental pollution and hazards.

Lead Exposure   One such consequence involves lead exposure (World Health Organization 2013). Millions of people around the world are exposed to lead from its use in gasoline (banned in most nations but still used in six nations), paint (again banned in wealthy nations but used in much of the developing world), and water pipes, and from certain mining, manufacturing, and smelting operations. As chapter 5 noted, lead exposure is especially dangerous for children and can lead to serious cognitive and behavioral problems, along with many health problems, including anemia and kidney dysfunction. Lead exposure accounts for some 150,000 deaths every year around the globe, most of these in the developing world.

Air Pollution   Another consequence of worldwide environmental inequality involves air pollution. Air pollution exists around the world, but pollution levels are especially high in the huge cities of China, India, and other middle-income and low-income nations. Traffic in these cities is extremely congested, and vehicles there often lack the pollution controls found in the United States and other wealthy nations. Pollution from fossil fuel and industrial plants is also widespread and again lacks the controls found in wealthy nations, as ineffective as these controls often are. As a result, air pollution in these nations' cities is considered a very serious health hazard. The lack of adequate health care in these cities for people who do incur pollution-caused disease worsens this situation even further and adds to the disproportionate impact that air pollution has on the world's poor. Air pollution from outdoor and indoor (e.g., the use of solid fuels for cooking and heating) sources kills some seven million people every year, more than one-third of them in China, India, and other Asian nations (Wong 2014).

China's air pollution is so serious that Chinese scientists liken it to a "nuclear winter" that disrupts photosynthesis and threatens food supplies (Kaiman 2014). Of 74 cities monitored by the Chinese government for air quality, 71 had dangerous levels of air pollution in 2013 (Wong 2014). In early 2014, the level of certain dangerous air particles in Beijing, the nation's capital with 20 million people, was twenty times higher than the safe level recommended by the World Health Organization. The U.S. embassy's measure of six pollutants in Beijing has reached a score as high as 750, more than twice the 300 score considered "hazardous" (Killalea 2014). The situation in Beijing has prompted the Shanghai Academy of Social Sciences to declare the city virtually "uninhabitable for human beings" (Kaiman 2014).

Toxic Waste   Many poor nations also face a disproportionate number of environmental hazards stemming from factories and other industrial operations. These factories routinely dump toxic chemicals and other substances into the ground and waterways of poor nations' villages and small towns. A notable example involves the Lanxi River in China's Hunan Province (Keyi 2014). Factories along the river have dumped agricultural and industrial waste into it for many years. Several villages along the river, and between 200 and 400 villages overall in China, have been dubbed "cancer villages" because dumping has greatly elevated their rates of cancer. About half of China's rivers and lakes are unsafe for drinking, swimming, or other contact; almost 300 million Chinese drink contaminated water. As a result of their polluted water, rural Chinese have higher rates than urban Chinese of intestinal and stomach cancer.

Writer Sheng Keyi recalls her childhood in a village along the Lanxi River, when people would routinely bathe in it and drink from it. Now, she says, the river "has become a lifeless toxic expanse that most people try to avoid. Its water is no longer suitable for fishing, irrigation or swimming. One villager who took a dip in it emerged with itchy red pimples all over his body" (Keyi 2014:SR4). The villagers dug wells for new sources of water but found the groundwater unsafe to drink because of abnormally high levels of ammonia, iron, manganese, and zinc.

The toxic waste problem extends far beyond China's borders. One study tested soil and water samples at 373 toxic waste sites in India, Indonesia, and Pakistan (Chatham-Stephens et al. 2013). The study concluded that almost 9 million people living near these sites were being exposed to chromium, lead, pesticides, and other toxic substances. Two-thirds of the people exposed to lead at these sites were children and women of child-bearing age.

Electronic Waste   A growing environmental problem in the developing world is *electronic waste*. Our televisions, computers, smartphones, tablets, and other electronic devices contain many toxic substances, including lead and mercury, and need to be disposed of very carefully. If merely placed into landfills or other similar areas, they eventually leach their dangerous substances into the ground and groundwater. Humans then become exposed to these substances and can become very sick, with many deaths resulting. Unfortunately, much of the electronic waste recycled or discarded in wealthy nations ends up in the developing world. One study estimated that almost one-fourth of electronic waste in wealthy nations finds its way to China, India, and five West African nations (Benin, Ghana, Ivory Coast, Liberia, and Nigeria) (Bradley 2014). Once this waste reaches these nations, the equipment is dismantled in rather crude, unsafe ways to capture its valuable metals, and the remainder is then dumped and often burned. Any burning releases toxic substances into the air. One study found that mercury levels in drinking water in an area of India where e-waste recycling was occurring were 700 times higher than the level India deems safe.

Natural Disasters   Developing nations are also at greater risk from natural disasters such as drought, earthquakes, hurricanes, landslides, and floods. As climate change has brought on drought and other environmental problems, developing nations have also become more vulnerable to the impact of climate change (The World Bank 2014b). In addition to their poor health care systems, a major reason for these nations' heightened risk is their weak infrastructures. When disasters occur, they simply lack the means and resources to deal with the disasters: their poverty increases the destruction caused by disasters and makes it difficult to help people and otherwise recover from a disaster. Natural disasters are thus a much more serious public health problem in developing nations than in wealthy nations.

A poignant example involves the low-income nation of Haiti, which suffered a severe earthquake in January 2010 that killed more than 200,000 people, injured hundreds of thousands more, left 1 million homeless, and helped set off a cholera epidemic the following October. This destruction was far worse than that caused by similar earthquakes in wealthy nations, as Haiti's decrepit housing and inadequate public services contributed greatly to its level of destruction (Basheka 2011). International relief aid came into Haiti at first, but several years later Haiti had still not recovered from the earthquake's devastating impact (UNOCHA 2014).

Substandard Health Care

The woeful status of health care in the developing world also helps account for its high rate of disease and death from disease. Simply put, developing nations often are able to provide only substandard health care, as they lack the personnel, equipment, and facilities to deal effectively with disease and other health problems that occur.

An example involves the Ebola virus that began this chapter's discussion. This virus is transmitted via fluid (mucus, saliva, sweat) contact, not through the air. As deadly as Ebola is once someone contracts it, its method of transmission makes it possible to contain it if proper equipment and facilities are available and appropriate procedures, including strict quarantine followed. U.S. health officials are confident that they could contain the virus if there were an outbreak in this nation because the United States has the proper equipment and facilities and because hospital personnel could be counted on to follow appropriate procedures (Leonard 2014).

The situation in Africa is very different. As a news report explained after the Ebola virus broke out there in early 2014, "The ability of countries at the bottom of global development rankings, with some of the world's weakest health systems, to contain such a virulent disease is a major concern" (Nossiter 2014:A1). For example, some Ebola patients were quarantined inside their homes instead of hospitals, and law enforcement personnel let family members and neighbors visit Ebola patients and have actual contact with them even though no visits should have been permitted. An official with Doctors Without Borders, the international medical aid organization, said, "It's not astonishing that it is spreading. You've got to attend to the smallest details" (Nossiter 2014:A1). Complicating the situation was that many townspeople refused to believe that their neighbors even had the virus.

India's health care system also illustrates how the world's poor have worse health in part because they have substandard medical care. India is the world's second largest nation, with a population of about 1.3 billion. Although India is classified as a middle-income nation, tens of millions of its citizens live in extreme poverty, and many of the remainder are still very poor. India's huge cities have hospitals and other health care facilities, but most of these facilities lack the personnel and equipment to deal with the high numbers of patients. Rural areas in India simply lack facilities, equipment, and personnel altogether or have health care that is woefully inadequate. An investigative reporter summarized the situation as follows: "India's massive population, it would seem, is the largest obstacle to running an efficient state health care plan for the poor. At every stop in the investigation, themes of overcrowding, overworked medical staffs and failing equipment dominated conversations. At smaller rural primary health centers throughout India, the doctor-to-patient ratio can be as high as 75,000 to one, according to the doctors who work there" (Hayden 2014b).

Worse yet, many health care facilities in India refuse to treat patients. One reason for their refusal is that the patient has a communicable disease like HIV or tuberculosis that health care workers fear contracting. Another reason is that the patients belong to the "wrong" caste or religion as far as health care workers are concerned. Fearing discrimination or refusal, many patients refuse to go to a hospital in the first place (Hayden 2014b).

Substandard health care throughout India is common. For example, the investigative reporter just mentioned visited the pediatric ward at one rural hospital (Hayden 2014a). There he saw dozens of newborns' mothers crammed into unclean hallways smelling of urine and lined with walls marked by bloodstains. Many mothers held their babies atop sheets made out of candy and Oreo cookie wrappers. Because of the conditions in India, many newborns arrive with serious health problems. In this hospital, there were about 15 newborns in intensive care for every doctor, a shocking ratio reflecting the number of sick newborns and India's lack of rural physicians. Not surprisingly, India has a high infant mortality rate, reaching 30 infant deaths (before age 1) per 1,000 live births in Delhi, the highest rate for any of India's cities. Every year about 300,000 newborns die in India the day they are born; this number accounts for almost one-third of such deaths worldwide (Save the Children 2013).

HIV and AIDS

The epidemic of HIV and AIDS in the developing world reflects and illustrates many of the problems this chapter has outlined regarding the dire state of health and health care in low- and middle-income nations. HIV and AIDS have certainly constituted significant health problems in the United States and other wealthy nations since the 1980s, but the HIV rate and AIDS death toll in the developing world make the terrible situation wealthy nations have experienced seem relatively mild by comparison.

HIV/AIDs has killed more than 25 million people worldwide since it emerged in the early 1980s. Approximately 35 million people around the world, including more than 3 million children, have HIV today; this number includes some 2 million people who become infected every year (World Health Organization 2014d). Africans account for almost three-fourths of all HIV patients. Some 1.5 million people, including 190,000 children, die from AIDS annually, with four-fifths of these deaths occurring in Africa. As these numbers indicate, HIV/AIDS have stricken Africa far worse than any other region. Thanks to massive prevention and treatment efforts by international health organizations, new HIV infections and AIDS deaths have declined over the past several years, but the HIV/AIDS problem in Africa and some other locations remains horrific. Around the world, 52% of HIV patients are women, but in Sub-Saharan Africa, this figure is almost 60%.

Several factors contribute to the HIV/AIDS problem in the developing world (UNAIDS 2013; World Health Organization 2014c):

- One of the major ways HIV is transmitted is via unsafe sex, but condom use in the developing world remains uncommon.
- As noted earlier, health care workers in India, at least, often refuse to treat HIV and AIDS patients for fear of becoming infected themselves.
- The widespread presence of prostitution in many developing nations helps HIV to spread more easily.
- Many of the nations with high HIV/AIDS rates experience political unrest or ethnic conflict that makes it difficult for health organizations to implement their efforts.

* The great gender inequality for women in the developing world renders them more at risk than men for HIV, in part because men control sexual relationships and commit rape and other gender-based violence against them.
* Most developing countries have laws that allow for the prosecution or overlook the persecution of gays, drug users, prostitutes, and other people at high risk of contracting or transmitting HIV; these laws make it difficult for those individuals to take certain measures to help prevent HIV infection or to seek medical care if they do contract HIV.
* Many developing nations ban certain actions, such as the provision of clean needles and syringes, that help to prevent the spread of HIV.
* Because many people in the developing world are illiterate or almost so, they are often ignorant of the dangers of HIV/AIDS and the ways in which HIV is transmitted. As evidence, only one-third of young people surveyed in developing nations know how HIV is transmitted, a figure that declines to only one-fifth among young women in some African nations.
* Because of lax procedures, HIV is transmitted in health care settings in developing nations via careless blood donation, storage and transfusion; injections with used needles or syringes; and other ways.
* Although antiretroviral therapy (ART) is a proven preventive against HIV and is commonly used in wealthy nations, ART is much less available and therefore much less used in developing nations.

* Even when ART is available in these nations, many HIV patients do not take their medicines correctly, putting themselves and others at risk.

Documenting Global Health Disparities

All the problems discussed so far in developing nations help account for many types of shocking health disparities around the world. We can illustrate these disparities by examining some basic indicators of health and disease for the standard income groupings of nations discussed earlier: low income, lower-middle income, upper-middle income, and high income.

Life Expectancy

Perhaps the most telling indicator is life expectancy at birth. This measure takes account of deaths at various ages beginning with infancy and of deaths for various reasons. Figure 6.2 shows average life expectancy for the four groups of nations. Women in high-income nations can expect to live 21 years longer on average than women in low-income nations. The

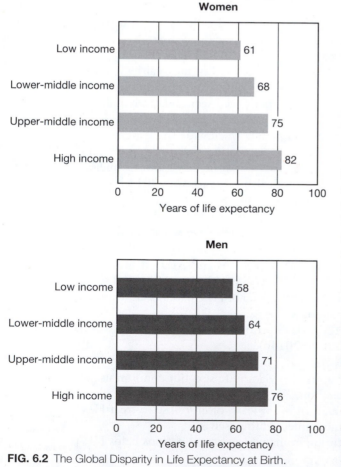

FIG. 6.2 The Global Disparity in Life Expectancy at Birth.

Source: The World Bank. 2014. *World Development Report 2014.* Washington, DC: The World Bank.

corresponding difference for men is 18 years. Combining these two numbers, overall life expectancy in poor nations is almost 20 years shorter than in wealthy nations. The situation is even worse in many African nations, where life expectancy is in the 50s for both sexes. In a few African nations, such as Sierra Leone and Zambia, it is under 50.

HIV/AIDs

As we have seen, the developing world has higher rates of HIV/AIDs for many reasons. Figure 6.3 shows the HIV/AIDS rate per 100,000 population for the four income groups of nations. The rate in low-income nations is many times higher than the rate in high-income nations.

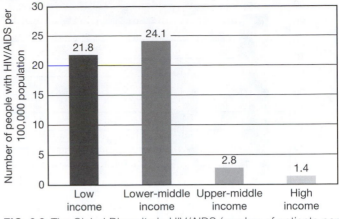

FIG. 6.3 The Global Disparity in HIV/AIDS (number of patients per 100,000 population).

Source: World Health Organization. 2014. *World Health Statistics 2014.* Geneva: World Health Organization.

Tuberculosis

Tuberculosis (TB) is a serious, sometimes fatal, respiratory disease caused by a bacterium and is highly contagious because it spreads through the air when someone coughs, sneezes, or speaks. However, most people who breathe in TB bacteria do not become sick because their immune systems are able to stave off the bacteria. People who are unhealthy to begin with are less able to do this because of their weakened immune systems and thus are more at risk for TB. A century or more ago, TB was the leading cause of death in the United States, but it is now rare in this and other wealthy nations thanks to improvements in social conditions and to advances in scientific medicine. However, it remains a serious threat in the developing world because of the general unhealthiness found there, because of overcrowding and other conditions that help to spread TB bacteria, and because of the substandard medical care characteristic of developing nations.

Figure 6.4 depicts the global disparity in TB rates per 100,000. The rate for low-income nations is eleven times higher than the rate for high-income nations.

Child Mortality

Another telling indicator is child mortality, which is the annual number of deaths before age 5 for every 1,000 live births. Because of malnutrition, malaria, and other diseases, many mothers in low-income nations give birth to sickly babies, as we mentioned earlier in regard to India. Whether or not

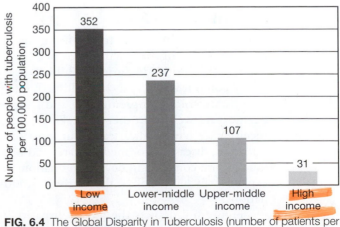
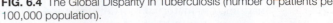

FIG. 6.4 The Global Disparity in Tuberculosis (number of patients per 100,000 population).

Source: World Health Organization. 2014. *World Health Statistics 2014.* Geneva: World Health Organization.

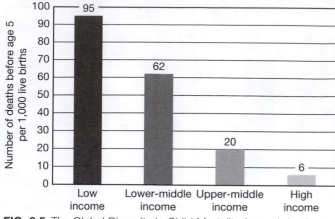

FIG. 6.5 The Global Disparity in Child Mortality (annual deaths per 1,000 live births).

Source: The World Bank. 2014. *World Development Report 2014.* Washington, DC: The World Bank.

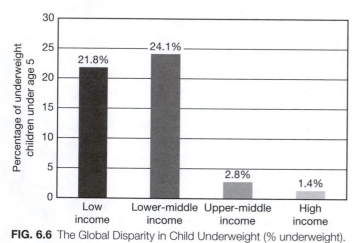

FIG. 6.6 The Global Disparity in Child Underweight (% underweight).

Source: World Health Organization. 2014. *World Health Statistics 2014.* Geneva: World Health Organization.

newborns have health problems when they are born, they often suffer malnutrition, diarrhea, parasitic disease, and other serious health problems in their early years. Once sick, the health care they receive is often substandard, as we have seen. For all these reasons, child mortality in low- and middle-income nations is shockingly high. The relevant rates appear in Figure 6.5. In low-income nations, 95 children for every 1,000 live births (equivalent to almost 10% of all live births) die before age 5. The corresponding rate for wealthy nations is only 6 deaths per 1,000 births. Doing a little math, the child mortality rate in low-income nations is sixteen times greater than the rate in high-income nations.

Child Underweight

As discussed earlier, many children die because of malnutrition and diarrhea and other diseases causing malnutrition. Therefore, the percentage of underweight children (under age 5) is a critical indicator of health risk. Figure 6.6 shows that this percentage is much higher in the developing world than in the high-income nations.

Maternal Mortality

Maternal mortality refers to death during childbirth, and is commonly measured as the number of maternal deaths per 100,000 live births. More than 500,000 women die worldwide during childbirth every year. Their deaths stem from pregnancy complications and/or childbirth complications. Sometimes these complications are totally unpredictable and happen to women even though they have been eating well and otherwise taking care of themselves, and even though they receive excellent medical care. But most of these complications result from malnutrition, disease, poor medical care, and other problems, which, as you know, are much more common in developing nations than in wealthy nations. This situation explains why almost all of the yearly 500,000 maternal deaths occur in developing nations.

Figure 6.7 depicts the global disparity in maternal mortality. In low-income nations, the maternal mortality rate is 410 per 100,000 births, equivalent to 4 deaths for every 1,000 births. In contrast, the rate in high-income nations is only 16 per 100,000. The rate in low-income nations is thus almost 26 times larger than the wealthy nations' rate. The two groups of middle-income nations also have much higher maternal mortality rates than the wealthy nations.

Natural Disaster Deaths

As discussed earlier, low-income nations are at much greater risk for disease and death from natural disasters. International organizations estimate the number of deaths from natural disasters each year in each country, and then determine the average annual number of deaths per one million population. This rate permits comparisons across the nations of the mortality risk from natural disasters. Figure 6.8 provides this comparison. The annual natural disaster death rate in low-income nations is 22 times greater than the rate in high-income nations. The U.S. rate is only 1.4, equivalent to about 400 deaths per year from natural disasters. If the U.S. rate were as high as the low-income nation rate, its number of annual deaths would be about 15,000. As high as the 50.5 death rate is for low-income nations, a few individual nations have much higher rates than that figure for their entire group. For example, Myanmar's rate exceeds 270, while Sri Lanka's rate exceeds 170.

Births Attended by Skilled Health Personnel

We have emphasized that health care in much and almost certainly most of the developing world is substandard. Many indicators of the quality of health care exist, but a very telling indicator, and one that helps account for the maternal mortality disparity we saw, is whether skilled health personnel attend a birth. Many mothers in the developing world give birth

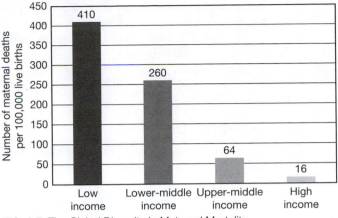

FIG. 6.7 The Global Disparity in Maternal Mortality.

Source: The World Bank. 2014. *World Development Report 2014*. Washington, DC: The World Bank.

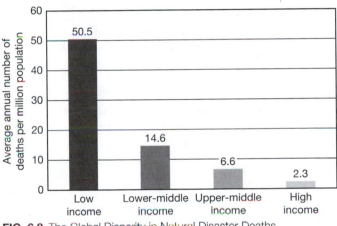

FIG. 6.8 The Global Disparity in Natural Disaster Deaths.

Source: The World Bank. 2014. *World Development Report 2014*. Washington, DC: The World Bank.

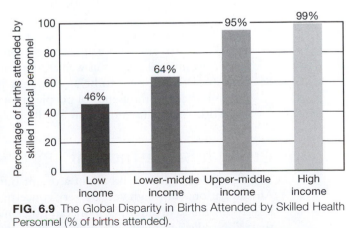

FIG. 6.9 The Global Disparity in Births Attended by Skilled Health Personnel (% of births attended).

Source: World Health Organization. 2014. *World Health Statistics 2014*. Geneva: World Health Organization.

without the assistance of such personnel, and these mothers and their babies are much more likely to develop complications and die as a result.

Figure 6.9 shows the percentage of births attended by skilled health personnel. Although virtually every birth in high-income nations enjoys the assistance of medical professionals, many fewer births in the developing world receive these professionals' help.

Conclusion

Global health disparities tragically illustrate the impact of poverty and other social conditions on health and disease, a central theme of medical sociology. Through no fault of their own, billions of people in low-income and medium-income nations face conditions that cause them to be sick and many of them to die. International efforts during the past few decades have greatly decreased the death and suffering in the developing world, but this chapter has shown that devastating health disparities still remain.

Summary

1. The world's nations are very unequal in wealth, resources, and influence. Billions of people live in very poor conditions unimaginable to people in wealthy nations.
2. A common typology of global inequality divides nations into four groups: high income, upper middle income, lower middle income, and low income. The low-income nations are primarily found in Africa and parts of Asia.
3. Modernization theory implicitly faults low-income nations for being so poor, while dependency theory attributes their poverty to exploitation by wealthy nations and by multinational corporations.
4. Global health disparities exist primarily because of world poverty and the deplorable conditions in which the billions of the world's poor live.
5. Children and women in low-income nations are especially vulnerable to a range of diseases and other health problems. Disease and malnutrition in children lead to many deaths and can have permanent consequences even if they survive. Women in low-income nations live in very patriarchal societies that make them vulnerable to HIV, domestic violence, and other serious health problems.
6. Environmental pollution and hazards also cause much disease and death. Toxic dumping into rivers and other waterways in low-income nations is a major cause for concern.
7. Another problem in low-income nations is substandard health care. Health care is lacking altogether in many rural regions, and is often substandard where it does exist in rural regions as well as in urban areas.
8. HIV/AIDS continues to be an epidemic in low-income nations, where AIDS kills hundreds of thousands of people annually. About 35 million people around the world, including more than 3 million children have HIV.

Giving It Some Thought

You're talking with a friend about a recent outbreak of cholera and diarrhea in an African nation. Although you are very concerned about this epidemic, your friend is less troubled and finally says, "Why can't they just take better care of themselves over there?" Needless to say, you're a bit shocked by this callous remark. What do you do or say next?

Key Terms

dependency theory, 95

global inequality, 93

global stratification, 93

modernization theory, 95

7 Medical School and the Training of Physicians

Health and Illness in the News

Amid a nationwide increase in deaths from opiate overdoses, Harvard Medical School students urged their school in spring 2016 to increase the amount of material on opioid addiction in its curriculum. Meanwhile, a White House official criticized medical schools for having "little or no education within medical school curriculums around addiction and safe prescribing." Disagreeing with this assessment, an official with the Association of American Medical Colleges responded, "Virtually all medical schools are covering both substance abuse and pain management in both preclinical coursework as well as in the clinic." (Bailey 2016)

This news story reminds us of the importance of providing medical students the knowledge and skills they need to become effective physicians. When we think of medical education in medical schools, we probably have at least three types of learning in mind: (1) learning about anatomy, physiology, and other scientific fields to give medical students a scientific knowledge base for their future practice of medicine; (2) learning how to diagnose and treat a very wide range of health problems; and (3) learning how to conduct a number of medical procedures ranging from drawing blood to doing surgery.

These are all essential features of a good medical education. But medical sociologists would add a fourth, less "official" type of learning that medical students experience, and that is *socialization* into the medical profession. This chapter discusses this important aspect of medical education after first reviewing the history of medical education and its status today. This discussion will show that medical students learn much more than scientific medicine during their years in school.

Development of Medical Schools and Medical Education

The medical school is a relatively recent establishment in the course of human history. As chapter 2 emphasized, medical knowledge before the rise of scientific medicine during the eighteenth and nineteenth centuries was woefully inadequate, and the healing powers of physicians were very limited. With hindsight, because there was hardly any medical knowledge to learn, medical schools perhaps were not even that helpful. Some medical schools did develop by the end of the Middle Ages, but these schools' students were able to learn little of practical value since so little was known then about the actual causes of disease and how best to treat it.

With this backdrop in mind, the first medical school during the Middle Ages was established in the southern Italy city of Salerno during the ninth century. The Salerno school soon attracted medical students from much of Europe. These students read writings of the ancient scholars such as Galen and Hippocrates and dissected pigs, monkeys, and other animals. During the next two centuries, Salerno graduates established other medical schools in England, France, Spain, and Portugal. Italy gained several important new medical schools during the fifteenth century. Additional medical schools were founded across Europe over the next few centuries. This period also saw the beginning of professional medical societies. Partly because of these societies' influence, England and some other nations began to require aspiring physicians to have a degree from a medical school or university and to pass a licensing exam prepared by the appropriate medical society. As scientific medicine began to develop during the eighteenth century, the curriculum and training at European medical schools became more complex and rigorous, a trend that intensified during the nineteenth century thanks to the rapid advances in scientific medicine discussed in chapter 2.

Medical Education in Early America

Aspiring physicians in early colonial America initially trained as apprentices to practicing physicians, but their training was often inadequate. Some practicing physicians provided excellent instruction for their students, but others provided little or no instruction. This fact led some aspiring physicians to sail to England or other European nations to train at medical schools there.

The first medical school in the colonies was established in 1765 at the College of Philadelphia. This school's founder, John Morgan, and its initial faculty had received their medical degrees at the University of Edinburgh in Scotland and then received clinical training in London hospitals. Their experiences in Edinburgh and London led them to favor their new medical school's association with a university and also to favor clinical training for their students. Their school accordingly soon joined with the University of Pennsylvania and provided its students clinical training at a nearby hospital founded by Benjamin Franklin. By 1813, four additional U.S. universities had medical schools: Columbia, Dartmouth, Harvard, and Yale; a few other universities established medical schools during the next several decades.

The curricula of these early university-affiliated medical school curricula consisted of two years of courses taught by part-time faculty, followed by working with physician preceptors for awhile. These schools' training lagged behind their European counterparts in not requiring coursework in the latest scientific developments and in not requiring four years of coursework (Bonner 1995). In another difference, whereas medical students in France and Germany had access to human cadavers for dissection in anatomy classes, American (and also British) students had much less access due to their societies' moral and religious qualms about human dissection. Because of similar qualms, American and British students were also much less likely than their French and German counterparts to receive any gynecological or obstetrical training or even to see a woman in labor (Bonner 1995).

Nineteenth-Century Developments

The university-affiliated medical schools were relatively expensive to attend, and they officially or unofficially were not open to African Americans and women. These problems motivated the rise of independent, for-profit medical schools (called **proprietary schools**) in many cities around the country during the first half of the 1800s. These schools greatly outnumbered university-affiliated medical schools by the middle of the century. The proprietary schools were less expensive to attend than the university-affiliated schools, and several of them primarily admitted and educated African Americans or women, respectively.

Despite these important virtues, proprietary schools typically offered an inferior education compared to that found in the university-affiliated schools. One problem was their for-profit status. The typical propriety school was owned by about eight or ten faculty members, whose major reason for opening the schools was to make profit. Because proprietary schools' profits depended on students in their schools paying tuition and fees, the schools needed to maximize the number of admitted students and to ensure these students could stay without fearing suspension or dismissal for academic difficulties.

Accordingly, the propriety schools had weak, if any, admission standards, and many of their students had only an elementary school education. Their students attended lectures by part-time faculty for a year or two and usually never saw a patient. As one medical historian has summarized this situation, "Entrance requirements were nonexistent, and the courses taught were superficial and brief. The typical path to a medical degree consisted of two 16-week sets of lectures, the second term identical to the first term. Instruction was almost wholly didactic, including lectures, textbook readings, and enforced memorization of the innumerable facts. Laboratory and clinical work were not to be found" (Ludmerer 2010:193).

Despite the growth of university-affiliated and proprietary medical schools in the early 1800s, apprenticeship continued to be a common form of training for aspiring physicians. After a suitable apprenticeship period, these individuals would simply declare that they were physicians and begin practicing medicine, as the licensing of physicians was still unknown. Many individuals did the same without even having an apprenticeship. Meanwhile, and as just noted, many students were graduating from proprietary schools with an inferior education.

In response to these problems, state medical societies began to call for the licensing of new physicians through examinations, and Connecticut in 1821 became the first state to require licensure. Other states slowly followed suit. When the American Medical Association (AMA) was founded in 1847, one of its chief aims was to lobby for examination-based licensure, along with improving medical education more generally.

A rather embarrassing fact of medical education during the 1800s concerns the behavior of medical students. Both in Europe and the United States, medical students were widely known for their rowdy behavior. Most medical students were young men, and they behaved as young men of the time often behaved. They drank a lot and were widely regarded as "being immature, unruly, quarrelsome, and ungovernable" (Bonner 1995:215). According to one report from that era, "Steeplechasing in the dissecting room, cheating on the Latin examination, flirting with the barmaid, gin-and-water until three o'clock in the morning [are] the stereotypical activities of the British student of medicine" (Bonner 1995:215).

Medical faculty at the University of London during the 1850s routinely had to deal with students who fought in laboratories, vandalized lecture hall walls, engaged in drunken behavior, and used profanities. American medical students had a similar reputation. An 1856 Philadelphia newspaper account called some medical students there "the roughest we ever saw . . . hair as long as that of a savage . . . sword canes, dirk knives, revolvers, attire very unfashionably made, hard swearing, hard drinking, coarse language, tobacco quids, and pools of tobacco spittle . . . medical students are a contemned [contemptible], despised, disrespected class" (Bonner 1995:216). The rigors of medical education, including eight or more hours a day (including Saturdays) of lectures and other instruction and several more daily hours of studying, may have contributed to the rowdy behavior for which medical students were known (Bonner 1995).

During the nineteenth century, medical school education continued to be limited for women and African Americans to the proprietary schools open to them. Elizabeth Blackwell, the first American women to graduate from a medical school, attended Geneva Medical College in the upstate New York town of Geneva and received her M.D. degree in 1849 after graduating first in her class. Blackwell had applied to and been rejected by sixteen medical schools because of her sex before being admitted to the Geneva school. A statue in her honor now stands on the campus of Hobart and William Smith Colleges, the site of the now defunct Geneva Medical College. A plaque in front of the monument says in part, "Her Life was devoted to women's and children's health care, reproductive education, and opening the medical profession to women."

Medical education also continued to be limited for African Americans to a few proprietary schools. This situation improved with the establishment in 1869 of Howard University in Washington, DC. One of the nation's historically black colleges, Howard initially included a college of medicine, along with a college of liberal arts. It educated the bulk of African American physicians for the next century and remains an important site of medical education for the African American community today.

Developments during the 1870s and Beyond   Several key developments in medical education occurred during the 1870s. Influenced by the increasing rigor of medical education in European medical schools, the medical schools at Harvard University, the University of Michigan, and the University of Pennsylvania added a third year to their required course of study for a medical degree, included new scientific fields into the curriculum, mandated laboratory instruction for the first time, and hired full-time faculty (Ludmerer 2010). Another key development was the construction by the University of Pennsylvania medical school of a *teaching hospital*. This was the first such hospital in the United States and is the model today for medical schools around the country.

As the 1880s began, only a few American medical schools were associated with universities and thus lagged behind many of their European counterparts. One reason for this fact was that few research universities as we now know them existed then in the United States, whereas many renowned universities had long existed in Europe. Research universities in the United States grew in number after the 1880s, thanks in part to decisions by the very wealthy industrial families of the time to begin their own universities or to donate large sums of money toward the establishment of other universities. A notable example of the former is Stanford University, which was begun in 1891 by railroad tycoon Leland Stanford and his wife Jane as a memorial to their 15-year-old son, who had died of typhoid fever. Their new university acquired an existing medical college in 1908. By the end of the nineteenth century, advances in scientific medicine such as germ theory (see chapter 2) led to the rise of new fields such as bacteriology, biochemistry, and pathology. Some European medical schools incorporated these advances into their curricula, but American schools were slower to do so.

A leading U.S. school for this incorporation was the Johns Hopkins University School of Medicine, founded in 1893. This new school had stricter admission stan-dards, including an undergraduate degree and a firm grounding in biology, chemistry, and physics, than many other schools, and a curriculum that incorporated the latest discoveries in scientific medicine and required four years of instruction. It featured small classes and instruction with patients, in contrast to the large lectures found in many other medical schools. Johns Hopkins was also the first university-affiliated medical school to admit women, as three women were in the school's entering class in its first year of operation. This important development occurred because four wealthy grown daughters of the university's trustees said they would donate a signifi-cant sum of money, about $13 million in today's dollars, to help open the medical school on the condition that it admitted women. They also insisted on the entrance requirements just mentioned.

By the early 1900s, other university-affiliated medical schools had strengthened their admission criteria and the rigor of their curriculum, and proprietary schools began to close down as they became unable to meet the growing expectations for medical education in view of the many advances in scientific medicine that had occurred during the past half century (Ludmerer 2010). These trends accelerated with the publication of the famous Flexner Report, to which we now turn.

The Flexner Report

In the early 1900s, the AMA asked the Carnegie Foundation to examine the status of medical education in the United States and Canada. The Carnegie Foundation hired Abraham Flexner, an education reformer, in 1908 to lead this study, which was published in 1910 (Flexner 1910). Widely called the Flexner Report, this study was highly critical of the quality of medical education at the time and advocated several reforms that were adopted widely. The Flexner Report is now considered perhaps the most important development in the history of American medical education.

Flexner had studied medical education in France, Great Britain, and Germany, and he learned more about their medical education as he readied his report. He was especially influenced by Germany's model, which was established during the 1880s and stressed rigorous laboratory training in the biological sciences as preparation for later clinical training in hospitals and an undergraduate degree for admission. This was a model already in place at the Johns Hopkins medical school, which had also been influenced by Germany's model.

Flexner explicitly chose John Hopkins' model as the "gold standard" against which to compare the quality of education in other North American medical schools (Duffy 2011). He visited all 155 medical schools in the United States and Canada and evaluated them using criteria such as their admission standards, the status of their laboratories and other physical facilities, and the quality of their instruction. He then divided all the schools into three categories: (1) schools whose quality rivaled that of Johns Hopkins; (2) schools with inadequate curriculum that could be improved with sufficient strategic financing; and (3) schools that were so substandard that they should be shut down. Most schools fell into the latter two categories, and the Flexner Report recommended that the 155 North American medical schools be reduced to only 31 through closure or absorption by other medical schools.

Coupled with stricter state licensing laws after its publication, the Flexner Report soon led to the closing of about one-half of the 155 medical schools, almost all of them the proprietary schools. As a retrospective on the centennial of the report commented, "The Flexner Report of 1910 transformed the nature and process of medical education in America with a resulting elimination of proprietary schools and the establishment of the biomedical model as the gold standard of medical training" (Duffy 2011:269).

The Flexner Report led to many reforms in the remaining medical schools, including stronger admission standards involving an undergraduate degree, laboratory-based education during the first two years of medical school, and clinical training thereafter. The report also called for medical school professors to have their full salaries paid by their schools. Before this time, many professors had relied on patient care as a major source of their annual income. The Flexner Report said this arrangement diverted the professors' time, energy, and attention from their instruction, and it urged that suitable salaries be provided instead by their schools. Because this recommendation would reduce the time medical professors spent with patients, some respected critics said the recommendation would cause medical professors to lose sight of patients as human beings. The Carnegie and Rockefeller Foundations donated large sums of money to help implement the Flexner's Report recommendations, including the one for full salaries paid by medical schools, and this salary model became adopted throughout the country, along with the other recommendations (Duffy 2011).

Medical Schools Today

There are now 145 accredited medical schools in the United States offering the M.D. degree and another 17 accredited schools in Canada (2015 figures). During 2015–2016, the U.S. schools enrolled almost 87,000 students. That same year, 52,536 college students sent almost 782,000 applications to these medical schools, for an average of almost 15 applications per applicant. From this group of applicants, 21,643 were accepted into at least one medical school, and 20,627 individuals eventually matriculated at a medical school (Association of American Medical Colleges 2016).

Although these figures mean that 41.1% of all applicants were accepted into at least one medical school, the acceptance rate at most individual medical schools was far lower than that, with many schools accepting fewer than 10% of their applicants. The typical medical school receives 4,500 applications, even though their entering classes will number at most a few hundred students and sometimes fewer than 200 depending on the school (Chen 2013). As these numbers indicate, it is difficult to gain admission to any one medical school. For example, the acceptance rate at Minnesota's Mayo Medical School was only 1.8% for fall 2015 admission, and several more schools had acceptance rates of under 4%, including the schools at Brown, Florida State, George Washington, and Stanford Universities (Smith-Barrow 2016).

Medical schools have a fairly common curriculum required by accreditation standards heavily influenced by the 1910 Flexner Report. After entering medical school, the typical student takes two years of courses (mostly large lectures) in basic sciences, including anatomy, biochemistry, microbiology, and physiology, and then takes a national examination in order to qualify to continue in school. The student then has two years of clinical instruction at a teaching hospital in a number of specialties, including anesthesiology, dermatology, internal medicine, obstetrics and gynecology, pediatrics, and surgery.

During these two years, students fulfill a *rotation*, or **clerkship**, in about 8–10 of these specialties. As you might have seen on TV shows set in hospitals, students go in small groups on *rounds* with their clinical instructors into patients' rooms. The instructors continuously quiz the students about the patients' symptoms and diagnosis and about their views on what tests and other medical procedures ought to be performed and about other aspects of how the patients should be treated. At the end of these two clinical years, students again take a national examination. Assuming they pass, they obtain their M.D. degree and then do a residency at a teaching hospital. Most residencies last three years (the first year is often called an *internship*), but students wishing to practice certain medical specialties often have residencies that last as long as seven years.

Sociodemographic Profile of U.S. Medical Students

Medical school officials recognize that a diverse study body improves the medical school experience and ultimately the quality of patient care. African American and Latino physicians, for example, are more likely to practice in areas populated by African Americans and Latinos, respectively, and thus are an important source of health care for the people in these areas. Women physicians are sometimes thought to offer better patient care than male physicians in some respects, especially for female patients (see chapter 8). Before the 1970s, very few women or people of color attended medical school, as most medical schools had official or unofficial policies that simply restricted medical school admission to white males. These policies have since vanished, and today's medical students are much more diverse than a few decades ago, if not as diverse as the U.S. population itself. In view of the importance of diversity in medical school enrollments, let's take a brief look at medical students' sociodemographic backgrounds today (Association of American Medical Colleges 2016).

Gender   Of the 86,746 students enrolled in U.S. medical schools in 2015–2016, 46.8% were women, and 53.2% were men. Although the women's percentage of is slightly lower than its height of 48.5% in 2005, it remains much higher than the 26.5% representation of women in medical school in 1980 and their 9.6% representation in 1970 (see Figure 7.1). Although women's proportion of medical students is somewhat lower than their proportion of the U.S. population, the gender composition of medical students does reflect the gender composition of medical school applicants, as women comprised 45.8% of applicants for fall 2015 admission.

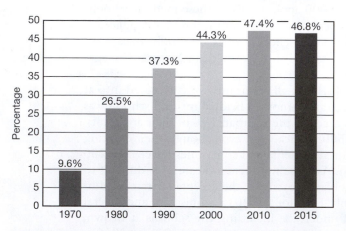

FIG. 7.1 Women's Percentage of All Medical Students, Academic Years 1970–2015.

Sources: Based on Jolliff, Lauren, Jennifer Leadley, Elizabeth Coakley, and Rae Anne Sloane. 2013. *Women in U.S. Academic Medicine and Science: Statistics and Benchmarking Report 2011–2012*. Washington, DC: Association of American Medical Colleges; https://www.aamc.org/data/facts/enrollment-graduate/158808/total-enrollment-by-medical-school-by-sex.html.

Sexual Harassment   One problem that women medical students and residents face, as women do in other school and occupational settings, is sexual harassment, which appears to be more common during students' last two years of clinical instruction than in their first two years of classroom instruction (Wear, Aultman, and Borges 2007). An early study of this situation involved a survey of 82 internal medicine residents (33 women and 49 men). Almost 75% of the women said they had been sexually harassed (e.g., offensive comments, unwanted attention, verbal and/or physical advances, sexual bribery) during medical school and/or during their residency, compared to only 22% of the men (Komaromy et al. 1993). Somewhat later, 156 students (67 women and 89 men) were surveyed at two medical schools. Seventy percent of the women had experienced sexual harassment and/or gender discrimination, compared to only 25% of the men (Nora et al. 1996). Surveys of students at 14 medical schools that were done shortly after these earlier studies similarly found that 69% of the women had experienced sexual harassment and/or gender discrimination (Nora et al. 1996).

However, some evidence suggests that sexual harassment of medical students has declined somewhat during the past decade. This evidence comes from a questionnaire given to all medical students nationwide when they graduate (Mavis et al. 2014). In 2000, 13% of the graduating students reported that they had experienced "unwanted sexual advances"; by 2011, this figure had declined to 8%. Similarly, in 2000, 26% of the graduating students reported that they had been the target of "sexist remarks or names"; by 2011, this figure had declined to 20%.

Despite these modest declines, sexual harassment remains a significant problem in medical education today and has been termed "a disturbing phenomenon in an environment ostensibly devoted to health and healing" (Wear, Aultman, and Borges 2007:26) Like sexual harassment that occurs in other settings, most sexual harassment of medical students goes unreported. Several reasons explain why many medical students who are harassed decide not to report their harassment: they may fear retaliation, they may think that medical school officials will fail to take action, or they may not want people to know what happened (Wear, Aultman, and Borges 2007).

Race and Ethnicity   The majority of medical students are non-Latino whites, but many also come from other racial/ethnic backgrounds (see Figure 7.2). About one-fifth of medical students are Asians or Pacific Islanders; this percentage is much higher than the 5.3% Asian and Pacific Islander share of the U.S. population. On the other hand, African Americans and Latinos, who comprise about 13% and 16%, respectively, of the U.S. population, are underrepresented in medical schools by more than half. This underrepresentation reflects these groups' relatively low socioeconomic status and lower levels of academic achievement stemming from that status. The 2015 proportion of African American and Latino students is only marginally higher than the 1980 proportion. Meanwhile, the one-fifth figure for Asians and Pacific Islanders represents a steep increase from their 3.0% representation in medical schools in 1980.

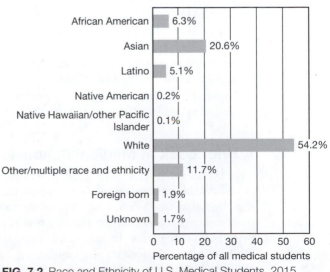

FIG. 7.2 Race and Ethnicity of U.S. Medical Students, 2015.
Source: Based on https://www.aamc.org/download/321540/data/fact-stableb5.pdf.

Socioeconomic Status   Most medical students come from rather wealthy families. To discuss this fact more precisely, it will be helpful first to define what is meant by family income *quintiles*. In measuring the income distribution of U.S. families, it is customary to divide families into five groups, or quintiles, according to their income. The 20% of families with the highest incomes form the top quintile, while the 20% of families with the lowest incomes form the bottom quintile, and so forth. With this description in mind, it is worth noting that more than 75% of accepted medical students come from families in the upper two quintiles (which by definition comprise only 40% of families), while fewer than 10% come from the lowest quintile (which by definition comprises 20% of families) (Grbic, Jones, and Case 2013). In addition, about 28% of applicants have parents with a doctorate or professional degree, and another 40% have parents with a master's or bachelor's degree. Adding these figures together, more than two-thirds of applicants have parents with at least a bachelor's degree (Grbic, Jones, and Case 2013).

Although the entrance of low-income and minority individuals into medical school represents a significant achievement given their disadvantaged backgrounds, they are at greater risk than their more advantaged counterparts for leaving medical school before acquiring their degree. The medical school attrition rate is only about 3%, meaning that about 3% of students who enter medical school eventually leave for financial or other reasons. But this rate is higher for low-income students and those of color (Brewer and Grbic 2010). This disparity concerns medical school officials because it lowers the diversity of the medical school student body.

This brief sociodemographic profile of medical students shows that low-income individuals and people of color (other than Asians and Pacific Islanders) are underrepresented in medical school admissions and enrollments and thus in the medical profession itself. This fact has implications for the availability of physicians and the quality of medical care for these underrepresented communities.

To address this underrepresentation, some medical schools have become more flexible with their admissions criteria. Traditionally, medical schools have relied almost exclusively on applicants' undergraduate grade point averages (GPAs), grades in science classes, and scores on the Medical College Admission Test (MCAT) to decide which small percentage of their applicants they will invite for interviews for further consideration. Because race and socioeconomic status may influence students' rankings on these criteria, some schools have adopted an approach called *holistic review* that takes into account applicants' personal backgrounds and experiences. This approach has led to higher numbers of admitted students who are persons of color and who come from low-income backgrounds. As a director of admissions at a medical school using holistic review explained, "No one is saying that skills and inclination in science is [*sic*] not important. But in this rapidly evolving and diverse society, they are insufficient" (Chen 2013).

A Brief Look at Medical School Faculty

Two broad categories of medical school faculty exist: basic sciences and clinical sciences. As their names imply, *basic sciences* faculty teach the courses students take during their first two years, and *clinical sciences* faculty provide the clinical instruction that students receive during the last two years in school. Thousands of faculty comprise both categories. In 2014, full-time basic sciences faculty numbered 18,822, while clinical sciences faculty numbered 139,646. Faculty in certain other areas, including dentistry and veterinary sciences, numbered 1,363. Adding these figures, the total number of full-time medical school faculty was 159,831 (Association of American Medical Colleges 2015).

Medical schools value a diverse student body, and they also value a diverse faculty. In this regard, a diverse faculty is thought to improve the medical school experience by providing students with diverse role models and possible mentors. Unfortunately, although medical schools have made significant strides in diversifying their faculty, diversity is lacking in some areas, as we shall now see.

Gender   Of the total number of medical school faculty, 61,924 faculty are women, and 97,769 faculty are men. Women thus comprise almost 39% of medical faculty, while men comprise about 61%. Because women are slightly more than half the population and almost half of all medical students, they are underrepresented among medical faculty.

Women medical faculty experience certain problems beyond their underrepresentation. These problems include gender discrimination and sexual harassment. A national survey of a random sample of 3,332 medical faculty found significant differences between female and male faculty in reports of these problems (Carr et al. 2000). To measure gender discrimination, one item in the survey asked, "In your professional career, have you ever been left out of opportunities for professional advancement based on gender?" A majority of women faculty, 60%, responded "yes" or "probably" to this question, compared to only 9% of male faculty. Doing some quick division, women faculty were thus about almost seven more likely than male faculty to report experiencing gender discrimination. Another question asked to measure sexual harassment was: "In your professional career, have you encountered unwanted sexual comments, attention, or advances by a superior or a colleague?" Slightly more than half, 52%, of the women faculty responded "yes" to this question, compared to only 5% of male faculty. Women faculty were thus about ten times more likely than male faculty to report being sexually harassed.

In other dimensions of medical faculty's experiences, recent national survey evidence finds that women faculty are more dissatisfied than male faculty with certain aspects of their lives as faculty members (Pololi et al. 2013). They report fewer opportunities for career advancement than men report, and they are less likely to feel that their schools' policies are "family-friendly." Other research has found that women faculty's salaries are lower than male faculty's salaries and that they face more difficulty in being promoted (Chen 2012b).

Race and Ethnicity   African Americans and Latinos are underrepresented among medical faculty, just as they are among medical students. Figure 7.3 shows that African Americans and Latinos each comprise fewer than 4% of medical faculty. In contrast, Asians, who comprise 14.6% of faculty, are overrepresented in the faculty compared to their proportion of the national population, just as they are among medical students. But because Asians are a disproportionately large proportion of medical students, it is not surprising that they are also a disproportionately large proportion of medical faculty.

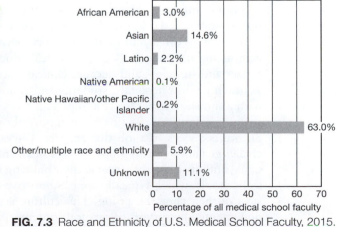

FIG. 7.3 Race and Ethnicity of U.S. Medical School Faculty, 2015.

Source: Based on Association of American Medical Colleges. 2014. *U.S. Medical School Faculty, 2014.* https://www.aamc.org/data/facultyroster/reports/420598/usmsf14.html.

The Lives and Experiences of Medical Students

Ask any medical student what it is like to be a medical student and you will no doubt hear about unbearable pressure and continuous exhaustion. From the day they enter medical school until the day they finish their residency, most medical students lead grueling lives, to say the least. Although many students had high undergraduate GPAs and thus ranked among the "best and the brightest" of undergraduates, they find their coursework incredibly demanding because of the sheer amount of information they are expected to know in minute detail and because of the national examination they must take after their first two years in school. Their two clinical years that then follow are little better, because students constantly have to be on their toes for their clinical instructors' quizzing. This "quizzing" often amounts to very intense grilling, with considerable pressure on students to come up with correct answers.

Stress, Fatigue, and Burnout

All these aspects of medical school education create considerable stress for many medical students. The financial costs of medical school contribute to even further stress, because many medical students have to take out huge loans to pay for the cost of their medical education. Average tuition for the four years of medical school is more than $200,000 and as high as $300,000 at some medical schools. By contrast, medical schools in other nations often cost much less because their governments heavily subsidize tuition. Yearly tuition in Canada averages less than $10,000 in U.S. dollars, and medical students in France and some other European nations pay virtually nothing.

Some U.S. students (and their parents) can afford to pay some or even all of their tuition, but others need to take out loans for the full amount, with almost 90% of students acquiring at least some debt. Because tuition and other costs rise every year, today's medical students are experiencing "skyrocketing medical debt," according to one report (Durisin and Nisen 2013). By the time they graduate, their median student loan debt (including debt from their undergraduate education) is $170,000, a figure the report called "astronomical." This debt prompts many medical students to shun primary care in favor of a specialty, such as orthopedic surgery, that typically earns a very high income (Phillips et al. 2009). More important for our discussion, debt also contributes to the stress they already feel from the medical school "grind" more generally.

For some medical students and residents, another source of stress is family responsibilities. Medical students and residents who are married, cohabiting, and/or have children often find themselves torn between their family roles and their medical training obligations. Because medical education requires long hours of attending classes and studying, and because clinical instruction and residencies require at least as much time in hospitals, students and residents typically have little time to spend with a spouse, partner, or children. This fact can cause strain in the students' various social relationships. As one news report about medical residents put it, "Working 80 hours a week in a job that requires physical stamina and unwavering focus can challenge family relationships in ways small and large" (Kowalczyk 2013a).

Another source of stress is the "bullying culture" (Chen 2012a) in many medical schools, which typically appears most strongly during students' third year, the start of their clinical training. This culture is a long-standing problem that was first documented by surveys of medical students about two decades ago. Many third-year students report in surveys then and now that they experience verbal harassment and other mistreatment, including threats made about their careers, during their third-year clerkships. This mistreatment primarily comes from their clinical instructors, who are residents and older physicians. The students normally keep quiet about their mistreatment: some fear retaliation if they disclose the mistreatment, and others may simply feel that the mistreatment is a normal part of medical school training. Yet, mistreatment adds to their stress and may undermine their self-confidence and success in their clerkships and later residencies (Fried et al. 2012). One medical school administrator commented on this problem, "We're talking about the really hard task of changing a culture, and that has to be done on a national level. There are a lot of really good people and role models out there. But the culture for all these years has been to just take the mistreatment and not say anything. It wasn't right back then, and it shouldn't be tolerated anymore" (Chen 2012a).

The high level of stress found in many medical students has the same effects as high levels of stress in the general population (see chapter 5): it promotes a variety of physical and mental health problems among medical students, including sleeplessness, depression, a loss of self-esteem, and, for women, disruption of menstrual cycles (Kollipaka et al. 2013; Sohail 2013). These problems may then affect medical students' academic performance, and any academic problems that do result may in turn increase their stress levels in what is surely a vicious circle.

Medical Student Burnout   The term medical student burnout refers to the mental, emotional, and physical stress and exhaustion that many medical students experience during their preclinical and clinical years and during their residencies. Students experiencing burnout typically feel emotionally drained, and they also experience a sense of low self-competence and begin to treat their patients very impersonally.

Several studies document the extent and impact of burnout (IsHak et al. 2013). These studies suggest that at least half of medical students experience burnout at some point during their medical training and that burnout sometimes leads to sleeping problems, mental disorders including depression, and suicidal thoughts. Students in their preclinical years are less likely to experience burnout if they perceive that faculty are helping them, and students in their clinical years are less likely to experience burnout if they have fewer overnight shifts. In one study of seven medical schools, 11.2% of students reported having considered suicide; students experiencing burnout were 2–3 times more likely to belong to this troubled group (Dyrbye et al. 2008). After finding a burnout rate of 71% among third-year medical students at Mount Sinai School of Medicine in New York City, one study concluded, "Medical student burnout is quite common, and early efforts should be made to empower medical students to both build the knowledge and skills necessary to become capable physicians, as well as withstand the emotional, mental, and physical challenges inherent to medical school" (Mazurkiewicz et al. 2012:212).

As this comment suggests, burnout stems largely from the nature of medical education, but personal factors may also make burnout more or less likely. A study of almost 300 medical students found that their motivation for applying to medical school predicted their likelihood of burnout: students whose interest in medicine stemmed from personal illness or the illness/death of a family member were more likely to experience burnout than those whose interest in medicine stemmed from other reasons like altruism and intellectual curiosity (Pagnin et al. 2013).

If burnout might reflect medical students' motivation for entering medicine, it can also affect which medical specialties they decide to pursue. In a study of 165 fourth-year medical students, those who had experienced burnout were more likely to choose specialties like dermatology and pediatrics with fewer demands on their time than specialties like internal medicine and surgery with long and unpredictable work schedules (Enoch et al. 2013).

Medical Residents   Medical students' residencies after their four years in medical school offer little relief to the problems just discussed. If anything, the demands on students' time and energy become even more severe during their residencies than they were during their four years of medical school. In fact, the fatigue that medical residents routinely experience is a subject of considerable concern and debate. Many residents routinely work 80 hours per week and have shifts that may last up to 30 hours straight. This schedule often leaves them sleepless and utterly exhausted. Many medical school officials say that this type of schedule is necessary for residents to acquire a sufficient amount of knowledge about the practice of medicine. But other medical experts worry that residents' tiring schedules endanger patient care and patient health by increasing their likelihood of committing medical errors or accidents.

In response to this concern, the Accreditation Council for Graduate Medical Education (ACGME) in 2003 reduced the maximum weekly hours that residents could work from a higher maximum to its present 80 hours and the length of shifts to their present maximum of 30 hours.

In 2008, however, the federal Institute of Medicine (IOM) issued a report, "Resident Duty Hours: Enhancing Sleep, Supervision, and Safety," whose title evoked the problems that residents' schedules continued to pose even with the reduced maximums (Ulmer, Wolman, and Johns 2008a). This report said that the 2003 standards of 80-work weeks and 30-hour shifts were still too long and endangered patients. In response, ACGME in 2011 reduced the shift length of first-year residents to 16 hours and of more senior residents, who comprise most residents, to 28 hours.

These changes did not win over the critics of medical residents' exhausting schedules. As an internal medicine resident who called these changes "still very dangerous for patients" explained:

> Residents make life and death decisions, often in the middle of the night. The work is constant, and the possibilities for mistakes are almost limitless. A misplaced decimal point in a prescription order can make all the difference. And it is important to remember whom the decisions of these young doctors affect. Residents are caring for real people—someone's parent, someone's son, someone's friend, someone who will leave a lot of people devastated if things go wrong. It is imperative that residents are alert and are able to think clearly and intervene appropriately. As the IOM concluded, during these long shifts residents are simply too tired to maintain peak performance, and, as a consequence, patient care suffers. (Fodeman 2011)

The IOM report called for additional reforms of medical residents' schedules. These reforms included:

- periods of days off after long shifts to let residents get enough rest and sleep
- restrictions on their moonlighting hours in other employment
- reductions in their patient caseloads
- increased supervision of their performance, and
- better communication when handovers (turning a patient's care over to another doctor when a resident goes off duty) occur.

The report's authors went on to conclude, "The nation must take a hard look at its residency programs—including hours, schedules, supervision, patient caseloads and handovers—and ensure that they serve both patient and resident safety today and educational needs for tomorrow. Altering the hours of resident work alone is not sufficient to maximize safety and learning. Until these changes take place, residency programs are not providing what the next generation of doctors or their patients deserve" (Ulmer, Wolman, and Johns 2008b:3). In view of the IOM report, medical residency programs must continue to institute appropriate reforms that will protect patients' health while still ensuring that medical residents acquire an excellent medical education.

Adding to the medical residents' problems is the strain caused by their family relationships as discussed earlier. Because residents do work up to 80 hours per week, they have precious little time and energy for spouses, partners, or children. When they do spend time with these significant others, they often find it difficult to keep their minds off their work, which means they are likely thinking about illness and death at the time they should be enjoying the company of their loved ones. As a news report summarized this problem, "Spouses wind up eating alone many nights. They often relocate for the training slot, sometimes putting their own career on hold. At work, residents witness illness and death day after day, which can sap energy for conversations at home. And when the couple are both residents, they can be on opposite schedules, requiring them to vacation separately" (Kowalczyk 2013a).

All these problems lead to a high rate of clinical depression among medical residents. Almost one-third of residents will experience depression at some point during their residencies, a rate that is four times higher than that of all U.S. adults (Mata et al. 2015).

The Socialization of Medical Students

Stress, fatigue, and burnout are significant facts of life for many medical students, but so, too, is the *socialization* they experience after they first enter medical school. **Socialization**, or the learning of a culture's norms, values, and attitudes, is a central concept in the discipline of sociology. Most sociological discussions of socialization emphasize the importance of parents, schools, peers, and religion as agents of socialization for younger children and adolescents alike. However, socialization also continues during adulthood. For example, people who enter various occupations learn the culture of their workplaces and the formal and informal rules they should follow to ensure they do well at their jobs and establish good coworker relationships. Socialization is certainly a lifelong process, even if it is most important during our younger years.

With this backdrop in mind, it should come as no surprise that sociologists and other scholars have long been interested in the socialization of medical students, with some early studies of medical school socialization appearing several decades ago (Becker et al. 1961; Merton et al. 1957). When college graduates enter medical school, their main goal is to acquire the scientific knowledge they will need to be able to practice medicine. But along the way, they also learn certain norms, values, and attitudes during their preclinical years, their clinical years, and their residencies. These norms, values, and attitudes reflect two dynamics: (1) the special nature of the subject matter, scientific medicine, that medical students are learning, and (2) the fact that clinical students and residents interact with hospital patients with serious illnesses and injuries, including patients who die despite the best efforts of the students/residents and other medical professionals.

A famous scene in the 1970s' M*A*S*H television show that was set in the Korean War conveys this fundamental fact of medical training and medical practice. After the show's physician star, Hawkeye Pierce, was unable to save the life of a close friend who had been wounded, Hawkeye's commander, Colonel Henry Blake, tries to console him by saying, "Look, all I know is what they taught me at command school. There are certain rules about a war. Rule number one is young men die. And rule number two is doctors can't change rule number one" (Wikiquote 2014).

Detached Concern   Medical school and clinical training are far from a battlefield, of course, but the patients whom medical students see still are often seriously ill or injured, and some of them do die. Anyone with a heart would ordinarily find it emotionally difficult to interact with a patient with a serious condition and even more difficult to have that patient die. Yet, as Hawkeye and his colleagues found on the Korean battlefield, medical professionals simply cannot let every serious condition and patient death "get to them" emotionally, because otherwise they will eat themselves up inside and suffer emotional and mental trauma. As a self-defense mechanism against such trauma, medical students begin early in their education and especially during their clinical years to develop **detached concern** (Halpern 2011).

A key aspect of medical students' socialization, detached concern involves a fair amount of emotional distance from patients in which the patients are depersonalized and treated less as people than as medical puzzles to be solved. During their clinical years, medical students observe detached concern in action as they accompany their clinical instructors during rounds. These experienced physicians often talk to the students about intimate aspects of the patient's condition right in front of the patient, and they often say very little to the patient and otherwise treat the patient impersonally. Such socialization helps students learn to view a patient as "just another case," and this view helps them to minimize or avoid the emotional anguish they might otherwise feel from their patients' suffering and occasional deaths.

Although detached concern does help medical students and the physicians they later become to avoid emotional trauma, the depersonalization it involves may affect their care of patients, who often feel their doctors treat them impersonally and insensitively (see chapter 8). This so-called *empathy gap* (Kowalczyk 2013b) on the part of medical students goes beyond patients' feelings: because studies link physician empathy to better health outcomes for patients, medical students' empathy gap may compromise patient welfare. Interestingly, studies find that students' scores on empathy assessments (which ask them to indicate their level of agreement with questions such as "Physicians should try to put themselves in the patient's position when caring for them") *drop* after they enter medical school. This drop is particularly noticeable during their third year of schooling, which, not coincidentally, is also their first year of clinical instruction, when they begin seeing patients (Kowalczyk 2013b). Medical education and the development of detached concern thus seem to reduce medical students' empathy.

This consequence prompts critics to call for measures to help medical students achieve a better balance between their need for detached concern and patients' need for more personal treatment by their physicians (Halpern 2011). In response to this criticism, some medical schools have begun efforts such as role-playing to improve students' empathy (Kowalczyk 2013b). A physician who favored these efforts commented, "Students come in with a lot of idealism. They want to be of help and service. And then something starts to happen when they are exposed to clinical care. We need better curriculum and education on how to manage those feelings" (Kowalczyk 2013b).

A recent account described a particular manifestation of detached concern (Morris 2013). At Harvard Medical School, many students look forward eagerly to participating in the school's organ transplant observation program, in which students travel with physicians to obtain an organ from a patient who just died and/ or to observe an actual transplantation. During one class, students applauded loudly when a pager signaled that its wearer had been chosen to perform one of these activities. When the instructor realized what was happening, he was shocked at the students' excitement and reminded them that someone had probably died very recently. A member of the class described what happened next: "The room fell quiet. We shifted uncomfortably in our seats. Dozens of Type A medical students, we were ashamed of what we had just done" (Morris 2013:A23). This student added, "In medicine, a lot of our training depends on the misfortune of others. Without sick people, we cannot learn to diagnose and treat. But we sometimes forget to manage our enthusiasm for the science of disease and, in doing so, ignore the human suffering that comes with the experience of disease" (Morris 2013:A23).

Tolerance of Uncertainty   Another key aspect of medical students' socialization stems from the complexity of the medical knowledge they are expected to learn and from scientific medicine's inability to prevent and cure every serious health problem. In a classic article, sociologist Renée C. Fox (1957) wrote that medical students are "training for uncertainty," to quote the title of the article. By this Fox meant two things. First, medical knowledge is so vast that students can never fully learn everything there is to learn about medicine. As Fox (1957:209) put it, their "mastery of all that is known in medicine will never be complete" regardless of how intelligent they are. Second, scientific medicine, despite its incredible advances since its inception, still does not understand many aspects of the causes of serious medical problems and the best way to treat these problems.

These two circumstances mean that medical students eventually learn that their own knowledge of medicine will be uncertain for two reasons: (1) their own inability to know everything known to scientific medicine; and (2) scientific medicine's inability to know everything about the causes and cures of disease and illness. Not only do students learn these two types of uncertainty, they also come to accept this double-sided uncertainty as inevitable. This aspect of medical students' socialization is called **tolerance** (or **acceptance**) **of uncertainty**.

This tolerance comes with a difficulty, wrote Fox: when medical students find they do not know something they ideally should know, such as how best to treat a specific medical condition, they sometimes have trouble deciding whether their ignorance stems from their inability to master something that scientific medicine does know, or instead from scientific medicine's own lack of knowledge on this matter. As Fox (1957:212) put it, they are initially "unsure where [their] limitations leave off and the limitations of medical science begin." Over time, however, they eventually come to understand whether their lack of knowledge stems from their own lack of learning or, instead, from scientific medicine's limitations. More importantly, they realize that lack of knowledge matter is much more likely to stem from scientific medicine's ignorance than from than from their own ignorance. This realization helps medical students to develop an "affirmative attitude" regarding uncertainty (Fox 1957:217) that in turn helps boost the students' self-confidence and makes them better able to practice medicine.

Conclusion

Medical schools have changed in many ways over the decades, but they are still grappling with how to obtain student bodies that reflect the diversity of America. For their part, medical students go through several years of very intense training on their quest to enter the medical profession. In addition to their formal learning in medicine, medical students also learn certain values and attitudes as part of the socialization process that occurs in medical schools. Although students obtain an excellent education in medicine, many experience high levels of stress, bullying and sexual harassment, and other problems that add to the burden they already face in learning a vast body of knowledge. Because the quality of medical practice depends heavily on the quality of physicians, it is important that medical schools institute appropriate reforms to ensure that medical students' stress is kept as minimal as possible and that they develop sufficient empathy for their patients.

Summary

1. Some medical schools developed in Europe by the end of Middle Ages, and several more were established over the next few centuries. Because medical knowledge at that time was so limited, however, their students did not learn much that was of practical value.

2. The first medical school in colonial America was established in 1765 at the College of Philadelphia. By 1813, Columbia, Dartmouth, Harvard, and Yale universities also had medical schools, and a few other universities also established medical schools over the next several decades.

3. Proprietary medical schools outnumbered university medical schools by the mid-nineteenth century. Although these schools were more affordable and some admitted African Americans or women, they typically offered an inferior education to that found in the university schools.

4. Despite the growth of medical schools during the nineteenth century, apprenticeship continued to be a common form of training for aspiring physicians in the United States. By the end of the century, however, many states had begun to require licensure and medical school degrees.

5. The 1910 Flexner Report criticized the quality of medical education at the time and advocated several reforms that were eventually adopted by medical schools across the nation.

6. Today's medical schools have a rather common curriculum required by accreditation standards. After entering medical school, the typical student takes two years of courses, then takes a national examination, and then has two years of clinical instruction at teaching hospitals in which they perform clerkships.

7. Women, people of color, and low-income students are underrepresented among the 86,000+ students in U.S. medical schools. At the same time, people of color and especially women are much better represented now than they were several decades ago.

8. Many medical students experience considerable stress because of the complexity of their training, the long hours they spend studying and in clerkships and residencies, the high cost of their education, and the bullying and harassment they sometimes experience.

9. In addition to their scientific education, medical students also learn certain attitudes and values as part of their socialization, including detached concern and tolerance of certainty.

Giving It Some Thought

You are a third-year medical student and are now in the third week of your first clerkship. A senior resident taking you and some other students on rounds ridicules you when you are slow to answer a question about a patient. You feel humiliated, and you notice some of the other students grimacing in sympathy. What, if anything, do you do about the verbal harassment you just experienced? Explain your answer.

Key Terms

clerkship, 114

detached concern, 122

medical student burnout, 119

proprietary schools, 110

socialization, 121

tolerance of uncertainty, 123

Physicians and Their Interaction with Patients

8

LEARNING QUESTIONS

1. What are the major characteristics of professions?

2. How well trained were the various health care providers during the U.S. colonial period?

3. What were the advantages and disadvantages of the professionalization of medicine during the nineteenth century?

4. Why has the medical profession's dominance declined since the 1950s?

5. What are the major differences between the paternalistic and egalitarian models of physician-patient interaction?

6. How do patients' gender and race sometimes affect the quality of their medical care?

Health and Illness in the News

Dr. Carroll Frazier Landrum, 88, makes old-fashioned house calls in the poverty-stricken town of Edwards, Mississippi, but with a twist: he practices his medicine out of his 2007 Toyota Camry. His many patients consider him a lifesaver, with one of them commenting, "I love that he's here. He may not cure cancer, but he's cured a lot of people of basic things. There's a lot of poverty in Edwards. There are many, many people here who do not have transportation to Vicksburg, Clinton, Jackson, and he truly serves a purpose. And there are people who come to him who would not get medical treatment otherwise."

In early 2015, however, Landrum told a reporter that the Mississippi State Board of Medical Licensure was seeking to revoke his right to practice medicine because his practice was out of his car. Landrum said he was just trying to help the poor patients he sees each week. As he told the reporter, "I've always had a heart for the poor. I grew up poor, and when the doctor would come to us, and he was happy to see us, I pictured myself doing that some day. I try not to ever turn people away—money or no money—because that's where the need is." (Bowman 2015; Holley 2015)

This poignant news story reminds us that physicians help people and save lives. It also reminds us that the poor often lack essential health care because of their poverty. This chapter describes the status of physicians in the United States today and takes a careful look at their interaction with patients. We will see that although physicians often work long, exhausting hours and perform a needed and even heroic role, their interaction with patients is sometimes less than ideal and, in particular, affected by issues of social class, race and ethnicity, and gender.

The Profession of Medicine

Many people work in many occupations, but only certain occupations, including medicine, law, and teaching, are considered professions. What, then, is a profession, and why is it important to know that physicians are members of a profession?

A **profession** is commonly defined as an occupation that is highly skilled and that requires prolonged training. That is certainly a good definition, but sociologists emphasize additional characteristics of professions that help us understand how and why members of professions perform their duties and interact with colleagues, the public, and other parties (Dingwall and Lewis 2014; Freidson 1988).

The most important characteristic is **autonomy**. In this context, autonomy means that a profession is largely free (from governmental influence or control) to determine all of the following: (1) the needed education and other standards, including examinations and licensure, for entrance into the profession; (2) the rules that govern the behavior of a profession's members; and (3) the discipline that should occur if any members violate these rules. The first point on entrance standards helps professions to achieve their goal of *monopolizing knowledge*, a concept to which we return shortly. The second and third points on rules and discipline refer to *self-regulation*, or the idea that professions are largely free to investigate alleged violations of their rules of conduct and to apply whatever sanctions, including loss of the license to practice, should these violations be proven.

Another characteristic of a profession is that its members possess **specialized knowledge** that is difficult to master (Hodson and Sullivan 2012). It is certainly not easy to learn the complexities of scientific medicine that medical students must master, and neither is it easy for law school students to learn the complexities of the law. Lacking appropriate professional education and training, the average citizen cannot hope to comprehend medicine, law, or the specialized knowledge possessed by any other profession. In the case of medicine, specialized knowledge takes two forms: (1) the vast body of facts and principles found in the basic medical sciences such as anatomy, physiology, and biochemistry; and (2) the techniques, such as surgery or listening to hearts and lungs, that physicians and other medical professionals use to diagnose and treat patients. Professions' mastery of specialized knowledge contributes to their general prestige in society.

A third characteristic of professions is their **professional culture**. This concept refers to the distinctive language (*jargon*), lifestyles, values, and behavior that typify members of professions. Specific aspects of a professional culture include how to dress and how to interact with each other and with people outside the profession. Members of a profession begin to learn their professional culture during their professional education after obtaining a college degree. As chapter 7's discussion of socialization during medical school indicated, detached concern for patients is an example of one of the values that medical students learn.

A fourth characteristic of professions is the **authority** that professionals exercise over clients and over the subordinate occupational groups with whom professionals interact. In the case of physicians, the clients just mentioned are their patients, and subordinate occupational groups include nurses, laboratory technicians, and hospital volunteers. Professionals' authority stems from their specialized knowledge and from their professional cultures. As sociologists Randy Hodson and Teresa A. Sullivan

(2012:264) observe, hospital physicians' specialized knowledge justifies their delegation of everyday patient care (bathing, bedpan emptying, feeding, etc.) to nurses or other staff: "The rationale is that delegation frees the professionals for the more highly skilled work for which they alone were trained."

The final characteristic of professions is altruism, or the idea that professions' primary goal is to help the clients they serve and in this way to help society as a whole. Physicians, attorneys, and members of other professions certainly often enjoy high incomes, but they and their professional associations are quick to emphasize that their chief concern is to aid their clients and to serve the public good.

The characteristics just identified join to produce a common goal of professions, **monopolizing knowledge** (Hodson and Sullivan 2012). Professions typically not only determine their entrance standards but also ensure that people not meeting these standards are not permitted to perform the duties associated with the profession. Another way of saying this is that professions normally try to hold a monopoly over the practice of their duties. Thus individuals must go to medical school, pass various examinations, and complete residencies before they can receive a license to practice medicine, and state laws prevent anyone who does not go through this long, intense process from practicing medicine. Professions argue that this form of control is meant to produce the most skilled practitioners (physicians, attorneys, etc.) possible, but it is also true that limiting the supply of practitioners yields higher incomes for the relatively few who meet the entrance standards. This point is relevant for the history of the medical profession in the United States, to which we now turn.

The Rise and Decline of the Medical Profession in the United States

Sociologist Paul Starr (1982) described the history of the medical profession in his classic 1982 book, *The Social Transformation of American Medicine*, which won the 1984 Pulitzer Prize for General Non-Fiction. The following synopsis draws on his and other accounts (Breslaw 2014; Rutkow 2010) and begins with the colonial period to provide a backdrop for the professionalization of medicine a century later.

Recall from chapter 7 that apprenticeship was a common path for aspiring physicians in early America. Although many physicians during this period obtained degrees from university-affiliated medical schools, many others obtained their degrees from propriety medical schools, which often provided an inferior education. Many other people simply declared that they were physicians after serving an apprenticeship or even after not serving an apprenticeship at all. This general situation meant that many U.S. physicians were poorly trained, to say the least, to practice medicine. American physicians with formal medical school training in Europe, such as Benjamin Rush (1745–1813), the leading American physician of the colonial period and a signer of the Declaration of Independence, still knew woefully little of real value for healing people because the advances of scientific medicine were still a century away. Rush, for example, joined many other physicians of the era in believing that *bloodletting* and *purging* (forced bowel movements) were the best cures for most diseases, when in fact these practices almost certainly worsened many patients' conditions and even helped kill them.

Despite the eminence of Rush and other American physicians who had gone to medical school in Europe, the primary source of medical care for most colonists was their families, specifically the wives, mothers, and other women in their families. These women, like women for centuries before them, practiced **domestic medicine** by drawing on folk wisdom received from their mothers that in turn had been received from their grandmothers and earlier generations of women.

Colonial women made medical potions from various herbs and plants, attended to wounds and injuries of family members, and in other respects were the primary caretakers of their family's health. To some extent domestic medicine was a communal affair, as women from one family would commonly provide medical advice to women from another family and help with the family's practical medical care when requested.

The popularity of domestic medicine, the existence of many self-proclaimed physicians without formal training, and the general poverty of many families all meant that physicians during early America generally had relatively low incomes and that their occupation lacked the prestige it has today. As scientific medicine advanced during the nineteenth century (see chapter 2), however, so did the prestige of physicians. They established several state and local medical societies before the Civil War and lobbied state legislatures to set up licensing requirements for physicians. As chapter 7 recounted, Connecticut became the first state in 1821 to require licensure for the practice of medicine.

Impact of the American Medical Association

The founding of the American Medical Association (AMA) in 1847 accelerated this process, as one of the AMA's key goals was to lobby states to require examination-based licensure. As states increasingly required a medical school degree for entrance into the medical profession (see chapter 7), the AMA played no small role in this new requirement. By the end of the nineteenth century, most states had begun to require medical school degrees and appropriate examinations and licensure for the right to practice medicine. The practice of medicine, then, had become largely professionalized by the end of that century.

The AMA's efforts to tighten standards for the practice of medicine stemmed largely from two motivations that recall the professional characteristics outlined earlier in this chapter. First, the AMA altruistically wanted to produce the best-trained physicians possible in order to produce the best patient care possible; in particular, it wanted to prevent people untrained in medicine from practicing medicine. Second, but less altruistically and more materialistically, the AMA also wanted to reduce the supply of physicians and other practitioners of medicine in order to increase physicians' incomes: the fewer the people who provide a service, in this case medical practice, the more they can charge for their services. These twin goals, altruism and materialism, motivated the AMA's largely successful efforts by the end of the nineteenth century to monopolize medical knowledge and practice. As two medical sociologists have put it, the medical profession succeeded in "putting competitors and quacks out of business" (Timmermans and Oh 2010:96).

This success did not come easily, however. Many laypeople and state legislators distrusted "official" physicians and continued to believe in the effectiveness of domestic medicine and other ways of healing. However, advances in scientific medicine after the mid-nineteenth century, and especially Pasteur's formulation during the 1870s of the germ theory of disease (see chapter 2), increased public confidence in scientific medicine and, in turn, lent credibility to the AMA's efforts to professionalize medicine. The publication in 1910 of the celebrated the Flexner Report (see chapter 7) on medical education in America strengthened medical education standards and hastened the demise of proprietary medical schools. The AMA soon won the right from the states and federal government to establish these new education standards and also standards for the examination and licensing of new physicians. This development marked the ascendancy of the medical profession and of the AMA as its leading proponent.

The Downside of Professionalization

While most readers probably welcome the professionalization of medicine as described in the preceding pages, the AMA's success did come with a price. Although the AMA's efforts improved the practice of medicine, they also increased the cost of much medical care because there were now fewer people allowed to practice medicine. Many people who previously could afford medical care could now no longer do so (Starr 1982).

The Displacement of Midwives   The health of one large segment of the population, pregnant women, was also compromised, because one of the strategies of the AMA and smaller medical societies involved securing a monopoly over the medical treatment of pregnant women and the delivery of their babies. This important development merits further discussion, which draws on two highly praised accounts (Ehrenreich and English 2005; Wertz and Wertz 1989).

For much of human history, and certainly for the United States during its early years, women gave birth with the aid of other women from their families or nearby households. Physicians were usually not part of this equation. Some women became so skilled in assisting with childbirth that they took on this responsibility as their formal or informal occupation. The term **midwife** developed in the medieval period to refer to a woman with this vocation.

Through most of the nineteenth century, midwives remained the individuals who assisted with most births. Having little experience with childbirth or training in how to assist with it (see chapter 7), nineteenth-century physicians (almost all of whom were men) actually knew relatively little, and generally much less than what most midwives knew, about how to deliver a baby. Despite this fact, the AMA and other medical societies saw an opportunity to maximize physicians' incomes by wresting the function of childbirth assistance from midwives and claiming it as their own. They did so by asserting that they, not midwives, were most qualified to help deliver babies, and they lobbied state legislatures to require a medical degree for childbirth assistance. Most state legislatures established such a requirement between 1900 and 1930, which in effect outlawed midwifery, put midwives out of work, and gave physicians a near monopoly over childbirth. Because physicians charged more money than midwives for their services and were also less skilled than midwives back then in delivering a child, pregnant women and their families suffered in two ways from the monopolization of childbirth by the medical profession.

Justifying Women's Exclusion from College   The ascendancy of the (male) medical profession harmed women in other ways. As medicine became professionalized by the late nineteenth century, the increasing prestige and authority of physicians increased their influence not only over medical practice, but also over certain aspects of public policy. Claiming special insights gleaned from their medical training, physicians increasingly commented on nonmedical matters that the physicians claimed still had a medical dimension.

One of these matters concerned the issue of whether women should be allowed to go to college. Reflecting the sexism of the era, many leading physicians claimed that women should not go to college for at least two reasons (Ehrenreich and English 2005). First, they could not be expected to do well in college because of their supposed delicate natures, and, moreover, they would not do well on exams during "that time of the month," that is, during their menstrual flow. Second, the pressures of college would disrupt their menstrual cycles and cause gynecological and reproductive problems. A popular book in the 1870s by a Harvard University medical professor even claimed that a woman who went to college would be putting the health of her uterus at severe risk of atrophy, and other physicians claimed that women who went to college might lose their ability to lactate and could even have their breasts disappear! All of this was nonsense, of course, but colleges and universities cited these physicians' claims as reasons to refuse admission to women.

Decline of the Medical Profession's Dominance

Despite these problems, the ascendancy of the medical profession continued well into the twentieth century, and the profession in general and the AMA, in particular, reached a position of dominance by the 1950s. This era has been called the *golden age of doctoring* (McKinlay and Marceau 2002). The medical profession was highly respected, patients rarely challenged physicians, and the AMA was a very effective lobbying group in advancing the professional and economic interests of the medical profession.

Since that era, the medical profession has become less dominant for several reasons (Timmermans and Oh 2010). First, *patient health movements* developed in the 1960s and 1970s that criticized physicians for ignoring the health needs of many kinds of patients (Brown et al. 2010). A key movement here was the women's health movement that began in the 1970s. This movement charged the medical establishment with neglecting the gynecological and obstetrical needs of women and with clinging to outmoded conceptions of women's health. With the aid of a pamphlet, *Our Bodies, Ourselves* (Boston Women's Health Book Collective 1973), that grew into a best-selling book, the women's health movement urged women to take control of their own health and to challenge physicians, almost all of whom were still men at the time, who ignored or even belittled their health concerns (Anspach 2010).

Second, many patients by the 1980s began to take a more active role in managing their health, in choosing which physicians to visit, and in raising questions about their physicians' instructions (Timmermans and Oh 2010). This change accelerated during the 1990s and 2000s with the advent of the Internet, which allowed patients to learn about their medical issues as never before and to become even more active in their own health care (Vanderminden and Potter 2010). With the aid of the Internet, laypeople were now able to read about their health problems and treatment options, and they were also able to participate in online patient forums and support groups on almost every health problem imaginable. These Internet activities gave patients new confidence to ask questions when they visit their physicians and more generally to play a more active role in improving their health (Conrad and Stults 2010). As Stefan Timmermans and Hyeyoung Oh (2010:597) summarize this development, "The growth of the Internet gave patients easy access to information on medical practitioners, health care policies, and general medical knowledge, facilitating patients' abilities to engage in consumerist practices and equipping them with decision-making leverage during patient-doctor interactions." With patients more empowered in all these ways, the authority of physicians and the medical profession declined accordingly.

A third factor in the decline of the medical profession's dominance was the steep rise in national health care costs and expenditures that began during the 1960s and lasted until the current decade (see chapter 12). This sharp increase brought new criticism to the medical profession and led to efforts by the federal and state governments to control medical costs through managed care and other arrangements and policies.

A final factor was a spate of news stories about unethical medical experiments, dangerous drugs that had been allowed to be marketed, and medical malpractice lawsuits (Timmermans and Oh 2010). These stories all suggested that the medical profession could not be trusted to protect the public's health.

Partly because of all of these currents, public trust in the medical profession declined after the mid-twentieth century. In the mid-1960s, about 72% of the public expressed trust in physicians as measured in national surveys; by the early 1980s, this figure had declined by almost half to only 37% (Timmermans and Oh 2010).

Medical Malpractice

We mentioned earlier that news stories about medical malpractice helped to reduce the dominance of the medical profession and Americans' trust in physicians. Allegations of **medical malpractice**, or negligent treatment by a health care professional that harms a patient, are common against physicians, with many malpractice lawsuits filed each year. The average physician can expect to be sued for malpractice at least once every seven years (Glatter 2013). Malpractice claims are usually filed about two years after the alleged malpractice occurred and usually take several years to resolve: *dismissed cases* (that is, those dismissed by a judge) take up to two years; *settled cases* (where the plaintiff patient and defendant physician reach an agreement out of court) take two to three years; and *adjudicated cases* (those that go to trial) take up to four years. All these figures mean that the average physician spends many years over a forty-year career dealing with open malpractice claims. Not surprisingly, these claims cause physicians much stress (Glatter 2013).

Of the malpractice claims that a judge does not dismiss, about 95% are settled out of court, and the remainder go to trial and are decided by a jury or a judge. In 2014, more than 12,000 malpractice cases were settled or adjudicated, and total payouts for these cases amounted to about $3.9 billion (Gower 2015).

To prevent malpractice lawsuits, physicians often practice **defensive medicine** by ordering diagnostic tests and other procedures that are probably or certainly medically unnecessary. Even so, physicians order these tests to prevent patients from later alleging that the physician was negligent for not ordering the tests. Defensive medicine adds billions of dollars to the nation's health care bill, with estimates ranging between $46 billion and $200 billion or more annually, equal to 2% of all health care expenditures (Glatter 2013; Mello et al. 2010). This sum costs health insurance companies much money, and it also costs consumers by driving up their health insurance premiums and through any payments they may owe for defensive testing even if they are insured.

In addition to this problem, juries have sometimes awarded millions of dollars to plaintiffs in malpractice and other lawsuits, with several celebrated examples involving trivial injuries (physical or otherwise) to the plaintiffs. In response, the medical profession, business leaders, and other parties have called for *tort reform* involving such measures as limiting the amount of punitive damages that civil juries may award to plaintiffs. Influenced by the celebrated examples just mentioned, the U.S. Congress and several state legislatures did pass legislation along these lines during the past two decades (Labaton 2005).

However, social science evidence suggests that concern over civil jury awards in medical malpractice lawsuits is exaggerated (Haltom and McCann 2004). In the nation's 75 largest counties, 1,156 malpractice cases were disposed of by trial in 2001, the last year for which the federal government has reported data (Cohen 2004). Plaintiffs won in only 311, or about 27%, of these cases. The median award plaintiffs received for both compensatory damages (for lost wages, medical expenses, etc.) and punitive damages (that are meant to punish the defendant and send a message to other potential offenders) was $422,000. Punitive damages were awarded in

15, or only 5%, of the 311 cases that plaintiffs won, and the median amount of these damages was $187,000.

Although the amount of these awards is higher than that for other lawsuits combined (Cohen 2004), it reflects the seriousness of the harm, almost always death or permanent injury/disability, done to the patient. And although malpractice suits distress physicians and promote defensive medicine, the low number of plaintiff victories and punitive damages does suggest that concern about jury verdicts in malpractice cases may be overstated.

In this regard, it is also worth noting that most malpractice victims never bring a lawsuit, with one study finding that only 16% of patients who suffered permanent injuries ended up suing their physician (Haltom and McCann 2004). Other evidence suggests that fewer than 5% of all medical errors, minor and serious, generate a malpractice lawsuit (Glatter 2013). These findings suggest that most physicians who commit possible malpractice need not be concerned about being sued, even if malpractice payouts do amount to almost $4 billion annually.

Malpractice and the Medical Profession's Autonomy   In addition to not being sued, physicians who commit malpractice often do not even have to worry about being disciplined by the medical profession. Recall that autonomy is the most important defining characteristic of professions, which are largely free to determine entrance and practice standards for their profession and to deal with violations of professional standards of conduct. The latter dimension of autonomy means that professions are largely free to police themselves when these violations are suspected. This self-policing is thought to make sense because professions' specialized knowledge makes their members best able to understand the complex aspects of their professional responsibilities, to decide whether any suspected violation has indeed occurred, and to determine the appropriate sanctions for any violator.

Professional self-policing might indeed make sense for these reasons, but only if professions can be trusted to serve the public good by carefully investigating alleged professional misconduct and applying appropriate sanctions, including loss of the right to practice. However, much evidence indicates that the medical, legal, and other professions often overlook misconduct or treat it very lightly in terms of sanctions, applying a mere "slap on the wrist" when a more serious sanction would be in order. Critics thus say that professional self-policing is akin to the proverbial fox guarding the chicken coop.

Much evidence of this problem exists for the medical profession. Many physicians do not report the medical errors that they think other physicians have committed (Campbell et al. 2007). Just as police do not like to "rat on" other police who have been corrupt or brutal, so do physicians not like to publicize other physicians' misconduct, and they may also fear being sued for bringing charges of misconduct. *Hospital review committees* are supposed to review any evidence of medical errors and to report any malpractice to their state medical boards. But hospitals often fail to report any malpractice they uncover, preferring to deal with the problem internally by, for example, telling the offending physician to find employment elsewhere. When the state boards do hear of misconduct, they often fail to investigate cases or impose a relatively minor sanction when they conclude that a physician acted negligently (Leibert 2010). One reason for this failure is that many state boards are underfunded and understaffed and thus lack the resources for thorough investigations.

A recent investigative report provided alarming evidence of this problem. The report concluded that "thousands of doctors who have been banned by hospitals or other medical facilities aren't punished by the state medical boards that license doctors" (Eisler and Hansen 2013). In one case, a state board cited a Texan physician several times for various violations but let him continue to practice. Eventually, a patient died from a dangerous mixture of medications that he had prescribed for her. The board finally revoked his license four years after this death. The victim's mother said, "If the board had moved faster, my daughter would still be alive. They knew this doctor had all these problems . . . (and) they did nothing to stop him."

Physicians' Lawsuits against Patients   Ironically, some physicians have begun suing patients and/or patients' families. Patients or families who are dissatisfied with their physician's care have written about their grievances on Internet blogs or on Twitter and other social media. In return, some physicians targeted by the blogs have sued the bloggers for defamation. In one example, a Boston physician sued a blogger for $100,000 after the blogger had complained about the stroke his wife, a cancer patient, suffered during surgery performed by the physician and about her subsequent death. Criticizing the lawsuit, the blogger said, "It's difficult to believe we have a legal system that allows people to be sued for expressing their grief" (Kowalczyk 2013). Physicians say patient privacy laws prevent them from responding to negative reviews in blogs or elsewhere on the Internet, such as on Angie's List or Yelp.

A Profile of Physicians Today

Today the United States has about one million physicians with an M.D. degree (*allopathic* physicians). This number has roughly doubled since 1980, when the United States had almost 470,000 physicians. Of the one million physicians today, only about 770,000 are actually practicing medicine, the remainder having retired or left medicine for other reasons (American Medical Association 2015). Physicians who are currently practicing medicine are called **active physicians**. Approximately 60,000 osteopathic physicians, whom chapter 9 discusses, also practice medicine.

Chapter 7 outlined the great increase in the number of women medical students during the past few decades. Not surprisingly, the number of women physicians (active or inactive) has greatly increased as well, rising by 500% from about 54,000 women physicians in 1980 to more than 310,000 today. Whereas slightly less than 12% of all physicians in 1980 were women, today about one-third are women, and a full 46% of physicians under age 35 are women (Roter and Hall 2015). Because women comprise almost half of all medical students, they will comprise an increasing proportion of the medical profession as older physicians, most of whom are men, retire and pass away. A later section in this chapter discusses women physicians further.

Chapter 7 also pointed out that the proportion of medical students who are African American, Latino, or Native American remains well below their proportion in the general population. It should not surprise you, then, to hear that today fewer than 10% of active physicians are African American, Latino, or Native American, even though these three backgrounds account for almost one-third of the population. This low number reflects the many inequalities faced by racial/ethnic minorities in the United States today and in the past. Although this low number may be understandable for this reason, it has important implications for racial health disparities in the United States. This is because physicians of color are more likely than white physicians to want to practice in areas with high numbers of persons of color (Ansell and McDonald. 2015). As we comment further below, these areas often lack sufficient numbers of physicians because most physicians prefer to practice in more advantaged areas. To help improve health care in these areas, then, it is critical that the medical community do everything reasonably possible to increase the ranks of medical students and physicians of color during the coming decades.

About one-fourth of active physicians are international medical graduates (IMGs), which means that they received their medical degree from a school in a nation other than the United States and then came to the United States to serve their residency and/or to practice medicine. The IMG proportion of active physicians ranges widely among the medical specialties, from a low of about 5%–6% in dermatology and orthopedic surgery to a high of about 50% in geriatric medicine and 45% in nephrology (the medical specialty regarding kidney problems) (Association of American Medical Colleges 2014).

Types of Physicians

There are many types of physicians based on the kind of work they do. A common typology divides physicians' practices into four major categories (Association of American Medical Colleges 2015):

- *Primary Care*: general and family practice, internal medicine, pediatrics, geriatric medicine (approximately 241,000 physicians overall)
- *Medical Specialties*: allergy and immunology, cardiology, critical care, dermatology, endocrinology, hematology and oncology, infectious diseases, neonatal-perinatal medicine, nephrology, pulmonology, rheumatology (126,000 physicians)
- *Surgical Specialties*: general surgery, colorectal surgery, neurological surgery, obstetrics and gynecology, ophthalmology, orthopedic surgery, otolaryngology, plastic surgery, thoracic surgery, urology, vascular surgery (155,000 physicians)
- *Other Specialties*: anesthesiology, emergency medicine, neurology, pathology, physical medicine and rehabilitation, psychiatry, radiology, and other specialties (246,000 physicians)

The income that all these physicians earn from their practices varies greatly. Specialists generally earn much more money than primary care physicians, and certain specialists earn much more money than other specialists. For example, the median annual compensation of primary care physicians is about $221,000, while the corresponding figure for all physicians in medical specialties is almost $400,000, or almost twice as much (2012 data). The median annual compensation for selected practices appears in Table 8.1.

TABLE 8.1	**Median Annual Compensation for Selected Medical Practices, 2012**
Type of Practice	
Anesthesiology	$431,977
General surgery	367,885
Obstetrics/gynecology	301,737
Internal medicine	224,110
Psychiatry	220,252
Pediatrics/adolescent medicine	216,069
Family practice (without obstetrics)	207,117

Source: Bureau of Labor Statistics, U.S. Department of Labor, *Occupational Outlook Handbook, 2014–2015 Edition*, Physicians and Surgeons, on the Internet at http://www.bls.gov/ooh/healthcare/physicians-and-surgeons.htm (visited March 22, 2015).

The Physician Shortage

Although the United States currently has hundreds of thousands of physicians, this number is insufficient to meet the demand for their services. The Association of American Medical Colleges (2015) concluded in a recent report that "the demand for physician services is growing faster than supply. While growth in the supply for APRNs [advanced practice nurses] and other health occupations may help to alleviate projected shortfalls to an extent, . . . the nation will likely face a growing shortage in many physician specialties—especially surgery-related specialties." Projected to range between about 46,000 and 90,000 physicians by 2025, this shortage reflects the fact that the growth in the number of physicians will lag behind the growth in demand for their services due to population growth and the aging of the huge baby boom generation.

A physician shortage already exists in many areas of the United States: rural areas and poor urban areas. This problem stems from the fact that physicians do not always practice where they are needed the most. Whether they have been practicing for many years or are fresh out of medical school and residencies, most physicians prefer to live and practice in suburbs and the wealthier segments of urban areas (Burrows, Suh, and Hamann 2012). This fact means that physicians underserve rural areas and the poor, inner-city neighborhoods of urban areas.

To illustrate, about 20% of the U.S. population lives in rural areas, but only about 11% of physicians practice in rural areas. Because rural physicians tend to be nearer retirement age than urban physicians, their likely retirement in the years ahead may well increase the rural physician shortage. This shortage is critical for yet another reason: because poverty rates are higher among rural residents than urban residents, rural residents are often in worse health than urban residents and already lack access to adequate health care because they often live long distances from the nearest health care provider, hospital, or clinic. Because of these problems, the current shortage of rural physicians is especially harmful, and any increase in this shortage will only add to the health problems that rural residents already face. An estimated 7,000 additional physicians are needed to address the current physician shortage in rural counties (Petterson et al. 2013), and this shortfall will likely increase in the years ahead.

A physician shortage also exists for poor urban communities. Inner-city hospitals and clinics are often woefully understaffed, and physicians tend not to locate their offices within the poor neighborhoods of the nation's cities. At the same time, the residents of these neighborhoods are likely to be in worse health and thus in need of medical services. An estimated 13,500 additional physicians are needed to address the current physician shortage in inner-city neighborhoods (Petterson et al. 2013). This shortfall will again probably worsen in the years ahead.

The current physician shortage is especially significant for primary care, in view of the importance of primary care for people's general health. In this regard, the United States lags far behind other democratic nations. It has only 30 primary care physicians for every 100,000 residents, compared to 80 per 100,000 in the United Kingdom and 159 per 100,000 in France (Consumer Reports 2013).

To help address the physician shortages in rural and inner-city areas, it is important for medical schools to increase their recruitment of new students from these two locations. This is because new physicians who hail from these locations are more likely to want to return to them to practice (Walker et al. 2010). In this regard, the federal government needs to provide greater financial incentives (e.g., helping to pay off loans) for medical school graduates who decide to practice in rural or inner-city areas.

Women Physicians

The increase since the 1970s in the number of women physicians has prompted the medical profession and medical scholars to pay attention to these physicians' experiences. As the old saying goes, women have come a long way in the medical profession, but still have a long way to go. The problems they encounter as women during medical school and residencies (see chapter 7) often continue after they become practicing physicians (Anspach 2010). In these and other respects, their experiences as physicians reflect those facing women in other jobs and careers (Coontz 2014).

Career Advancement   For example, the early career phase is very important for someone's later career advancement. Yet women in medicine and many other occupations typically begin their careers at an age when it is biologically advantageous for them to have children, that is, their late 20s and early 30s. Once they become pregnant and have a child, women generally find themselves having to balance their career and family more often than men do. Pregnancy leads some women to eventually reduce their working hours before their child is born and most women to take at least a few weeks off after giving birth. Although many new mothers go back to full-time work soon thereafter, other women reduce their hours or suspend their careers altogether to raise their child. When mothers do work full-time, they are still more likely than fathers to take a child to and from day care or school, to medical appointments, and so forth. These situations all mean that women interrupt their careers more often than men do or at least cannot devote their full attention to their careers even if they are working full-time. These factors in turn help to account for women's lower salaries compared to men and make it more difficult for them to advance their careers.

The experiences of women physicians reflect these gender dynamics (Shams and El-Masry 2015). Like women in other occupations, women physicians typically have their first child at the beginning of their careers or even during medical school or residencies. Once the child is born, they find it more difficult than their male counterparts to balance career and family. As one physician has observed, "This period in a woman's life coincides with medical school, residency, and fellowship training, when work demands are high and finances are strained, with little money available to hire support personnel" (Verlander 2004:332). Women physicians generally spend more time than male physicians on parenting, and they are also more likely than male physicians to interrupt their careers for family reasons by working fewer hours or not at all for a period of time. Among physicians who are currently practicing, it is estimated that women work seven fewer hours per week than men (Williams, Pecenco, and Blair-Loy 2013). Like women in many other occupations, these gender differences in working patterns lead women physicians overall to lag behind their male counterparts in many aspects of career advancement.

In a related problem, women physicians who reduce their hours because of pregnancy, childbirth, and/or parenting needs have sometimes incurred the wrath of colleagues who resent having to take on the any medical responsibilities that the woman has had to give up. These colleagues also sometimes doubt the woman's commitment to her medical career (Verlander 2004). These problems again reflect the problems that women in other occupations often encounter.

The Gender Wage Gap   Women physicians' greater family responsibilities and fewer hours worked contribute to a large gender wage gap in the medical profession: male physicians earn much more money annually than female physicians, who earn only about 80% of what male physicians earn (Williams, Pecenco, and Blair-Loy 2013). Yet even when the different hours that female and male physicians tend to work are statistically controlled (meaning that physicians who work the same hours are in effect being compared), male physicians still earn about $56,000 more annually than female physicians (Seabury, Jena, and Chandra 2013).

A major reason for this gender gap is the fact that women physicians tend to concentrate in the medical specialties that earn less money, while male physicians tend to concentrate in the specialties that earn much more money (Riska 2010). For example, women comprise 60% of the nation's pediatricians but less than 20% of the nation's general surgeons (Association of American Medical Colleges 2014), whose annual compensation is much higher. The fact that women tend to concentrate in the lower-paying medical specialties helps to account for the gender wage gap they experience. Such **gender segregation** in the medical profession also occurs among other occupations. Most secretaries are women, for instance, whereas most carpenters are men. Gender segregation in the workforce helps explain why women earn less money than men from their jobs, and it also helps explain why women physicians earn less money than male physicians.

Yet, women earn less than men even within specific medical specialties. For example, even though 60% of pediatricians are women, these women still earn only about two-thirds the income earned by male pediatricians. In fact, women physicians earn less than male physicians even when age, specialty, and hours are statistically controlled. This fact indicates that other factors, such as possible gender discrimination or gender differences in salary-negotiating effectiveness, also account for the gender wage gap in the medical profession, although the exact mix of factors remains to be determined (Williams, Pecenco, and Blair-Loy 2013).

Physician-Patient Interaction

Medical sociologists have long been interested in understanding and explaining the interaction between physicians and patients. Talcott Parsons' (1951) famous concept of the *sick role*, discussed in chapter 4, assumed that it was best for patients and hence for society if patients occupy a very subordinate status in this interaction. Writing in 1951, Parsons thought that patients would maximize their health by always listening to their doctor and not questioning their doctor's advice and instructions.

Models of Physician-Patient Interaction

The Paternalistic Model   Parsons and other medical scholars at the time he developed the sick role concept favored the traditional, hierarchical model of the physician-patient relationship in which the physician is the "boss" and the patient the passive, obedient "follower." They believed that this type of relationship would help ensure that patients would be as healthy as possible. This so-called **paternalistic model** continued to be the favored model among physicians and medical scholars for several decades and is still a common model today. In this model, patients' visits with doctors tend to be brief, only about 15–20 minutes, and even hurried. The physician dominates these visits by asking the patient a series of questions and expecting and receiving concise answers. Patients are not given much, if any, time to ask questions and may even be intimidated by a physician's authoritarian manner from trying to clarify a physician's explanation or asking about other matters. In this model, physicians also do not inquire about family, work, and other nonmedical factors that may be affecting the patient's health or have the potential to do so.

As this brief description implies, physicians' communication styles contribute to the degree to which physician-patient interaction follows the paternalistic model. Although these styles have begun to change, as we will discuss shortly, several studies have found that physicians still tend to dominate conversation during office visits, often interrupting patients and not giving patients time to ask questions or to discuss their health concerns (Karnieli-Millera and Eisikovitsb 2009). Physicians use medical terms that the average patient cannot understand and, consciously or not, have a communication style that can be authoritarian and even intimidating to patients.

The Egalitarian Model   The paternalistic model began to fall out of favor among health scholars beginning in the 1960s and 1970s as the dominance of the medical profession began to decline because of the developments discussed earlier. All these developments helped erode the traditional patriarchal model of the physician-patient relationship in favor of a more *patient-centered* model, often called the **egalitarian model**. In this model, patients take a more proactive role in the physician-patient relationship through such activities as reading on the Internet about their health problem, asking their physician questions about the physician's diagnosis and treatment recommendations, and actively making decisions about medication and other treatment. At the same time, physicians under this model take the time to listen and respond to any concerns patients might raise and treat the patient as an equal in health care decision making (Elwyn et al. 2014). In this model, the physician's manner is decidedly nonauthoritarian so that patients will feel as comfortable as possible to ask any questions that might come to mind, in disclosing symptoms they might otherwise have kept hidden, and in voicing concerns about their health and aspects of their treatment (Levinson, Lesser, and Epstein 2010).

Research finds that the egalitarian model helps enhance the health of many patients compared to the paternalistic model (Draeger and Stern 2014; Rosen 2014; Roter and Hall 2013). A significant reason for this benefit is that patients whose interaction with physicians follows this model tend to be more satisfied with their physician overall and thus to follow the physician's advice and instructions regarding their health (Fuertes et al. 2015). Recognizing this benefit, health scholars encourage physicians to communicate with their patients more as equals than as subordinates and to help them feel at ease to ask questions and to express their feelings and concerns (Smith and Kirkpatrick 2013).

As beneficial as the egalitarian model might be, certain factors unfortunately make it difficult for many instances of physician-patient interaction to actually follow this model (Lovell, Lee, and Brotheridge 2010). First, office visits with personal physicians usually average only about 20 minutes (Chen, Wildon, and Jha 2009). This fact of scheduling may be necessary for physicians to see all their patients, but it leaves precious little time for the more extended conversation that ideally occurs under the egalitarian model. Second, office visits are just that, office visits, rather than home visits. The days of physicians visiting someone's home, where a patient will feel most comfortable, are long gone despite some signs of a recent comeback, and the mere fact of sitting in a medical office makes many patients uncomfortable and less likely to want to converse at length. Third, many patients are feeling pain or other discomfort, making them less able to engage in the extended conversation favored by the egalitarian model. Fourth, many physicians remain authoritarian in their manner and, consciously or not, make their patients reluctant to discuss their symptoms and to ask questions.

Gender, Race and Ethnicity, and Physician-Patient Interaction

In some science fiction world, people would always relate to other people in the same way regardless of their gender, race and ethnicity, or other aspects of their social backgrounds. Unfortunately, that world does not exist: in the real world in which we all live, gender, race and ethnicity, and other social factors do affect how we interact with each other. Before the 1980s, blatant sexism and racism often characterized social interaction in the United States, as scholarly accounts, novels, films, and TV shows have so often documented. Although gender and racial/ethnic prejudice and discrimination still remain, America thankfully has come a long way in the past few decades. For example, sexist and racist remarks that a generation or two ago were rather commonplace would almost certainly trigger shock and dismay today. Even so, gender and race and ethnicity continue to affect social interaction in many, often subtle ways, even if the participants in the interaction are not aware of this effect.

Medical sociologists and other health scholars have begun to pay attention to this dynamic in physician-patient interaction. Their research shows that gender and race and ethnicity indeed make a difference. In particular, the gender of both the physician and the patient may affect how the physician interacts with the patient and what tests and treatment the physician may suggest for the patient. Meanwhile, the race and ethnicity of the patient may similarly affect the physician's interaction and decisions regarding tests and treatment.

This body of research is important for at least two reasons. First, it reminds us that gender and race and ethnicity continue to influence how Americans interact with one another. Second, and more important for medical sociology, it suggests that physicians unconsciously make decisions and suggestions that may compromise the health of women and of persons of color. We review this body of research briefly, starting first with gender before turning to race and ethnicity.

Gender   The research on gender tries to answer two questions. First, does physicians' gender influence how they interact with patients and the advice and recommendations they may give to patients? Second, does patients' gender affect how physicians interact with them and the advice and recommendations their physicians may provide? Research on both questions finds that physician-patient interaction is indeed often *gendered* in the ways described.

The Impact of Physicians' Gender   Let's first consider the issue of whether and how physicians' own gender may affect their interaction with patients and their recommendations for tests and treatment. The large increase of women in the medical profession during the past few decades almost inevitably meant that scholars would become interested in this possible gender effect. Accordingly, scholars have observed or recorded (with the permission of the physicians and patients) actual office visits. They then analyze the visits to see whether female and male physicians tend to have different communication styles and whether patients respond differently to female and male physicians. Patients are also either surveyed or interviewed to see what they think of their physicians and other aspects of their medical care.

This growing body of research generally finds that physicians' gender does make a difference in these ways (Roter and Hall 2015). To be more specific, women physicians tend to have better communication skills and to be more patient centered than male physicians. This difference is thought to stem from gender socialization since childhood that produces differences between the sexes more generally in communication and social interaction. As a recent review of the research concluded:

> In some very important ways, women are better doctors than men and they were better even before going to medical school. . . . Decades of research . . . show that women in general are more relationship-oriented and egalitarian in their attitudes and conversational style, more expert in 'reading' others' personality and emotions, more skilled in nonverbal communication, and higher scoring on measures of emotional intelligence compared to men. (Roter and Hall 2015:273)

Reflecting these gender differences, women physicians tend to spend more time than male physicians with patients and are more likely to voice empathetic comments about the patients' welfare. They are also more likely to advise patients about their lifestyles and mental health. In turn, patients "open up" to female physicians more than to male physicians by talking about their symptoms, feelings, and other aspects of their lives (Roter and Hall 2015). They may also be more likely to accept advice regarding exercise and nutrition and the control of diabetes when it comes from female physicians than from male physicians (Kluger 2013; Schieber et al. 2014). Ironically, even though women physicians are more patient centered and effective as just described, patient satisfaction with female and male physicians is about equal, meaning that "patients don't give women doctors the credit they deserve" (Roter and Hall 2015:273).

The Impact of Patients' Gender   We earlier recounted the women's health movement of the 1970s that called attention to the women's health concerns that male physicians often ignored or belittled. Although the medical profession has become more enlightened about women's health needs since the 1970s, research continues to show that women's health concerns are often not taken seriously and, in this regard, receive worse health care than men. For example, female patients are more likely than male patients to say that male physicians were condescending and dismissive of their health concerns (Anspach 2010). Research also finds that physicians are more likely to disregard possibly serious health symptoms presented by women than those by men.

Research on this latter topic involves several methodologies. One methodology examines hospital records to see whether female and male patients who present with similar symptoms (cardiovascular symptoms are most often studied) are recommended for similar diagnostic testing and medical procedures. Another methodology has physicians view videos of female and male patients (either real patients or actors) who discuss their symptoms (cardiovascular symptoms are again most often studied), and the physicians are then asked to indicate what, if any, diagnostic tests they would order for the patient. The various types of research often, but not always, find that physicians are less likely to suggest appropriate diagnostic testing and treatment for female patients than for male patients (Anspach 2010).

Researchers on this topic assume the physicians are not being consciously sexist. Rather, they think that physicians are somehow not regarding the women's symptoms as serious as the men's symptoms, and that physicians (in regard to the cardiovascular symptoms research) may be thinking that the women's symptoms stem from anxiety or other emotional issues rather than from cardiovascular problems. In this regard, a 1990s' study of emergency-room chest-pain treatment found that men were more likely to receive heart medication and consultations, while women were more likely to be given antianxiety medication (Lehmann et al. 1996). Regardless of the actual reasons for this important gender difference in cardiovascular care, an unfortunate conclusion is that "there is considerable evidence that women are less likely than men to be treated aggressively for heart disease" (Anspach 2010:237) and that this disparity may shorten their lives.

Race and Ethnicity   Most research in this area concerns the degree to which physicians treat African American and non-Latino white patients differently by, for example, providing less medical attention to African American patients than to white patients with the same symptoms. Research on this topic involves methodologies similar to those for the gender differences in medical care just discussed, and the findings of this research mirror those for gender.

To be more specific, and focusing on cardiovascular symptoms (the subject of much of the research), physicians are less likely to order appropriate diagnostic testing and procedures for African American patients than for white patients with similar heart symptoms. In particular, African Americans are less likely than whites to receive or be recommended for procedures such as angioplasty, cardiac catheterization, and coronary bypass surgery, even among patients with similar incomes (Smedley, Stith, and Nelson 2003). In one study, several hundred physicians viewed videos of African American and white patients who were in fact trained actors, although the physicians did not know this. The "patients" all presented with similar symptoms, including chest pain. Even so, physicians were less likely to recommend cardiac catheterization for the African American patients than for the white patients (Schulman et al. 1999).

Other research has shown that racial bias also reduces the chances of African Americans receiving a kidney transplant. Patients who need kidney transplants must be put on a kidney transplant list to await a kidney from a live or recently deceased donor. Physicians consider many factors when they decide whether a kidney patient is a good candidate for a transplant list, including the patients' age and general health and likelihood of taking good care of themselves after receiving a new kidney. Race should not be one of these factors. Nonetheless, some research has found that African American kidney patients are less likely than white patients to be put on transplant lists (Patzer et al. 2012).

Researchers on this type of bias assume that it does not reflect conscious racial discrimination by physicians. Instead, they say it reflects unconscious racial bias, also known as *implicit bias,* which is also thought to underlie racial discrimination in employment and other areas of social life (Fisher and Borgida 2012). Physicians do not consciously feel that African American lives are less important than white lives. Instead, they may have other beliefs that play a role, such as (in regard to the heart studies) the belief that African Americans are more to blame for their poor heart health or might not take good care of themselves even if they did receive appropriate coronary treatment. It is likely that these types of beliefs or other unconscious racial biases help account for the racial discrimination that does occur in physician-patient interaction.

Regardless of the exact reasons for this discrimination, a conclusion from a systematic review of hundreds of studies on this subject is that "minority patients received fewer recommended treatments for diseases ranging from AIDS to cancer to heart disease" (Ansell and McDonald 2015:1087). These racial disparities remain even among patients with similar incomes and insurance status (having or not having insurance and type of insurance if they do have it). Physicians' implicit racial biases are thus thought to help account for the large, persistent racial disparity in health in the United States that chapter 5 discussed (Ansell and McDonald 2015).

Conclusion

The medical profession has come a long way since the colonial period. By the mid-twentieth century, it had achieved a position of dominance in the practice of medicine in the United States in the "golden age of doctoring." Since that era, certain developments have challenged the medical profession's dominance. Patient health movements charged that physicians had neglected their concerns and for this and other reasons compromised their health. New research evidence indicated that an egalitarian model of physician-patient interaction was better for patients' health than the traditional paternalistic model.

The medical profession began to change in other ways as well. Dominated by white males before the 1970s, the medical profession has since seen a large increase in the number of women physicians and a much smaller increase in physicians of color. Despite these strides, the profession's demographic makeup still does not begin to reflect that of the American population.

Troubling evidence of unconscious gender and racial biases in physician-patient interaction persists. In particular, physicians tend to provide a lower quality of care to women and to African Americans who present with symptoms of heart disease and other potentially serious health conditions. This evidence points to the need for the medical profession to educate its members about their biases and in this and other ways to ensure that patients are treated the same regardless of their gender and race.

Summary

1. The major defining characteristics of professions include autonomy, specialized knowledge, professional culture, authority, altruism, and the goal of monopolizing knowledge.

2. During the colonial era and through the early nineteenth century, many people practiced medicine with little or no formal medical training. The primary source of medical care for most colonial families was the women in these families.

3. Medicine became professionalized by the end of the nineteenth century thanks to the efforts of the AMA and other medical bodies to tighten education and licensure standards. Although this professionalization generally improved the practice of medicine, it also made health care more expensive and restricted the ability of midwives to help women give birth.

4. About one-third of the approximately one million allopathic physicians today are women, representing a large increase since the 1970s. At the same time, the increase in physicians of color since the 1970s has been rather minimal.

5. Physician shortages generally exist today across the United States, but especially in rural areas and in poor urban neighborhoods. The general physician shortage should become worse a decade from now thanks to the retirement or death of many physicians by that time.

6. Women physicians face many of the same problems that women medical students do. In addition, they have more problems than male physicians in balancing their careers with their family obligations, and their salaries are lower than those of male physicians.

7. The traditional model of physician-patient interaction favored a paternalistic role for the physician. Research evidence suggests that an egalitarian model is more likely to increase patient satisfaction and patient compliance with physicians' instructions and, for these reasons, to enhance patient health.

8. Women physicians tend to be more patient oriented than male physicians, but patients are not generally more satisfied with women physicians than with male physicians.

9. Research evidence suggests that physicians are more likely to provide a lower standard of care for female patients than for male patients and for African American patients than for white patients. These disparities are thought to stem from unconscious gender and racial biases on the part of physicians.

Giving It Some Thought

You are one of five new physicians in a large medical practice. Of the five new physicians, three are women and two are men. After having separate informal conversations with each of the other four new physicians, you have realized that the three new women physicians have annual salaries that are about $2,000 lower than those of the two new male physicians. What, if anything, do you do with this new knowledge?

Key Terms

active physicians, 133
altruism, 127
authority, 126
autonomy, 126
domestic medicine, 127
defensive medicine, 131
egalitarian model, 138
gender segregation, 137

medical malpractice, 131
midwife, 129
monopolizing knowledge, 127
paternalistic model, 137
profession, 126
professional culture, 126
specialized knowledge, 126

Other Health Care Providers
Conventional and Alternative

LEARNING QUESTIONS

1. Why is nursing interesting from a theoretical perspective?

2. What are the different types of nurses?

3. Why will the nursing shortage worsen, and what are the effects of the nursing shortage?

4. Why do many hospital nurses experience stress and burnout?

5. Why is good oral health important for more general physical health?

6. Which complementary and alternative medical approaches show promise of being effective?

Health and Illness in the News

Rosemary White-Traut, a Chicago hospital nurse, noticed a long time ago that mothers of premature babies were afraid to handle their newborns and just let them sleep in their incubators. This practice concerned White-Traut because she assumed that the babies would feed more and otherwise prosper if their mothers cradled them, talked to them, and did everything that parents of healthy newborns should ideally do. White-Traut developed an instructional program to help these mothers overcome their fears and to interact with their infants. She then found that the babies whose mothers had this training tended to grow more (weight and length) than premature newborns whose mothers did not have the training. The National Institutes of Health published White-Traut's research on this topic in spring 2015. (Novak 2015)

Physicians are certainly not the only health care providers. Nurses, who comprise the largest health care occupation, are the unsung heroes of the health care system. They work in hospitals, physicians' practices, health care clinics, schools, nursing homes, and many other settings. They labor long hours for wages that are lower than they should be and often spend much time caring for patients with serious problems. Many other health care occupations also exist. Most of these occupations provide **mainstream health care**, which is health care based on the biomedical model and widely regarded as normal and conventional. Other individuals and occupations provide **complementary and alternative health care** (also called *complementary and alternative medicine*, or CAM), which is health care that is considered outside the boundaries of standard medical treatment. This chapter examines both types of health care.

Mainstream Health Care

The types of mainstream health care providers are far too numerous to list them all here, but they include dentists and dental hygienists and assistants, nurses, optometrists and opticians, osteopathic physicians, pharmacists, podiatrists, physical and occupational therapists, psychologists, and registered dietitians. We begin with nurses in view of their critical importance to the entire population and the amount of research that exists on nursing and nurses.

Nurses and Nursing

As a health care profession, nursing is interesting from a theoretical perspective. This interest stems from the fact that nursing is indeed a profession in many ways, as it fits the definition of a profession presented in chapter 8: an occupation that is highly skilled and that requires prolonged training. Nursing also possesses several of the defining characteristics of professions that chapter 8 identified, including specialized knowledge, professional culture, and altruism. However, nursing does not fully demonstrate the two remaining characteristics, autonomy and authority. The reason for this is that nurses are subordinate to physicians and thus lack complete autonomy in the practice of their occupation, even if they often exercise independent decision making. By the same token, nurses do not exercise authority over physicians (even if they do exercise authority over patients), so they have only limited authority.

Although nursing is a profession, then, nurses do not enjoy *full* professional status. The fact that almost all nurses are women and the majority of physicians are men aggravates this situation, given women's subordinate status to men in society more generally. These two facts—nursing's limited professional status and nursing's gendered composition—color both the history of nursing and the present situation of nursing. To provide a context for the status of nursing today, we first review nursing's history (D'Antonio 2010; Judd and Sitzman 2014; Reverby 2013).

A Brief History of Nursing   Nursing is a relatively recent profession. Recall from chapter 8 that women were their families' primary health care providers in colonial America and for centuries earlier in other parts of the world. This fact raises an interesting question: Why was it women rather than men who served their families' health care needs? The answer to this question is that people back then (and many people still today) considered women as inherently more gentle and caring than men and thus better suited to attend to their families' health care. As a result, women were expected to care for their husbands, children, and aging parents.

Some women also provided health care outside the walls of their own family's dwelling. Women who were proficient in various aspects of health care would help other families deal with their medical needs. In line with the old saying that "it takes a village," these women saw their health care provision as a way to help their communities, and sometimes they received small payments for their services. Other women became midwives (see chapter 8). During the nineteenth century, many American women also performed various health care duties, often involving menial labor, in hospitals, private homes, or other settings. Although some of these duties were what we would now call nursing duties, most of these women had no formal training in nursing and were not formally nurses in the way that term implies today.

As the medical profession advanced during the nineteenth century, women's customary role as health care providers could have meant that they would attend medical school in great numbers and become a key part of the medical profession. However, as chapter 7 emphasized, most medical schools refused to admit women, as the dominant ideology of the time was that women belonged in the home. Because of this ideology and the medical schools' restrictions, an untold number of women who might have wanted to become physicians never were able to pursue their dreams. The same fate awaited the many midwives who lost their jobs as the medical profession slowly but surely gained a monopoly over obstetrics (see chapter 8). Any midwives who might have wanted to become physicians so that they continue helping women with pregnancy and childbirth would have again found medical school doors closed to them because of their sex.

Florence Nightingale's Early Influence For all these reasons, nursing became the only occupation that women interested in health care could realistically expect to pursue. Formal training of nurses in the United States and thus the development of nursing as a profession took hold gradually during the nineteenth and early twentieth centuries. A key figure in the nursing's development was the celebrated Florence Nightingale (1820–1910), an English woman acclaimed as the founder of the nursing profession. (In honor of Nightingale, new nurses today commonly recite the Nightingale Pledge, in which they promise to follow high standards of care and to be devoted to the nursing profession.)

Nightingale gained fame during the Crimean War of 1853–1856, in which Great Britain joined with France, Sardinia, and Turkey to fight Russia. During this war, she trained and managed a team of nurses who provided critical care to wounded soldiers. This level of care made clear to British citizens nursing's potential to deal with health problems in the civilian population. Meanwhile, the publicity Nightingale gained for her work during the Crimean War allowed her to expand nursing training in England after the war ended. In 1860, she established the world's first nonreligious nursing school at St. Thomas' Hospital in London. This school soon spurred the establishment of nursing schools in other European nations. In many ways, the development of nursing as a profession had begun.

In just a few years, a war on the other side of the Atlantic Ocean also advanced the development of nursing as a profession. That war, of course, was the Civil War, the bloodiest war in American history. Nurses proved indispensable aid during the Civil War by tending to the tens of thousands of wounded on battlefield after battlefield. As with the Crimean War, the nurses' success indicated to Americans the potential of nursing to help the general population. Three schools of nursing opened in 1873 in Boston, New Haven, and New York, respectively. Influenced by the post-Civil War women's rights movement to pursue a career, the students at these schools tended to come from relatively wealthy families.

These schools ignited a nursing school boom in the United States, with the number of schools, most of them run by hospitals, exceeding 1,700 by 1920. Although they were called "schools," many of these units actually provided only minimal medical training to their nursing students. Instead, they mainly coordinated the care that the students provided to patients. Accordingly, much of what the students did was menial labor rather than real health care.

Given the popular assumption back then that women were naturally more caring, these nursing students were expected to work an exhausting 10–12 hours daily without complaint even though they were generally not paid for their work. As historian Susan Reverby (2013:275) observes of the hospitals' motivation for establishing nursing schools, "Administrators quickly realized that opening a 'nursing school' provided their hospitals . . . with a young, disciplined, and cheap labor force. . . . The service needs of the hospital continually overrode the educational requirements of the schools." Reverby (2013:276) adds that hospitals were able to exploit the nursing students' labor because of their gender: "And because the work force was almost entirely women, altruism, sacrifice, and submission were expected, encouraged, indeed, demanded."

After these nurses completed their hospital school training, the hospitals would usually not hire them because then they would have to be paid. This situation forced the new nurses to work in private homes or for local health agencies. In this regard, they had to compete for employment with women who were calling themselves nurses even though they had had no formal training.

The Twentieth Century   Concerned by this situation, nursing reformers, including the American Nurses Association (ANA), which began as the Nurses Associated Alumnae in 1896 and was renamed in 1911, sought to establish licensure standards for nursing so that hospitals would have to train their nurses well enough to meet these standards. Their efforts succeeded, and most states had imposed licensing requirements by the end of the 1920s. However, because these requirements were rather weak, they did not really improve the training of nurses very much.

The ANA continued its efforts to advance nursing training and, in turn, to improve nursing's professional status. By the 1960s, some colleges and universities had established nursing degrees, and their ranks grew rapidly over the ensuing decades. So, too, did the requirement of a college degree for the practice of nursing. As women began attending college more than in the past thanks in part to the contemporary women's movement that began in the late 1960s, the new college nursing programs initially attracted many of these new students. Ironically, however, as career opportunities opened up to women in traditionally male occupations, enrollment in the college nursing programs waned to an extent. Despite this development, the new college programs and stricter education and other licensure requirements furthered the professionalization of nursing and improved nursing's professional status.

A Profile of Nurses Today   The United States now has about 4 million nurses. This huge number is roughly four times greater than the number of physicians, and it makes nursing one of the very largest of all U.S. occupations. Nurses around the nation work in a variety of health care settings, including hospitals, health clinics, physicians' offices, colleges and universities, nursing homes, and private homes. This section takes a brief look at the types of nurses and at their sociodemographic backgrounds.

Types of Nurses   The standard classification of nurses reflects the kind of formal education they receive and the duties they then perform as nurses. Three major categories of nurses exist under this classification. We present these categories in order of increasing educational requirements and complexity of professional duties (Bureau of Labor Statistics 2015; Kaiser Family Foundation 2015).

Licensed practical nurses (LPNs; also called *licensed vocational nurses*) rank at the bottom of the nursing hierarchy. To say LPNs rank at the bottom should certainly not be taken as an insult. Instead, this statement merely indicates that LPNs receive less education than other nurses and exercise less complex duties as they practice their profession. LPNs typically have a high-school degree, take a one-year state-approved program of classroom and clinical instruction, and must pass a national examination. They provide very basic nursing care and work under the supervision of physicians and registered nurses. The median annual wage (2012 data) of LPNs is about $42,000, and there are more than 730,000 LPNs in the United States.

Registered nurses (RNs), the bulk of the nursing profession, typically have one of the following: (1) a two-year college degree in nursing, (2) a four-year college degree in nursing, or (3) or a diploma from an approved nursing program, usually run by a hospital. Their education consists of courses in the basic sciences and in nursing care as well as clinical instruction. RNs perform a variety of complex patient-care duties and have a very demanding job. The number of RNs, whose median wage is about $65,000, is about 3.1 million.

Advanced practice nurses (APNs) are the most highly trained nurses. They typically have a master's degree or the equivalent training and perform highly skilled duties depending on their particular training. APN is actually a miscellaneous category that includes *clinical nurse specialists* (in such areas cardiac care or oncology); *nurse anesthetists* (who assist with anesthesia), *certified nurse midwives* (who assist with childbirth), and *nurse practitioners* (who perform many traditional physician duties). The number of APNs of all types exceeds 150,000, and their median annual wage exceeds $96,000.

Nurse practitioners (NPs) are often confused with *physician assistants* (PAs). PAs are not nurses, but their responsibilities do mirror those of NPs, so this confusion is understandable. A major difference between the two professions is that NPs work independently of or in collaboration with a physician (depending on a particular state's regulations), while PAs work under the supervision of a physician. Most of the more than 160 accredited PA programs in the United States offer a master's degree, which is the typical level of education that PAs receive. There are about 90,000 PAs in the nation, and their median annual wage is about $91,000.

Some tension has developed recently between physicians and NPs. The reason for this tension is that NPs perform many traditional physician duties. Recognizing this fact, health reform advocates have called for the greater use of NPs in primary care settings for three reasons: (1) to help compensate for physician shortages (see chapter 8); (2) to treat the millions of newly insured people under the Affordable Care Act (Obamacare); and (3) to lower the cost of primary care, since NPs earn much lower incomes than physicians do (Chen 2013).

Physician organizations oppose this view and say that NPs are simply not qualified to replace physicians. Nursing organizations reply that research shows that NPs' primary care is as good as physicians' primary care and that physicians fear loss of income from the greater use of NPs (Tavernise 2015). Commenting on this debate, one health economist concluded, "The doctors are fighting a losing battle. The nurses are like insurgents. They are occasionally beaten back, but they'll win in the long run. They have economics and common sense on their side" (Tavernise 2015).

Sociodemographic Backgrounds of Nurses Who are the nation's nurses? It is helpful to know the sociodemographic composition of nurses in terms of gender, race and ethnicity, and education.

Gender Starting with gender, about 91% of all RNs and 92% of all LPNs are women, meaning that 8%–9% of all RNs and LPNs are men (Landivar 2013). This latter percentage represents an increase from 1970, when only about 3% of all nurses were men. Many nursing schools refused to admit men before a 1981 U.S. Supreme Court ruling that this refusal was unconstitutional; it is also true that before the 1980s, nursing was considered a "women's job" more than it is now. Men comprise a much greater proportion (41%) of nurse anesthesiologists. Although men comprise only a small proportion of all nurses, male RNs earn about $5,100 more annually than female RNs (Muench et al. 2015). The reasons for this gender pay gap remain unknown but probably reflect those discussed in chapter 8 for the gender pay gap among physicians. For example, female nurses may lose work time and pay because of their family responsibilities, and they may have lower pay simply because of a "lingering bias that a man is more of an expert because he's a man," as one nursing professor put it (Saint Louis 2015:A20).

Race and Ethnicity. Turning to race and ethnicity, nurses are not very representative of the diversity of the U.S. population. Although people of color comprise more than one-third of the general population, they comprise only 19% of RNs (American Association of Colleges of Nursing 2014a). To be more precise, 83% of RNs are white, but only 6% are African American, 3% are Latina/o, 6% are Asian, and the remaining 3% are Native American, Native Hawaiian or Pacific Islander, or members of other backgrounds. The nursing profession recognizes the need to increase representation of underrepresented racial/ethnic groups in the profession and has implemented several measures, including the use of scholarships, to attract people from these groups into nursing schools (American Association of Colleges of Nursing 2014a).

Education. The United States has more than 1,900 accredited nursing schools, almost half of which offer a baccalaureate degree. Most schools are affiliated with a college, university, or hospital. Depending on their affiliation and the nature of their programs, nursing schools offer a diploma, two-year associate's degree, or four-year baccalaureate degree. In 2010, about 144,000 individuals took the national nursing examination for the first time. Of this number, about 40% had attended a bachelor's program, and the remaining 60% had attended a program offering an associate's degree or diploma (National Center for Health Workforce Analysis 2013).

As these figures indicate, the majority of new nurses do not have a four-year college (baccalaureate) degree. Because some nurses obtain further formal education after entering the nursing profession, it is instructive to examine the highest level of education obtained by nurses of all ages combined. A recent national survey of RNs found that 40% had a diploma or associate's degree, 59% had a baccalaureate or master's degree in nursing or another field, and 1% had a doctoral degree in nursing or another field (Budden et al. 2013). By contrast, fewer than one-third of nurses in 1980 had a baccalaureate degree.

This increase in the proportion of nurses with at least a baccalaureate degree is significant for at least two reasons. First, as nurses achieve a higher level of education, the status of the nursing profession should rise as well. Second, and probably more important, the American Nurses Association (2015) and the Institute for Medicine (2011) emphasize the need for baccalaureate training for nurses in view of the increasing complexity of medicine and the increase in the number of older people as the baby boom reaches its older years. The increasing educational levels of the nursing workforce, then, will help meet the nation's many health needs in the years ahead.

Nursing's Challenges and Opportunities   Nursing today continues its efforts to enhance its professional status and to advance other professional needs such as higher wages. This section examines some of the major challenges and opportunities faced by nurses and the nursing profession.

A Nursing Shortage   Chapter 8 emphasized that the United States now has a physician shortage, particularly in rural communities and poor urban areas, and that this shortage will worsen over the next decade as many older physicians retire. A nursing shortage also exists now, and this shortage, too, promises to worsen over the next decade as hundreds of thousands of nurses retire. Because nurses provide so much care and services for patients in hospitals and other settings, this shortage worries nursing officials and health care administrators. Of special concern is the fact that the baby boom generation will continue reaching its older years during the next decade and experiencing the health problems that often come with old age. Because of their sheer numbers, these older baby boomers will need more nursing care and services than any prior generation of older Americans. For this reason, the nursing shortage is especially worrisome.

By 2022, more than one million job openings are projected for registered nurses due to the retirement or death of current nurses and the need for additional nurses to address the current nursing shortage (American Association of Colleges of Nursing 2014b). It is estimated that 260,000 nursing openings will go unfilled by 2025 due to the lack of nurses. To address this shortage, the United States needs to graduate an additional 30,000 nurses annually, an increase of 30% over the current number of graduates, for the foreseeable future. Unfortunately, nursing schools must reject 80,000 qualified applicants annually (2012 data) for lack of faculty, classroom space, and other constraints.

The nursing shortage is thought to have several consequences (American Association of Colleges of Nursing 2014b). First, it almost certainly increases the stress on current nurses as they juggle patient caseloads that are heavier because of the shortage. Second, much research finds that these heavy caseloads significantly impair the quality of patient care and raise the risk of death for hospital patients. Third, the stress and other problems stemming from the shortage are thought to be prompting many nurses to retire from nursing.

Stress and Burnout We just mentioned that the nursing shortage increases nurses' stress, especially hospital nurses' stress. Although this increase is very worrisome, it is also true that nursing is highly stressful even with average patient caseloads: even though these caseloads are only average, they still keep nurses extremely busy and leave them rather exhausted. A survey of 122 hospital nurses identified two additional sources of stress in addition to their caseloads: (1) the nurses' belief that they were not able to deal adequately with the emotional demands of patients and their families; and (2) the nurses' frequent need to help patients who are dying and to communicate with families of patients who have just died (Gray-Tofta and Anderson 2002). Nurses with higher stress were more likely to be dissatisfied with their job and also to resign their position.

Interviews with and observations of nurses in hospitals and other settings routinely document the stress and other problems that nurses face in their daily jobs (Robbins 2015). The emotional trauma that hospital nurses often experience is evident in the recollection of a new hospital nurse who had just dealt with her first dying patient, an infant in neonatal intensive care. The baby died in her arms after the parents withdrew life support. The nurse recalled,

> Right then and there, I just got a knot in my stomach because I knew that this was my first time. *Don't cry; don't do anything*—it was like I was really trying to talk myself into holding back from feeling anything. And then the parents didn't want to hold him, and as bad as I felt and as teary eyed as I was, I decided I wanted to hold him; somebody had to hold him. I just felt it was unfair to allow him to die alone. Since then, I have gone through this experience two or three more times. And it gets easier—not so much easier emotionally, but you are in better control of it. You might cry only one or two tears instead of bawling your eyes out. It is not as gut wrenching as it is the first time. It never feels better—it

is just easier to hold back until you are driving home by yourself and nobody can see you crying. (Gutkind 2013:vi–vii)

Illness and Injury Adding to nurses' stress are the physical demands and risks of their job. Because they often have to lift heavy patients, they often experience back, neck, and shoulder pain. In addition, nurses are commonly exposed to infectious diseases and to needles and other instruments that can cause injuries. Meanwhile, their high levels of stress and burnout can impair their immune systems and leave them prone to various illnesses. All these problems translate to a high risk for illness and injury among hospital nurses. This risk is so high that nurses rank fifth among all occupations in workdays missed because of workplace injuries and illnesses (American Nurses Association 2011). A national survey of nurses found that three-fourths were concerned about the effects of stress, almost two-thirds were concerned about incurring a musculoskeletal injury, and more than 40% were concerned about acquiring an infectious illness. More than half had experienced musculoskeletal pain during the past year from their job, and more than half had also been threatened or verbally abused (American Nurses Association 2011).

Lack of Full Autonomy Earlier we pointed out that although nursing is a profession, nurses lack the full autonomy normally associated with the definition of a profession. This situation has existed ever since nursing began as a profession, and it continues to concern the ANA for at least three reasons (Weston 2010).

First, the lack of full autonomy means that nursing enjoys less professional status than it would enjoy if nurses had more autonomy. Second, nurses differ in the degree of autonomy they enjoy (due to differences in hospital operating procedures and individual physicians' inclinations), and nurses who have less autonomy are less satisfied with their jobs than nurses with more autonomy. Third, because nurses are so often on the frontlines of patient care, they are often called upon to exercise independent judgment amid dire circumstances, and sometimes they even have to correct physicians' mistakes regarding medication and medical procedures. To the extent this is true, patient care is likely to be enhanced in such circumstances if nurses can proceed appropriately without having to wait for a physician's approval. As one physician has written, "Nurses' observations and suggestions have saved many doctors from making fatal mistakes in caring for patients. Though most physicians are grateful for such aid, a few dismiss it—out of arrogance and a mistaken belief that a nurse cannot know more than a doctor" (Altman 2014). Unfortunately, physicians have been known to bully nurses who question a physician's judgment. This situation is unfortunate as it intimidates nurses from pointing out possible physician mistakes. As one oncology nurse has observed, "The silencing of nurses inevitably creates more opportunities for error" (Brown 2013:SR5).

Nurses' Subordination to Physicians Most nurses feel that physicians do not show them enough respect (Chambliss 2008; Leape et al. 2012). To the extent this perception is accurate, it stems in no small degree from the fact that nurses are subordinate to physicians. This subordination occurs for two reasons. The most important reason is that physicians supervise nurses, as just discussed. The second reason arises from the gendered nature of the typical physician-nurse relationship. Recall that most nurses are women and that the majority of physicians continue to be men. Ever since nursing began as a profession, the most common dynamic of physician-nursing interaction, then, has had female nurses work under the supervision of male physicians, reflecting a gender hierarchy still found so often in the larger society (Ulrich 2010).

The hierarchical nature of physician-nurse interaction thus reflects nursing's lower autonomy and professional status, but it also reflects the hierarchical gender dynamics found in the larger society. Fortunately, the gendered nature of physician-nurse interaction has lessened during the past few decades as nurses have become more assertive about their work responsibilities in line with society's changing gender roles, as male physicians have become less patriarchal in their interaction with female nurses, and as more women have become physicians. Some evidence indicates that women physicians treat nurses in a more egalitarian way than male physicians do (Porter 2001).

Other Mainstream Health Care Providers

The fact that so many different mainstream health care providers exist in addition to nurses and physicians reminds us that people have many different health care needs. This section outlines several of these occupations and draws on the Bureau of Labor Statistics' *Occupational Outlook Handbook* for much of its information (Bureau of Labor Statistics 2015).

Dentists and Dental Hygienists and Assistants You have probably heard many times since childhood that you should brush your teeth at least twice a day, floss daily, and see a dentist twice a year. This is sound advice. Oral health and health care are increasingly recognized as vital components of the body's overall health status. Poor oral health not only contributes to many mouth-related problems, ranging from cavities to gum disease to the loss of all natural teeth, but can also release harmful bacteria into the rest of the body and raise the risk of heart disease, stroke, and uncontrolled diabetes. This *mouth-body connection* is the subject of increasing attention from physicians, dentists, and other health care professionals and researchers (Duran-Pinedoa and Frias-Lopez 2015). Against this backdrop, dentists and dental hygienists should be regarded as some of our most important health care providers, even if no one seems to like going to the dentist.

Dentists receive either a Doctor of Dental Surgery (DDS) or Doctor of Dental Medicine (DMD) four-year degree from an accredited dental school, which they typically enter after receiving a bachelor's degree, and then must pass appropriate written and clinical examinations before receiving their license. Just as physicians may engage in general practice or instead a specialty, so can dentists. Dental specialties include *orthodontics* (with which many readers of this book are all too familiar!), *oral and maxillofacial surgery*, *pediatric dentistry*, and *endodontics* (root canal procedures). There are about 150,000 dentists in the United States, and their median annual pay is about $150,000 (2012 data). Women comprise almost one-fourth of all dentists and about 40% of new dentists. The major national organization of dentists is the American Dental Association (ADA). Like the parallel organizations for physicians (American Medical Association) and nurses (American Nurses Association), the ADA engages in many kinds of advocacy efforts to advance the professional interests of its members and of the dentistry profession more generally.

More than 60 dental schools operate in the United States and another 10 schools in Canada. Several states have three or more dental schools, but some states, including New Hampshire, North and South Dakota, and Vermont have no dental school. The American Dental Education Association (ADEA) is the governing organization for all North American dental schools.

Dental hygienists are key figures in many and probably most dental practices. They clean teeth, examine patients for evidence of cavities and other oral health problems, and educate patients about dental care. Their licensing requirements include graduation (associate's degree) from an accredited dental hygiene school and passing of appropriate written and clinical examinations. There are almost 200,000 dental hygienists in the United States, and their median annual pay is about $70,200.

Dental assistants engage in important tasks for a dentist's office that do not include actual patient care. These tasks include sterilizing dental instruments and laying them out for use by a dentist or dental hygienist, preparing materials to create temporary crowns, processing dental X-rays, and record keeping. Some states require dental assistants to graduate from an accredited dental assistant program and pass an examination, but other states have no licensing requirements. The accredited programs found in some states are typically located at a community college and involve 1–2 years of coursework depending on the state. There are slightly more than 300,000 dental assistants in the United States, and their median annual pay is about $35,000.

Opthalmologists, Optometrists and Opticians   Eye care is also important. Ophthalmologists are physicians (MD degree) who specialized in ophthalmology. They are licensed to perform eye surgery and to treat serious vision problems in other ways. Although ophthalmologists are certainly important for eye care, most people, children and adults alike, with normal vision problems (i.e., near-sightedness and far-sightedness) see an optometrist for their eye care.

Optometrists examine our eyes for these problems, but they also examine our eyes for more serious problems such as glaucoma and corneal issues. As many readers of this book again know all too well, optometrists also prescribe contact lenses and eyeglasses for patients who need vision correction. Optometrists receive a Doctor of Optometry (OD) degree from a four-year Doctor of Optometry program, which students typically enter after receiving a bachelor's degree elsewhere. There are slightly more than 33,000 optometrists in the United States, and their median annual pay is almost $100,000. The national organization for the nation's 20 optometry schools is the Association of Schools and Colleges of Optometry.

Opticians (also called *dispensing opticians*) provide patients with eyeglasses and contact lenses based on prescriptions issued by optometrists or ophthalmologists. Some states require licensure, while other states do not. Many opticians typically have a one-year or two-year degree from a community college, while other opticians have a high-school degree and receive on-the-job training while working under an optician's supervision. About half the states require licensure for opticians. There are about 68,000 opticians in the United States, and their median annual pay is about $33,300.

Osteopathic Physicians   There was a time when *osteopathic physicians* (also called *osteopaths*) were considered alternative health care providers and even quacks. That time is long past, as osteopaths work today alongside traditional allopathic physicians in hospitals, physician practices, and other medical settings. Osteopathic physicians prescribe medications and in other respects perform the same tasks that allopathic physicians perform, including surgery.

Osteopathic students comprise about one-fourth of all medical students in the nation today and receive their education and training from one of the nation's 33 osteopathic medical schools, which offer a four-year curriculum similar to that offered by traditional medical schools. Upon graduation and passing of a national examination, they receive the Doctor of Osteopathic Medicine (DO) degree and then complete an internship and residency program that takes from two to seven years. In all these respects, their education and career path parallels that of allopathic medical students. The major national organization of osteopaths is the American Osteopathic

Association. Like other professional organizations, it undertakes various efforts to advance the professional interests of its members and of osteopathy more generally.

The United States now has more than 90,000 osteopathic physicians, practicing and no longer practicing, in the United States, compared to about ten times that number of allopathic physicians (American Osteopathic Association 2014). They are found in every state, although historically they have tended to practice in the Northeastern and Midwestern states. Slightly more than one-third of all osteopaths are women, and almost half of osteopathic students are women. These figures are very similar to those for allopathic physicians. Of the approximately 22,000 osteopathic students, 2.7% are African American; 19.3% are Asian or Pacific Islander; 3.6% are Latino; 0.5% are Native American; and 67.2% are non-Latino White (2012–2013 data). These figures are again similar to those for allopathic students.

Osteopathy's overall philosophy of health and medical treatment derives from the views of its founder, Andrew Taylor Still (1828–1917), a nineteenth-century U.S. physician. Still believed that musculoskeletal problems underlie many physical health problems because they impede normal blood flow, and he also thought that medications and alcohol harmed the body's health and were generally immoral to ingest. He founded the world's first osteopathic medical school in Kirksville, MO, in 1892.

Historically, osteopathic physicians have differed from allopathic physicians in certain ways that account for their earlier perception as alternative providers. These differences reflect Still's beliefs as the founder of osteopathy. Compared to allopathic physicians, osteopathic physicians traditionally have taken a more holistic approach to health by emphasizing preventive medicine (such as a good diet and proper posture) more than allopathic physicians have emphasized. In another important difference, they have also emphasized the proper alignment of the body's musculoskeletal system for overall physical health and the body's ability to heal itself. Some and perhaps many osteopaths thus practice *osteopathic manipulative medicine* by using their hands to pressure, bend, and stretch patients' joints and muscles.

Despite these historic differences, the two types of physicians today are rather indistinguishable and, as noted earlier, work alongside each other in various medical settings. Accordingly, chapter 8's discussion of physicians is also relevant for osteopathic physicians, even if that discussion relied primarily on studies of allopathic physicians because they comprise the bulk of all physicians.

Pharmacists As you are no doubt aware, *pharmacists* dispense prescriptions for medicine provided by physicians or other health care providers who are authorized to write prescriptions. They also routinely answer consumers' questions about medications and other health concerns. Pharmacists are found in almost every community and work not only in drugstore chains like CVS, Walgreens, and Rite Aid, but also in the pharmacy sections of Walmart and other big box stores and of supermarkets. They also work in hospitals and health clinics. Their sheer ubiquity makes pharmacists significant members of the nation's health care system.

Aspiring pharmacists attend an accredited pharmacy school to obtain the Doctor of Pharmacy (Pharm.D.) degree. To receive their license, which is required by every state, they also must pass two examinations in pharmacy knowledge and pharmacy law, respectively. The more than 120 accredited pharmacy schools throughout the nation receive their accreditation from the Accreditation Council for Pharmacy Education (ACPE); the schools' governing body is the American Association of Colleges of Pharmacy (AACP). Pharmacy schools exist in every state except for Alaska and Delaware and comprise more than 62,000 students and 6,000 faculty. Many require a four-year college degree for admission, but others require only two years of college. Almost all pharmacy schools have a four-year curriculum, while a few enable students to graduate within three years. Whatever the length of their education, students typically take courses in basic sciences, pharmacology, and medical ethics, and they also perform an internship in a pharmacy, hospital, or other setting.

The United States has almost 300,000 pharmacists, whose annual median pay is about $117,000. Their major professional association is the American Pharmacists Association (APhA), founded in 1852 in Philadelphia and headquartered today in Washington, DC.

Physical Therapists   Physical therapy is another important and increasingly common health care occupation. Thanks in large part to the aging of the baby boom generation, employment of physical therapists is expected to grow more rapidly than employment for other occupations within the next decade. Physical therapists help people to recover from injuries and relieve the pain and difficulty of movement arising from arthritis, diabetes, and other chronic illnesses. They work in hospitals, nursing homes, physician practices, and other health care settings. There are more than 200,000 physical therapists in the United States, and their median annual pay is about $80,000.

Physical therapists must be licensed in every state. To receive their license, they must obtain the Doctor of Physical Therapy (DPT) degree from more than 200 physical therapy programs accredited by the Commission on Accreditation in Physical Therapy Education. These programs' admission requirements include a bachelor degree, and they typically have a three-year curriculum that includes courses in the basic sciences and in biomechanics and pharmacology and a clinical internship. Once they receive their degree, physical therapists may choose to apply for a one-year clinical residency in which they acquire additional skills and knowledge. Whether or not they choose to pursue a residency, all physical therapists must pass a national examination to receive their license, and some must also satisfy additional requirements depending on the state in which they wish to practice.

The American Physical Therapy Association (APTA) is the major professional association of physical therapists. APTA emphasizes the benefits of physical therapy for many conditions, including the fact that physical therapy is often an effective alternative to prescription drugs and/or surgery for back pain, knee pain, and other conditions.

Podiatrists   Podiatrists treat various problems of the foot, ankle, and lower leg. These problems include in-grown toenails, fungus and other diseases, and certain deformities. Podiatrists may prescribe medications and perform surgery, and they may also recommend corrective devices for the foot.

Aspiring podiatrists obtain a Doctor of Podiatric Medicine (DPM) degree after receiving a bachelor's degree (or at least three years of undergraduate work) and then complete a three-year residency. There are only nine accredited podiatric medicine colleges in the United States; these schools are found in Arizona, California (two schools), Florida, Illinois, Iowa, New York, Ohio, and Pennsylvania. The typical DPM program involves a four-year curriculum that includes the basic sciences during the first two years and clinical rotations during the last two years. To receive their license, new podiatrists must pass a national examination; some states also require their own examination.

There are about 11,000 podiatrists in the United States, and their median annual pay is about $116,000. Their employment prospects are much better than average during the next decade, thanks again to the aging baby boom generation. Podiatrists' national professional association is the American Podiatric Medical Association (APMA), headquartered in Bethesda, MD.

Complementary and Alternative Medicine (CAM)

If scientific (biomedical) medicine is mainstream medicine and vice versa, then it is fair to say that CAM existed before scientific medicine developed and continues to exist today. Since before the dawn of scientific medicine, individuals have attempted to use nonscientific and nonbiomedical means to heal other people. Many such alternative measures are still popular today, and in fact have gained popularity since the 1960s as criticism of the medical profession and health care system grew (see chapter 8).

The terms *complementary medicine* and *alternative medicine* are both used to refer to unconventional and nonstandard methods of healing and thus are fairly synonymous and used as such here. That said, "complementary medicine" technically refers to alternative treatments that are used *along with* conventional, biomedical treatments, while "alternative medicine" refers to treatments that are used *instead of* conventional treatments (Shi and Singh 2015). *Integrative medicine* is often used as a synonym for complementary medicine or for CAM as a whole (Baer 2010).

Many CAM therapies exist, including acupuncture, biofeedback, chiropractic, deep breathing, herbal and other natural dietary supplements, homeopathy, massage, meditation, prayer, and yoga. These therapies are widely used even though scientific evidence for their effectiveness is lacking overall. The use of these therapies derives from several reasons (Shi and Singh 2015). First, many patients, such as those with chronic pain, have not been helped by conventional biomedical therapies and turn to CAM for relief. Second, patients with certain conditions may wish to try CAM as a last-ditch alternative to surgery and/or risky medications. Third, patients feel that CAM providers will pay more attention to them than physicians normally do. Finally, CAM is generally less expensive than biomedical therapy and thus may potentially save patients much money if it can help them.

Five medical problems lead all others as the conditions for which patients seek CAM relief: allergies, arthritis, backaches, fatigue, and headaches (Su and Li 2011). Although health insurance plans often cover chiropractic, they generally do not cover other CAM therapies. As this situation suggests, chiropractic is increasingly being regarded as a conventional therapy, much as osteopathy was originally regarded as an alternative form of care and now is regarded as a conventional form.

The growing popularity of CAM has led mainstream health providers to take a greater interest in CAM rather than rejecting it out of hand. The federal government established the Office of Alternative Medicine in 1993. Five years later, the office was renamed the National Center for Complementary and Alternative Medicine, and in 2014 was renamed again as the National Center for Complementary and Integrative Health (NCCIH; https://nccih.nih.gov). This center, whose 2015 fiscal year budget was $124.1 million, funds research on CAM's effectiveness and gathers and provides information about CAM to health professionals and to the public.

Despite this growing acceptance of CAM, the medical profession historically had resisted CAM and dismissed many CAM therapies as no more than quackery. In fact, one aspect of the rise of the medical profession during the nineteenth century involved its efforts to convince the public to favor biomedical means of healing over the traditional, alternative means to which they were long accustomed. Thus the American Medical Association and other physician organizations emphasized the scientific basis for the biomedical model and this model's greater effectiveness in curing disease. A major goal of these organizations' successful efforts to secure state licensing standards for the practice of medicine (see chapter 8) was to prevent individuals from practicing the traditional, nonbiomedical health care that had been the norm historically. As sociologist Terri A. Winnick (2013:283) has summarized these efforts, "As the sole arbiter of science, regular medicine was able to blithely dismiss competing philosophies and treatments as unscientific. More importantly, they were also able to align themselves with the state and seek its protection over their work."

As CAM became more popular since the 1960s, however, the medical profession has begun to embrace at least some CAM therapies as acceptable means of healing. The term "complementary" implies this growing acceptance, as complementary measures are meant to accompany biomedical therapies and vice versa. Two reasons account for this growing acceptance (Baer 2010). First, the medical profession saw the "writing on the wall" and realized that it could lose patients if it rejected CAM altogether rather than incorporating CAM into the treatment of patients. Second, many physicians and nurses began to recognize that some CAM practices might indeed be effective and that the complementary use of these practices would enhance patients' health. In any event, CAM is now a growing part of the curriculum in medical schools and especially nursing schools and the subject of sessions at conferences and workshops that physicians and nurses attend (Bayer 2010).

Prevalence of CAM

The National Health Interview Survey (NHIS), which has long been one of the nation's leading sources of data on the population's health and use of health services, is now also a leading source on the use of CAM. In coordination with the NCCIH, the NHIS has included items on CAM use in its huge national survey several times since 2002. In 2012, the adult U.S. population as represented in the survey reported significant use of several CAM approaches during the past year (see Figure 9.1). The percentages reported in Figure 9.1 translate to millions of Americans. For example, the 17.7% of the survey's sample who used dietary supplements (those that are nonvitamin and nonmineral) during the past year is equivalent to about 41 million adults; the 8.4% who used chiropractic or osteopathic manipulation is equivalent to about 19 million adults; and the 1.5% who tried acupuncture translates to 3.5 million adults. Overall, one-third of adults used some form of CAM during the past year, a proportion equivalent to about 78 million adults.

Sociodemographic Characteristics and CAM Use

Not surprisingly, our sociodemographic backgrounds affect our likelihood of using the various CAM approaches.

The most striking difference is seen with education. Higher levels of education strongly predict CAM use, as almost 43% of people with college degrees used CAM during the past year, compared to less than 16% of those without a high-school degree (see Figure 9.2).

Another strong predictor of CAM use is poverty status. Fewer than 21% of poor adults used any CAM approach during the past year,

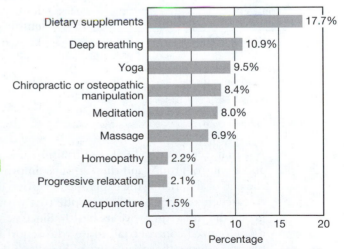

FIG. 9.1 Percentage of Adults Using Selected Complementary and Alternative Approaches during Past Year, 2012 National Health Interview Survey.

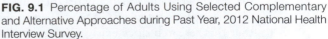

Source: Clarke, T. C., L. I. Black, B. J. Stussman, P. M. Barnes, and R. L. Nahin. 2015. *Trends in the Use of Complementary Health Approaches among Adults: United States, 2002–2012.* Hyattsville, MD: National Center for Health Statistics.

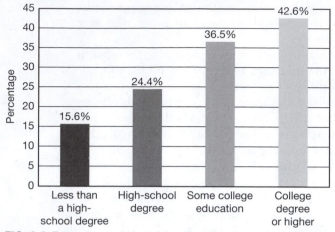

FIG. 9.2 Education and Use of Any Complementary and Alternative Approach during the Past Year, 2012 National Health Interview Survey.

Source: Clarke, T. C., L. I. Black, B. J. Stussman, P. M. Barnes, and R. L. Nahin. 2015. *Trends in the Use of Complementary Health Approaches among Adults: United States, 2002–2012.* Hyattsville, MD: National Center for Health Statistics.

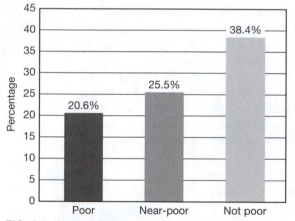

FIG. 9.3 Poverty Status and Use of Any Complementary and Alternative Approach during the Past Year, 2012 National Health Interview Survey.

Source: Clarke, T. C., L. I. Black, B. J. Stussman, P. M. Barnes, and R.L. Nahin. 2015. *Trends in the Use of Complementary Health Approaches among Adults: United States, 2002–2012.* Hyattsville, MD: National Center for Health Statistics.

compared to 38% of adults who are not poor (see Figure 9.3).

A third strong predictor is race and ethnicity. Non-Latino whites are more likely than African Americans or Latinos to have used any CAM approach during the past year (see Figure 9.4).

As these data suggest, the people who are most likely to use CAM are non-Latino white, college educated, and not poor. Gender and age also predict any CAM use, but the differences here are less striking than those we have seen for education, poverty status, and race and ethnicity. Regarding gender, 37.4% of women used any CAM approach during the past year, compared to only 28.9% of men. Turning to age, the proportions using any CAM approach during the past year are 32.2% for adults aged 18–44, compared to 36.8% for adults aged 45–64 and 29.4% for adults 65 and older.

Effectiveness of CAM

We noted earlier that scientific evidence of the effectiveness of CAM is lacking overall. Many individuals who try CAM find it helpful, which is wonderful for them, but their reports do not amount to sound scientific evidence. This is because of the well-known **placebo effect,** the idea that people might feel healthier from trying a new health approach such as CAM or from taking a new medication simply because they expect the new approach or medication to make them feel better. For this reason, *randomized control trials* are the "gold standard" in medical research (see chapter 1). These trials include at a minimum an experimental group and a control group, and these groups' improvement in health are then compared at the end of the trial. If the experimental group improves more than the control group, researchers can reasonably conclude that whatever was "done to" the experimental group did in fact improve its health. Since people who try CAM are not involved in a randomized control trial, those who report benefits may simply be experiencing a placebo effect rather than any real benefit of their CAM approach.

Scientific studies of CAM's effectiveness are still rather meager. To the extent that this research does exist, it suggests that certain CAM approaches may indeed be effective. For example, one very popular dietary supplement, fish oil, may reduce blood pressure and inflammation (Clarke et al. 2015). Several studies also suggest that yoga may reduce cardiovascular risk factors (blood pressure, body weight, and total cholesterol) and relieve depression and other psychiatric disorders (Cabral et al. 2011; Chu et al. 2014). Research also suggests that acupuncture may relieve chronic pain of the lower back, neck, or knee and reduce the frequency of migraine and tension headaches (Pendrick 2013), while mindfulness meditation may relieve chronic insomnia, chronic pain, depression, respiratory infections, and ulcerative colitis (Goyal et al. 2014; National Center for Complementary and Integrative Health 2015). On the other hand, although there are relatively few rigorous studies of chiropractic, the available research indicates that the spinal manipulation it involves does not relieve lower back pain (Rubinstein et al. 2012), even though many chiropractic patients say it does.

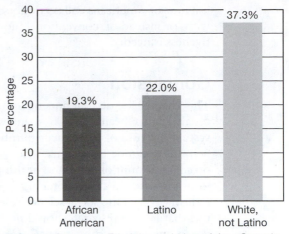

FIG. 9.4 Race and Ethnicity and Use of Any Complementary and Alternative Approach, 2012 National Health Interview Survey.

Source: Clarke, T. C., L. I. Black, B. J. Stussman, P. M. Barnes, and R.L. Nahin. 2015. *Trends in the Use of Complementary Health Approaches among Adults: United States, 2002–2012.* Hyattsville, MD: National Center for Health Statistics.

Apart from fish oil, there is scant research on the effectiveness of nonvitamin/nonmineral dietary supplements. This is unfortunate, since the almost one-fifth of American adults who use these supplements spend some $33 billion annually on them (O'Connor 2015b). The dietary supplement industry is largely unregulated, thanks to a 1994 federal law that exempts the industry from the scrutiny of the Food and Drug Administration (FDA). As a result, the industry is allowed to market products without the products having been tested for efficacy and safety. This allows supplement companies to typically make claims of effectiveness for which scientific evidence is lacking, and it also allows them to market products that simply do not contain what their labels say they contain (O'Connor 2015a). Worse yet, there is growing evidence that many supplements may be unsafe and cause serious health problems, including those involving the heart, liver, and kidneys.

For example, several weight-loss and workout supplements contain a potentially harmful chemical, β-methylphenethylamine (BMPEA), that is almost identical to amphetamine (O'Connor 2015). The use of BMPEA can increase the risk of high blood pressure and cardiovascular problems. After the presence of BMPEA was publicized in 2015, several supplement store chains said they would no longer sell products containing this chemical, and the FDA warned several companies to remove BMPEA from their products. In another example, many people with celiac disease, an intestinal autoimmune disorder aggravated by the consumption of gluten, take probiotic supplements. However, more than half of the most popular probiotic supplements contain gluten (O'Connor 2015a)!

The highly regarded periodical *Consumer Reports* (2010) has identified a dozen common ingredients in dietary supplements that may be especially harmful to the health of people who take supplements containing them. These ingredients are: conite, bitter orange, chaparral, colloidal silver, coltsfoot, comfrey, country mallow, germanium, greater celandine, kava, lobelia, and yohimbe. The supplements containing these ingredients are marketed for a variety of health conditions, including inflammation, pain, and erectile dysfunction. However, their possible dangers include cancer, kidney damage, nausea, stroke, and even death.

These dangers suggest great caution in the use of dietary supplements. Other CAM approaches appear to be safe, and, as we have seen, several may be effective based on a relatively small amount of sound research on this issue. Because tens of millions of Americans will no doubt continue to use CAM approaches in conjunction with, or instead of, conventional biomedical therapy, more research on CAM's effectiveness is needed.

Conclusion

This chapter focused on nursing and other nonphysician mainstream health care and on alternative health care. In many ways, nurses are the backbone of the health care system because of their sheer numbers and because of the multifaceted, hands-on help they provide to patients. The work they do is quite difficult, and it causes them no small amount of stress and health problems. The other mainstream health occupations discussed in this chapter also comprise a valuable component of the health care industry. Very little social science research has been carried out on these occupations, but that lack of research should not be interpreted as suggesting these occupations are in any way unimportant. Complementary and alternative medicine has grown in popularity during the past few decades and now comprises a multibillion dollar industry that is used by tens of millions of Americans. Although dietary supplements are generally ineffective and even unsafe, several other CAM therapies show promise of being effective.

Summary

1. Nursing is a profession that lacks full autonomy because nurses are subordinate to physicians. As a result, nurses do not enjoy full professional status.
2. Florence Nightingale established the world's first nonreligious nursing school in London in 1860. The first American nursing schools opened in 1873 in Boston, New Haven, and New York, respectively. The number of U.S. nursing schools exceeded 1,700 by 1920.
3. The United States now has about 4 million nurses. The types of nurses include licensed practical nurses, registered nurses, and advanced practice nurses. More than 90% of all nurses are women.
4. The current shortage of nurses promises to worsen over the next decade as nurses retire. This situation is especially worrisome because the baby boom generation will continue to swell the ranks of older Americans during the next decade. The nursing shortage adds to the stress that nurses already face and compromises patient care.
5. Hospital nursing is highly stressful and is a major reason for nurses' dissatisfaction with their jobs. A key source of this stress is the emotional difficulties nurses face in dealing with patients with serious health problems and with those who are dying. Hospital nurses are also at a high risk for illness and injury from various aspects of their nursing duties.
6. Nurses' subordination to physicians reflects both the professional aspects of these two occupations but also the gender hierarchy still found in the larger society. The gendered nature of physician-nurse interaction has fortunately lessened during the past few decades.
7. Other mainstream health providers include dentists and dental hygienists and assistants, optometrists and opticians, osteopathic physicians, pharmacists, physical therapists, and podiatrists. These and many other health care occupations provide very important health care for the general population.
8. Complementary and alternative medicine (CAM) has grown in popularity during the past few decades. Millions of Americans use at least one form of CAM.

9. Some scientific evidence points to the effectiveness of several CAM approaches, including meditation and yoga. However, there is little research that dietary supplements are effective, and several supplements are thought to pose serious health risks.

Giving It Some Thought

You are a registered nurse in a medium-sized hospital. A physician instructs you to provide a patient a certain amount of a specific medication twice daily. When it is time for the first dose a few hours later, you notice that the physician listed an amount of medication that in your opinion far exceeds a safe dosage. You contact the physician and ask if he might have made a mistake in prescribing the dosage. He replies somewhat angrily, "Just do as I instructed!" What do you do next?

Key Terms

advanced practice nurses, 148

complementary and alternative health care, 144

licensed practical nurses, 147

mainstream health care, 144

placebo effect, 158

registered nurses, 148

10 Hospitals and Other Health Care Settings

LEARNING QUESTIONS

1. Why did hospitals increase in number after World War II, and why have they declined in number since the 1970s?

2. What are the major recent trends in the hospital industry?

3. How many deaths occur from hospital errors every year?

4. How and why do hospitals' nursing shortages affect patient care?

5. Why are hospital charges in the United States so high?

6. How good is the quality of care in nursing homes?

Health and Illness in the News

In May 2015, the California Department of Health fined a dozen hospitals for potentially fatal or harmful errors. In one case, a surgical team had left a plastic clip inside a patient's skull. In another case, hospital staff failed to properly treat a patient who fell in a shower; the patient was declared brain dead a few days later. In a third case, a surgical team left an item inside a patient after a hysterectomy. A fourth case involved a patient who died after a surgical team's error led the patient to receive an intravenous drug used for anesthesia after the surgery had ended; the drug led to internal bleeding and brain damage that proved fatal. The fines for each incident were between $50,000 and $100,000. (Goodman 2015; Halstead 2015)

Hospitals save lives, but they also cost lives. They are places where medical miracles occur, but they are also places where fatal mistakes are made. They are filled with caring staff, but they also employ staff who could use some lessons in caring. Most of us were born in a hospital, and many of us will die in a hospital. From birth to death, hospitals touch the lives of almost every American and treat millions of patients every year. They employ more than 5 million people ranging from janitors to medical staff to administrators, and they take in some $1 trillion of the nation's health care expenditures. Without question, hospitals are a major component of the health care industry and absolutely critical to the nation's health.

This chapter examines the structure and functioning of hospitals and takes a critical look at their patient care. The chapter also examines other health care settings, including nursing homes and small medical clinics. By the conclusion of this chapter you should have a good understanding of some of the major problems and challenges facing these health care settings today and for the foreseeable future. We begin with hospitals and devote the bulk of the chapter to them.

Hospitals

As you undoubtedly know, a **hospital** is an institution that provides medical treatment and nursing for people who are sick or injured. The American Hospital Association (AHA) requires such a setting to have at least six inpatient beds for it to be considered a hospital. Hospitals as we now know them are relatively modern organizations that resulted from the rise of scientific medicine in the late nineteenth century. They grew rapidly in number from that period into the 1980s but then declined somewhat for reasons to be discussed in the next section's recounting of the history of hospitals. Their rise and recent decline reflect important developments in health care, as the next section will indicate.

A Brief History of Hospitals

The origins of hospitals go back to ancient times (Risse 1999). If we think of a hospital as a location where people go to stay while physicians try to heal them, hospitals in some form, however rudimentary, were found in the ancient civilizations of Egypt, Greece, India, and Rome. During the Middle Ages, the Catholic Church and other religious orders established hospitals where monks and nuns provided religious solace and medical and other care for the poor, homeless, and other people in need. Because medical knowledge of any real use was so scant during that period, the medical care these religious figures provided was rather ineffective, even if the patients of their hospitals were helped and comforted in other ways. These medieval hospitals are thus best regarded as vehicles for carrying out medieval Christianity's commitment to charity rather than as vehicles for providing effective medical care.

The first "real" hospitals developed during the Renaissance in Italy and then elsewhere in Europe, and nonreligious hospitals existed by the 1700s in several European cities. Wealthy individuals built many of these hospitals to serve their communities and to earn some money. By the early 1800s, France became the world's leading nation for the development of hospitals. This development reflected two historical events. The first was the French Revolution of 1789, which left in its wake the idea that the state should take care of its citizens; the building of hospitals was a significant manifestation of this idea. The second event, or rather set of events, was the many wars that France fought under the leadership of Napoleon during the early nineteenth century. To treat all the wounded soldiers from all these wars, Napoleon built several hospitals. The establishment of French hospitals during this period reflected the first sustained government financing and management of hospitals in the Western world. The French hospitals encouraged physicians to specialize in surgery, and they also provided patients for the clinical training of France's medical students (Krause 1977).

As scientific medicine developed rapidly during the latter nineteenth century, so did hospitals. Germ theory and other discoveries of scientific medicine during this period indicated that medical care could finally help cure people and ease their symptoms. The development of nursing as a profession and of formal nursing education (see chapter 9) also meant that trained nurses could be available for patient care in hospitals. By the early twentieth century, hospitals had become firmly established in the industrial world.

Hospitals in Early America The establishment of hospitals in early America lagged behind their establishment in Europe (Rosenberg 1987). By the mid-1700s, several colonies had established two types of hospitals that were "hospitals" in name only. The first type was a building that was meant to isolate people with contagious diseases like leprosy, with little medical care provided. The second type was essentially an *almshouse*, a building for housing and taking care of the poor and homeless, rather than a hospital *per se*. Benjamin Franklin and Dr. Thomas Bond, a Quaker who had studied medicine in London and become familiar with the hospitals there and in France, founded the first colonial *medical* hospital in Philadelphia in 1751. This new Pennsylvania Hospital's mission was to provide medical care to people who were both sick and poor. It initially was housed in a private home until land was purchased and a new building opened in 1755.

Other hospitals developed in early America through the early to mid-1800s. Following the Pennsylvania Hospital model, they primarily treated poor patients. Perhaps because they cared only for poor patients, these hospitals had few resources and "deplorable conditions" (Shi and Singh 2015:86), including inadequate sanitation and ventilation and untrained nurses. The majority of patients who entered them died in them. Meanwhile, middle- and upper-class patients were cared for in their homes and even had surgery performed there.

The Post-Civil War Period Beginning in the 1870s, the same developments that spurred the building of hospitals in Europe also spurred the building of hospitals in the United States. Based on their funding and operation, these hospitals took three forms: (1) *proprietary* hospitals paid for and managed by wealthy individuals, including physicians; (2) *municipal* hospitals, paid for with tax dollars and managed by local communities; and (3) *Catholic* hospitals, paid for and operated by the Catholic Church. Conditions in these hospitals were better overall than those before this time. The proprietary hospitals and, to some extent, the Catholic hospitals primarily treated fairly wealthy patients, while the municipal hospitals primarily treated low-income patients.

Many hospitals of all these types were built in the United States during the approximate half-century from the 1870s through the 1920s. The growth of hospitals during this period was truly remarkable. In 1872, the United States had only 178 hospitals; this number rose to 4,359 by 1909 and 6,665 by 1929 (Shi and Singh 2015). By the end of this period, then, the nation had 37 times as many hospitals as it had at the beginning of this period. The number of hospital beds during this era correspondingly rose from about 36,000 in 1872 to 900,000 in 1929.

The Great Depression began in 1929. Hospitals were among the many businesses that had to close their doors during the next decade, with the number of hospitals falling to 6,189 institutions by 1937. The Depression also forced hospitals to rely increasingly on patient fees for their funding, even though patients were now less able to afford hospital fees because of the Depression. Hospitals also took on many more charity cases because of the Depression, adding to the hospitals' financial burdens.

All these currents helped lead to the nation's first widespread system of private health insurance (Shi and Singh 2015). The key development here was the establishment in 1929 of hospital care insurance for Dallas, Texas, public school teachers to help them afford medical care at their city's Baylor University Hospital. Following this example, other hospitals also began to offer medical services to the public in return for monthly payments (*premiums*). These plans soon became the model for the development of Blue Cross health insurance, which originated in Minnesota in 1933 and in effect (and with the help of the American Hospital Association) combined the individual hospitals' plans from various regions into a single network. This early Blue Cross model covered only hospital expenses, not physician fees or other medical expenses. The development of health insurance for hospital care during this period provided a needed source of financial support for the nation's hospitals and helped them weather the storm that was the Great Depression.

The Post–World War II Period   World War II followed the Great Depression. During the approximately 16 years that these two epic events encompassed, hospital construction came to a standstill. This problem created a shortage of hospital beds by the end of the war in 1945 and led Congress to pass the Hospital Survey and Construction Act (better known as the Hill-Burton Act after its Congressional sponsors) in 1946. As its formal name implies, this legislation gave the states large sums of federal money to build new hospitals. These funds spurred the building of hospitals throughout the nation during the next two decades. Another spurt of hospital growth occurred after the advent of Medicare and Medicaid in 1965, as these new plans meant that many more older and poor citizens could afford hospital care than before.

Hospitals Since the 1970s   Since the 1970s, however, the number of hospitals has declined rather dramatically (see Figure 10.1), falling from 7,156 in 1975 to 5,724 in 2011, a drop of 20%. The number of hospital beds has similarly declined from almost 1.5 million in 1975 to 924,000 in 2011, a loss of 37% of beds.

These steep declines stemmed from several factors that decreased the demand for hospital beds and thus led to a loss of hospital revenue that forced many hospitals to close (Shi and Singh 2015). First, many more patients began to use outpatient services to save the incredibly high costs of hospitals' inpatient care. Second, and again to save costs, health insurance companies began to insist under the new *managed care* concept that patients receiving inpatient care leave hospitals sooner rather than later or receive care outside a hospital altogether. Third, recognition grew that hospitals can be dangerous places in which to stay (a problem we discuss later), and patients ironically began to limit their stays when possible in order to protect their health. Fourth, the development of home health care and other nonhospital services meant that patients had alternatives to hospitals. Some could avoid hospitals altogether, and others could be discharged from hospitals earlier because adequate continuity of care could now be provided outside the hospital.

As well, Congress passed the 1982 Tax Equity and Fiscal Responsibility Act (TEFRA) that changed how Medicare reimbursed hospitals. Before 1982, Medicare would reimburse hospitals reasonable charges for each day a patient spent in the hospital, for each test or procedure performed, and for the various other expenses hospital stays incur. Under this so-called *cost-plus* method, there was little incentive for hospitals to limit an individual patient's hospital stay or the tests and procedures performed. Quite the contrary: the longer the stay and the more services provided, the greater the reimbursement. To reduce Medicare costs, TEFRA shifted

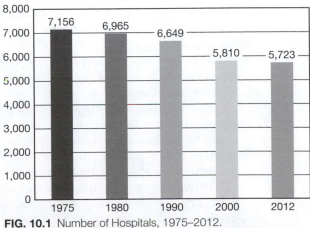

FIG. 10.1 Number of Hospitals, 1975–2012.
Source: National Center for Health Statistics. 2015. *Health, United States, 2014.* Hyattsville, MD: Centers for Disease Control and Prevention.

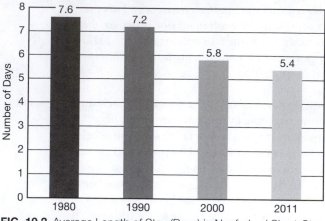

FIG. 10.2 Average Length of Stay (Days) in Nonfederal Short-Stay Hospitals, 1980–2011.

Source: National Center for Health Statistics. 2015. *Health, United States, 2014.* Hyattsville, MD: Centers for Disease Control and Prevention.

Medicare reimbursement from the cost-plus method to a **prospective payment system** (PPS). Under PPS, Medicare reimbursed hospitals a fixed amount per inpatient regardless of how long the patient stayed in the hospital and regardless of how many tests, procedures, and other services were performed. This new system reduced hospitals' reimbursement (and hence income) and led them to limit the number of days a patient stayed (Balotsky 2005).

All these factors reduced the number of hospital patients and especially their length of stay in a hospital. As Figure 10.2 illustrates, the average patient spent 7.6 days in a hospital in 1980. That figure has fallen and now stands at only 5.4 days. Fewer patient-days translated to a serious loss of income for many hospitals and thus to their closures or mergers with other hospitals.

Hospitals in the United States Today

The United States now (2012 data) has 5,686 hospitals that house some 914,000 hospital beds (American Hospital Association 2015a). Let's examine some important features of these hospitals.

Types of Hospitals   Hospitals are commonly classified according to many factors, such as whether they are public or private, whether they are for-profit or nonprofit, whether they are short-stay or long-term institutions, and whether they have a small number of beds or large number of beds. A common classification takes into account whether hospitals are public or private and whether they are for-profit or nonprofit (Shi and Singh 2015). Based on these features, the nation has three types of hospitals.

Public hospitals (also called *government hospitals*) are owned and managed by local governments (city or county), state governments, or the federal government. Local hospitals tend to serve low-income patients and are often found in the low-income sections of large cities. These hospitals were hit especially hard by the developments described in the previous section that led to hospital closures. State hospitals tend to be large mental health institutions, while federal hospitals serve designated populations such as military veterans and Native Americans. Public hospitals of all types comprise about 30% of all hospitals (American Hospital Association 2015a).

Private nonprofit hospitals (also just called *nonprofit hospitals*) are owned and operated by private groups, secular or religious (if religious, usually the Catholic Church). Because these hospitals exist to benefit the community, they are considered charities and do not pay taxes to the local, state, or federal governments. These hospitals comprise about 51% of all hospitals.

Private for-profit hospitals (also just called *for-profit hospitals* or *proprietary hospitals*) are owned and operated by private investors, who may be individuals, partnerships, or corporations. As their name implies, for-profit hospitals aim to make a profit for their investors. These hospitals have increased in recent decades even as the total number of hospitals has fallen, and they now comprise almost one-fifth of all hospitals. Despite concerns that for-profit hospitals may cut corners in the name of profit and thus compromise patient care, the latest evidence indicates that their patient care is similar to that provided by nonprofit hospitals (Joynt, Orav, and Jha 2014).

Across the United States, most hospitals overall (87% of all hospitals) are **community hospitals**, defined as nonfederal, short-term hospitals open to the general public. By definition, the federal hospitals that serve designated populations are not community hospitals, and neither are prison hospitals and long-stay hospitals.

It is also useful to classify hospitals by their type of service. Most hospitals are **general hospitals**, as they provide a range of services for a range of medical conditions. In contrast, **specialty hospitals** treat patients with specific medical conditions. Examples include children's hospitals, psychiatric hospitals, and rehabilitation hospitals.

Three additional types of hospitals are worth mentioning even if they also fall under the classification schemes just discussed (Shi and Singh 2015). **Teaching hospitals** are affiliated with a medical school. As such, they provide training to medical students and opportunities for health care research. **Church-affiliated hospitals** are sponsored by and operated by the Catholic Church or other religious denominations. Although these hospitals are open to the public, various aspects of their operation may reflect the religious beliefs of the sponsoring denomination. Finally, **osteopathic hospitals** developed after the founding of osteopathy in the late nineteenth century (see chapter 9) and originally reflected osteopathic principles. Today, however, the few remaining osteopathic hospitals are for all intents and purposes no different from conventional (allopathic) hospitals.

The Structure of Hospitals   Hospitals are *bureaucracies*. This means that they are characterized by: (1) *hierarchy*, or a chain of command in which a relatively few people at the top supervise many more people below them; (2) *specialization*, or a division of labor in which specific people perform specific tasks; (3) *written rules and regulations*; and (4) *record keeping*, especially of records related to patient care. As emphasized by Max Weber (1978 [1921]), one of the founders of sociology, bureaucracies are also characterized by (5) *impartiality and impersonality*. Weber thought that impartiality in hiring, promotion, and firing was important for the success of large formal organizations, but he also worried that bureaucracies could be very impersonal.

Contemporary scholars emphasize that bureaucracies can be not only impersonal but also alienating (Adler 2012). Clients or customers of bureaucracies, including patients of hospitals, all too often "get lost in the shuffle" and find that they are treated rather impersonally or even forgotten. These experiences can lead to a sense of alienation and dissatisfaction with a bureaucracy's services. Hospital patients on gurneys who are left alone in a hallway while awaiting a medical test or procedure know about this problem all too well.

Contemporary scholars emphasize that *red tape* can also characterize bureaucracies. Bureaucracies can have so many rules and regulations, however important and well intended, that it may take very long for them to accomplish their tasks. Hospital patients who have to go through many hoops to get some answers about their billing also know about red tape all too well.

Beyond these basic characteristics of hospitals as bureaucracies, hospitals also have an interesting governing structure (Griffin 2012). Because hospitals are in essence businesses but also medical institutions, they typically have a dual system of governance, divided between *administration* and *medical staff*. A chief executive officer (CEO) heads administration, while a medical director or chief of staff heads the medical staff. Both these persons and the divisions they head in turn report to the hospital's *board of trustees* that heads the entire hospital. The trustees typically include business and community figures, the CEO, and at least one physician. The medical staff is generally self-governing and organized into departments based on medical specialties. Each department has its own *chief of service*, just as most academic departments have their own chairperson or head of department depending on the title used at a particular college or university.

Sometimes the administrative and medical divisions live in an uneasy alliance. As two health scholars point out, "Such a dual structure is rarely seen in other businesses and presents numerous opportunities for conflict between the CEO and the medical staff" (Shi and Singh 2015:319). For example, the CEO may wish to keep costs low for understandable reasons, while the medical director may wish to purchase the latest medical technology to enhance patient care. More generally, nurses, pharmacists and other hospital health professionals in a sense have two masters: the hospital's administration and its medical staff. As a result, they may face competing influences, or *cross pressures*, from these two authorities as they go about their daily schedules. The hospital's pharmacy may be asked by medical staff to remain open for longer hours, but told by hospital administration that this would not be economical. There is an old saying that no one can serve two masters, and hospital structure and hospital life often illustrate this adage all too well.

Trends in the Hospital Industry   We noted earlier that the number of hospitals and hospital beds has fallen since the 1970s. Two other important trends in the hospital industry are worth noting. One trend is the *growth of multihospital chains.* Before the 1960s, a hospital was typically individually owned and independent of other hospitals. This situation began to change in the late 1960s and 1970s as hospital consolidation occurred from the rise of multihospital chains. A **multihospital chain** (also called a *multihospital system*, or *MHS*) consists of two or more hospitals owned and operated by a central organization, much as retail chains such as McDonald's, Rite Aid, or Walmart consist of many individual stores owned and ultimately run by a corporation. Those stores resemble each other physically much more than hospitals in an MHS resemble each other, but the overall concept is similar. MHSs are either for-profit chains or nonprofit chains. Two of the for-profit chains each include more than 130 hospitals and are the largest MHSs, while many of the remaining chains each include several dozen hospitals.

The major reason for the growth of MHSs has been economic. Simply put, an MHS has much more economic clout than an individual hospital. This clout makes an MHS better able to negotiate with health insurance companies for higher reimbursement rates, and it makes an MHS better able to negotiate with suppliers of hospital equipment and other products for lower prices.

The growth of MHSs has been rather dramatic. Before the 1970s, just a few of the nation's hospitals were part of an MHS. By 2004, 49% of hospitals belonged to MHSs, and this figure rose to 63% by 2012. This trend accelerated in 2010 with the advent of the Affordable Care Act (ACA) (Obamacare), which put pressure on hospitals to cut expenses and gave hospitals incentives for quality of care that are theoretically better met by MHSs than by individual hospitals (Sanofi-Aventis 2015).

Despite this hope, the quality of care (as measured by patient readmission rates, mortality rates, and patient satisfaction) varies greatly among MHSs, with some exhibiting much lower quality of care than others (Yonek, Hines, and Joshi 2010). There is also evidence that hospital consolidation raises hospital care costs rather than lowering them, most likely because consolidation reduces competition among hospitals (Gaynor and Town 2012). This evidence suggests that the growth of MHSs is ironically achieving the opposite consequence of one of the major rationales for their growth. In other problems, some large MHSs have been accused of admitting patients who did not need admission, of exaggerating emergency room patients' conditions in order to receive higher insurance reimbursement, and of performing unnecessary and even dangerous cardiac procedures on patients (Abelson and Creswell 2012; Creswell and Abelson 2012a, 2014).

A second, related trend in the hospital industry is the *acquisition of physician practices*. Hospitals have increasingly been acquiring physician practices that were previously owned by the physicians themselves. Motivated by the ACA, these acquisitions are meant to foster a greater integration of health care delivery. Such integration should, in theory, increase quality of care and also limit costs by reducing duplication of tests and treatments and by transferring some hospital services to physicians' offices.

In practice, however, these acquisitions may in fact be increasing medical costs, again because of reduced competition and also because hospitals charge insurers higher rates for physicians' services than physicians charged before their practices were acquired (Medicare Payment Advisory Commission 2012). In a study of California health care costs, per-patient costs were highest in MHS-owned physician practices, next highest in physician practices owned by a local hospital, and lowest in physician-owned practices (Robinson and Miller 2014). Some physicians in practices acquired by hospitals say they have been pressured to perform unnecessary tests and procedures and to admit patients to their hospitals who do not need admission (Creswell and Abelson 2012b). All this evidence again suggests that this particular trend may be producing the opposite consequences of what it should be accomplishing.

Hospital Employment, Admissions, and Costs   All these aspects of the types of hospitals, recent trends in the hospital industry, and hospitals' governing structures are important to understand. But perhaps the most significant feature of hospitals is that the U.S. hospital industry is an incredibly huge enterprise responsible for the employment and health of tens of millions of Americans and the expenditure of hundreds of billions of the nation's health care dollars. The hospital industry employs almost 4.9 million people (2015 data) in a great variety of professional and blue-collar positions. Some 35.4 million people (2012 data), including repeat admissions, are admitted to all U.S. hospitals annually, and 126 million people (including repeat visitors) visit hospital outpatient departments annually. The care for all these patients costs the nation more than $900 billion annually, almost one-third of the nation's entire health care expenditure (American Hospital Association 2015a). Any changes that occur in hospitals' structure, functioning, effectiveness, and financing cannot help but have significant implications for people's health and for the nation's health care.

Problems in U.S. Hospitals

As hospitals attend to the health care needs of millions of Americans and to the need to control health care costs, they also grapple with several problems that threaten the health of millions of Americans. We examine some important problems here briefly.

Nursing Shortages   One fundamental problem that hospitals face now and for the foreseeable future is a shortage of nurses. As chapter 9 explained, a nursing shortage exists now nationwide and promises to worsen over the next decade, thanks to the number of nurses who will be retiring and to the inevitable aging of the baby boom generation. Hospitals have also limited their employment of nurses to save costs.

This situation has worsened the nursing shortage, a fact that brings to mind another old saying: penny wise and pound foolish. As a state nursing association official warns, "The biggest change in the last five to 10 years is the unrelenting emphasis on boosting their [hospitals'] profit margins at the expense of patient safety. Absolutely every decision is made on the basis of cost savings" (Robbins 2015:A25).

Because of the nursing shortage, hospital nurses have much higher caseloads than optimal. These caseloads induce much stress and burnout and lead many nurses to retire. Worse yet, heavy nursing caseloads are a significant risk for factor patients' health and even raise the risk of their dying. As one nursing writer has commented, "Dozens of studies have found that the more patients assigned to a nurse, the higher the patients' risk of death, infections, complications, falls, failure-to-rescue rates and readmission to the hospital—and the longer their hospital stay" (Robbins 2015:A25). Although nurses should ideally attend to no more than four or five "regular" (i.e., not in intensive care or the emergency room) patients at a time, nurses often have caseloads double this optimal size. According to the nursing writer just quoted, nurses who complain about understaffing face censure from hospital administrators. Agreeing with this sentiment, a national nursing union official said, "It happens all the time, and nurses are harassed into taking what they know are not safe assignments. The pressure has gotten even greater to keep your mouth shut. Nurses have gotten blackballed for speaking up" (Robbins 2015:A25).

Hospital Errors and Infections A word to the wise: if you want to be as healthy as possible, stay out of the hospital or leave a hospital as soon as possible after receiving care there. This is harsh advice, to be sure, but not unduly alarmist, because there is growing evidence that hospitals are, in fact, dangerous places.

Hospitals make mistakes. Or to be more precise, hospital physicians and other hospital employees make mistakes. As the news story that began this chapter reminds us, surgeons can leave objects inside patients, and physicians and nurses can commit other errors that harm and even kill patients. Surgeons sometimes operate on the wrong part of a patient's body. Patients sometimes do not get needed medical care. The wrong medication is sometimes given to a patient or an accidental overdose of a proper medication is administered. Physicians and nurses often fail to wash their hands, allowing deadly bacteria to be transmitted to patients. Other types of mistakes also allow deadly bacteria to be transmitted. All these errors arise from carelessness. They are more frequent than otherwise because physicians often do not get enough sleep (see chapter 8) and because nurses, as just discussed, have caseloads that are heavier than they should be.

Tens of thousands of patients die each year from hospital errors. Estimates of the number of annual deaths from these errors range from a low of 44,000, according to an influential Institute of Medicine (2000) report; to 250,000, according to a recent analysis by Johns Hopkins University researchers (Makary and Daniel 2016); to a high of 440,000, according to an article in the *Journal of Patient Safety* (James 2013). This latter estimate, which many health policy experts consider reliable (Allen 2013), is equivalent to an average of 1,205 hospital patient deaths per day. This estimate would make hospital errors the third-highest cause of death in the United States, trailing only heart disease and cancer. As a columnist for the business publication *Forbes* pointed out, this estimate "means that hospitals are killing off the equivalent of the entire population of Atlanta one year, Miami the next, then moving to Oakland, and on and on" (Binder 2013).

Infections from lack of hand washing cause at least 75,000 of the deaths from hospital errors every year. Some evidence indicates that in the absence of pressure from hospitals to have clean hands, hospital physicians and nurses fail to wash their hands in more than two-thirds of their patient interactions; physicians are worse than nurses in this regard (Hartocollis 2013).

The exact number of annual deaths from hospital errors deaths will perhaps never be known. Hospital medical records often lack information about errors because of hurried record keeping, because hospital personnel do not realize an error occurred, or because these personnel may not wish any errors to be recorded (Allen 2013). In fact, a report by the U.S. Department of Health & Human Services (HHS) (2012) estimated that hospital employees report only 14% of all medical errors and, worse yet, asserted that hospitals typically fail to change the practices that led to the errors.

Whatever the actual number of deaths, hospital errors also harm many more people who do not die. Consumers Union (2012), the publisher of *Consumer Reports*, estimates that medical errors (including infections) harm 9 million hospital patients, or one-fourth of all inpatients annually. These medical errors cause health complications that incur treatment expenses in the billions of dollars every year, including some $30 billion just for the health problems resulting from infections (Hartocollis 2013). These expenses are passed along to private insurance companies, the federal government (Medicare and Medicaid), and often patients themselves. Health insurance premiums and perhaps even federal payroll (FICA) taxes are higher than they should be because of medical errors. This situation in turn means that medical errors cost many Americans much money even if they or their families do not experience medical errors themselves.

Ironically, hospitals profit from medical errors because they can then bill insurers for treating the complications stemming from errors (Kliff 2013). As one news report summarized this situation, "Hospitals make money from their own mistakes because insurers pay them for the longer stays and extra care that patients need to treat surgical complications that could have been prevented" (Grady 2013:A15). This in turn means that reducing errors would lose hospitals money because they receive a separate payment for each service they perform. This fact creates a financial disincentive to reduce errors. If instead hospitals were to receive a set payment for every patient or surgery, they would have a financial incentive to reduce errors because they would then have to pay the cost themselves of treating error-based complications. The ACA is attempting to address this situation in certain ways (see chapter 13).

Hospital errors are not inevitable. There are known protocols that can be followed, such as mandatory hand washing and counting hospital instruments after surgeries to make sure none is missing, that can greatly reduce the number of errors. Unfortunately, and as the HHS report indicated, many hospitals have done woefully little to prevent errors. According to the *Forbes* columnist cited earlier, "There's little excuse for this record of abject failure, and the misery and death of millions." The columnist continued that "a plethora of research and case studies have emerged with proven strategies for improving hospital safety. The hospitals that put a priority on safety and use these proven techniques show results, and their patients are safer. Those that minimize the importance of patient safety kill more of their patients" (Binder 2013).

One more word to the wise: be careful of teaching hospitals in July. There is some evidence of the so-called **July effect**, the idea that errors occur more often in July in teaching hospitals because that is when new medical residents begin working in hospitals after their academic training has ended (Young et al. 2011). These new physicians have typically had an excellent education, but they are still, after all, new, and more likely than experienced physicians to make errors. They also often know much less than veteran nurses about many aspects of patient care. As one oncology nurse has described this situation, "Any nurse who has worked in a teaching hospital is likely to have found July an especially difficult month because . . . the first-year residents are calling the plays, but they have little real knowledge of the game" (Brown 2012).

Rural and Inner-City Hospitals   U.S. hospitals differ greatly in quality. As we have just seen, some make more errors than others. Some hospitals have the latest equipment and technology and physicians and nurses who went to the top medical and nursing schools; other hospitals lack the latest equipment and technology and have physicians and nurses whose education was at less prestigious schools. Some hospitals are bright and gleaming and almost cheerful places to visit (especially considering that they are hospitals), while others are dark and grim and gloomy.

Rural Hospitals   To the extent that hospitals differ in quality, two groupings of hospitals have special problems through no fault of their own. The first grouping consists of rural hospitals. These hospitals are typically small and cater to almost 51 million people, who tend to be older and poorer than nonrural residents and who often must travel long distances (American Hospital Association 2015b). Whereas large hospitals in suburban and urban areas often have many highly skilled staff in virtually every medical specialty, rural hospitals may lack physicians and nurses in several specialties or at most have only one or two professionals in a given specialty. Because rural areas often have trouble attracting professionals to move to their locations for new employment, rural hospitals have the same problem in attracting physicians and nurses (see chapter 8).

Rural hospitals also often do not have the latest equipment and technology or at least do not have the full range of equipment and technology found in larger, wealthier hospitals. People go to rural hospitals to have babies delivered and minor surgeries performed, but more complex surgeries are often beyond these hospitals' capabilities. Although rural hospitals certainly perform a vital function for rural areas, they simply cannot afford to provide the range and quality of care found in many suburban and urban hospitals.

Because rural hospitals are small and underfinanced, they have been struggling in recent decades and vulnerable to closure. As a recent news report noted, rural hospitals "suffer from multiple endemic disadvantages that drive down profit margins and make it virtually impossible to achieve economies of scale" (Gugliotta 2015). These disadvantages include their high numbers of older and uninsured patients, their need to pay physicians higher salaries to induce them to work in a rural area, and their inability to provide certain medical services, such as knee replacements, that are especially lucrative.

In just the five-year period from 2010 to 2015, 48 rural hospitals were forced to shut their doors. The majority of these closures were in the South, including ten in Texas. In addition to the problems they face as just described, rural hospitals were especially affected by the ACA for three reasons (O'Donnell and Ungar 2014). First, the ACA reduced federal payments to hospitals for treating uninsured patients because it was assumed that states would expand their Medicaid programs. However, many states, including most Southern states, declined to do this, and rural hospitals have suffered the consequences. Second, the ACA provided financial penalties for hospitals when patients must be readmitted soon after they are released. Because rural hospitals treat so many low-income and older patients, they tend to have higher readmission rates and thus have again suffered more than their fair share of financial penalties. Third, the ACA mandated new electronic recordkeeping, which can easily cost $1 million or more for a small hospital. Some rural hospitals simply were unable to find the funds for this purpose.

Inner-City Hospitals   The second grouping of troubled hospitals consists of inner-city hospitals. Many of the nation's top hospitals are found in urban areas, but the quality of hospitals differs greatly within urban areas. Those that are located in low-income, inner-city areas are often underfinanced and understaffed. They are also often over-crowded, as the low-income populations they treat have more than their fair share of health problems (see chapter 5). Because these hospitals also tend to be in high-crime areas, they also have more security problems than hospitals located elsewhere.

A major reason for the critical financial situation of many inner-city hospitals is the clientele they serve (Thomas 2014). Their patients tend to be poor or low-income and to be either uninsured or covered by Medicaid (which covers poor and low-income individuals and families) rather than private insurance and unable to pay anything for hospital services (or for that matter, for physician services). This means that the hospitals receive reimbursement for the services they provide their patients primarily from Medicaid. However, Medicaid provides lower reimbursements than those received from private insurance or Medicare. This fact means in turn that inner-city hospitals, all things equal, have a lower revenue stream than hospitals that serve wealthier patients.

Just as many rural hospitals have had to close, so have inner-city hospitals, a trend that worsens the physician shortage already plaguing inner-city neighborhoods (see chapter 8). The number of hospitals in 52 large U.S. cities fell to 426 in 2010 from a high of 781 in 1970 (Thomas 2014). By contrast, almost two-thirds of the 230 hospitals that opened between 2000 and 2014 were in suburban areas or wealthier urban areas. The closure of so many hospitals in poor urban neighborhoods leaves their residents without a nearby hospital, even though they are much more likely than people living in suburbs or wealthy urban neighborhoods to be unhealthy. Simply put, hospitals are departing the urban neighborhoods whose residents are most likely to need hospital care. One health writer likens this situation to closing fire stations in neighborhoods with high rates of fires and opening them in neighborhoods with low rates of fires (Thomas 2014). Because residents of inner-city neighborhoods tend to be people of color, the closure of so many hospitals in these areas has a disproportionate racial/ethnic impact.

Several of the inner-city hospitals that have closed have simply moved to the suburbs or to wealthier urban neighborhoods (Galewitz 2015). These locations provide the hospitals with a better revenue stream from what hospitals call a better *payer mix*, as their patients are much more likely to be covered by private insurance, and a more appealing setting for attracting physicians and nurses to their workforce. As one public health professor describes this dynamic, "You move to where the money is" (Galewitz 2015). But this dynamic in turn means that these hospitals are abandoning the poor and people of color.

Emergency Room Care
Many emergency rooms (ERs) are overcrowded, and patients often have to wait a long time for critical care. Moreover, hospitals often board ER patients, who are disproportionately low-income and/or elderly, in crowded hallways instead of admitting them to a room. The reason for this is that hospitals prefer to hold rooms for wealthier patients covered by private insurance, which has higher reimbursements than Medicaid or Medicare (Chen 2011).

In a related issue, ER staff are so busy that they have little time to do anything more than treat patients' immediate problems (Chen 2014). In particular, they have little or no time to talk with patients about their family situation, income, medications, and other aspects of their lives that may be promoting or prolonging their health problems. They also have few or no resources to help coordinate a patient's care after the patient goes home from the ER.

These issues pose special difficulties for elderly patients who visit the ER. These patients often have several chronic illnesses, take many medications, and have at least some dementia (Chen 2014). To address these difficulties, health policy experts in geriatric care urge ERs to hire geriatric specialists and to make a better effort in coordinating home care among other measures.

Issues with Hospital Charges   One of the dirty little secrets of hospital care is that hospitals often have incredibly different charges for the same procedures even if the hospitals are in the same geographic region (Brill 2013; Kliff and Keating 2013). For example, one hospital in Virginia charges about $26,000 for a lower limb replacement, while another hospital charges almost $120,000. Two Dallas-area hospitals charge $43,000 and $161,000, respectively, for lower limb replacements. Around the nation, hospital charges for joint replacements range enormously from a low of $5,300 to $223,000; simple pneumonia cases range from $5,100 to $124,000. Medicare and private insurance typically reimburse hospitals much less than they charge, but the disparities in hospital charges remain striking nonetheless, and patients sometimes have to pay some of the charges themselves in deductibles and copayments that may amount to hundreds or thousands of dollars.

Hospital charges in general are very high even for minor procedures, especially for ER care. In one hospital's ER, the charge for three stitches to heal a knee injury was $2,229, and the charge to close a toddler's head gash with some skin glue was $1,696 (Rosenthal 2013b). The average American inpatient in 2013 paid an average of more than $4,000 for each day in a hospital, compared to only about $800 in many other wealthy democracies. Some U.S. hospitals charge more than $12,500 daily.

Several factors explain the higher charges of U.S. hospitals (Rosenthal 2013b). One factor is the dominance of multihospital chains, described earlier, as these chains use their clout to negotiate higher reimbursement rates from insurers. Another factor is the fact U.S. hospitals charge for every little thing, including a single aspirin, whereas hospitals in other democracies do not charge for basic items and services. Also, U.S. hospitals are much freer than other nations' hospitals (whose costs are constrained by government regulations) to charge whatever they think the market will bear, regardless of the actual cost of the goods and services they provide. As one public health professor points out, "The charges have no rhyme or reason at all. Why is 30 minutes in the operating room $2,000 and not $1,500? There is absolutely no basis for setting that charge. It is not based upon the cost, and it's not based upon the market forces, other than the whim of the C.F.O. of the hospital" (Bernard 2012:B1). All these factors help explain some exorbitant hospital charges, including charges in a particular California hospital of $37 for one Tylenol with codeine pill (market price = $0.50), $154 for a neck brace (market price = $20), and $543 for a breast-pump kit (market price = $25) (Rosenthal 2013b).

Other Health Care Settings

However important hospitals are for tens of millions of people, they are just one of the many types of health care settings that exist. A common setting, of course, and one with which most readers are familiar, is a private physician's office. But other health care settings also treat millions of people every year. This closing section of the chapter briefly examines a few of these settings.

Ambulatory Care Facilities

Ambulatory care facilities are settings that provide health care to patients who are not inpatients—that is, they arrive at the facility, are examined and/or treated, and then depart. The traditional physician's office is an ambulatory facility, but in recent decades other types of ambulatory facilities have developed. They are becoming increasingly popular, as they provide many forms of health care for much less expense than hospital care and thus save consumers, private insurers, and the federal and state governments much money (Weber et al. 2015). They also help take pressure off from hospital emergency rooms, which treat many patients who have only minor problems at a much higher cost than in ambulatory facilities. Three increasingly popular types of ambulatory facilities are *urgent-care centers, retail store clinics,* and *surgicenters.*

Urgent-Care Centers   Urgent-care centers (also called w*alk-in centers*) provide a wide range of minor medical services, with or without an appointment, including diagnostic testing with X-ray machines and other technology. A mixture of physicians, nurse practitioners and/or physician assistants, and nurses staffs urgent-care centers. Some centers are independently owned or part of an urgent-care center system owned by private investors or insurance companies, and some centers are owned by hospitals. Many centers are open at night and/or on weekends, making them attractive alternatives for people who incur health problems outside of the normal workweek or for those whose schedules do not permit them to seek health care during normal working hours. They are intended for minor acute health problems rather than chronic problems.

For better or worse, urgent-care centers present competition for hospitals and private physicians and threaten these providers' revenues, as they offer lower-cost care than hospitals and provide care in nonbusiness hours without the need to wait for an appointment. As an example of their lower cost, a typical acute bronchitis case costs an average $814 in hospital emergency rooms nationwide, but only $122 nationwide in urgent-care centers; a middle-ear infection costs almost $500 in an emergency room versus only $100 in an urgent-care center (Creswell 2014). This increased competition has led many hospitals and hospital systems to establish their own urgent-care centers or to consider doing so (Stempniak 2015). As one news headline put it, the "race is on to profit from rise of urgent care" (Creswell 2014:A1). This race is no surprise, since urgent-care centers take in an estimated $14.5 billion of revenue annually. Most centers do not treat uninsured patients unless they can pay themselves, and most also do not accept Medicaid and thus do not treat many low-income clients. They thus have a wealthier clientele than do many hospitals and a more stable revenue base.

One potential problem with urgent-care centers is that many states do not license and regulate them (Creswell 2014), raising questions about their quality of care. Perhaps not surprisingly, some private physicians think urgent-care centers provide inferior care. As one family physician explained, "The relationship I have with my patients and the comprehensiveness of care I provide to them is important. While there is a role for these centers, if I were sick I'd rather see my regular doctor, and I hope my patients feel that way" (Creswell 2014:A1). However, a study by the RAND Corporation found that the quality of care at urgent-care centers was similar to that at physicians' offices (Mehrotra et al. 2009).

Retail Store Clinics   Another type of ambulatory care facility that is becoming more popular is the **retail store clinic**, found in big box stores like Target and Walmart or in stores owned by CVS, Rite Aid, Walgreens and other pharmacy chains. Typically staffed by a nurse practitioner or physician assistant or occasionally a physician, these clinics provide a lower level of care than that found at urgent-care centers. They examine patients for minor conditions like sore throats, rashes, and headaches, screen them for high blood pressure and cholesterol, and provide common vaccinations. However, they typically lack the diagnostic technology found at urgent-care centers or at many private physician offices. Because the stores in which these clinics are found are in so many locations and are open during the evenings and weekends, they are a popular alternative for health care for people with minor conditions. The RAND study just mentioned also found that the quality of care at retail store clinics was similar to that at physicians' offices.

Surgicenters Surgicenters (also called *ambulatory surgery centers*, or ASCs) are independent health care facilities that provide surgical services on an outpatient basis for relatively minor types of surgery and medical procedures (e.g., a broken finger or colonoscopy). Surgicenters are staffed by physicians, nurses, and other medical personnel typical of those found in hospital surgical departments. Most surgicenters are owned by physicians, but hospitals, seeing a source of revenue, now have joint ownership of almost one-fourth of all surgicenters and own 2% of surgicenters outright (Ambulatory Surgery Center Association 2013). The first surgicenter was founded in Phoenix, AZ, by two physicians in 1970, and the number of surgicenters has grown rapidly since then to more than 5,300 today.

Surgicenters' costs are lower than hospital costs for equivalent surgeries, partly because they have fewer overhead costs and partly because their surgical procedures take less time than those at hospitals (Munnich and Parente 2014). For example, Medicare pays surgicenters an average of $964 for outpatient cataract surgery, compared to $1,670 at hospitals (Ambulatory Surgery Center Association 2013). As a result, surgicenters save Medicare more than $2.6 billion annually compared to what their surgeries would have cost at hospitals. Adding in savings to private insurance companies and to patients themselves (coinsurance and deductibles), surgicenters have saved the nation many billions of dollars since they began in 1970.

Although surgicenters have saved so much money because they have drawn patient visits from hospitals, they have also drawn patient visits from physician offices. Many procedures that used to be performed in physician offices are now being performed in surgicenters. However, surgicenters charge much more than physician offices for these procedures. One example involves a woman who needed two colonoscopies performed by the same physician a month apart (Rosenthal 2013a). The first colonoscopy was performed in a surgicenter that charged $9,142 for the procedure; the second colonoscopy was performed in the physician's own office, which charged $5,233 for the procedure. So, while surgicenters have saved much money compared to hospital expenses, they have also cost more money compared to physician office expenses.

Nursing Homes

Nursing homes are facilities that provide extensive, long-term medical care and practical support for their residents. Most nursing home residents are 65 and older and have chronic medical (including mental health) problems that render them unable to live by themselves. Some residents are younger than 65 but still have medical problems that make them unable to live independently. Nursing homes differ in the level of care they provide, with some focusing on *skilled nursing care* (including such care as physical and respiratory therapy and dialysis) for patients discharged from a hospital, and others providing mainly *intermediate care* or *custodial care* (helping with daily living activities such as bathing and eating).

The United States now has 15,640 nursing homes (2014 data) that contain almost 1.7 million beds, for an average of 106 beds per nursing home (Centers for Medicare & Medicaid Services 2016). More than two-thirds (69%) of nursing homes are for-profit; one-fourth are nonprofit; and 6% are government owned.

About 81% of nursing home beds are occupied at any one time, meaning that almost 1.4 million people live in nursing homes at any one time. Almost 3% of the 65 years and older population lives in nursing homes, and one-tenth of people 85 years and older reside in these facilities; as many as 40% of people 65 years and older can expect to spend at least some time in a nursing home. Women comprise two-thirds of nursing home residents because they outlive men, and almost 80% of nursing home residents are non-Latino whites. About 80% of nursing home residents have difficulties performing daily living activities such as bathing and using the bathroom, and two-thirds have moderate or serious cognitive impairment. Slightly more than one-third of residents are severely incontinent (bladder and/or bowel problems), and one-fourth receive an antipsychotic medication at least weekly.

Nursing Home Costs   Nursing home care is costly. The nation spends about $156 billion annually on nursing care facilities and continuing care retirement communities (National Center for Health Statistics 2015). A private nursing home room costs $250 daily (2015 data), while a semi-private room costs $220 daily (Genworth 2015). Doing a little math reveals that nursing home costs average between about $81,000 and $91,000 annually. The average resident stays in a nursing home for 835 days (2.3 years), although any one resident may stay from just several weeks to five years or more (Mullin 2013). Doing some more math again, this means that nursing home costs for the average resident will range between about $184,000 and $209,000.

Most nursing home residents and their families cannot come close to paying this huge expense. Medicare pays only for 100 days, and only for convalescent care following discharge from a hospital state that lasted at least three days. Further, Medicare pays only for skilled care, not for custodial care. These restrictions mean that many nursing home residents do not even qualify for Medicare aid or reach the maximum 100 days and then pay out of pocket. In either circumstance, many nursing home residents quickly deplete whatever savings they have and then have their care paid by Medicaid. Some insurance companies now provide long-term care insurance that pays for all nursing home costs. However, the premiums for this insurance are high, more than $5,000 annually for a married couple. Most people cannot afford these premiums and thus do not acquire long-term care insurance.

Nursing Home Quality of Care   Another major concern about nursing homes is their quality of care, which is often substandard. Many nursing homes simply are not safe places for their residents, as their staff may neglect residents' care and even abuse them. In this regard, research evidence suggests that for-profit nursing homes offer lower quality of care than nonprofit nursing homes, although mixed evidence overall precludes any firm conclusions (Comondore et al. 2009).

State agencies paid by Medicare inspect nursing homes annually and look for problems known as *deficiencies*. The nursing homes are then ranked on an A to L scale, with A denoting the most minor deficiencies and L the most serious deficiencies. Table 10.1 shows how the Centers for Medicare & Medicaid Services (CMS) classifies these rankings. Most (81%) nursing homes receive a ranking of either D or E, meaning they pose potential for more than minimal harm, while 4.4% receive rankings of actual harm or immediate jeopardy. Only 10% of nursing homes receive the lowest set of rankings (A,B,C) indicating only potential for minimal harm (Centers for Medicare & Medicaid Services 2013b), The two most common deficiencies found in the annual inspections involve the risk for accidents and for infections (Ornstein 2012).

| TABLE 10.1 | Severity Grid for Rating Nursing Home Deficiencies |

Ranking	Severity Assessment
J,K,L	Immediate jeopardy to resident health or safety
G,H,I	Actual harm that is not immediate jeopardy
D,E,F	No actual harm with potential for more than minimal harm that is not immediate jeopardy
A,B,C	No actual harm with potential for minimal harm

Source: Centers for Medicare & Medicaid Services. 2013. *Nursing Home Data Compendium 2013 Edition*. Washington, DC: U.S. Department of Health & Human Services.

These rankings are sobering, but even more sobering are data from the Office of Inspector General of the U.S. Department of Health & Human Services. This office reported that one-third of skilled nursing home residents suffered some type of harm, including an infection or medication error, in just the one month, August 2011, for which data were examined. More than half of those harmed needed hospitalization, and 1.5% of skilled nursing home residents died from a harm they suffered. As a news report described this general situation, "The injuries and deaths were caused by substandard treatment, inadequate monitoring, delays or the failure to provide needed care, the study found. The deaths involved problems such as preventable blood clots, fluid imbalances, excessive bleeding from blood-thinning medications and kidney failure" (Allen 2014). The fact that so many problems were found in just a single month is not only sobering, but also rather frightening.

Home Health Care and Hospice Care

Rising health care expenses have helped make *home health care* and *hospice care* more popular in recent years, just as they have made ambulatory care facilities more popular.

Home Health Care   **Home health care** involves health care that occurs in the home of a chronically ill patient or in the home of the patient's caregiver. The patient in this situation is usually an elderly person, but she or he may also be a younger person with a physical or mental disability or other chronic health problem. The traditional caregivers in home health care have been a member of the patient's immediate or extended family. Usually this person is a woman, for example, the daughter or daughter-in-law of the patient. As almost anyone who has been a caregiver will attest, caregiving in home health care can be time-consuming, stressful, and grueling. Even so, the family may not be able to afford institutional care or may feel that the patient will find the home setting more comfortable and less intimidating than an institutional setting.

Recognizing both the burden on caregivers and the burden of rising health care costs, the health care industry has in recent years implemented a greater use of formal home health care involving visits by nurses and other health professionals (employed by more than 12,000 home health agencies nationwide) to a patient's home. If patients can be helped this way in their homes instead of being hospitalized or put in a nursing home, health care expenses are much lower. Changes in Medicare since the 1980s have enabled such home care to receive Medicare reimbursement (Shi and Singh 2015). This form of home health care includes nursing services such as changing dressings and monitoring medication, and also other services such as physical therapy and speech therapy. Thanks to developments in health care technology, this more formal home health care also includes specialized therapies such as oncology therapy and dialysis. In 2014, some 3.5 million patients received formal home health care that provided $83 billion in payments to home health care agencies; Medicare and Medicaid paid for 80% of these expenses (Centers for Medicare & Medicaid Services 2014).

Hospice Care   **Hospice care** refers to care for terminally ill people who are expected to live no longer than six months. Although some 3,700 hospice facilities exist, hospice care can also occur in a home, nursing home, or retirement center. Because by definition a hospice patient is dying, most hospice care consists of *palliative care* (management and relief of pain and other symptoms), as well as psychosocial and spiritual support for the patient (Shi and Singh 2015).

In 2014, between 1.6 and 1.7 million people received hospice care (National Hospice and Palliative Care Organization 2015). The median number of days for which they received care was 17.4, and the average number of days, a much higher figure since many patients live for several months, was 71.3. Almost 36% of all patients received their hospice care in a private residence, 14.5% received it in a nursing home, and 32% received it at a hospice facility. Most (84%) of hospice patients are 65 years and older, and 41% are 85 years and older. Slightly more than one-third of hospice patients are dying from cancer, 15% are suffering from dementia, and 13% are suffering from heart disease. Medicare paid about $15 billion for hospice expenses in 2013.

This $15 billion figure is a lot of money, but hospice care actually saves much money compared to traditional hospital care for terminally ill patients, who continue to be given expensive medications, tests, and treatments with life-saving technology. A recent study found that patients are more likely to choose hospice care when their physicians recommend it and that physicians' recommendations are a more important factor in this choice than the patients' age, gender, or race (Lazar 2015). The study also found that physicians working in for-profit hospitals were less likely than those working in nonprofit hospitals to recommend hospice. The study's author noted that physicians are trained to try to save lives, but that it would be in the best interests of terminally ill patients and would also save health care costs if more physicians began recommending hospice care.

Conclusion

Hospitals provide many types of medical care to millions of Americans every year at a cost of hundreds of billions of dollars. Yet certain problems limit the ability of hospitals to help as many patients as possible and even endanger patients' health and lives. These problems include errors that may kill as many as 440,000 patients annually, a nursing shortage, and a shortage of hospitals in rural and inner-city areas. Rising medical costs have made ambulatory care facilities more popular, as these facilities provide adequate care for minor health concerns at a lower price than hospital services would cost. Nursing homes are a critical component of the nation's health care system, but they cost patients and their families tens of thousands of dollars and often provide substandard care. Home health care and hospice care provide patients reasonable, less costly alternatives than hospital care for a wide range of medical and other services.

Summary

1. The first real hospitals developed during the Renaissance in Italy and then elsewhere in Europe. By the early 1800s, France became the world's leading nation for the development of hospitals.

2. The first colonial medical hospital was founded in Philadelphia in 1751. Hospitals in early America primarily treated poor patients and often had decrepit conditions.

3. The United States had more than 6,500 hospitals by 1929. The Great Depression that began that year spurred the development of the nation's first private insurance plans that helped people afford hospital costs. The number of hospitals soared after World War II before declining for several reasons after the 1970s.

4. Hospitals are commonly classified as public (government) hospitals, private nonprofit hospitals, and private for-profit hospitals. Most hospitals are general hospitals as they treat people for a range of medical problems, but some specialty hospitals focus on specific conditions.

5. Hospitals are bureaucracies with a dual line of authority along administrative and medical lines. These two lines of authority sometimes can be in tension.

6. About two-thirds of hospitals now belong to multihospital chains, and hospitals are also increasingly acquiring physician practices. Although both these trends should theoretically hold health care costs down, evidence indicates that they are prompting higher costs.

7. Significant hospital problems include a nursing shortage, errors that kill as many as 440,000 patients annually, and a lack of hospitals in rural and inner-city areas.

8. Ambulatory care facilities such as urgent-care centers, retail store clinics, and surgicenters provide a range of health care services at a lower cost than hospital care.

9. Nursing homes provide a valuable service but at the same time often provide health care that is substandard. Home health care and hospice care also provide a valuable service and one that saves patients, their families, and the health care system considerable costs.

Giving It Some Thought

Your spouse is in the hospital for fairly minor surgery and is staying one night in the hospital after the surgery has been completed. A physician comes to check on your spouse that night. You notice that the physician does not go to the room's sink to do any hand washing. Because you know that lack of hand washing in hospitals is a major source of harmful and even deadly infections, you're wondering how clean the physician's hands are. Do you say anything?

Key Terms

ambulatory care facility, 174

church-affiliated hospitals, 167

community hospital, 167

general hospital, 167

home health care, 178

hospice care, 179

hospital, 163

July effect, 171

multihospital chain, 168

nursing home, 176

osteopathic hospital, 167

private for-profit hospital, 166

private nonprofit hospital, 166

prospective payment system, 166

public hospital, 166

retail store clinic, 175

specialty hospital, 167

surgicenter, 176

teaching hospital, 167

urgent-care center, 175

Health and Health Care in the World's Wealthy Democracies

11

LEARNING QUESTIONS

1. What are any five peer nations of the United States?

2. What is the Bismarck model of health care?

3. How does Canada's health care system differ from the United Kingdom's health care system?

4. Why do the health care systems of Canada and the United Kingdom have lower costs than the U.S. system?

5. What does the U.S. health disadvantage mean?

6. Why does the United States have worse health than other nations?

Health and Illness in the News

With Great Britain about to have a national election in May 2015, both the Conservative and Labour parties agreed on at least one thing: to spend more money on the nation's health care system that provides free health care for everyone. The head of a British health care charity said that political leaders view Britain's National Health Service (NHS) as "the most revered public institution in this country." An NHS official had earlier called the NHS "an international icon of the British social conscience" that "replaces fear with hope." (Castle 2015)

The United States has much better health and much better health care than the low-income nations discussed in chapter 6. But that is no cause for celebration: given these nations' wretched living conditions and other problems, the United States certainly should have better health and health care than they do. Moreover, and more relevant for this chapter, the United States lags behind its peers, the world's wealthy democracies, in many indicators of health and health care.

A major reason for this situation is that the United States is the only wealthy democracy lacking universal health coverage for all its citizens. **Universal coverage** means that 99%–100% of these nations' citizens have all or most of their *basic* health care (also called *core* care, and including most medical services and sometimes dental and/or vision care) covered by insurance (OECD 2013). By contrast, many Americans are uninsured or underinsured and cannot afford health care that would be free in Great Britain, as the opening news story suggests, and free or very afford-able in other wealthy democracies.

Therein lies a sad tale that this chapter will describe. We begin by describing the health care systems of the world's wealthy democracies before presenting several comparisons of health and health care that will not favor the United States.

The Health Care Systems of Wealthy Democracies

The United States is an exceptional nation in many ways, both good and bad. Its lack of universal health coverage is one unfortunate way it stands out among the world's wealthy democracies that are its peer nations. This fact has fundamental implications for the quality of health in the United States. To help understand these implications, we need first to understand how the health care systems in peer nations work. Fur-ther information about these systems may be found in a variety of sources (Budrys 2016; Harrison 2015; Mossialos et al. 2015; Reid 2010).

Before proceeding, it makes sense to identify the wealthy democracies that are the proper peer nations for comparison. These nations include Canada; the nations of Western Europe and Scandinavia; Israel; Japan; and the "down under" nations of Australia and New Zealand. Table 11.1 lists the full range of countries that are com-monly considered the peer nations of the United States for comparisons of health and health care, education, and other social indicators.

As further backdrop for the discussion of other nations' health care systems, it is helpful to note that the United States spends far more on health care than its peer nations. Its annual per capita spending on health care of $8,745 is the highest of all the wealthy democracies and about 2–3 times as high as that for many Western European nations (2012 data). Figure 11.1 shows a comparison of per capita health care spending for six selected nations: Canada, France, Germany, Sweden, the United Kingdom, and the United States, which easily spends more per capita than the other five nations in this comparison.

Not only does the United States spend much more per capita on health care, it also spends a much higher percentage of its gross domestic product (GDP) on health care. This percentage is at least 1.5 times higher than every other peer nation and about twice as high as some peer nations. Figure 11.2 shows the comparison for our selected nations.

With this background material in mind, we now turn to their various health care systems and will see how, unlike the United States, they provide free or affordable health care to all their citizens.

TABLE 11.1 **The World's Wealthy Democracies**

1. Australia	9. Ireland	16. Norway
2. Belgium	10. Israel	17. Portugal
3. Canada	11. Italy	18. Spain
4. Denmark	12. Japan	19. Sweden
5. Finland	13. Luxembourg	20. Switzerland
6. France	14. Netherlands	21. United Kingdom
7. Germany	15. New Zealand	22. United States
8. Greece		

Source: OECD. 2015. *Health at a Glance 2015: OECD Indicators*. Paris: OECD Publishing.

Models of Health Care Systems

Health writer T.R. Reid (2010) reminds us that a nation's health care system inevitably reflects the nation's history, politics, economy, and values. Despite this fact, health care systems around the world generally follow one of four models. The models reflect two primary considerations: (1) whether the government or private sector pays for most health care through insurance or direct payments to health providers, and (2) whether the government or private sector is the provider of most health care (by owning and operating hospitals and employing most physicians, nurses, and other health care providers) (DPE Research Department 2014; Reid 2010; Stevens 2010). As we shall see, these considerations in turn are very relevant for the cost of health care and for the degree to which people can afford health care. We now turn to these four models (Reid 2010).

The Bismarck Model

The **Bismarck model** (also called a *multi-payer health insurance model*) takes its name from Otto von Bismarck, the nineteenth-century Prussian chancellor who established the welfare state. The health care systems of Belgium, France, Germany, Japan, and Switzerland follow this model. Health care

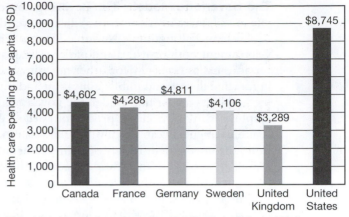

FIG. 11.1 Health Care Spending Per Capita in Selected Nations.

Source: Based on Mossialos, Elias, Martin Wenzl, Robin Osborn, and Chloe Anderson (eds.). 2015. *International Profiles of Health Care Systems, 2014: Australia, Canada, Denmark, England, France, Germany, Italy, Japan, The Netherlands, New Zealand, Norway, Singapore, Sweden, Switzerland, and the United States.* New York, NY: The Commonwealth Fund.

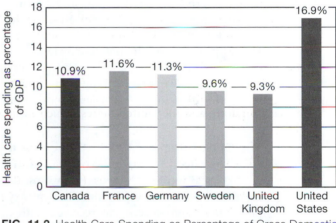

FIG. 11.2 Health Care Spending as Percentage of Gross Domestic Product.

Source: Mossialos, Elias, Martin Wenzl, Robin Osborn, and Chloe Anderson. 2015. *International Profiles of Health Care Systems, 2014: Australia, Canada, Denmark, England, France, Germany, Italy, Japan, The Netherlands, New Zealand, Norway, Singapore, Sweden, Switzerland, and the United States.* New York, NY: The Commonwealth Fund.

providers in this model are generally privately employed (i.e., the government does not own most hospitals and does not employ most physicians), and health insurance is also private (i.e., provided by private companies rather than the government). Employers and employees together pay for this model's health insurance. Citizens are required to belong to a health insurance plan, and the plans, even though they are private, are also nonprofit for the core care they insure. In the Bismarck model, governments typically strongly regulate costs and other aspects of health care provision even if this provision is largely private. As a result, the various plans pay for health care at a fairly uniform rate, greatly reducing administrative costs for billing (DPE Research Department 2014).

The Beveridge Model   The **Beveridge model** (also called a *national health service model*) takes its name from William Beveridge, a social reformer whose work led to the United Kingdom's National Health Service (see below). In this model, the government both provides and pays for health care. Taxes pay for this government service, just as taxes pay for other government services such as policing, fire fighting, mail delivery, and public education and public libraries. Patients do not receive medical bills. Under this model, the government owns most or all hospitals and also employs many physicians; private physicians do practice and receive government reimbursement. Because health care in this model is essentially a government enterprise, the government largely determines medical costs and thus keeps these costs as minimal as possible. In addition, because there is little or no private insurance, the high marketing and administrative costs associated with private insurance are lacking. For these reasons, health care costs under the Beveridge model tend to be relatively low, and certainly lower than those under the system of private, for-profit insurance that characterizes the United States. The wealthy nations that use the Beveridge model include the United Kingdom, Italy, New Zealand, and Spain. This model is an example of what is meant by a *single-payer* system.

The National Health Insurance Model   The **national health insurance model** combines aspects of the Bismarck and Beveridge models. Health care providers are primarily private employees (Bismarck), but the government (national and/or local governments) pays for most or all of health care (Beveridge), making this model another example of a single-payer system. Like the Beveridge model, the national health insurance model has relatively low costs because insurance is not-for-profit, because administrative and marketing costs are low, and because the government can determine what it is willing to pay for medical services. Canada is probably best known for its national health care model, but Australia, Denmark, and Sweden also use this model.

The Out-of-Pocket Model   In the **out-of-pocket model**, most health care is privately provided, and citizens pay for most of their health care themselves. This model characterizes most of the world's nations, that is, those that are too poor to provide health care for their populations and typically lack even private health insurance. People in these nations generally receive health care pay only if they can afford to pay for it themselves (*out-of-pocket*). This means that wealthy people can receive health care because they can afford it, while the masses of poor people receive little or no health care at all.

The U.S. Model   The U.S. health care model is unusual because it actually combines aspects of all four models just described (Reid 2010). It follows the Bismarck model (private provision and private insurance) for most people under age 65. At the same time, it also follows the Beveridge model (government provision and government insurance/payment) for three groups of people: Native Americans, active military personnel, and military veterans; all three groups receive free care from the federal government. Next, with Medicare the United States follows the national health insurance model for people aged 65 and older. Finally, the United States follows the out-of-pocket model for its many uninsured residents and also for many insured Americans who incur copayments, coinsurance, deductibles, and other out-of-pocket expenses.

The U.S. model is a hybrid model for all these reasons. It is also a unique model, and not in a good way, because it does not include universal health coverage. As two health scholars explain, "Most developed countries have national health insurance programs run by the government and financed through general taxes. Almost all citizens in such countries are entitled to receive health care services. Such is not yet the case in the United States, where not all Americans are automatically covered by health insurance" (Shi and Singh 2015:2). The idea that everyone should have health coverage is "the underlying moral principle of the health care system in every rich country—every one, that is, except the United States" (Reid 2010:23). The United States stands alone among wealthy nations in not observing this moral principle.

The U.S. model also differs from peer nations in one other feature, and that is the lack of a unified system for coordinating and financing health care. As health writer T.R. Reid (2010:21) explains, "And yet we're like no other country because the United States maintains so many separate [health] systems for separate classes of people, and because it relies so heavily on for-profit private insurance plans to pay the bills. All the other countries have settled on one model for everybody, on the theory that this is simpler, cheaper, and fairer. With its fragmented array of providers and payers and overlapping systems, the U.S. health care system doesn't fit into any of the recognized models [of peer nations]." Chapter 12 further discusses the fragmented nature of U.S. health care.

With this international context in mind, we now turn to brief descriptions of several peer nations' health care systems. They all feature better health and health care overall than the United States at a much lower cost.

The Health Care Systems of Selected Nations

Canada   It makes sense to start with Canada, and not just because it is near the beginning of the alphabet. Because Canada is the northern neighbor to the United States and features the national insurance model, its health care system has captured much interest as a possible exemplar for the United States. As such, much attention has focused on the possible merits and drawbacks of a Canadian-style system for the United States.

Canada's national insurance system is actually only quasi-national, as it is technically based in Canada's ten provinces and three territories, each of which sets its own standards for insurance payments and other matters within the framework established by the federal government. However, because the differences among the provinces and territories are limited, our discussion here will treat Canada as having in effect an actual national system.

The origins of Canada's system are worth noting. These origins lie in the decision of the province of Saskatchewan in the late 1940s to establish a government single-payer system, funded by taxes, in which the province paid for hospital care. The inspiration for this decision came from Saskatchewan's premier (governor), Thomas Clement Douglas (Reid 2010). As a boy in his native Scotland, Douglas suffered a serious knee injury that left him limping and on crutches because his family could not afford surgery. After his family moved to Canada a year later, a Canadian surgeon chose Douglas as the subject for a novel surgical technique and repaired the knee completely. After he became premier, Douglas remembered his family's inability to afford his knee surgery and resolved that no family in his province should go without needed medical care because it was too expensive. As he later recalled, "I felt that no boy should have to depend either for his leg or his life upon the ability of parents to raise enough money. I came to believe that people should be able to get . . . health services irrespective of their individual capacity to pay" (Reid 2010:127).

The new Saskatchewan model won acclaim and was eventually adopted and expanded to all of Canada in the 1960s. For more than half a century, the provinces and territories have paid for all core medical services; most hospitals continue to be privately owned, and most physicians continue to be privately employed. Patients are not billed for their core costs and instead show their provincial health card to their health care providers, who are reimbursed regularly by their province or territory on a **fee-for-service** basis (i.e., a separate charge for each office visit, each test, and each medical procedure. Private health insurance is available to help pay for noncore medical costs such as dental and vision care and prescriptions, although some provinces pay some of these costs for some of their residents: about two-thirds of Canadians buy private insurance or have employer plans to cover these supplemental costs (Kliff 2012a). Because the Canadian provincial and territorial governments together insure Canada's entire population of more than 35 million, they have much leverage in negotiating charges with hospitals, physicians, and other health care providers. This leverage helps keep Canada's health care costs lower than they would otherwise be.

We will see later in this chapter that Canada ranks higher than the United States on a variety of health outcomes and health care measures. One area in which it ranks lower is waiting times for nonurgent care: elective surgery (e.g., hip replacement, cataract surgery), nonurgent tests and procedures, and appointments with specialist physicians. Although waiting times vary by province, on the whole Canadians wait longer for nonurgent care than Americans do. In national surveys conducted by the Commonwealth Fund, 18% of Canadians say they have to wait at least four months for elective surgery, compared to only 7% of Americans; 29% of Canadians say they have to wait at least two months for a specialist appointment, compared to only 6% of Americans (Mossialos et al. 2015). Canada's longer times have received much attention in popular press comparisons of the two nations' health care systems (Barua 2014).

Two points are worth noting in regard to Americans' faster waiting times for nonurgent care. First, the U.S. health care system might be faster than Canada's for nonurgent care, but it is not necessarily faster than other nations' universal health care systems. The percentage of respondents in several such nations (France, Germany, the Netherlands, Sweden, Switzerland, and the United Kingdom) who report the long waiting times just described are generally no higher, and sometimes lower (depending on which waiting-time issue is being compared), than the U.S. percentages (Mossialos et al. 2015). It is also true that in the United States, Medicare, which is essentially national insurance for people aged 65 and older and thus similar to Canada's model for everyone (see chapter 13), does not produce longer waiting times for patients than is true of privately insured people.

Thus, Canada's longer waiting times are *not* an inherent function of universal health care *per se,* nor of its particular version of a single-payer model, but rather a function of Canada's decisions regarding the allocation of health care resources (Carroll 2012). In effect, Canada has set a global budget for what it wants to spend on health care and has erred on the side of having fewer specialists but more primary physicians (Kliff 2012b), because primary physicians are less expensive, and primary care also plays a critical role in a nation's health. Canada's choice to favor primary care over specialist care has arguably contributed to its good health outcomes but also to its waiting times for nonurgent care.

Second, although Canada has longer waiting times for nonurgent care, it still exhibits better health and health care outcomes than the United States. In this regard, only 13% of Canadians say they are unable to afford needed medical care, including prescriptions, during the past year, compared to 37% of Americans (Mossialos et al. 2015). So while many Canadians may wait long times for nonurgent care, tens of millions of Americans are receiving no care at all.

Health policy scholars continue to debate the relative merits of the two nations' health care systems. Still, Canada's universal access to care remains a compelling point in its favor. As an American health journalist has noted,

In Canada there are no financial barriers to care at the point of service as there are and will continue to be in the U.S. Canadians don't pay coinsurance of 30 percent or 50 percent if they have an outpatient procedure or go to an urgent care clinic, charges that are becoming increasingly common here. They don't worry about paying a gigantic bill if they happen to use an out-of-network doctor or hospital. The publicly funded system north of the border bases patients' access to medical services on need, not on the ability to pay (Lieberman 2014).

The journalist also noted that Canada's health care system treats all Canadians equally, with no one having more access to core care than anyone else based on income. By contrast, wealthier Americans can afford insurance with lower deductibles and copayments and for this and other reasons are much better able to afford health care. And because so many Americans receive health insurance through their employment, some simply have better insurance coverage than others because of the specific coverage their employer happens to offer.

In a final word on Canada, it is also worth noting that Canadians are more satisfied than Americans with their nation's health care system. Almost half (48%) of Canadians say their health system "works well," compared to only 25% of Americans; conversely, only 9% of Canadians say their health system needs to be "completely rebuilt," compared to 27% of Americans (Mossialos et al. 2015). As well, 57% of Canadians say they are "very satisfied or "satisfied" with their health care system, compared to only 25% of Americans (Kliff 2012a),

France France has one of the world's best health care systems from all indications. It ranks highest among 11 wealthy democracies on a composite "healthy lives" score based on amenable mortality, infant mortality, and life expectancy at age 60, although it ranks lower on access (affordability) to health care (Davis et al. 2014). France achieves its excellent "healthy lives" score even though it spends less than half per capita on health care than the United States does (see Figure 11.1). What can we learn from France's example?

France follows the Bismarck model of health care. As discussed earlier, this means that France's health care system generally features private insurance and the private provision of health care. Most physicians are private employees, while the hospital industry features a mixture of public and private hospitals. All French citizens are required to have health insurance for core medical services, which they purchase from *sickness insurance funds.* (The government pays for insurance for low-income residents and for their dental and vision care.) Physicians charge patients on a fee-for-service basis. Most French citizens obtain their health insurance through their employment and share the cost of their health care premiums with their employer via payroll deductions. In most of these respects, the French model is remarkably similar to the U.S. model.

However, there are significant differences. The premiums the French pay are much lower than what Americans usually pay. Moreover, whereas Americans often pay hundreds or thousands of dollars in deductibles, the French pay no deductibles at all. In the United States, when people lose their job, they also lose the health insurance that they probably had from their employment and have to purchase another insurance plan if they can afford it (unlikely if they are unemployed), hope they qualify for Medicare, or wait until they find another job with an employer that provides health insurance. In France, if people lose their job, the government picks up their former employer's share of their health insurance premium, and the person continues to be insured. U.S. health insurance companies often take a very long time to reimburse physicians and hospitals, while the French sickness insurance funds reimburse within a week.

In another significant difference, most U.S. private health insurance is for-profit, but the French sickness insurance funds are nonprofit plans. This fact means that the French plans' "main concern is not providing a return to investors but, rather, paying for people's health care" (Reid 2010:51). A concern for profit is a major reason U.S. health insurance companies have long refused to cover some or all of many hospital and other health care charges that Americans incur. Before the advent of Obamacare, they also declined new coverage for people with preexisting conditions and canceled coverage if someone was incurring too many medical expenses. Under Obamacare, they can no longer do these things (see chapter 12). In contrast, the French sickness insurance funds have not taken these measures precisely because they are nonprofit, and they routinely cover whatever charges are submitted (Reid 2010). Because the French funds are nonprofit, they also do not spend money on advertising, on reviewing and denying claims, and on certain other matters; this fact helps to make their administrative costs (and thus premium costs) much lower than those of U.S. insurance companies. In yet another difference, French patients are free to see almost any physician or visit any hospital they wish, whereas U.S. insurance plans often limit patient choice to "in-network" providers by charging patients much more for "out-of-network" providers or not covering out-of-network care at all.

One additional difference is worth noting. The French government closely controls and limits what providers may charge, whereas the U.S. government has weak or no controls by comparison. As a result, charges from physicians, hospitals, and pharmaceutical companies are much lower than they would otherwise be, saving the insurance plans and patients' much money compared to the U.S. system.

France accomplishes all its advantages compared to the U.S. system with waiting times that are similar to those in the United States. As noted, it also does so at less than half the cost per capita that the United States pays.

Germany France's Bismarck model also distinguishes Germany, where the model essentially originated under von Bismarck's reign. The two countries' health systems are thus similar in fundamental respects. German health insurance is private; physicians are typically privately employed; and hospitals are a mix of public and private institutions. All Germans are required to buy insurance from one of some 160 quasi-public, nonprofit private insurance plans called *sickness funds*, all of which provide the same broad coverage and charge the same premiums, split between employers and the insured (Khazan 2014). Germans pay 8.2% of their wages (via payroll deduction) under about $62,000 annually for their premiums, and employers pay another 7.3%. The wealthiest Germans are not required to obtain insurance from a sickness fund and instead may subscribe to private insurance from a for-profit company; they must have insurance whichever arrangement they choose. Most people eligible for the private, for-profit insurance still choose the sickness funds; about 90% of Germans subscribe to the sickness funds and 10% to the for-profit funds (Underwood 2009). The government pays for insurance for children and unemployed adults. Small copayments exist only for some prescriptions and for hospital stays (about $15 per day) (Mossialos et al. 2015). There are no deductibles.

All the sickness funds provide coverage for core medical services as well as dental and vision care, psychiatric care, physical therapy, and prescriptions (and thus provide more coverage than France does). Because Germany has plenty of hospitals and physicians, waiting times for medical care are generally low. Like French patients, German patients can visit any physician or hospital they prefer.

In a significant difference from the French system, the German national government generally does little to control medical costs. Instead, the sickness funds within each of Germany's sixteen states negotiate rates, many of them fee-for-service, with physicians and hospitals for their own state. The funds have a fair amount of leverage, but less than the government would have. Along with Germany's rather extensive coverage, this fact means that German medical costs tend to be relatively high among wealthy democracies and certainly higher than France's costs, if much lower than the United States (see Figure 11.1).

Because Germany's sickness funds, like France's, are nonprofit, they again do not review and deny claims, since they fairly automatically reimburse any hospital or physician charges. This fact saves many administrative costs, as is also true of France. Again like France, when Germans lose their jobs, they continue to be insured because the German government pays their insurance premiums.

The health systems of Canada, France, and Germany all provide universal coverage, and they all achieve health outcomes that are generally better than those achieved by the United States and for far less money. People in these three nations do not go bankrupt because of medical expenses, which many Americans have trouble paying (see chapter 12). Like the residents of all wealthy nations with universal coverage, Canadians, the French, and Germans are all much less likely to forgo medical care for cost reasons, as we shall see later in this chapter. Although Canada, France, and Germany achieve their universal coverage in different ways and differ in other respects, they still overall provide examples of health care systems that rank higher than the U.S. health system at a far lower cost.

Sweden   Sweden's health care system generally follows the Beveridge model. It provides universal coverage and does so via public insurance and a mixture of public and private hospitals and physicians: hospitals are mostly public, and so are many physicians. (The number of private physicians means that Sweden also follows the national insurance model to some degree.) Health care is decentralized and financed through taxation by the nation's 21 county councils (equivalent to U.S. states or Canadian provinces) and 290 municipalities. The county councils pay for a wide range of medical services, including prescription drugs and dental care up to age 20, for their general populations, while the municipalities pay for the care of the elderly and disabled. Copayments are small and limited to about $125–$150 annually. Swedes thus pay very little out-of-pocket for their health care.

Most Swedish physicians are salaried rather than receiving a fee for every service if there were a fee-for-service model. They are also paid through a **capitation** system determined by the county councils and municipalities. Under this system, which is the opposite of a fee-for-service model, physicians receive a set fee for a patient rather than a separate fee for each test, procedure, and other service that might be performed. Because this dual salary and capitation model means that physicians generally have no financial incentive to order tests and procedures that might be unnecessary, it helps to keep health care costs lower in Sweden than in the United States (Frank 2013). And. because Sweden's health care system relies on public insurance run by government units that are nonprofit by definition, these units do not haggle over claims in the way that the U.S. private, for-profit insurance companies often do (Frank 2013).

Sweden pays less than half per capita on health care than the United States does and has better health outcomes and health system rankings. Only 6% of Swedes forgo needed care for cost reasons, compared to 37% of Americans (Mossialos et al. 2015). Although other differences between the two nations may help account for Sweden's better health outcomes, there is no evidence that its system of universal coverage and national insurance is compromising the health of its residents. Quite the contrary: as an American economist who visited Sweden observed, "The Swedish system performs superbly, and my Swedish colleagues cited evidence of that fact with obvious pride" (Frank 2013:BU6). The economist added that the evidence from Sweden and other wealthy nations belies the belief of many Americans that adopting a European-style health care system in the United States would cause all sorts of problems.

United Kingdom   The United Kingdom (UK) also features the Beveridge model of health care: the UK government employs many physicians and operates most hospitals and also pays for all core medical services. Because the UK model involves government-run health care, it (along with Sweden and the other nations with the Beveridge model) manifests what is often called *socialized medicine.*

This term is often used by critics of the UK/Beveridge model to criticize it, but the United States features many services and institutions that are government-run without anyone calling this socialism: the Post Office, the military and National Guard, public schools, public libraries, policing, fire fighting, and even the public works departments of cities and towns that fix potholes, pave roads, and perform other tasks. These examples suggest that a government-run health care system is no more "socialistic" than government-run postal services or public schools or public libraries. In this regard, recall that the U.S. government provides free medical care for military personnel, military veterans, and Native Americans. The physicians and nurses who provide this care are typically government employees. Is this socialism? As Reid (2010:106) pointedly asks, "If this [the Beveridge model] is un-American, why did we choose it for America's military veterans?"

The UK health care system began in the late 1940s and grew out of an influential 1942 report on social insurance by William Beveridge, a political official and social reformer. This system operates as follows. Its National Health Service (NHS) pays fully for a wide range of core medical services (including prescriptions, dental care, and some vision care) through taxation. Medications prescribed by hospitals are free, while outpatient prescriptions require a $12 copayment. However, because there are no prescription copayments for children, people aged 60 and older, pregnant women and recent mothers, low-income persons, and many chronically ill persons, most prescriptions end up costing nothing (Mossialos et al. 2015).

Apart from the prescription copayments, UK residents pay no copayments and no deductibles for their medical care. As Reid (2010:105) observes, "People go their entire lives without ever paying a doctor or hospital bill; in Britain, this is considered normal." Because there is no billing for medical services and no review (and possible denial) of standard insurance claims, UK's administrative costs for health care are low, helping to account for its low per capital spending (see Figure 11.1).

The UK government operates most hospitals and employs many (salaried) physicians, nurses, and other health care providers. Its NHS employs more than 1.6 million people, including about one-third of primary physicians and almost all specialist physicians. UK residents register with a primary physician, who gets paid on a capitation basis: the physician receives a fee for every patient, regardless of whether the physician actually sees the patient. This system helps keep medical costs lower than a fee-for-service system, and it also gives primary physicians a financial incentive to keep patients as healthy as possible (since they get paid even if they do not see a patient). Beyond that, UK physicians also receive an extra fee if their patients do remain healthy (Reid 2010). About 11% of Britons pay for private insurance, which helps them pay for private hospitals and over-the-counter medicines and may yield them faster waiting times with health providers.

How well does the UK "socialist" model work? Quite well. In the Commonwealth Fund's comparison of eleven wealthy democracies, the UK ranked first in each of the following areas: quality of care, access, and efficiency. It also ranked second in equity (income differences in access), though only tenth in health outcomes (but ahead of the United States, which ranked eleventh). The United Kingdom's overall ranking still led all the other ten nations (Davis et al. 2014). In the Commonwealth Funds surveys, only 4% of UK residents say they have to forgo needed medical care because of cost, compared to 37% of Americans. The British Medical Association (BMA, the equivalent of the American Medical Association) applauds the UK health care system, with its chairperson saying, "The NHS is not perfect. But the market-style philosophy [private, for-profit insurance] of the U.S. is a lesson we could do well without" (Harrell 2009).

Now that we have learned something about the health care systems in several peer nations, it is time to see how the United States fares in comparisons of health and health care among the wealthy democracies. *Spoiler alert*: it does not fare well.

Comparing the Wealthy Democracies

Sometimes money isn't everything. The United States spends some $2.9 trillion annually (2013 data) on health care and, as we have seen, much more per capita than any other wealthy democracy. The huge U.S. expenditure would perhaps make sense if it generated better health outcomes: it would be nice to think that we get what we pay for, to paraphrase an old saying. However, that is not the case. The title of a recent report from the U.S. Institute of Medicine (Woolf and Aron 2013) summarizes the harsh reality: *U.S. Health in International Perspective: Shorter Lives, Poorer Health*. Although the United States spends much more than its peer nations on health care, it has worse health and health care outcomes on average.

Comparing Health in Wealthy Democracies

We can document this fact with several measures of health outcomes that are commonly used to indicate the quality of nations' health care systems. This type of comparison is not an exact science because nations differ in many ways (e.g., poverty rates, dietary habits, social support mechanisms) that may affect health outcomes. Thus, differences in health outcomes cannot be attributed solely to differences in health care systems. With this caveat in mind, let's examine some comparisons of important health outcomes.

Life Expectancy   Life expectancy at birth is a common measure for comparing the health of people in different nations (see chapter 6). Using this critical measure, the United States has worse health than its peer nations. In these nations, life expectancy at birth exceeds 80 years on average, while it is below 80 in the United States. Moreover, while life expectancy worldwide has increased since 1970, this increase has been more modest in the United States than in its peer nations (OECD 2013). Figure 11.3 illustrates life expectancy at birth for our selected nations. As this figure shows, Americans can expect to live 2.3 fewer years on average than Canadians, and 3.5 fewer years than residents of France.

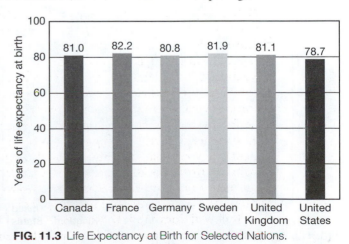

FIG. 11.3 Life Expectancy at Birth for Selected Nations.

Source: OECD. 2015. *Health at a Glance 2015: OECD Indicators*. Paris: OECD Publishing.

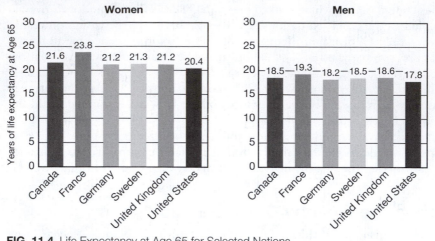

FIG. 11.4 Life Expectancy at Age 65 for Selected Nations.

Source: Based on National Center for Health Statistics. 2015. *Health, United States, 2014.* Hyattsville, MD: Centers for Disease Control and Prevention; OECD. 2013. Health at a Glance 2015: OECD Indicators. Paris: OECD Publishing.

It is also useful to compare life expectancy at age 65, or how long people can expect to live on average after reaching age 65. By that time of life, people in different nations are on the same playing field, so to speak, since differences in infant and childhood mortality, homicide rates, and other causes of death that mostly affect people under age 65 do not enter into life expectancy calculations as they do for life expectancy at birth. Once again, however, we see that Americans are at a disadvantage, as those who reach age 65 can expect to live fewer additional years than their counterparts in other wealthy democracies. Figure 11.4 shows the comparisons for our selected nations.

Infant Mortality and Low Birth Weight   Infant morality, the number of infant deaths (before age 1) per 1,000 live births, is another common and critical indicator of health disparities (see chapter 6). The U.S. infant mortality rate is higher than that for all its peer nations and up to 2–3 times higher than some of these nations (see Figure 11.5 for selected nations).

Low birth weight (under 5.5 pounds) is a related indicator of infant health and a strong predictor of health problems during infancy and childhood. The United States has the highest percentage of low birth weight infants among all the wealthy democracies (see Figure 11.6 for selected nations).

Diabetes   International comparison data also exist for specific health problems. We do not have space here to provide all the comparisons that exist, but will take the time to examine diabetes. Diabetes is an increasingly common chronic

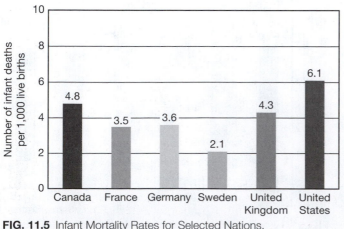

FIG. 11.5 Infant Mortality Rates for Selected Nations.

Source: National Center for Health Statistics. 2015. *Health, United States, 2014.* Hyattsville, MD: Centers for Disease Control and Prevention.

disease that causes various health complications and shortens lives. Because proper diet and weight can prevent Type-2 diabetes for many people, this disease is of particular interest to many public health scholars. Among the world's wealthy nations, the United States has the highest rate of diabetes among adults aged 20–79 and a rate that is twice as high as a few of these nations. Figure 11.7 provides the diabetes comparison for our selected nations.

Obesity   Another set of health risk factors of special interest to public health scholars is obesity and overweight. These factors may promote diabetes, as just noted, and also heart disease and other serious health problems (see chapter 3). For this reason, a nation's obesity rate is an important indicator of the poor health of its residents. In this regard, the United States holds the dubious honor of ranking the highest by far among the wealthy democracies (and also all OECD nations) in its percentage of obese adults, and it has a rate that is three times as high as some of these nations (see Figure 11.8 for selected nations).

We have seen that the United States is worse than its peer nations on various health indicators. Calling this the **U.S. health disadvantage**, the report by the Institute of Medicine cited earlier concluded that "on nearly all indicators of mortality, survival, and life expectancy, the United States ranks at or near the bottom among high-income countries," and it called attention to a "pervasive pattern of poorer health, more injuries, and shorter lives in the United States than in other high-income countries" (Woolf and Aron 2013:56,87). The report noted that the United States ranks lower

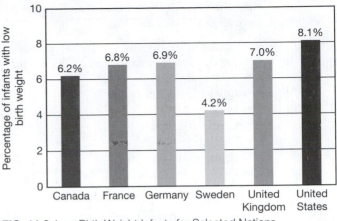

FIG. 11.6 Low Birth Weight Infants for Selected Nations.

Source: Based on OECD. 2015. *Health at a Glance 2015: OECD Indicators*. Paris: OECD Publishing.

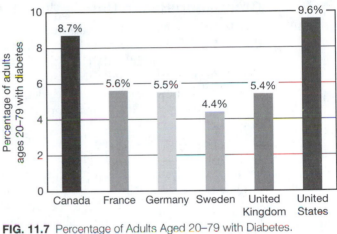

FIG. 11.7 Percentage of Adults Aged 20–79 with Diabetes.

Source: Based on OECD. 2013. *Health at a Glance 2013: OECD Indicators*. Paris: OECD Publishing.

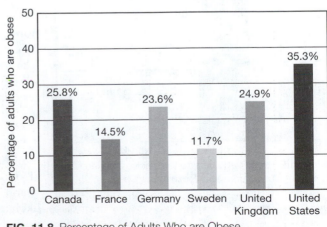

FIG. 11.8 Percentage of Adults Who are Obese.

Source: Based on OECD. 2015. *Health at a Glance 2015: OECD Indicators*. Paris: OECD Publishing.

than the average of its peer nations on the following health areas, some of which we have already examined:

- Infant mortality and low birth weight
- Adolescent pregnancy and STDs
- HIV and AIDS
- Obesity and diabetes
- Heart disease
- Chronic lung disease
- Disability
- Injuries and homicides
- Drug-related deaths

The Institute of Medicine report added that the United States does have lower cancer and stroke death rates and ranks well in terms of control of blood pressure and cholesterol, but it emphasized that this nation still ranks lower than its peer nations on most health indicators.

Comparing Health Care in Wealthy Democracies

If there are many indicators of the quality of health, there are also many indicators of the quality of health care. One important indicator involves *access to care*. For example, even if a nation like the United States might have the world's best physicians and best medical technology, this status loses meaning if many people cannot afford health care or otherwise do not have adequate access to health care.

The Commonwealth Fund, a private U.S. foundation, has conducted surveys of physicians and of the populations of eleven wealthy nations (Australia, Canada, France, Germany, Netherlands, New Zealand, Norway, Sweden, Switzerland, United Kingdom, United States), and it has also gathered other kinds of data. A Commonwealth Fund report that analyzed all these data before the full advent of Obamacare reached a striking conclusion about U.S. health care: "The U.S. is last or near last on dimensions of access, efficiency, and equity" (Davis et al. 2014:7).

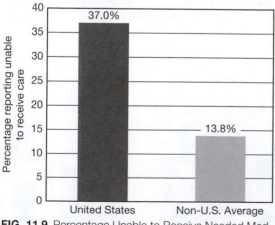

FIG. 11.9 Percentage Unable to Receive Needed Medical Care During Past Year Because of Cost.

Source: Based on Mossialos, Elias, Martin Wenzl, Robin Osborn, and Chloe Anderson. 2015. *International Profiles of Health Care Systems, 2014: Australia, Canada, Denmark, England, France, Germany, Italy, Japan, The Netherlands, New Zealand, Norway, Singapore, Sweden, Switzerland, and the United States.* New York, NY: The Commonwealth Fund.

For example, the Commonwealth Fund's surveys ask respondents to indicate whether they were unable to receive care (visiting a physician, filling a prescription, getting other care) during the past year because of cost. An average of 13.8% of the respondents in the ten non-U.S. nations reported this problem, compared to more than one-third (37%) of American respondents (see Figure 11.9). Americans were thus almost three times more likely than residents of the other nations to report being unable to receive needed medical care for cost reasons.

The United States trails its peer nations in indicators of the quality of health care beyond affordability For example, Americans discharged from hospital care report being more likely than people in any peer nation to have post-discharge complications and to need to be readmitted to a hospital (Woolf and Aron 2013). In another example, health scholars have estimated the number of deaths from about three dozen causes that could be prevented by better (more timely and more effective) health care. The United States has a higher rate of such preventable deaths (*amenable mortality rate*, the number of preventable deaths per 100,000 people) than any of the fifteen peer nations with which it has been compared (Nolte and McKee 2011). Finally, U.S. respondents in the surveys conducted by the Commonwealth Fund are more likely to report poor coordination by the health care system of their chronic illnesses, poor communication from health care providers, and medical errors. Perhaps not surprisingly, U.S. respondents and physicians are both more likely than their counterparts in other wealthy nations to be dissatisfied with the health system of their nation (Woolf and Aron 2013).

The news regarding health care is not all bad for the United States. For example, Americans in the Commonwealth Fund report were more likely than residents of most of the other nations to say they were able to see a specialist within two months. However, they were also *less* likely than residents of most of the other nations to be able to see a doctor or nurse the same day for which they sought more immediate care. Another way of saying this is that the United States has faster specialty care but slower primary care (Woolf and Aron 2013). The report's conclusion regarding the status of U.S. health care bears repeating: "The U.S. is last or near last on dimensions of access, efficiency, and equity" (Davis et al. 2014:7).

Explaining the U.S. Health Disadvantage

We have seen that the United States far outspends other wealthy democracies on health care, yet has worse health and health care overall. This paradoxical situation begs an explanation. Although it is difficult and perhaps impossible to identify the exact reasons for this situation, several factors do seem to help explain the health disadvantage of the United States (Woolf and Aron 2013).

Lack of Universal Health Coverage   According to many health scholars, a major factor, and one this chapter has stressed throughout, is the fact that the United States is the only wealthy democracy without universal coverage of health care costs for basic (core) medical services (i.e., the full gamut of physician examinations, diagnostic testing, and surgery and other procedures, but often not including prescriptions and dental and vision care).

As we saw earlier, the different nations have different ways of achieving universal coverage. Some governments pay for health care themselves and finance this form of national health insurance with income taxes and/or payroll taxes. Other governments require everyone to be insured, and families then pay for private insurance themselves, often with government subsidies and even full government payment for children's health insurance. Although private insurance in some of these nations technically comes from for-profit companies, government policies and regulations mean that these companies generally do not make much, if any, profit from their insurance for core care. Instead, their profit comes from supplementary coverage for services such as dental care, vision care, and prescriptions (Jacobson 2010).

In contrast, about 16% of the U.S. population, amounting to some 50 million Americans, was uninsured before the 2010 passage of the Affordable Care Act (Obamacare); that percentage is now (2015) down to 11.5% (Cohen and Martinez 2015). This situation stems from the unique reliance of the United States on private, for-profit insurance, either through employers or through self-insurance, with government insurance only for people aged 65 and older (Medicare) and many, but far from all, low-income persons (Medicaid). The U.S. reliance on private, for-profit insurance inevitably means that many Americans are uninsured because they cannot afford insurance or choose not to pay for it. Either because they are uninsured or because they still cannot afford some forms of health care even if they are insured, many Americans forgo needed health care, as we saw earlier in this chapter. This fact in turn helps lead to poorer health outcomes and thus the U.S. health disadvantage. Chapter 12 discusses U.S. health insurance further.

On a related matter, Americans pay a much greater share themselves of health care expenses (via copayments, coinsurance, deductibles, and other out-of-pocket payments) than do peer nations' residents, as whatever insurance Americans do have often falls short of covering the total expense. As the Institute of Medicine summarizes this point, "Cost sharing is common in the United States, and high out-of-pocket expenses make health care services, pharmaceuticals, and medical supplies increasingly unaffordable" (Woolf and Aron 2013:106).

Lack of Adequate Primary Care Another reason for the U.S. health disadvantage is the lack of adequate **primary health care** (health care delivered by primary care physicians such as family physicians and general practitioners) (Avendano et al. 2009). Public health scholars emphasize that good, available primary care is essential for preventing health problems from arising and for treating the problems that do arise (Shu 2012; Starfield, Shu, and Macinko 2005). Despite this fact, the United States has neglected primary care. As a recent report observed, "Although primary care is fundamental to a well-functioning health system, the U.S. has undervalued and underinvested in it for decades" (Abrams et al. 2015:4).

A common measure of the availability of primary care is the number of primary care physicians compared to an area's population size. Based on this measure, the United States lags behind all its peer nations for two related reasons. First, the United States has lower **physician density** (the number of all physicians compared to population size) than any peer nation but Japan (Woolf and Aron 2013). Second, the United States also has the lowest proportion of its physicians engaging in primary care than any of its peer nations (Woolf and Aron 2013). These two facts translate to lower availability of primary care physicians as measured by the number of primary care physicians per 100,000 residents. Figure 11.10 shows a comparison of this availability for our six selected nations; the United States again fares worst in this comparison.

High Cost of Health Care Whether health care is affordable depends on at least two factors: (1) how expensive it is, and (2) how well people are able to afford whatever health care does cost. We have already observed that Americans are less able to afford health care than peer nations' residents because the United States lacks universal health coverage and health insurance. But they are also less able to afford health care because U.S.

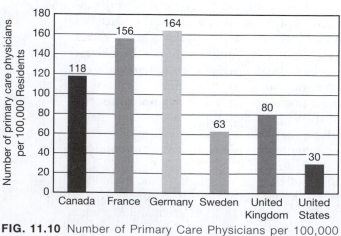

FIG. 11.10 Number of Primary Care Physicians per 100,000 Residents.

Source: http://stats.oecd.org/index.aspx?DataSetCode=HEALTH_STAT#

health care costs are much higher than peer nations' costs, as chapter 12 discusses further. As that discussion will make clear, U.S. health care is much more expensive than peer nations' health care for several reasons. Suffice it to say here that the high cost of U.S. health care helps explain the U.S. health disadvantage (Woolf and Aron 2013).

Poverty   A fourth factor that helps explain the U.S. health disadvantage is the high degree of poverty found in the United States. The U.S. poverty rate is much higher than in other wealthy democracies, and the United States also lags behind its peer nations in providing many kinds of social and economic support services for its low-income population (Woolf and Aron 2013). Because we have seen earlier in this book (chapter 5) that poverty and low income are important predictors of poor health, the high U.S. poverty rate and the lack of social and economic support services help explain why Americans are generally less healthy than the residents of peer nations.

This point merits further attention. Poverty does help explain the worse health of the United States, and its impact should not be minimized. However, it is also true that upper-middle-class and upper-class Americans are less healthy than their counterparts in peer nations (Woolf and Aron 2013). This comparison underscores the fact that other aspects of U.S. health care and Americans' lives must be explaining the worse health of Americans. Expanding on this point, the Institute of Medicine noted that Americans have the highest rate of obesity among peer nations, as we have already seen, and higher rates of drug abuse (Woolf and Aron 2013). But the report also noted that Americans who are not overweight and who do not smoke tobacco are still less healthy overall than their counterparts in peer nations. The reasons for their worse health remain unknown.

In a related point, the United States is more diverse racially and ethnically than its peer nations. As we have seen in earlier chapters, people of color in the United States are less likely to have health insurance and more likely to have worse health. These twin facts raise the possibility that the racial/ethnic diversity of the United States helps explain its health disadvantage. However, non-Latino white Americans, including wealthy non-Latino white Americans, still have worse health overall than their counterparts in peer nations (Woolf and Aron 2013). This fact is similar to the one noted for poverty and again points to the significance of other factors for the U.S. health disadvantage.

These considerations all indicate that the U.S. health disadvantage arises from a complex set of factors and that no one factor can be held responsible. As the Institute of Medicine report noted, "It is highly likely that the U.S. health disadvantage has multiple causes and involves some combination of unhealthy behaviors, harmful environmental factors, adverse economic and social conditions, and limited access to health care" (Woolf and Aron 2013:208).

Conclusion

The United States remains the world's only wealthy democracy without universal health coverage and some form of universal health insurance. Despite the fact that the United States greatly outspends its peer nations on health care, it ranks at or near the bottom on most measures of health outcomes and health care performance. The peer nations achieve universal coverage in different ways, but their example points to various policies and strategies that the United States might adopt to improve the nation's health.

Summary

1. Although the United States spends much more per capita on health care than other wealthy democracies, it ranks near or at the bottom of its peer nations on many measures of health outcomes and the quality of health care systems.
2. Several models of national health care systems exist based on whether the government pays for health care and whether the government owns most hospitals and employs most physicians and nurses.
3. The health care systems of Canada, France, Germany, Sweden, and the United Kingdom all achieve universal coverage in different ways, and they all have health care systems that rank higher than the United States at a much lower cost per capita.
4. In one of the most important measures of the quality of health care, Americans are much more likely than the residents of other wealthy democracies to be unable to receive needed medical care because of its expense.
5. Possible reasons for the health disadvantage of the United States include its lack of universal health coverage, its lack of primary care physicians, its high medical costs, and its high poverty rate. Yet, even wealthier Americans have poorer health than their counterparts in peer nations.

Giving It Some Thought

Your family earns about $60,000 a year, enough to make ends meet but not enough to cover unusual expenses. Your health insurance has a $4,000 deductible. After your partner is diagnosed with cancer and undergoes chemotherapy and much hospitalization, you quickly use up your deductible and incur $10,000 of additional expenses that you cannot afford to pay. What do you do?

Key Terms

beveridge model, 184

bismarck model, 183

capitation, 189

fee-for-service, 186

national health insurance model, 184

out-of-pocket model, 184

physician density, 196

primary health care, 196

U.S. health disadvantage, 193

universal coverage, 181

The U.S. Health Care System

12

LEARNING QUESTIONS

1. Why is the U.S. health care system not really a "system?"

2. What share of health care spending comes from the various levels of government?

3. What does underinsurance mean, and what is its impact?

4. How do social inequalities reproduce themselves in health care?

5. Why are prices for health care and prescription drugs in the United States so high?

6. What are the major sources of waste in U.S. health care spending?

Health and Illness in the News

In May 2015, a breast cancer patient was scheduled to have a uterine mass removed at a Tucson, Arizona, hospital. She was told the night before the surgery that she had to pay a $1,000 copayment before the surgery could take place. Because she could not afford this payment and the hospital would not accept a partial payment, she canceled the surgery. "I got really angry," the patient recalled. "My doctor made it clear this is medically necessary." The woman's medical expenses as a cancer patient during the past year had already reached about $10,000, and she was having trouble paying all her bills. After a newspaper contacted the hospital, a hospital official apologized to the patient, who had her uterine surgery a month later and then began paying the $1,000 bill over time. (Innes 2015)

The United States has some of the best hospitals, physicians, and medical technology in the world. As the Arizona cancer patient's sad story reminds us, it also has patients who cannot afford needed medical care and who go into deep debt as a result. This chapter examines the U.S. health care system. It presents some important facts and figures about U.S. health care and examines some significant problems in the delivery of health care services to Americans.

The U.S. Health Care "System"

Many books describe the structure and operation of the U.S. health care system in minute detail. Because this is not one of these books, our goal in this chapter is simply to outline major aspects of U.S. health care and to examine important issues regarding health care delivery.

One key thing to know about the U.S. health care system is that it is not really a "system." The term *system* implies a collection of elements that work together in tight coordination to achieve a common goal. U.S. health care does not fit this definition because the United States in fact has numerous health care "systems." The national government delivers one version of health care; each of the fifty states delivers its own version of health care; and the nation's countless counties, cities, and towns all deliver their own health care to some degree.

This situation reflects the federal system of government that characterizes the United States. Under federalism, the various states are largely free to govern their own affairs on many matters, and health is one of these matters. Accordingly, the U.S. federal government plays a more limited role than other democratic governments (see chapter 11) in all aspects of health care: how health care is funded and operated, what health care should cost, and which health care goals are prioritized and how these goals are achieved. Under this federal system of government, U.S. health care is largely decentralized rather than nationally coordinated.

Other factors also account for the federal government's limited role in health care (Johnson and Kane 2010). Going back to the colonial period and revolution against England, Americans have long valued individualism and distrusted big government. Because of these related values, Americans tend to believe that individuals are largely responsible for their own fate and that the government should do relatively little to help people who have not been able to help themselves. In these respects, Americans differ markedly from their counterparts in other wealthy democracies, who tend to take a more *collectivist* orientation in believing that individuals are often harmed by forces beyond their control and that the role of government is to help those in need. The national health care systems in these peer nations reflect this orientation, while America's individualism and distrust of government have impeded the development of a similar system.

Another factor explaining the decentralization of U.S. health care is capitalism. Compared its peer nations, the United States has perhaps always placed more faith in and reliance on private enterprise and the profit motive to guide the nation's affairs. This reliance helps to further explain the limited role of the federal government in health care and also America's unique reliance on for-profit, private health insurance in lieu of national public insurance.

A final factor explaining the limited government role in health care involves the political influence of well-financed interest groups. Specifically, private insurance companies and the American Medical Association and other physician organizations were able to defeat several attempts during the last century to bring national health coverage to the United States (Quadagno 2006). Chapter 13 discusses this historical dynamic in further detail.

With this overview in mind, we now turn to some important facts and figures about U.S. health care before discussing several problems of health care delivery.

U.S. Health Care by the Numbers

The U.S. health care system is so immense that it is helpful to consider the amount of money it involves, the number of people it employs, and the number of patients it treats. This section presents some important basic information about American health care.

The Cost of Health Care

The United States spent $2.9 trillion on health care in 2013, or $9,255 per person. As chapter 11 highlighted, this expenditure is easily the highest among the world's wealthy democracies. Table 12.1 shows how this multi-trillion dollar expenditure was achieved. As you can see, about half of U.S. spending on health care goes to hospitals and physicians and clinics. Large amounts are also spent on other types of health care. It all adds up to some $2.9 trillion, an almost unimaginable figure. Note that *net cost of private health insurance* is the fourth-highest expenditure at $174 billion. This cost is the difference between the total amount of premium payments and the total amount paid out in benefits for health care performed. This difference thus consists of such private insurance items as administrative costs (billing and advertising), profits, and dividends to stockholders. A discussion later in this chapter on the high cost of health care will refer back to this net cost of private insurance.

Sources of Health Care Spending   Now that we have seen where health care spending goes, it is helpful to see the sources for all this spending. Table 12.2 lists these sources. Note that private insurance is the largest source of health care payments at $962 billion. This amount for private insurance equals one-third of all health care spending, the highest such proportion among wealthy democracies, all of which except for the United States rely on taxation to finance some form of universal coverage for core medical services (see chapter 11). The private insurance amount thus underscores the key role played by private insurance in the U.S. health care system.

Note also from Table 12.2 that individuals and families pay $339 billion in out-of-pocket costs. This works out to about $1,045 per capita. Adjusted for cost-of-living differences, this per capita cost is second only to Switzerland among wealthy democracies and much higher than the average for ten peer nations including Switzerland (see Figure 12.1). This high U.S. out-of-pocket cost reflects in part the copayments, coinsurance, and deductibles that Americans often pay and that their peer nations' counterparts do not pay (see chapter 11). The difference in Figure 12.1 between the United States and its peer nations' average is $399 out-of-pocket spending per

TABLE 12.1	U.S. Health Care Spending by Category, 2013 (billions of dollars)
Hospital care	$937
Physicians and clinics	$587
Prescription drugs	$271
Net cost of private health insurance	$174
Investment (research, buildings, equipment)	$165
Nursing care and continuing care retirement facilities	$156
Other health care (e.g., schools, ambulances, substance abuse, etc.)	$148
Dental services	$111
Other professional services (e.g., optometry, physical therapy)	$80
Home health care	$80
Government public health	$75
Non-durable medical products (e.g., over-the-counter medicines, medical instruments)	$56
Durable medical equipment (e.g., eyeglasses, contact lenses)	$43
Government administration	$37

Source: Centers for Medicare & Medicaid Services. 2013. "National Health Expenditures 2013 Highlights." www.cms.gov.

TABLE 12.2	Payment Sources of U.S. Health Care Spending, 2013 (billions of dollars)
Private health insurance	$962
Medicare	$586
Medicaid	$450
Out-of-pocket	$339
Other third-party payers and public health activity	
(e.g., worksite health care, workers compensation, vocational rehabilitation, school health)	$312
Investment	$165
Other government health insurance	
(e.g., Department of Defense, Veterans Affairs)	$106

Source: Centers for Medicare & Medicaid Services. 2013. "National Health Expenditures 2013 Highlights." www.cms.gov.

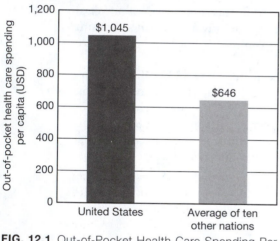

FIG. 12.1 Out-of-Pocket Health Care Spending Per Capita, Most Recent Year Available.

Note: Non-US nations include Australia, Canada, Denmark, France, Germany, Italy, New Zealand, Sweden, Switzerland, United Kingdom
Source: Based on Mossialos, Elias, Martin Wenzl, Robin Osborn, and Chloe Anderson. 2015. *International Profiles of Health Care Systems, 2014: Australia, Canada, Denmark, England, France, Germany, Italy, Japan, The Netherlands, New Zealand, Norway, Singapore, Sweden, Switzerland, and the United States*. New York, NY: The Commonwealth Fund.

capita. This means that an American family of four would save almost $1,600 annually in out-of-pocket spending if this aspect of U.S. spending were no higher than the peer nation average.

Sponsors of Health Care Spending It is useful to examine whether the types of *sponsors*, or entities, that finance the nation's health care bill (through insurance premiums, out-of-pocket costs, tax payments, and/or tax revenue) are private or public (government). Table 12.3 shows the relevant information.

Several items from Table 12.3 are worth noting. First, private business provides the funds for about one-fifth ($620 billion/$2.9 trillion) of all health care spending. Because the United States relies far more on employer-based health insurance than other wealthy democracies, private businesses in the United States bear more than their fair share, so to speak, of health care financing. According to many economists and health policy analysts, this burden reduces the wages employers can afford to pay and raises the prices they must charge for goods and services (Burtless and Milusheva 2013; Gottschalk 2008). Americans thus pay a hidden cost for the unique employee-based, private insurance model of the United States (Kliff 2013).

Second, private households provide the funds for more than 28% ($824 billion/$2.9 trillion) of all health care spending. This is a higher proportion than private households in other wealthy democracies provide, thanks again largely to the U.S. private insurance model.

Third, because private businesses and private households provide so much of the funding for the U.S. health care bill, the various levels of government provide relatively little compared to the norm for other wealthy democracies. When we add up the amounts in Table 12.3 for the levels of government and do a little arithmetic, public funding pays for about 43% of the U.S. health care bill. By contrast, public

TABLE 12.3	Types of Sponsors of National Health Expenditure, 2013 (billions of dollars)
Private	
Private business (e.g., employer contributions to private health insurance premiums and to Medicare payroll taxes, workers compensation, disability insurance)	$611
Household (e.g. employee contributions to employer-sponsored health insurance, individual health insurance, payroll taxes for Medicare, out-of-pocket health spending)	$824
Other private revenues (e.g., philanthropic support, investment income)	$218
Public	
Federal government (e.g., Medicare and Medicaid expenditures, maternal and child health, Department of Defense, Veterans Affairs	$758
State and local governments (e.g., Medicaid expenditures, vocational Rehabilitation, public health activities)	$509

Source: Centers for Medicare & Medicaid Services. 2013. "National Health Expenditures 2013 Highlights." www.cms.gov/.

funding pays an average of about 75% of other wealthy and near-wealthy nations' health care bills (OECD 2013). In fact, the United States is the only wealthy democracy where public funding pays for less than 50% of health care spending.

Health Care Employment

Previous chapters have listed the numbers of physicians, nurses, and other health care providers in the United States. As those numbers indicated, the U.S. health care system is simply a massive employer that provides jobs to millions of people.

The U.S. Census gathers data on all occupations through its annual American Community Survey (ACS), a random sample of the American population. Table 12.4 reports ACS estimates of the number of people working in health occupations, including nurses and other employees who work in schools and other non-health care settings; these estimates exclude custodial workers and other people employed by the health care system whose duties do not involve any actual health care or services related to health care. According to these estimates, health care occupations employ more than 14 million people and account for 10.5% of the nation's entire workforce.

Health Care Visits

Most people seek health care at least once a year, and often much more often than once a year. The National Health Interview Survey (NHIS) asks respondents whether they had seen a physician or other health care professional (excluding dentists) or visited an emergency room during the past year, either for preventive services or because they had a health problem. Table 12.5 summarizes their responses. About 84% of Americans have at least one health care visit annually, and more than 12% have at least ten visits. Most Americans clearly have some contact with the health care system every year. In fact, the number of visits to physician offices and hospital outpatient and emergency departments exceeds 1.2 billion annually (National Center for Health Statistics 2015).

Health Insurance

Some of the most important numbers in the U.S. health care system concern health insurance. Before presenting some insurance numbers, it will be helpful to outline

TABLE 12.4	U.S. Health Occupations, 2010–2012 Estimates
Occupational Category	**Number of Employees**
Medical and health service managers	553,748
Psychologists, counselors, social workers	1,559,901
Health care practitioners	
Physicians	835,723
Registered nurses	2,801,108
Other (e.g., chiropractors, dentists, dietitians,	
Optometrists, pharmacists, physical therapists)	1,197,334
Health technologists and technicians (e.g., dental hygienists, paramedics, licensed practical nurses, laboratory technologists, medical records technicians, opticians)	2,223,372
Health care support occupations (e.g., dental assistants, home health aides, physical therapist assistants)	3,311,640
Personal care aides	992,467
Medical secretaries	630,527
Total	14,105,820

Source: National Center for Health Workforce Analysis. 2014. *Sex, Race, and Ethnic Diversity of U.S. Health Occupations (2010–2012)*. Rockville, MD: Health Resources and Services Administration, U.S. Department of Health and Human Services.

TABLE 12.5	Health Care Visits During Past Year (2013), All Ages
Number of Visits	**Percent**
None	16.1
1–3 visits	47.6
4–9 visits	24.0
10+ visits	12.3

Source: National Center for Health Statistics. 2015. *Health, United States, 2014*. Hyattsville, MD: Centers for Disease Control and Prevention.

the major types of health insurance in the United States, which fall into two broad categories: private and public (government).

Most people who have private insurance obtain it through their employer (*employer insurance*), while some pay for their insurance themselves entirely (*individual insurance*). They usually do so for one of three reasons: (1) their employer does not offer health insurance, which is true of many small businesses; (2) they are self-employed; or (3) they are unemployed.

In addition to private insurance, the United States has two major forms of public (government) insurance, Medicare and Medicaid (both listed in Table 12.2), for specific populations. **Medicare** is a federal program that provides basic medical services for everyone aged 65 and older; it also serves some younger disabled people and dialysis patients. Medicare does not normally cover long-term nursing care, most dental care, eye exams for prescription eyeglasses, dentures, hearing aids and hearing exams, foot care, personal care assistance, and some other services. Medicare patients also pay a monthly premium of at least $105 (higher for individual incomes beyond

$85,000 annually), coinsurance of 20%, and a $1,260 deductible for a hospital stay per benefit period (a sixty-day window).

Medicare does not provide automatic prescription drug coverage, but people aged 65 and older have the option of obtaining Medicare coverage for their prescriptions through plans run by private insurance companies. These plans have premiums; they also have a standard $320 deductible and 25% coinsurance up to a limit of $2,960 annually. Enrollees pay a greater share of their prescription costs after this limit until they reach a total of $4,700 in out-of-pocket spending. They then pay 5% of their prescription drug costs.

As all this information should imply, many Medicare enrollees incur significant out-of-pocket costs. To help pay these costs, many enrollees obtain private supplemental insurance that can still leave them with considerable out-of-pocket costs. As a result, enrollees' average annual out-of-pocket spending is almost $5,000 annually. Seniors in poorer health have higher out-of-pocket spending yet(Cubanski et al. 2015).

Medicaid is a combined federal/state program that provides core medical services (with some out-of-pocket spending) for some low-income children and parents, pregnant women, seniors, and people with disabilities. The individual states run their own Medicaid programs within guidelines established by the federal government. The federal government provides the states at least half of their Medicaid funding, and the states provide the rest of their Medicaid funding. Different states provide different amounts of funding and have different income-based eligibility requirements for Medicaid. This fact means that Medicaid eligibility and benefits vary from state to state, with some states being less generous than others and not covering someone who would have been eligible in another state. Because Medicaid benefits vary by state, so do out-of-pocket costs that Medicaid patients still must pay.

An example of state differences in Medicaid eligibility involves children aged 1–5 in four-person households. In 2014, such children in California would have qualified for Medicaid if their families' annual incomes were lower than $62,244, while their counterparts in Texas qualified only if their families' annual incomes were lower than $34,344 (Center for Medicaid & CHIP Services 2014).

A third and much smaller public health insurance program is the Children's Health Insurance Program (**CHIP**). This program provides core medical services (with out-of-pocket costs) to children whose families' incomes are fairly low but still too high to qualify for Medicaid. Some states also provide CHIP coverage for parents and pregnant women. Like Medicaid, CHIP's benefits and eligibility requirements vary by state.

With this backdrop in mind, let's examine the extent and types of insurance coverage in the United States. Table 12.6 presents insurance coverage data for 2014, the year the Affordable Care Act (Obamacare) took full effect. As you can see, a majority of Americans have private health insurance. The proportion of uninsured Americans was 10%. If we just consider people (children and adults) under age 65 since Medicare covers everyone aged 65 and older, the uninsured rate rises to 12%; if we limit the calculation to adults under age 65 since Medicare covers many children, the uninsured rate rises to 14%, or almost one of every seven adults. The total number of uninsured Americans of all ages in 2014 was 33 million.

Problems In U.S. Health Care Delivery

The United States provides some of the best health care in the world, but it also ranks lower than peer nations in many measures of health and health care (see chapter 11). Health scholars have identified many problems in U.S. health care delivery that ideally

TABLE 12.6	Health Insurance Coverage in the United States, All Ages, 2013

Source of Coverage	Percentage of People With This Coverage
Private plan	
Employer	48.2
Individual	6.0
Government plan	
Medicaid	14.7
Medicare	15.6
Other public	2.0
Uninsured	13.4

Source: Kaiser Family Foundation. 2015. Health Insurance Coverage of the Total Population. Retrieved from http://kff.org/other/state-indicator/total-population/#.

should be addressed if the nation wishes to improve its quality of health and health care. Earlier chapters of this book have already addressed several of these problems:

- Pharmaceutical companies' payments to physicians that may lead them to prescribe the companies' drugs rather than less expensive generic drugs (chapter 2);
- Physician shortages that reduce access to health care (chapter 8);
- Physician biases that may weaken their treatment of women and of people of color (chapter 8);
- Nursing shortages that compromise good health care (chapter 9); and
- Various hospital-related problems, including hospital errors, hospital shortages in rural and inner-city areas, and high hospital charges (chapter 10).

This section discusses additional problems in the U.S. health care delivery. As you will see, these problems overlap to an extent, but we will discuss them separately to highlight their key aspects.

Fragmentation and Lack of Coordination

The earlier discussion of the U.S. health care "system" pointed to the decentralized nature of American health care. This decentralization in turn leads to fragmentation and lack of coordination in the delivery of health care. As health scholars Leiyu Shi and Douglas A. Singh (2015:4) explain, "US health care delivery does not function as a rational and integrated network of components designed to work together coherently. To the contrary, it is a kaleidoscope of financing, insurance, delivery, and payment mechanisms that remain loosely coordinated. Each of these basic functional components—financing, insurance, delivery, and payment—represents an amalgam of public (government) and private sources." Because of this loose, complex structure and lack of central coordination, U.S. health care suffers from duplication, waste, and weak cost control (Shi and Singh 2015).

Decentralization leads to fragmentation for another reason, and that is the lack of uniformity in the cost and thus availability of health care. This cost varies greatly by region of the country and even among different hospitals and physicians within the same city (Brill 2013). The U.S. private insurance model compounds this situation, as the cost of health care for consumers varies according to the terms of their health insurance plans, assuming they have coverage in the first place: someone may pay virtually nothing for a given surgery or other medical procedure, while someone else may have to pay thousands of dollars. As a medical billing advocate points out regarding hospital charges, "If you line up five patients in their beds and they all have gall bladders removed and they get the same exact medication and services, if they have insurance or if they don't have insurance, the hospital will get five different reimbursements, and none of it is based on cost. The insurers negotiate a different rate, and if you are uninsured, underinsured or out of network, you are asked to pay full fare" (Bernard 2012:B1).

The potential to enjoy health care under the private insurance model also depends heavily on someone's ability to afford health care. Even among people with similar insurance terms, some individuals and families simply have less money and are less able to pay deductibles and coinsurance, as this chapter's opening news story illustrated. Then too, the nation's for-profit, insurance companies are notorious for questioning claims and limiting or denying coverage.

All these circumstances mean that Americans do not receive *uniform* health care. By contrast, peer nations' citizens do receive uniform health care because they all have health coverage and because the cost of specific medical services is generally the same across a given nation (Klein 2013a). If Americans cannot afford health care because of where they live, because of the terms of their health insurance, and/or because of their financial circumstances, a more fragmented and ineffective health care system is the consequence.

The general fragmentation of U.S. health care is reflected in the poor coordination of health care at the patient level (Elhauge 2013). An individual patient may see many physicians in a given year outside a hospital (Medicare patients see seven or eight physicians on average), and the physicians often do not communicate with each other. Physicians who treat the same patient in the same hospital also often do not communicate with each other. The result in either case is a lack of coordinated health care that may compromise patient health because it leads to medical treatment that is ineffective or even harmful. Ironically, physicians and hospitals that do coordinate health care risk losing income if they reduce patients' health problems. This means there is a financial incentive *not* to have better coordination, making it difficult to achieve more coordinated health care (Elhauge 2013).

Health Insurance Coverage: Uninsurance and Underinsurance

Much research documents the critical importance of insurance for helping people to afford health care, for helping them to maintain good health, and for helping them to avoid premature death. An estimated 44,000 Americans die prematurely every year because they lack health insurance and thus access to health care (Wilper et al. 2009).

Lack of health insurance is thus a critical problem for U.S. health care. As chapter 11 discussed, Americans are much more likely than people in peer nations to lack health insurance. This problem arises from the unique reliance of the United States on private insurance for people under age 65. This reliance has traditionally (i.e., before Obamacare) meant that many people go without any health insurance. This happens for several reasons:

- their employer does not offer health insurance, which is true of many small businesses;
- they cannot afford the insurance premiums even if their employer does offer insurance;
- they are self-employed or unemployed and cannot afford the premiums;
- they can afford the premiums, whether or not they have an employer, but choose to save the money and take the risk of being uninsured.

The result of all these circumstances is that, as Table 12.6 indicated, 10% of the U.S. population, or 33 million Americans, had no health insurance in 2014.

A related problem is **underinsurance**, which refers to the situation in which people are insured but still must pay high deductibles and/or much coinsurance and thus experience significant out-of-pocket costs. People who are underinsured experience problems similar to, if not as severe as, those who are uninsured: they may have to forgo needed medical care, and they may go into debt from health care costs.

The Commonwealth Fund terms an insured individual *underinsured* if any one of these three circumstances occurs: (1) out-of-pocket health care costs (excluding premiums) during the past year are at least 10% of household income; (2) out-of-pocket costs are at least 5% of household income if this income is below 200% of the federal poverty level; or (3) the deductible is at least 5% of household income. Based on this measure, national surveys conducted in 2014 and 2015 by the Commonwealth Fund found that almost one-fourth of insured American adults under age 65 (or 31 million adults) are in fact underinsured (Collins et al. 2015a, 2015b). Recalling the earlier note that 14% of adults under age 65 are uninsured, these figures mean that almost 4 in 10 American adults under age 65 are either uninsured or underinsured.

The 2014 Commonwealth Fund survey asked respondents if they had problems in the past year paying medical bills or were paying off medical debt. More than one-third (35%) of the American adults under age 65 in the survey reported having a medical bill problem or medical debt. The survey also asked respondents if they had to forgo needed medical care because of cost; more than one-third (36%) of American adults also reported this situation. Uninsured or underinsured adults were more than twice as likely as insured adults who were not underinsured to report all these situations. Meanwhile, in the 2015 Commonwealth Fund survey, one-fourth of insured adults under age 65 said it was "very difficult or impossible" to pay their premiums, and more than 40% said the same about their deductibles.

Other survey evidence underscores the fact that medical bills can be difficult for Americans to pay even when they have insurance. In a 2015 survey, one-fifth of insured Americans under age 65 reported having difficulty paying their medical bills during the past year (Sanger-Katz 2016). Almost two-thirds of people reporting this difficulty said they had drained their savings, and more than 40% said they either had to get a second job or work longer hours. A major problem here is the high deductibles of many insurance plans, a problem that chapter 13 discusses further.

Chapter 11's discussion of the world's wealthy democracies indicated that lack of health insurance and high health care costs help explain the U.S. health disadvantage. The numbers just presented show that many Americans go without needed medical care and suffer serious financial problems because of America's private insurance model and high health costs. Even among American adults who are insured and also not underinsured, more than one-fifth have to forgo needed medical care because of cost, and more than one-fifth also have financial problems arising from medical expenses (Collins et al. 2015). Medical expenses help account for almost two-thirds of the 1.7 million personal bankruptcies yearly and play the largest role in these bankruptcies (Mangan 2013). The citizens of other wealthy democracies worry much less, if at all, being able to afford their medical care (see chapter 11).

Social Inequalities in Health Care Delivery

The quality of health care delivery depends on two considerations: (1) the degree of access to health care, and (2) the quality of health care when it is accessed. Unfortunately, society's social inequalities reproduce themselves in health care delivery: access to health care and the quality of health care both generally vary according to social class, race and ethnicity, gender, and sexual orientation and gender identity. Chapter 5 documented how these social inequalities produce health disparities, while chapter 8 discussed physician biases that reduce the quality of care they provide for women and for people of color. Other social inequalities in health care delivery exist, as we shall now see.

Access to Health Care   Lack of health insurance is a common indicator and predictor of (lack of) access to health care. If so, social class and racial/ethnic differences in the lack of health insurance are troubling. As Figure 12.2 shows for people under age 65, low-income people are much more likely than wealthier people to be uninsured, and people of color are more likely than non-Latino whites to be uninsured.

Males are also somewhat more likely than females to lack insurance, perhaps reflecting men's "macho" belief (see chapter 4) that they need not worry about their health.

Another common indicator of access to health care is the number of annual health care visits someone makes. Recall that 84% of Americans have at least one health care visit every year. Given that most Americans do obtain health care annually, the 16% of Americans who have *no* health care visits are of special interest to health policy scholars. The reason for this interest is that a lack of health care visits may result in worse health, either because someone does not receive preventive health services or does not receive care for a health problem. The percentage of people under age 65 with no health care visits varies greatly by insurance status: 39% of the uninsured have no such visits annually, compared to only about 13% of the insured (National Center for Health Statistics 2015). In this age group, then, the uninsured are three times more likely than the insured to have no health care, even though their health is poorer on average.

Figure 12.3 depicts sociodemographic disparities in the lack of health care. These disparities partly reflect the differences in lack of health insurance shown in Figure 12.2 as well as the factors discussed in chapter 5's examination of health disparities.

The disparities shown in Figure 12.3 are again troubling. Because poverty and near-poverty are associated with worse health in many respects (see

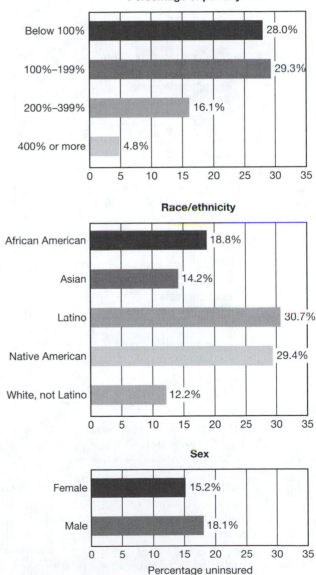

FIG. 12.2 Lack of Health Insurance Among Persons Under Age 65, By Selected Characteristics (% uninsured).

Source: National Center for Health Statistics. 2015. *Health, United States, 2014.* Hyattsville, MD: Centers for Disease Control and Prevention.

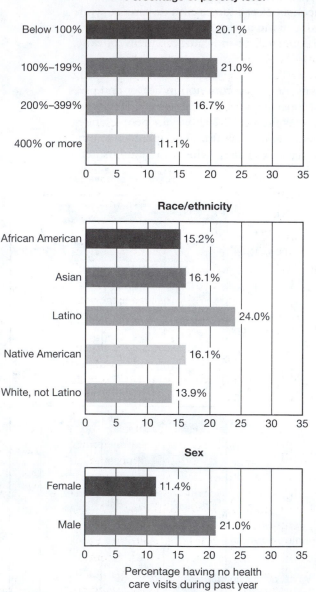

FIG. 12.3 Household Income, Insurance Coverage, and Health Care Visits, 2013 (% with no health care visits during past year).

Source: National Center for Health Statistics. 2015. Health, United States, 2014. Hyattsville, MD: Centers for Disease Control and Prevention.

chapter 5), it is especially important for low-income people to receive health care. Yet, the reverse is true: Americans living in poverty or near-poverty (up to 200% of the poverty level) are twice as likely as wealthier Americans (400% or more of the poverty level) to go without any health care. People of color are also more likely than non-Latino whites to go without health care. Meanwhile, males are twice as likely as females to have no health care visits, perhaps again reflecting their "macho" belief that they can ignore any health problems.

Sociodemographic disparities in health care disparities go beyond the lack of health insurance and health care visits. The National Health Quality and Disparities Report (QDR) assesses almost two dozen measures of health care access, including affordability and timeliness of access. Poor Americans (under the poverty level) have worse access than high-income Americans (at least 400% of the poverty level) on every single measure; African Americans and Latinos have worse access on about half the measures; and Asians and Native Americans have worse access on one-third of the measures (Agency for Healthcare Research and Quality 2015).

Quality of Health Care Sociodemographic disparities in the quality of health care are more difficult to study and document than disparities in access to health care. However, there is enough research on this topic for health scholars to conclude that the quality of health care is sometimes worse: (1) for low-income people than for wealthier people, (2) for people of color than for non-Latino whites, (3) for women than for men, and (4) for LGBT people than for straights.

Social Class and Race and Ethnicity The QDR also assesses dozens of measures of health care quality, and these measures again provide evidence of sociodemographic disparities. The QDR's quality measures are too numerous to list here, but include such things as: the quality of communication with health care providers; whether patients receive *effective* care (e.g., whether heart attack patients receive appropriate treatment within 90 minutes of arrival at a hospital); whether patients receive *coordinated* care; and whether patients receive *safe* care (e.g., whether they incur infections or pneumonia while in a hospital). Poor Americans experience worse quality on more than half the measures; African Americans and Latinos experience worse quality on about one-third of the measures; and Asians and Native Americans experience worse quality on about one-fifth of the measures. Illustrating the complexity of this research, Latinos, Asians, and Native Americans also experienced better quality of care on about one-fifth of the measures (Agency for Healthcare Research and Quality 2015).

As noted earlier, chapter 5 discussed other kinds of evidence pointing to racial/ethnic inequalities in health care quality. To recall, physicians are less likely to recommend appropriate medical testing and treatment of African American patients than they are for white patients. The reasons for this racial difference in medical treatment remain unknown but probably reflect unconscious racial bias and stereotyping by physicians. For example, physicians in one study described their African American patients as less intelligent than their white patients and more likely to abuse alcohol and other drugs (van Ryn and Burke 2000). Moreover, a survey of 222 white medical students and residents found that 40% of first-year students and 25% of residents falsely believed that African Americans' skin is thicker than whites' skin. Respondents who endorsed this and other false beliefs about biological differences between the races were also more likely to think that African Americans feel less pain than whites do (Hoffman et al. 2016). The latter stereotype may explain why much research finds that physicians are less likely to treat pain (by providing pain medication and, if provided, the appropriate amount of medication) reported by African American patients than by white patients (Hoffman et al. 2016).

Gender   Chapter 8 also recounted research that finds gender differences in the quality of health care (Anspach 2010, Read, and Gorman 2010). In this regard, recall two key findings. First, women patients are more likely than male patients to say that male physicians treat them condescendingly and play down their health concerns. Second, physicians are less likely to recommend appropriate testing and treatment for real or hypothetical female patients than they are for male patients. The reasons for these gender differences again remain unknown but probably reflect unconscious gender biases among physicians. Whatever the reasons, these gender differences in medical treatment "raise questions about medicine's scientific neutrality," writes sociologist Renee R. Anspach (2010:237), and provide "a powerful demonstration of a key discovery of medical sociologists: that medical decision making is a social process."

Women also suffer lower health care quality in another way. As chapter 5 discussed and as it is worthwhile reiterating, when women do not have health insurance or cannot afford health care even if they are insured, they lack access to contraception and gynecological care. This means they are disadvantaged in reproductive health care in a way that men are not. The women who experience this disadvantage are disproportionately poor and persons of color. These women thus experience what is termed *reproductive injustice* (Center for Reproductive Rights 2014): compared to wealthier white women, they are likely to have untreated gynecological problems and to have higher infant mortality rates.

LGBT Health Care   Relatively little research exists on possible health care disparities (access and quality) based on sexual orientation and gender identity. As chapter 5 noted, one reason for this deficit is that sexual orientation and gender identity until recently had not been included in the major national surveys, such as the NHIS, that are used to measure health care access and quality. The research that does exist still suggests that LGBT people are disadvantaged in the area of health care (Ard and Makadon 2012; Harvey and Housel 2014; Ranji et al. 2015).

One traditional reason for this problem is lack of health insurance. LGBT individuals are more likely than straight individuals to be poor or have low incomes and thus to be uninsured; this situation is especially true of the transgender population. Before the U.S. Supreme Court legalized same-sex marriage everywhere in 2015, individuals in same-sex relationships were also more likely than heterosexual spouses to lack health insurance because many employers did not insure LGBT spouses or partners. Partly for both these reasons, a survey taken a few years ago found that one-third of LGBT individuals with incomes under 400% of the poverty level were uninsured (Durso et al. 2013). Now that same-sex marriage is legal everywhere, health insurance coverage for LGBT people will almost certainly increase, as it did in New York after that state legalized same-sex marriage in 2011 (Gonzales 2015). To the extent this occurs, and to the extent that Obamacare is increasing insurance coverage for low-income people (see chapter 13), LGBT persons' health care access will increase as well.

Other LGBT-related health care disparities exist (Harvey and Housel 2014; Ranji et al. 2015). First, many health care professionals lack sufficient knowledge of the special health problems that the LGBT community experiences and the reasons for these problems (see chapter 5). As a result, LGBT persons may receive inadequate medical care. Some physicians have even uttered negative comments and refused to treat LGBT patients when the latter disclose their sexual orientation and gender identity. As a recent report noted, "Significant shares of LGBT individuals report negative experiences when seeking care, ranging from disrespectful treatment from providers and staff, to providers' lack of awareness of specific health needs. In a survey of LGBT persons, more than half of all respondents reported that they have faced cases of providers denying care, using harsh language, or blaming the patient's sexual orientation or gender identity as the cause for an illness" (Ranji et al. 2015:10).

Second, because older LGBT people are less likely to have children, they are more likely than their straight counterparts to lack practical help (e.g., being driven to a physician) when a health problem occurs. In addition, given the stigma that LGBT status still carries in the United States and elsewhere, some LGBT individuals are reluctant to seek health care for fear that health care providers may inquire about their sexual orientation and gender identity. Partly for this reason, LGBT individuals are more likely to go without health care. For example, lesbians have lower rates than heterosexual women of breast and cervical cancer screenings. In a related issue, health care intake forms commonly ask whether the patient's gender is female or male. LGBT people may find it difficult to answer this question, and LGBT health advocacy groups recommend that intake forms be revised to include a wider range of choices to help LGBT patients feel more welcome and comfortable (Ard and Makadon 2012).

The High Cost of Health Care

As mentioned earlier, the U.S. health care system suffers from high expenses that force people to forgo needed medical care and even drive them into debt. The incredibly high cost of U.S. health care helps explain why the United States spends so much more per capita on health care than its peer nations.

Dramatic evidence of the high cost of U.S health care can be seen when we consider the costs of various medical tests and procedures across the wealthy democracies. These tests and procedures cost much more in the United States than in its peer nations. Table 12.7 illustrates this problem with cost comparisons for selected tests and procedures in Canada and the United States. In every case, the U.S. cost greatly exceeds the Canadian cost.

Because hospital fees and physician fees are both higher in the United States than in peer nations, combined hospital and physician fees for medical procedures

TABLE 12.7	Average Cost of Selected Medical Tests and Procedures, Canada and United States, 2012 (U.S. dollars)	
	Canada	**United States**
Angiogram	$35	$914
CT scan, abdomen	$124	$630
CT scan, head	$124	$566
Physician fees, appendectomy	$408	$1,001
Physician fees, C-section	$606	$3,676
Physician fees, hip replacement	$697	$2,888
Physician fees, normal childbirth	$536	$3,096

Source: International Federation of Health Plans. 2012. *2012 Comparative Price Report: Variation in Medical and Hospital Prices by Country*. London: International Federation of Health Plans.

TABLE 12.8	Average Total Hospital and Physician Fees for Selected Medical Tests and Procedures, Spain and United States, 2013	
	Spain	**United States**
Appendectomy	$2,281	$13,910
Bypass surgery	$16,247	$75,345
C-section	$2,844	$15,240
Hip replacement	$8,010	$26,489
Knee replacement	$8,100	$25,398
Normal childbirth	$2,251	$10,002

Source: International Federation of Health Plans. 2013. *2013 Comparative Price Report: Variation in Medical and Hospital Prices by Country*. London: International Federation of Health Plans.

performed in hospitals are especially higher. Table 12.8 illustrates this situation with average costs from Spain and the United States for selected tests and procedures.

Prescription drugs also cost much more in the United States than in peer nations. For example, Gleevec, a cancer drug, cost the average U.S. patient $6,214 in 2013, compared to only $1,141 for the average Canadian patient; Copaxone, a multiple sclerosis drug, cost the average U.S. patient $3,903, compared to only $862 for the average English patient; and Humira, an acid reflux drug, cost the average U.S. patient $1,193, compared to only $881 for the average Swiss patient (International Federation of Health Plans 2013).

Reasons for the High Cost of U.S. Health Care   Why does health care of all types cost so much more in the United States than in peer nations? Several reasons come into play.

The Role of National Governments   The first reason reflects in the role played by peer nations' national governments. As chapter 11 explained, some national governments set the prices they will pay for health services (charges by physicians, hospitals, and other health care providers) and prescription drugs. Meanwhile, other national governments pressure health care providers and insurance companies to negotiate lower prices; because these governments provide some form of universal health care coverage, they have the clout to demand lower prices from health care providers and pharmaceutical companies, and they are very willing to exercise this clout (Squires 2012).

In contrast, less effective negotiation occurs in the United States, or none at all, leading to much higher prices for health care services and prescription drugs. As one health economist put it, "Other countries negotiate very aggressively with the [health care] providers and set rates that are much lower than we do" (Klein 2013b). Medicare and Medicaid do negotiate somewhat lower prices for health services for their patients However, as one news analysis noted, "outside that, it's a free-for-all. Providers largely charge what they can get away with, often offering different prices to different insurers, and an even higher price to the uninsured" (Klein 2013b).

The private insurance model helps account for this situation. The nation's many private insurance companies divide up the pool of the insured, reducing the clout that each company has when it negotiates separately with health care providers and pharmaceutical companies. As a result, whatever negotiation occurs is less effective in lowering prices (Consumer Reports 2014). Although the federal government should theoretically have much clout, the fact that it provides less than half of all U.S. health insurance gives it much less leverage than national governments elsewhere have. The federal government does use its leverage to reduce Medicare charges for health services compared to what private insurance companies pay, but federal law prohibits the government from negotiating with pharmaceutical companies for lower Medicare drug prices.

The Fee-for-Service Model   The second reason for the high cost of U.S. health care is the *fee-for-service* model on which the United States largely relies. As chapters 10 and 11 explained, physicians, hospitals, and other health care providers working under this model charge a separate fee for each service they provide for a given patient. These separate fees add up to yield high per-patient charges. Because health care providers are paid for everything they do, they in effect have a financial incentive for providing as many services as possible, and some of these services are simply not necessary. As one economic writer has put it, "The more they do, the more they earn" (Samuelson 2011). In contrast, several peer nations use the capitation model that provides a set fee per patient regardless of the number of services performed. As chapter 11 discussed, these nations' capitation models help keep their health care costs lower than otherwise. The fee-for-service model helps account for the volume of unnecessary medical testing, procedures, and other services, discussed later in this chapter.

Administrative Costs   The third reason for the high cost of U.S. health care departs from actual prices but again involves the private insurance model. This reason concerns *administrative costs*. Physicians, hospitals, and other health care providers typically bill and negotiate with many private insurance companies and spend much time and effort doing so. The average physician spends almost an hour daily dealing with insurance companies regarding payments, authorization for procedures, and other matters (Cutler et al. 2012). Health care providers employ extensive and expensive billing departments and other administrative staff to handle their dealings with private insurance companies and all the resulting paperwork (digital or hard copy).

Moreover, because private companies are for-profit, these companies spend much of their time dealing not only with health care providers but also with patients whose claims they routinely review and sometimes challenge or deny. This dynamic again involves a huge administrative staff and expense, and much more so than in a nation like Canada that has national health insurance. In just one example, as of a few years ago, the Duke University regional health system in North Carolina, which treats some 63,000 inpatients annually, employed 1,300 billing clerks (for 900 hospital beds!), while Canada's McGill University regional health system employed 12 billing clerks even though it handles almost 40,000 inpatients annually (Cutler 2013; McCanne 2009). Duke thus has roughly one billing clerk for every 48 inpatients, while McGill has roughly one billing clerk for every 3,300 inpatients. A McGill billing clerk thus attends to 69 times as many inpatients as a Duke billing clerk.

All these currents mean that a good chunk of the U.S. health care bill involves the sheer cost of all the administrative expenses incurred under the private insurance model on the part of health care providers and private insurance companies alike. In fact, it is estimated that administrative costs account for $361 billion, or more than one-eighth, of the U.S. annual health care bill. This amount is three times what is spent on cancer and twice what is spent on heart disease (Cutler et al. 2012). Peer nations spend a much lower proportion of their annual health care bills on administrative costs.

We can see evidence of the administrative and other expense of U.S. private insurance with some numbers appearing earlier in this chapter. Recall from Table 12.1 that the net cost of private insurance (administrative costs, profits, etc.) is $174 billion annually. In contrast, the cost for government administration of health care, most of it Medicare or Medicaid, is only $37 billion annually. Private insurance thus costs the nation almost five times as much as public insurance, even though private companies insure less than twice as many Americans as the federal government does (see Table 12.6), and even though the people whom the government insures tend to be much older (Medicare) and poorer (Medicaid) than those whom private companies insure.

Pharmaceutical Drug Prices   Earlier we mentioned that the United States pays far more than peer nations for pharmaceutical drugs, almost $300 billion annually (see Table 12.1). This topic merits further attention, as pharmaceutical companies argue that the high cost of research and development for a new drug justifies a drug's high price.

This argument has some merit at first glance. However, health economists reply that the high price of prescription drugs instead stems from a combination of other reasons (Llamas 2014; Nordrum 2015). First, the pharmaceutical industry lacks competition, as pharmaceutical companies are prohibited by federal regulations from producing a rival drug for five to seven years after a new drug is approved. As one health economist noted, "In drug companies, you do not have perfect competition—you have artificial monopolies" (Nordrum 2015).

Second, that pharmaceutical companies, unlike other businesses, do not fear their prices will be too expensive for consumers, because they just have to convince insurance companies to pay for their drugs. As a news analysis summarized this situation, "The price of medicine [in the United States] is not limited by two of the primary forces that keep the costs of most U.S. consumer goods in check—competition and affordability" (Nordrum 2015).

Third, and as discussed earlier, the federal government and private health insurance companies have relatively little leverage in negotiating for lower drug prices. Whereas pharmaceutical companies face much pressure in peer nations to have lower prices, they do not feel this pressure in the United States.

These circumstances all leave pharmaceutical companies relatively free to charge what they want in the American market. As another health economist explained, "I would argue that the [drug] prices that we have in the U.S. are not set by the market because we don't really have the conditions of a market. They're not set by the government because they can't negotiate the price. Essentially, we've chosen to let pharmaceutical companies write blank checks for their prices" (Nordrum 2015).

Free of normal free market considerations, pharmaceutical companies instead set their drug prices by considering what it would cost insurance companies to treat patients in the short term and long term if the health condition they suffer were not prevented, cured, or relieved by a new drug. Because their new drugs may save so much money, pharmaceutical companies feel emboldened to charge very high prices for their drugs. Faced with the prospect of paying huge costs for patients if the drug were not available, private insurers and the federal government feel pressured to go along with the pharmaceutical companies' demands for high prices (Nordrum 2015). As the news analysis cited earlier summarized this problem, "With no reason to stop, pharmaceutical companies will continue to price drugs based on the highest possible amount they believe insurers and governments will pay for those medicines" (Nordrum 2015).

A recent example of this dynamic involved a drug called Sovaldi, which received FDA approval in 2013 and which cures 90% of patients with hepatitis C, a debilitating and potentially fatal liver disease. Patients take a Sovaldi pill once a day for twelve weeks and then are cured. Because there are 3.2 million hepatitis C patients in the nation, the cost savings to insurance companies from this drug are incalculable. Drawing on the discussion just presented, it might not be surprising to know that Gilead, the company that markets Sovaldi, charged $1,000 per pill, or $84,000 for the full twelve-week treatment, when Sovaldi came on the market. Because insurance companies could potentially pay this high price for several million patients, it prompted heavy criticism from consumer groups and the insurance industry (Barrett and Langreth 2015).

Waste in Health Care Spending

Waste also contributes to the high cost of U.S. health care but is a sufficient problem in its own right to deserve separate attention here. **Waste** refers to several types of *needless* health care spending (Lallemand 2012):

- Spending on unnecessary or ineffective health care services (e.g., back surgery when physical therapy would have worked);
- Spending on medical care that is needed to treat complications from ineffective or uncoordinated care or from medical errors;
- Excessive spending arising from administrative complexity (e.g., a lack of standardized insurance forms because there are so many different private insurance companies);
- Higher prices stemming from a lack of competitive markets (because many medical service prices are not fully transparent and there is insufficient competition over pricing); and
- Fraudulent billing for medical services that were not provided.

A study by the Institute of Medicine (IM) estimated that almost one-third (30%) of the nation's health care bill fits this multifaceted definition of waste (Smith et al. 2012). Applying this estimate to the $2.9 trillion U.S. health care expenditure in 2013 yields a waste figure of some $870 billion annually. As just one example of waste, the IM study found that one-fifth of patients need additional medical visits or tests because their medical records or test results had not been transferred in time for an appointment. The study also cited the high number of medical errors during hospitalization (see chapter 10) that result in increased medical costs.

As noted earlier, the fragmentation and fee-for-service model that characterize U.S. health care help explain why there is so much waste in health care spending. The volume of unnecessary medical tests, procedures, and other services is especially notable. As a recent report noted, "Doctors often order tests and recommend drugs or procedures when they shouldn't—sometimes even when they know they shouldn't" (Consumer Reports 2012). Unnecessary tests, procedures, and medications cost the nation more than $200 billion annually (Smith et al. 2012). Perhaps even worse, unnecessary tests like X-rays and CT scans expose many patients to unnecessary and potentially dangerous amounts radiation, unnecessary surgery may lead to complications and even death, and unnecessary medications may lead to dangerous side effects.

An example of unnecessary radiation involves CT scans for lower-back pain. Although these scans do not help people with lower-back pain recover any faster, more than 2 million people with lower-back pain receive them annually. One study estimated that more than 1,000 of these people will develop cancer from their CT scanning (Consumer Reports 2012).

Many unnecessary surgeries also occur. Although numerous surgeries are absolutely necessary, many others are not necessary. Some physicians perform them because they feel the surgeries will help despite much medical evidence to the contrary; other physicians perform them simply to profit from them. Whatever the motivation, studies find that tens of thousands of surgeries, and perhaps more than 2 million annually, are clearly unnecessary (Eisler and Hansen 2013). These surgeries are thought to account for between one-tenth and one-fifth of cardiac procedures and spinal surgeries. Other common types of unnecessary surgery include cesarean sections, hysterectomies, and knee replacements. Unnecessary surgeries of all kinds cost the nation an estimated $150 billion annually and lead to many medical complications and an estimated 12,000 deaths annually from these complications (Eisler and Hansen 2013; Waldman and Armstrong 2010).

Health care fraud by physicians and other health care providers is also common and costly. These providers sometimes commit fraud via several types of schemes, including billing insurance payers (Medicare, Medicaid, or private insurance) for services for fictitious patients and for real patients' services that did not actually occur. The Federal Bureau of Investigation (2012) estimates that health care fraud of all types accounts for 3% to 10% of all health care spending annually. Because 2013 health care expenditures were $2.9 trillion, the FBI's estimate suggests that health care fraud amounted to at least $87 billion in 2013 and perhaps as high as $290 billion.

Conclusion

The U.S. health care system is the largest in the world, costing almost $3 trillion annually, employing more than 14 million people, and encompassing more than 1.2 billion health care visits annually. Because the federal government plays a smaller role in the operation and provision of health care than other national governments, the operation and provision of health care vary greatly by state and municipality. U.S. health care suffers from several problems, including fragmentation and lack of coordination, lack of health insurance and underinsurance, sociodemographic disparities in health care access and quality, and high cost and waste.

Summary

1. The U.S. health care system is not really a "system" because the federal government, the fifty states, and the nation's municipalities all deliver their own version of health care to some degree.

2. The federal, state, and local government pay for about 43% of the nation's health care budget. This proportion is much lower than the average of 75% for peer nations.

3. Americans' personal expenditures for health care in the form of premiums and out-of-pocket spending exceed those for the citizens of peer nations.

4. In 2013, the year before Obamacare took full effect, 13.4% of Americans lacked health insurance; this figure rose to 18.5% of adults under age 65. The number of uninsured Americans of all ages was about 42 million.

5. The U.S. health care system suffers from fragmentation and lack of coordination. The cost and availability of health care vary greatly by region of the country and within the same city. Cost and availability also vary according to the terms of private insurance plans and the incomes of American families and individuals. Health care is also often poorly coordinated at the patient level.

6. Uninsurance and underinsurance are another set of problems for U.S. health care. These twin problems mean that many people go without health care and/ or have trouble paying for health care.

7. Social inequalities reproduce themselves in health care delivery. Health care access and quality are generally poorer for low-income persons, people of color, and LGBT persons. Women also experience poorer quality of care than men in some ways.

8. Health care and prescription drugs are much more expensive in the United States than in peer nations. A major reason for this fact is that the national governments of peer nations more closely control the prices for health services and prescription drugs. Another reason is the fee-for-service model that characterizes much U.S. health care. A third reason for the high expense of U.S. health care is administrative costs, which are larger in the United States than in peer nations.

9. Waste, or needless health care spending, accounts for almost one-third of the nation's health care bill, or almost $900 billion annually. Examples of waste include unnecessary medical testing and ineffective medical care that results in the need for additional health services.

Giving It Some Thought

You are a 45-year-old primary care physician. A patient complains of back pain and wants to obtain a CT scan. You realize that the CT scan is not necessary because the patient's back pain will probably diminish and then disappear over the next few months, as most back pain does. At the same time, the patient is insistent, and as a physician you have always wanted to have a good relationship with your patients. What do you tell this back-pain patient?

Key Terms

CHIP, 205
Medicaid, 205
Medicare, 204

underinsurance, 208
waste, 216

Health Care Reform
Obamacare and Beyond

LEARNING QUESTIONS

1. Why did the Progressive Era fail to achieve national health insurance?

2. Why did employer-based health insurance arise during World War II?

3. Why did the administrations of Franklin Roosevelt and Harry Truman not achieve national health insurance?

4. What were the achievements and limitations of Obamacare by mid-2016?

5. What would be the advantages of Medicare for All?

6. Why does Obamacare not adequately address the social causes of health and illness?

Health and Illness in the News

After a U.S. Supreme Court ruling in 2015 upheld Obamacare's nationwide tax subsidies to help low-income people afford health insurance, Florida resident Jason Foster rejoiced. One of the millions of Americans who gained health insurance under Obamacare, Foster is a self-employed kidney transplant survivor who has to take antirejection drugs for the rest of his life. He would have lost his federally subsidized insurance had the Supreme Court ruled the other way. "If they repeal it, I lose the medication," he said. "I lose the coverage. I would get sick again. I would lose the kidneys that for me is almost a death sentence."

While Mr. Foster was celebrating being able to remain insured, a news report from Georgia stated that one-fifth of the state's adults remained uninsured despite Obamacare. A health policy writer noted, "That's a situation that's causing big bills in terms of those consumers, but also some financial hardship on the part of hospitals and other healthcare providers." The writer still applauded the Supreme Court decision for helping more than 400,000 low-income insured Georgians keep their insurance: "I think that it's very good news for struggling hospitals in rural areas and elsewhere, because if it had gone the other way they would have seen a lot more uninsured patients in their doors and in their emergency rooms." (Bevington 2015; Conlon 2015)

"It was the best of times, it was the worst of times," begins Charles Dickens' majestic *A Tale of Two Cities*. This famous opening line describes both the U.S. health care system and the Affordable Care Act's (Obamacare) attempt to reform it.

The United States offers some of the best medical care in the world. However, as the last few chapters have shown, the United States also has physician and nursing shortages; it ranks near or at the bottom among peer nations on many health care measures; it has tens of millions of uninsured or underinsured residents; and its health care is incredibly expensive and wasteful, and generally uncoordinated.

Enacted in 2010, Obamacare was intended to address these problems, and it has had some notable achievements. Sixteen million more Americans had health insurance by mid-2015 than before Obamacare took full effect in 2013 (Martinez and Cohen 2015). However, 28.5 million Americans remained uninsured by mid-2015 and millions more were underinsured, and the other health care problems just mentioned show little sign of abating in the foreseeable future. The twin news stories that opened this chapter underline the fact that Obamacare has succeeded but that this success has also been limited.

This chapter offers a critical look at health care reform. It examines Obamacare's key provisions and the reasoning underlying its controversial individual mandate and other stipulations, and it also examines Obamacare's impact and projected benefits and limitations for the years ahead. The chapter ends by discussing the merits of a single-payer system for the nation.

Origins of U.S. Health Insurance

To provide a proper context for the discussion, we first present a brief history of health insurance in the United States drawn from several accounts (Gordon 2004; Hoffman 2003; Moniz and Gorin 2014; Quadagno 2006; Starr 1982). National health insurance has been on the public agenda many times during the past century. This synopsis will help understand how the United States came instead to have its unique private insurance model and why it has been so difficult to upend this model despite the many problems it has created for the U.S. health care system and the health of millions of Americans. As one health policy professor has observed, "Inasmuch as history offers lessons about the contemporary prospects for health reform, optimism is not one of them. Still, that history is well worth knowing, both to appreciate what forces have stymied previous reform efforts and to understand the origins of the current system and its bewildering arrangements for insuring, paying for, and delivering medical care" (Oberlander 2005:1679).

Why did the United States end up with a private insurance model instead of the various forms of national health insurance and health care developed by other wealthy democracies? The answer to this question begins in the mid-1800s, when some U.S. companies began offering private insurance for injuries. By the end of the nineteenth century, some companies also had begun offering insurance for loss of income incurred by illness or disability (Moniz and Gorin 2014). These two types of limited policies were far from health insurance as we now know it, but they did help establish the idea that people could pay premiums in return for some economic benefit if they were injured or ill. The rudiments of a private insurance model thus existed by the beginning of the twentieth century, even if a full-fledged private insurance model was still several decades away.

The Progressive Era

At the same time, interest in a *national* insurance model financed and run by the state and/or federal governments began arising from a combination of several social forces. During the last few decades of the 1800s, industrialization and urbanization produced major social transformations and social problems such as poverty and crime. These problems led to the rise of the Progressive Era, named after a social reform movement that lasted from the late 1800s through the early 1920s. This movement criticized corruption by business and political leaders and sought to help the poor, children, and immigrants and racial minorities.

One focus of social reformers during the Progressive Era was health and illness. As chapter 2 recounted, urban living conditions during the second half of the nineteenth century produced deadly infectious diseases. Concern over disease and illness led to the rise of the public health movement (see chapter 2), and it also motivated Progressive Era reformers to try to help average citizens to pay for the medical care they so sorely needed.

A model for reformers' efforts lay in Western Europe, where several nations, including Austria and Germany as described in chapter 11, had all created national, compulsory health insurance programs by 1912. The United States had not yet followed their example because of reasons outlined in chapter 12: America's decentralized government, historic distrust of a national government, and faith in the private market. Encouraged by these nations' models, Progressive Era reformers tried to establish a similar model in the United States. Presidential candidate Theodore Roosevelt advocated one such model in 1912.

During this period, the sheer number of industrial accidents and high jury awards to plaintiffs injured in these accidents led most states to require businesses to provide workers' compensation in the form of automatic payments to employees for lost wages and medical expenses incurred by work-related accidents. The reformist American Association for Labor Legislation (AALL) helped achieve this new policy. Inspired by this success, AALL members and other reformers decided that it might also be possible to persuade the states to require all workers and their families to have health insurance. Arguing that healthy workers are more productive and less likely to have workplace accidents, AALL developed a proposal for required health insurance that would have paid for medical services, hospital care, and maternity services. State governments, employers, and employees would have financed this insurance. In effect, this would have been a national compulsory health insurance model similar to what now exists in some other democracies (see chapter 11). AALL hoped that its proposal's presumed benefits for employers would help it get enacted (Moniz and Gorin 2014).

These efforts by the AALL and other reformers instead met with strong opposition from big business and the private insurance industry. Until this time, the private insurance industry had offered life, fire, and casualty insurance, but not health insurance, which it considered too risky financially. Ironically, the debate over national health insurance made the private insurance industry realize that a heavy demand for health insurance might exist (Hoffman 2003). With potential profits in sight, the private insurance industry opposed any national health insurance model, and some companies began selling their first health insurance policies by the mid-1920s. A few national labor leaders, including famed Samuel Gompers, also opposed national health insurance on the grounds that it reflected governmental paternalism and implied that workers could not manage their own affairs. However, other national labor leaders and many local labor leaders favored a national model (Hoffman 2003).

National health insurance still had chances of succeeding, but world events soon intervened. Specifically, World War I began in 1914 and the United States entered the war in 1917 to fight Germany and Austria. Because these were the nations where national social insurance had begun during the late 1800s, national social insurance became stigmatized (Palmer 1999). Moreover, the Russian Revolution of 1917 led to a "red scare" in the United States that led to the arrests of thousands of social activists. Many of these activists' goals, including national insurance, became impossible to achieve. As one insurance executive said in 1917, national compulsory health insurance was "a communistic system . . . repugnant to American minds and destructive of American initiative and individuality" (Moniz and Gorin 2014:24). In 1920, moreover, the American Medical Association (AMA) issued a strong statement against national health insurance, as it feared that a national model would reduce physicians' incomes by controlling medical fees and also interfere with the physician-patient relationship (Quadagno 2006). Although more than a dozen states considered compulsory health insurance by the 1920s, not a single state enacted any insurance model along these lines. Once possibly close to enactment, national health insurance in the United States was now dead, or at least on life support.

The Great Depression and the New Deal

The issue of health insurance waned for a few years until the advent of the Great Depression, which lasted from 1929 to the entrance of the United States in World War II in 1941. As chapter 10 recounted, the deep unemployment caused by the Depression led to the nation's first real private health insurance plan in Dallas, Texas, to help schoolteachers pay for hospital care. This achievement soon spread to other hospitals in other states and became the model for the establishment of Blue Cross insurance in the early 1930s. This new insurance helped people pay for hospital care but not for physicians' services nor for other medical expenses. Blue Shield was then established in 1939 to pay for physicians' services. The creation of Blue Cross and then Blue Shield marked the beginning of the private insurance model in the United States. As two health scholars explain, "The establishment of Blue Cross and Blue Shield insurance plans laid the foundation for a third-party payment system, completely changed health care financing, and paved the way for employment-based insurance" (Shi and Singh 2015:27).

The Great Depression in effect created the first widespread private insurance plan, but it also led to new pressure for national health insurance. After President Franklin D. Roosevelt took office in 1933, he established his New Deal program of social and economic reform to help deal with the effects of the Great Depression. Perhaps the most significant New Deal accomplishment was the Social Security Act of 1935, which, as should be clear from its name, established the federal financial aid for people aged 65 and older that the United States has had ever since. This legislation passed despite conservative opponents' charges that Social Security was socialism. The legislation also provided unemployment insurance, benefits for injured workers, and funds for programs to enhance maternal and child health and to help people with physical disabilities.

As the Social Security Act was being developed, the White House initially considered adding national compulsory health insurance to the other provisions. In response, the AMA mounted an intense lobbying effort that led President Roosevelt to exclude health insurance from the final bill on which Congress voted, lest Congress defeat the entire bill. Roosevelt remained interested in compulsory health insurance during the next few years but still feared that any legislation related to it would meet defeat in Congress. When a New York senator introduced national health insurance legislation in 1939, the AMA and other medical bodies again lobbied against it, and the bill died in committee (Moniz and Gorin 2014).

The 1940s and 1950s

National health insurance went on the back burner after the United States entered World War II in 1941. A national health insurance bill was introduced in Congress in

1943, but it died in committee after opposition from the AMA. Ironically, however, the war generated interest in, and led to the development of, *private* health insurance. The reason for this was that the war produced shortages of civilian employees in the private sector because millions of Americans were fighting the war abroad or helping the war effort at home in war-related industries. The government had also imposed wage and price controls to curb wartime inflation. Because employers could not increase wages to attract the new employees they so urgently needed, some began offering health insurance as an inducement. This new type of health insurance proved popular, and it then became more popular after the war ended as employees began to expect employers to provide insurance.

Roosevelt planned to introduce new legislation after the war that would have provided national compulsory health insurance among other social benefits. After Roosevelt died in 1945, his successor, Harry S. Truman, introduced legislation for such insurance, but conservative opponents again termed it socialism and the AMA said it would make physicians "slaves" (Starr 1982:283). Truman's bill died, and when he reintroduced it a few years later, it again incurred charges of socialism and Communism from conservative opponents and the AMA, and it went nowhere.

Meanwhile, employer-based private health insurance continued to grow rapidly. A Congressional act in 1954 accelerated its ascent by making such insurance nontaxable for employees. This stipulation increased employees' interest in obtaining health insurance from employers (Moniz and Gorin 2014). The strong economy during the 1950s enabled employers to make their health insurance coverage more generous, and by the end of the decade employer-based, private health insurance coverage had become dominant throughout the nation. In effect, private insurance had triumphed over national public (government) insurance.

The 1960s: Medicare and Medicaid

Because national health insurance for all Americans had not been achieved, proponents thought it might be possible to secure national health insurance just for Americans aged 65 and older because they were already receiving Social Security. Interest in such a program grew through the 1950s, and this idea was included in the Democratic Party's 1960 presidential campaign platform. In the early 1960, the AMA again derided this program as socialism. President John F. Kennedy supported the idea, as did President Lyndon B. Johnson after Kennedy's 1963 assassination.

Congress finally passed legislation in 1965 that established Medicare for older Americans and Medicaid for many poor children, parents, pregnant women, and certain other persons. Private insurance industry opposition to this legislation was relatively muted, in part because the industry had little interest in insuring people who were old or poor (Hoffman 2009, 2010). Before 1965, the employer-based health insurance system had failed to help the elderly, the poor, and the unemployed because they were either not employed or had employers who did not provide health insurance. Medicare and Medicaid brought health insurance to these disadvantaged groups for the first time. Ironically, this achievement helped to reduce enthusiasm for national health insurance because elders and many of the poor were now covered (Quadagno 2006). Medicare and Medicaid thus "marked an incremental victory and larger defeat" (Gordon 2004:28) for the cause of national health insurance.

The 1970s and 1980s

During the 1970s, Senator Edward M. Kennedy, some other Democratic and Republican members of Congress, and Presidents Richard M. Nixon and Jimmy Carter all proposed forms of national health care with varying degrees of generosity; Kennedy's would have followed Canada's national insurance model (see chapter 11). None of this legislation succeeded, and President Ronald Reagan's election in 1980 again put national health insurance on the back burner for several years (Moniz and Gorin 2014).

Reagan's presidency ended in January 1989, and by that time rising health costs had generated new interest in national health insurance. A bipartisan Congressional committee established in 1988 included recommendations in its final report for required employer-based health insurance and government insurance for the unemployed, but Congress did not act on its recommendations.

1990s–2008

During the 1990s, interest grew among labor unions, some business leaders and physicians, and other parties in national health insurance based on Canada's model. President Bill Clinton introduced national health care legislation in 1993 that would have required employers to pay most of their employees' health insurance and the government to cover unemployed and poor individuals. Many liberals thought this plan did not go far enough toward Canada's single-payer model, while conservatives and private insurance and pharmaceutical companies strongly opposed it. The bill eventually crumbled in the face of this opposition. National health care again returned to the back burner, this time for more than a decade, before reemerging as an issue in the 2008 presidential election, won by Barack Obama.

The failure over a century to establish national health insurance left the United States with the system it has now, described by sociologist Jill Quadagno (2006:201) a few years before Obama's election as "a patchwork of public and private programs that provides some people with secure coverage but leaves others with sporadic periods of being uninsured and 45 million with no health insurance at all." It was this failed patchwork that President Obama began to tackle shortly after he took office in January 2009.

The Patient Protection and Affordable Care Act (Obamacare)

We have seen that a combination of factors thwarted efforts during the past century to establish a national health insurance model in the United States. These factors were a decentralized government, historic distrust of a national government, faith in the private market, and the opposition of powerful interest groups. We can add to this list two additional reasons. One reason is Americans' traditional aversion to taxes. Americans have never liked paying taxes, and to the extent that many proposals for national health insurance have relied on tax payments, Americans have disliked these proposals (Shi and Singh 2015). A second reason is bias against the poor and people of color (Gordon 2004; Quadagno 2006). Traditional bias against these two groups has historically prompted many Americans to oppose social welfare programs because these programs disproportionately help these two groups. This bias is yet another reason that has made national health insurance difficult to achieve, as this type of insurance again disproportionately helps the poor and people of color.

All these forces confronted President Barack Obama when he introduced his plan for health care reform early in his presidency. They generated one of the most contentious political debates of modern times before passage of the Patient Protection and Affordable Care Act (ACA), commonly called Obamacare, in 2010. Details of the politics surrounding the fight over and passage of Obamacare may be found elsewhere (Brill 2015; The Washington Post 2010).

Major Health Benefit Provisions of Obamacare

The Obama White House had several major goals in seeking its version of health care reform: (1) reduce the number of Americans without health insurance; (2) eliminate certain abuses by the health insurance industry, including refusing to cover people with preexisting conditions, canceling coverage for people with high medical expenses, and imposing annual and lifetime dollar limits on the cost of coverage; (3) increasing the use of preventive health services, especially for women in view of their gynecological and obstetrical needs; and (4) controlling health care costs.

The ACA's attempt to achieve these goals was so complex that the original legislation describing the ACA amounted to some 370,000 words, equivalent to more than 1,100 typed, double-spaced pages. Full details about the ACA may be found at http://www.hhs.gov/healthcare/rights/.) We certainly cannot outline every aspect of the ACA but will begin our discussion by listing many of the health care benefits Obamacare provides for the public, with certain restrictions. These benefits include:

- Dependent children can now remain on a parent's health insurance policy until they turn 26 years old
- Insurance companies cannot refuse to cover people with preexisting conditions
- Insurance companies may not cancel a policy for someone with high medical costs
- Annual and lifetime dollar limits on most health care benefits are now eliminated
- Insurance companies may no longer charge higher premiums for women than for men or for less healthy people than for healthy people
- Many preventive health care services are now free for all adults, including alcohol counseling, blood pressure screening, colorectal cancer screening, depression screening, diabetes screening, HIV screening, obesity screening and counseling, syphilis screening and STD prevention counseling, tobacco use screening and cessation interventions, and various immunizations
- Many preventive health services are now free for women, including anemia screening for pregnant women, breast cancer and cervical cancer screening, contraceptive methods and counseling except when insured by religious organizations or certain for-profit companies with religious objections, domestic violence screening and counseling, folic acid supplements for women who may become pregnant, gestational diabetes and hepatitis B screening for pregnant women, urinary tract screening for pregnant women, and well-woman visits
- Many preventive health visits are now free for children, including alcohol and other drug use assessment, autism screening, behavior assessments, blood pressure screening, depression screening for adolescents, hearing screening for newborns, HIV screening for newborns, a wide range of immunizations, lead screening for children at risk of exposure, obesity screening and counseling, STD screening and counseling, and vision screening.

The Individual Mandate

Perhaps the most controversial feature of the ACA was the so-called **individual mandate** that requires every American to have health insurance or else pay a tax penalty. As part of the mandate, the federal government and 16 state governments established online *health insurance exchanges*, or *marketplaces*, where individuals and families could shop for health insurance either because they were uninsured or because they wished different insurance coverage from what they already had. All the insurance providers in these marketplaces are private companies, as the White House plan rejected the idea of the federal government providing a government-funded "public option" as one of the insurance choices. Individuals and families with incomes under 400% of the federal poverty level are eligible to receive federal subsidies in the form of tax credits to help pay for the private insurance received from the marketplaces.

During the debate over the ACA, conservative opponents said the individual mandate reflected an out-of-control, federal government that in a socialistic maneuver was taking away the individual freedom of Americans to decide whether or not they wanted health insurance. However, the idea of an individual mandate is in fact consistent with conservative philosophy for the following reason: people without health insurance can visit a hospital emergency room and obtain medical and emergency care at public expense that is then passed on to people (in the form of higher charges and higher premiums) who are responsible enough to have insurance. As a result, people without insurance are essentially "free-loaders" who are not taking personal responsibility for their health care expenses and instead spreading the cost of their health care to other people. This general reasoning explains why almost every state requires every motor vehicle to carry various forms of insurance, so that people in an accident with an uninsured driver do not have to draw on their own insurance or potentially pay thousands of dollars in vehicle and health care expenses.

The other feature related to the individual mandate is the use of the health insurance marketplaces. Here again, this feature reflects conservative principles, in this case faith in market forces as commercial insurance companies compete in the marketplaces while consumers shop for their best prices (premiums, deductibles, coinsurance) and best coverage.

The conservative principles underlying the individual mandate and marketplaces explain why a conservative think tank, the Heritage Foundation, in fact proposed these general concepts in 1989 as a conservative alternative to the Clinton administration's proposal for national health insurance (Roy 2011). As a resident fellow at the American Enterprise Institute (AEI), another conservative think tank, observed in a 2012 op-ed entitled *The Conservative Case for Obamacare*, "The architecture of the Affordable Care Act is based on conservative, not liberal, ideas about individual responsibility and the power of market forces" (Kleinke 2012:SR4).

Reflecting these conservative ideas, Massachusetts Republican governor Mitt Romney championed and won the passage of a health care reform model in his state in 2006 that provided the model for Obamacare. This fact was widely noted during the 2012 presidential campaign in which Romney opposed Obama's reelection. The AEI op-ed writer just mentioned argued that Romney should have tried during the campaign to take credit for Obamacare rather than denying his model's influence on it because "Obamacare is, at its core, Romneycare across state lines" (Kleinke 2012:SR4). The writer also noted that many Democrats thought Obamacare did not go far enough by failing to establish a national insurance model.

The individual mandate also makes sense from the health insurance industry's perspective, which is why insurance companies eventually supported the ACA in the months leading up to its passage. Several related factors explain the insurance industry's support.

First, the mandate aimed to have millions of uninsured Americans enroll in a health insurance plan. Because there was no public option, the private insurance industry would gain many new customers and much revenue from this flood of the newly insured.

Second, many young people in good health chose to forgo health insurance before Obamacare. This was a problem for the insurance industry, because any insurance company's profitability depends on *not* paying benefits to most of the people it insures. In effect, the good fortune of people who do not need to use their insurance pays for the benefits their company provides to its customers who must use their insurance. For this reason, the insurance industry welcomed their new coverage of young people as required under Obamacare.

Third, recall that Obamacare provides many kinds of benefits for all adults, and also specific benefits for women and for children. These benefits all cost the insurance industry much money. Because the insurance industry is mostly for-profit, why, then, would it support Obamacare? The answer lies in the individual mandate. In return for accepting the need to pay for Obamacare's many benefits, the insurance company would again acquire millions of new customers.

As should be clear from this discussion, Obamacare was an attempt based on conservative principles to work within the existing private health insurance model to bring health insurance to uninsured Americans and to correct the coverage abuses inherent in a for-profit health insurance industry. The next section assesses Obamacare's achievements and limitations at the date of this writing.

Achievements and Limitations of Obamacare

As this chapter noted at the outset, Obamacare reflects the best of times and the worst of times. By mid-2016, five years after Obamacare's passage in 2010 and a year after the individual mandate took full effect, evidence showed that Obamacare had already succeeded in several ways in a relatively short time (Altman 2016; Pear, Sanger-Katz, and Abelson 2015). But there was also evidence that many health care problems as described in chapter 12 remained and would continue. We first assess Obamacare's achievements at this six-year benchmark and then its limitations. Because of the time it takes to accumulate and analyze data, the most recent data for this assessment are from 2015.

Achievements of Obamacare

The many ACA health benefit provisions listed earlier have helped countless Americans in many ways. For this reason, Obamacare should already be considered a huge success. For example, one study found that women's out-of-pocket spending on contraception declined steeply in the first half-year after the ACA's requirement for free contraceptive coverage took effect in 2013 compared to the same period a year earlier: their spending on contraceptive pills fell by about 50%, while their spending on intrauterine devices (IUDs) fell by 70% (Tavernise 2015a). Other evidence suggests that Obamacare's provisions have enabled young women to have cervical cancers diagnosed at an earlier stage than would have been possible before Obamacare (Tavernise 2015b). Because earlier diagnosis of cancer improves the chances of effective treatment and survival, Obamacare has likely been invaluable for many young women across the nation.

Beyond the gains from these provisions, a proper assessment of Obamacare involves whether it has succeeded regarding three criteria: (1) access to health care; (2) the cost of health care; and (3) the quality of health care. Evidence by 2015 showed promising results for the first two criteria but hardly any results at all, one way or the other, for the quality of care (Blumenthal et al. 2015).

Access Regarding access, a review of the relevant evidence concluded that "the ACA has brought about considerable improvements in access to affordable health insurance in the United States" (Blumenthal et al. 2015:2455). This conclusion reflects the fact

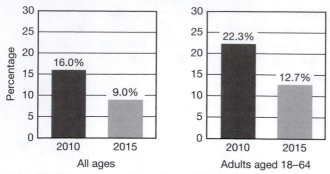

FIG. 13.1 Percentage of Americans Without Health Insurance, 2010 and 2015.

Source: Martinez, Michael E. and Robin A. Cohen. 2015. *Health Insurance Coverage: Early Release of Estimates from the National Health Interview Survey, January–June 2015.* Washington, DC: National Center for Health Statistics.

that Obamacare has expanded the ranks of the insured, with the White House estimating in spring 2016 that 20 million previously uninsured people had gained insurance under Obmacare (Altman 2016). Reflecting this estimate, Figure 13.1 shows that the *uninsurance* rate for Americans dropped considerably from 2010 to 2015 (see Figure 13.1). More generally, some 11 million Americans had bought health insurance through one of the marketplaces by mid-2015, and 87% of these customers qualified for federal subsidies (Blumenthal, Abrams and Nuzum 2015; Martinez and Cohen 2015).

A second sign of increased access involves Medicaid patients. A problem before Obamacare, and one that still exists, is that many physicians do not take Medicaid patients because Medicaid reimbursement rates are lower than those for Medicare and many private insurance plans. Obamacare required state Medicaid programs to reimburse primary care physicians at Medicare rates during 2013 and 2014. Evidence by 2015 found that the higher reimbursement rates were associated with increased availability of physician appointments for Medicaid patients (Polsky et al. 2015).

Cost   Another set of achievements, however preliminary, for Obamacare involves reduction in health care costs due to changes in the economics and processes of health care delivery (Blumenthal et al. 2015). For example, the ACA imposed financial penalties for hospitals with overly high readmission rates for Medicare patients. By 2015, such readmission rates had declined by more than 1%, equivalent to 150,000 fewer readmissions yearly, saving millions of dollars.

In an attempt to produce more coordinated care so as to enhance patient health and reduce wasteful spending, the ACA provided financial incentives to health care providers who formed Accountable Care Organizations (ACOs) for Medicare patients. An ACO consists of hospitals and physicians who provide coordinated medical care. These providers receive financial bonuses if and when certain benchmarks for patient health and health care costs are reached. By 2015, more than 400 ACOs were serving some 7.2 million Medicare patients, one-seventh of all people 65 and older (Abrams et al. 2015). The ACOs have had a mixed performance in cost savings but had still saved more than $1 billion during the two years after their inception (Blumenthal et al. 2015).

Other ACA reforms aim to reduce medical costs or at least the annual rise in medical costs. These reforms, which are being implemented selectively, include: (1) *medical home* models that encourage providers to provide coordinated preventive and medical services; and (2) *bundled payments* that provide a set fee to hospitals and physicians for an individual patient in lieu of fee-for-service payments (Abrams et al. 2015). It will take some years before adequate data on these reforms are available for assessment.

Potential evidence regarding Obamacare and cost control comes from data regarding increases in the nation's annual health care expenditure. As Figure 13.2 shows, this expenditure soared from 1980 through 2010 and continued to rise through 2013. However, the rise since 2010 represents an annual increase of 3.2%, lower than the annual increase of 5.6% during the 2000s. Thus, the rise of health care spending has slowed since the passage of the ACA. Moreover, per-capita Medicare spending has actually decreased somewhat since Obamacare's enactment. This trend prompted the Congressional Budget Office (CBO) to estimate that Medicare spending in 2020 will be $200 billion lower than the CBO estimated before the ACA's passage (Blumenthal et al. 2015).

Despite this evidence, it is too early to know (at the time of this writing) whether and to what extent Obamacare led to these changes in national health care spending. For example, this spending had slowed before Obamacare's enactment

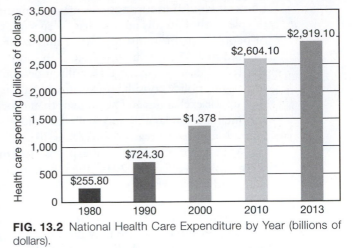

FIG. 13.2 National Health Care Expenditure by Year (billions of dollars).

Source: National Center for Health Statistics. 2015. *Health, United States, 2014.* Hyattsville, MD: Centers for Disease Control and Prevention.

because of the 2008 recession. However, several stipulations of the ACA, including those we described earlier in discussing cost control, probably also help explain these spending changes (Blumenthal et al. 2015).

Quality   It is also too early to know very much about what effect, if any, Obamacare has had on the quality of health care and thus on the quality of health. The results discussed earlier on lower hospital readmission rates for Medicare patients in the wake of financial penalties to hospitals for high readmission rates do point to better quality of care, but some years will have to go by before more definitive evidence emerges (Blumenthal et al. 2015).

Data are available on one important measure of the quality of health care and thus of health: hospital errors, which are a significant problem (see chapter 11). The ACA imposed financial penalties for hospitals with high rates of medical errors, and it also established other efforts to help hospitals reduce errors. Under Obamacare, the number of patients harmed by hospital errors has dropped—the first time this has ever happened. Specifically, the number of errors declined by 17% between 2010 and 2013, meaning that 1.3 million fewer hospital patients were harmed. This decline is estimated to have prevented 50,000 patient deaths (Abrams et al. 2015).

Health benefits can also be expected from the Prevention and Public Health Fund that the ACA created. As its name implies, this fund provides money to communities for public health efforts focused on the prevention of health problems. By 2015, communities had received more than $5 billion from the fund for such things as immunization programs and diabetes, tobacco use, and heart disease and stroke prevention efforts (Abrams 2015).

Two conclusions from this discussion of Obamacare's achievements are worth noting. First, it is far too early to have a definitive assessment of these achievements. Second, the data to date do point to several achievements and show promise for more achievements in the years ahead.

Limitations of Obamacare

Certain limitations of Obamacare have also become evident. Although it is again too early for a definitive assessment, these limitations are nonetheless troubling.

Lack of Health Insurance   A major limitation concerns the number of uninsured people. Although this number has fallen since the passage of the ACA, many millions of people remain uninsured. As of mid-2015, of the 28 million uninsured people eligible to enroll in a marketplace plan, only 10.1 million (slightly more than one-third) had done so, leaving 18 million people uninsured despite their eligibility. As one health policy consultant explained, "It has proven to be harder to get people to sign up for exchanges and keep them than experts expected. Hispanics, young people and men are still lagging in enrollment and it still seems like the exchanges have not figured out how to reach them" (Rau 2015).

Millions of people are still expected to remain uninsured a decade after Obamacare took full effect. In 2014, the CBO, mentioned earlier, estimated that if Obamacare did not exist, 57 million people under age 65 would have been uninsured in 2024. With Obamacare, the CBO estimated that 31 million people will remain uninsured in 2024 (Stein and Young 2014). Two-thirds of these latter people will remain uninsured because they did not sign up for coverage through an employer, the marketplaces, or Medicaid, while 30% will remain uninsured because they are undocumented immigrants and thus are not eligible for marketplace insurance nor for Medicaid.

A final 5% of these uninsured people are potentially eligible for Medicaid but live in states that did not expand Medicaid as the ACA intended. The ACA originally required states to expand their Medicaid eligibility so that nearly all low-income people under age 65 who were not previously eligible for Medicaid (e.g., nonpregnant, nondisabled adults without dependent children) could now receive Medicaid. In return, the federal government would pay the entire costs of this new coverage from 2014 through 2016 and 90% beginning in 2020. However, a 2012 U.S. Supreme Court ruling that upheld the individual mandate also overturned this state Medicaid expansion requirement (Musumeci 2012). As a result, by mid-2015, only 29 states and the District of Columbia decided to expand Medicaid along the lines originally required by the ACA. The decision by the majority of the states *not* to expand Medicaid prevented many of their residents from obtaining insurance as Obamacare intended.

Returning to the CBO's 2024 estimates, 26 million fewer people (57–31=26) will be uninsured in 2024 than if Obamacare had not been enacted. That is a notable achievement, but 31 million people will still be uninsured for the reasons just given. Their lack of insurance will continue to subject them to worse health outcomes and have many implications for the general status of the nation, including higher medical charges and more expensive premiums as explained earlier.

High Out-of-Pocket Costs   Another concern involves high deductibles and copayments for some of the marketplace plans (Pear 2015). When purchasing health insurance, there is usually a tradeoff between the price of premiums and the size of deductibles, coinsurance, and copayments: the lower the premium, the higher the deductibles/coinsurance/copayments, and vice versa. To save money, many people buying marketplace insurance have opted for plans with the lowest premiums and thus higher potential out-of-pocket costs. These so-called *bronze* plans cover only an average of 60% of medical costs, meaning that an individual or family with a bronze plan must pay for 40% of their medical costs. (Silver plans cover 70%, gold plans 80%, and platinum plans 90%.) Some of the people in bronze plans may not be able to afford the higher premiums of the other plans, while people may simply wish to save some money and take the gamble that they will not become sick or injured.

This issue aside, the old saying "penny wise, pound foolish" applies here: people with lower premiums for marketplace insurance are at risk for significant out-of-pocket costs if and when they do become sick or injured. For example, bronze plan deductibles average more than $5,000 yearly for an individual and more than $10,000 for a family. Because the limit in 2015 for marketplace out-of-pocket costs was $6,600 for an individual plan and $13,200 for a family plan, some people with bronze marketplace insurance potentially may have very high out-of-pocket expenses.

People with the other marketplace plans may also face such costs even though their plans are more generous. For example, a family of three with a $73,000 income and a silver plan pays almost $7,000 in premiums even with subsidies. If this family ends up paying its full limit of $13,200 in annual out-of-pocket costs, its total medical bill would surpass $20,000 (Rau 2015).

Fueling these concerns about the marketplace plans' costs, health insurance companies nationwide said in 2015 that they were seeking premium increases of 20% to 40% or more for their marketplace plans. The companies claimed that the new clients they acquired under the ACA were in worse health than the companies had anticipated. Critics noted that the insurance companies were doing quite well under Obamacare, with some companies' stock up by more than 50% in the first half of 2015, and that several company CEOs had received an annual compensation of more than $10 million (Hansen 2015).

Out-of-Network Coverage   A third concern involves out-of-network coverage (Pear, Sanger-Katz, and Abelson 2015). Many insurance companies have established *networks* of hospitals, physicians, and other health care providers: companies provide fewer benefits to patients using an out-of-network provider or sometimes restrict coverage to in-network providers altogether. Patients using out-of-network providers are thus often responsible for high out-of-pocket costs or even the full costs of their medical care. In this regard, several of the marketplace plans under Obamacare restrict coverage to in-network providers. Many people in such plans may not care if they must use in-network providers, but others may wish to use providers closer to home or with whom they have had a previous patient relationship. A real risk also occurs if patients mistakenly use an out-of-network provider and find themselves responsible for the full costs of their medical services.

Since the marketplace insurance plans began developing, several plans have changed which hospitals and physicians are in-network or out-of-network. Some people who signed with a plan because certain providers were in-network have been dismayed when these providers suddenly were not in-network. Some patients have even had trouble determining from their marketplace plan which physicians are in-network or out-of-network and have even been given wrong information (Rosenthal 2015). Some physicians complain that they themselves did not know how and why insurance plans were placing them in-network or out-of-network and were dismayed when they lost patients because the plans decided the physicians were out-of-network (WOAI 2015).

These last two problems, high out-of-pocket costs and out-of-network coverage issues, suggest to some critics that Obamacare "may in some ways be undermining its signature promise: health care that is accessible and affordable for all," according to a news analysis (Rosenthal 2015:SR1). Supporting this view, a national survey in 2014 found that 46% of Americans reported problems in affording health care, a rise of 10% from the year before (Rosenthal 2015). These problems will hopefully diminish as better standards are eventually established, but in the meantime they have caused many patients a good deal of concern and a good deal of money.

Toward Medicare For All

Obamacare is a noble attempt to achieve health reform within America's unique system of private insurance. The previous section documented Obamacare's initial achievements while also pointing to continuing problems of access and cost. As this chapter and the previous two chapters suggest, the private insurance model guarantees that these problems will continue:

- Because private insurers are for-profit, they will continue despite Obamacare to have premiums, deductibles, and coinsurance that are as high as they can secure, which will continue to impose financial burdens on many families and individuals and prevent them from obtaining needed medical care. These for-profit insurers will also continue to question patients' claims and physicians' requests for reimbursement. They will do so because for-profit health care is "inherently contradictory," as one policy professor has written, because "the more health care the insurance companies provide . . . the less profit they make" (Rodberg 2013). As a U.S. physician who moved to Canada commented, "I'm tired of doing daily battle with the same adversary that my patients face—the private insurance industry, with its frequent errors in processing claims; . . . outright denials of payment; . . . and costly paperwork that consumes about 16 percent of physicians' working time" (Queenan 2015).
- Because there are so many private insurers, the private insurance model produces huge administrative costs amounting to almost $400 billion annually (see chapter 12).
- Because the private insurance model is also largely employer based, health insurance for the majority of American adults under age 65 is linked to their employment. This fact constrains their employment choices, lowers their wages, and imposes significant costs on their employers in the form of health insurance premiums and administrative expenses related to providing insurance.
- The private insurance model also forces physicians to spend much of their time dealing with many insurance companies regarding permission to perform various procedures.
- Because the countless private insurance companies have relatively little clout in negotiating with hospitals and physicians for reduced costs, the cost of U.S. health care will continue to be higher than in peer nations, where the government negotiates on behalf of nearly every citizen.
- Because insurance companies restrict coverage to in-network providers, Americans will continue to be constrained in their choice of providers.

All these problems led to renewed interest in national health insurance, also called a *single-payer model*, while Obamacare was being debated before its passage and in the years since its passage. A national organization, Physicians for a National Health Program (www.pnhp.org), has long championed this model, which achieves universal coverage via government insurance for everyone. Because this is what the United States now has for people 65 and older through Medicare, many single-payer proponents label their model **Medicare for All**.

Medicare is not perfect: it does not cover long-term nursing care and dental care, for example, and older Americans may still have significant out-of-pocket costs (see chapter 12) (Davis et al. 2015). Still, Medicare provides older Americans good, timely medical care at a per-service cost that is lower than what private insurance achieves because of the federal government's clout in negotiating prices. Before Medicare began in 1965, almost half of Americans aged 65 and older had no health insurance; now almost every older person is insured. Before Medicare, elders had to pay more than half of their health care costs out-of-pocket; now they pay only 13% out-of-pocket. Medicare has by all accounts contributed greatly to the health of older Americans and is a considerable success. As a recent assessment concluded, "Medicare performs well compared with private insurance coverage. Medicare beneficiaries are less likely to report not getting needed care, less likely to experience burdensome medical bills, and less likely to report negative insurance experiences than those under age 65 insured by employer plans or individual insurance" (Davis et al. 2015:7).

Single-payer proponents argue that if Medicare is working this well for the older population, it makes sense to extend it to everyone under age 65. As one health economist states, "It is striking how many problems facing the Affordable Care Act would disappear if the nation were instead implementing Medicare for All—the extension of Medicare to every age-group" (Seidman 2015:909).

Many single-payer proponents look to Canada for their inspiration (Hackett 2009; Kliff 2012; Lieberman 2014; Maioni 2014; Nader 2013), even though Canada's national insurance model (also called *Medicare*) is technically based within its provinces and territories. These proponents point to the following advantages of Canada's national insurance model (some of which chapter 11 discussed) compared to the U.S. private insurance model:

- All Canadians automatically receive health insurance when they are born, guaranteeing universal coverage for a wide range of health services. As a result, all Canadians have the same access to free basic health care regardless of social class, race and ethnicity, or other sociodemographic factors, including where they live. They do not have trouble paying for their health care, as they merely use their health card whenever they obtain care. In contrast, access in the United States often depends on whether people have insurance (including whether they are employed) and how much they can afford if they do have insurance; health care is also much more expensive in some areas of the United States than in other areas.
- Because all Canadians have the same free insurance, no Canadian has health problems because of lack of insurance or underinsurance. In the United States, millions of people have worse health because of lack of insurance or underinsurance, and thousands die annually from lack of insurance.
- Because Canada essentially has one health insurer that is nonprofit, administrative costs are relatively low, physicians do not have to deal with a multitude of insurance companies, and patients do not have to haggle for full coverage for their claims. The exact opposite of all these dynamics characterizes the United States.
- Contrary to the U.S. experience, Canadians have a free choice of health providers (no provider is out-of-network).
- Canada's national system enables its government to reduce health care costs by setting fees for providers and by providing global budgets for hospitals within which hospitals must operate. In contrast, the decentralized, private insurance model of the United States enables higher prices for health care to prevail.

Single-payer proponents cite all these advantages in advocating a single-payer system for the United States. The physician mentioned earlier who was moving to Canada cited an additional advantage that goes to the heart of Canada's national insurance model: "I'm looking forward to being part of a larger system that values caring for the health of individuals, families and communities as a common good—where health care is valued as a human right" (Queenan 2015). Consumer activist Ralph Nader may have had this value in mind when he summarized the difference between Canada and the United States with this pithy statement: "In Canada, when you go to the doctor or hospital the first thing they ask you is: 'What's wrong?' In the United States, the first thing they ask you is: 'What kind of insurance do you have?'" (Nader 2013).

A *Medicare for All* plan based on both the Medicare of the United States and the Medicare of Canada would have the following features (Seidman 2015):

1. All Americans would be insured from birth and be given a national health card to provide them free health care from any health provider anywhere in the country.
2. This plan would be financed by taxes that would replace the premiums that individuals and employers are now paying and the significant out-of-pocket costs that many patients and their families are paying; wealthier people would pay higher taxes than poorer people.
3. Health care would continue to be delivered primarily by private hospitals and privately employed physicians.
4. Individuals would not have to worry about having a job with an employer that provided insurance, and employers would not have to spend the time, effort, and money for providing it.
5. Patients would have no out-of-pocket costs for basic medical services and could buy supplemental insurance, as Canadians do, for dental and vision care and other services that might not be covered by Medicare for All.
6. The federal government under Medicare for All would be able to use its new clout to negotiate and establish lower prices for health services and prescription drugs, helping greatly to rein in high health care costs.
7. Paperwork and other administrative tasks would be relatively minimal and thus far less costly than now.

Despite these many advantages, Medicare for All is not in the foreseeable future for the United States. The present political climate is certainly not ripe for a new health care model. Moreover, the private health insurance industry, pharmaceutical industry, and probably the American Medical Association would no doubt use their potent lobbying powers to fiercely oppose any plans to extend Medicare to the entire population. A single-payer option under Obamacare is a more plausible scenario, but even this much more limited option does not appear to be on the political horizon for many years to come.

Obamacare will likely improve Americans' health and help control medical costs as it enrolls more of the uninsured and moves toward coordinated care on a set-fee basis, with financial incentives to health providers for positive health and cost outcomes and disincentives for negative outcomes. The Kaiser Permanente health organization, which owns 38 hospitals, employs 18,000 *salaried* physicians in California and several other states, and supplies *nonprofit* insurance to its 10 million members, offers a worthy model for other health care providers to follow under Obamacare (Abelson 2013).

Yet, until the United States adopts some form of national insurance similar to what every other wealthy democracy now has, its quality of health and of health care will continue to lag behind peer nations. Americans will similarly continue to have worse health and access to health care because of their income, race and ethnicity, location of residence, and other sociodemographic factors. For a nation that aspires to "the pursuit of happiness" as written in our founding document, this situation must change before too many more years go by.

Postscript: A Sociological Prescription for Reducing the U.S. Health Disadvantage

Chapter 11 pointed out that Americans are less healthy overall than the residents of other wealthy democracies. In line with the Institute of Medicine, we called this difference *the U.S. health disadvantage*. Even if Obamacare brings health insurance to millions of Americans, as it seems to be doing, millions of Americans will remain uninsured or underinsured. Meanwhile, health care will continue to be very expensive, with significant out-of-pocket costs and millions of Americans having to take on medical debt or to forgo needed medical care. These facts guarantee that the U.S. health disadvantage will persist, even if Americans' health does improve because more people will be insured and because Obamacare provides so many preventive health care measures.

There is a further problem. As chapter 5 emphasized, *fundamental causes* of health inequalities will persist unless and until these causes themselves are addressed (Phelan, Link and Tehranifar 2010). Obamacare does little to address these causes. Even Medicare for All would not address these causes adequately, although it would make health care much more affordable and accessible. For all these reasons, the United States must not rely on its health insurance model alone to reduce the U.S. health disadvantage. Instead, it must also address the fundamental inequalities in society that produce worse health and health inequalities.

The public health model (see chapter 2) emphasizes the adage that an ounce of prevention is worth a pound of cure. Medical sociologists and public health scholars thus highlight the need to tackle the social causes of health and health problems to reduce health inequalities based on social class, race and ethnicity, gender, LGBT status, and other factors. If the United States could reduce poverty, racial/ethnic discrimination, and otherwise alleviate the social causes of health and illness, the health of Americans will improve.

It would be nice to wave a magic wand to have these things happen, but we do not live at Hogwarts Castle or in the Land of Oz. Fortunately, sociologists and other scholars have acquired a good deal of evidence on how to improve society in order to improve Americans' health. Along with the experiences of other wealthy democracies, many studies point to the potential of various programs and policies to address the social factors underlying the poor health of Americans generally and health inequalities in particular (Cancian and Danziger 2009; Eitzen 2010; Russell 2015; Sharkey 2013). A sociological prescription for reducing the U.S. health disadvantage would thus feature strategies to implement or strengthen these programs and policies, all of which address the social causes of health and illness. These strategies include:

- Increase job training, public works programs, and other efforts to enable the poor and low-income people to have decent-paying employment
- Provide other government aid to the poor and unemployed, including early-childhood intervention programs, as other wealthy democracies do much more effectively
- End racial segregation in housing and other forms of racial discrimination
- Reduce the environmental pollution in urban areas that impairs health, and address crime and other urban problems that produce stress and thus health problems
- Increase efforts to reduce rape and domestic violence, both of which disproportionately affect women and girls, and finance and expand rape crisis centers and domestic violence shelters
- Improve women's social and economic inequality
- Change male socialization practices so that males will be less likely to engage in risky behavior and more likely to seek needed health care
- Reduce prejudice and discrimination against the LGBT community
- Increase and strengthen early-childhood intervention programs for low-income children and their families

- Provide free or heavily subsidized high-quality day care to low-income parents
- Improve the nation's schools and otherwise help guarantee that all Americans receive as much high-quality formal education as possible
- Strengthen prenatal and postnatal nutrition and other services

All these strategies might also need a magic wand to achieve, for the United States does not seem likely to invest much more money and effort into these strategies than it is already doing. That is a shame, for every other wealthy democracy spends a much greater share of its national budget on these strategies, and particularly on helping their low-income residents, than the United States does, and they provide much more economic and social supports to their residents than the United States does (Russell 2015). Americans pay a heavy cost for our neglect of of people suffering from social inequalities, and poor health is just one of these costs.

Social science research and other democracies' experiences strongly suggest that addressing the social causes of health and illness will improve Americans' health. We know from this research and these countries' experiences what America must do as a nation. Whether we have the will and wisdom to do what must be done remains a fundamental question.

Conclusion

Although national health insurance has been on the political agenda for the past century, it has never been achieved for several reasons, including Americans traditional distaste for government programs and fierce opposition by the private insurance and pharmaceutical industries and the American Medical Association. Obamacare has brought health insurance to millions of Americans and shown promise of other achievements in cost and coordinated care. Nevertheless, millions of Americans remain uninsured despite Obamacare, and millions of Americans continue to have trouble affording their medical care. A single-payer insurance model like Canada's would help greatly to correct the many problems caused by the United States' decentralized, private insurance model. To improve the nation's health, any efforts to improve the health care system must be accompanied by efforts to address the social causes of health and illness. These latter efforts are essential to address health disparities caused by poverty, race and ethnicity, and other sociodemographic factors.

Summary

1. Progressive Era activists sought to bring national health insurance to the United States, but failed to do so for several reasons, including hostility toward Germany and Communism.
2. National health insurance was favored by the administrations of Franklin D. Roosevelt and Harry S. Truman but never adopted due to opposition from conservative members of Congress and lobbying efforts by powerful interest groups.
3. Medicare and Medicaid passed in 1965 and represented the first widespread health insurance by the federal government (Medicare and Medicaid) and state governments (Medicaid).
4. Obamacare's principles and structure reflect conservative philosophy and strategy and derive from the structure of a required insurance model established in Massachusetts under the leadership of Republican governor Mitt Romney.

5. Under Obamacare, millions of Americans had obtained health insurance by mid-2015, and certain Obamacare programs showed promise for reducing health care costs and enhancing coordinated health care.
6. Millions of people will remain uninsured under Obamacare, and millions more will have trouble affording health care and paying their medical bills.
7. Single-payer proponents point to Canada's national health insurance system as a model for the United States to adopt. This model would provide free health care with any health provider of a patient's choosing.
8. A sociological prescription for improving the health of Americans would involve strategies that address the social causes of health and illness. These strategies include efforts to reduce poverty and racial discrimination and efforts to achieve full gender inequality.

Giving It Some Thought

You went to medical school and did your residency, and you have now been a physician for six years in a small group practice. You initially enjoyed your new career, but for some time have been experiencing the same frustrations that the physician quoted in this chapter cited as her reasons for moving to Canada. You begin to wonder whether you should follow her example. What do you decide?

Key Terms

individual mandate, 225

Medicare for all, 232

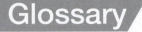

acculturation adoption by immigrants of the American culture and lifestyle

active physicians people with an M.D. degree who are still practicing medicine, having not retired or left medicine for other reasons

advanced practice nurses nurses who have a master's degree or the equivalent training and who perform highly skilled duties; they include clinical nurse specialists, nurse anesthetists, certified nurse midwives, and nurse practitioners

altruism as a characteristic of professions, the idea that professions' primary goal is to help the clients they serve and in this way to help society as a whole

ambulatory care facility a setting that provides health care to patients who are not inpatients

authority as a characteristic of professions, the dominance that professionals exercise over clients and over the subordinate occupational groups with whom professionals interact

autonomy as a characteristic of professions, the idea that a profession is largely free to determine all of the following: (1) the needed education and other standards, including examinations and licensure, for entrance into the profession; (2) the rules that govern the behavior of a profession's members; (3) the discipline that should occur if any members violate these rules.

Beveridge model a health care system in which the government pays for health care through taxation and also owns most hospitals and employs many physicians

binge drinking having five or more drinks on the same occasion on at least 1 day in the past 30 days

biographical disruption changes in a person's normal life activities and social relationships after a diagnosis of chronic illness

biomedical model the view that illness, disease, and other health problems have one or more specific medical causes and can be treated with appropriate medications and/or other medical procedures

Bismarck model a health care system in which citizens are required to have private, nonprofit health insurance and in which the provision of health care is largely private

capitation the payment to physicians of a set fee for a patient rather than a separate fee for each test, procedure, and other service that might be performed

cell theory the view that cells are the basic functional and structural unit for all organisms

CHIP the Children's Health Insurance Program that provides core medical services to children whose families' incomes are fairly low but still too high to qualify for Medicaid.

church-affiliated hospitals sponsored by and operated by the Catholic Church or other religious denominations

clerkship a clinical rotation during the third and fourth years of medical school in which students go on rounds with other students

community hospital a nonfederal, short-term hospital open to the general public

complementary and alternative health care health care that is considered outside the boundaries of standard medical treatment

concentrated disadvantage the combination in urban neighborhoods of problems such as extreme poverty, high unemployment, high crime rates, dilapidated housing, substandard schools, abandoned buildings, inadequate public funding, environmental hazards, weak social ties and mutual trust among neighbors, and much graffiti and vandalism

conflict theory the belief that society is dominated by individuals and groups with wealth, power, and other influences, and that many people lie at or near the bottom of society's social hierarchy

contested illness illnesses such as chronic fatigue syndrome and Gulf War syndrome that physicians cannot identify as medically caused

criteria of causality conditions that must be satisfied before it can be concluded that an independent variable affects a dependent variable

cumulative disadvantage the accumulation over the life course of the impact of stress and other childhood problems

defensive medicine the practice of ordering diagnostic tests and other procedures that are probably or certainly medically unnecessary

dependency theory the assumption that wealthy nations of Western Europe became wealthy because they colonized nations in Africa, South America, and other parts of the world centuries ago, took their natural resources, and enslaved many of their citizens or exploited their labor

dependent variable a variable that is affected by an independent variable

detached concern   medical students' emotional distance from patients

disease   the actual medical symptoms affecting an individual, and more generally a biological problem affecting the structure or functioning of some part of the body

domestic medicine   health care practiced by female family members drawing on folk wisdom received from their mothers that had been in turn received from their grandmothers and earlier generations of women

egalitarian model   A patient-centered model of physician interaction in which patients take a proactive role and physicians listen carefully to their health concerns

environmental inequality   the disproportionate impact of environmental problems on the health of people with low socioeconomic status and on people of color

environmental racism   the disproportionate impact of environmental problems on people of color

epidemiological transition   the shift in the nature of disease and illness from ancient times to the present day, thanks to basic changes in society and advances in scientific medicine and social epidemiology

epidemiology   the study of the causes and the distribution of disease and illness

fee-for-service   the payment to physicians of a separate fee for each office visit, each test, and each medical procedure that a patient experiences

functionalism   the belief that society's social institutions all help society to survive and even thrive, and that each social institution served several functions in this regard

fundamental cause   a social condition that influences the likelihood of many diseases, that does so for many reasons, that involves access to resources regarding health, and that has effects on health persisting over time even though intervening mechanisms may change

gender paradox   the fact that women outlive men but have worse health overall than men

gender segregation   the concentration of women into certain occupations and of men into certain other occupations

general hospital   a hospital that provides a range of services for a range of medical conditions

germ theory   the view that microorganisms cause disease

global inequality   the unequal distribution of nations in terms of wealth, power and influence, and resources

global stratification   the unequal distribution of nations in terms of wealth, power and influence, and resources

health behavior   the activities people do that either maintain or improve their health or potentially harm their health

health belief model   the assumption that promotive health behavior is more likely among individuals who perceive that they are susceptible to incurring a health problem, who perceive the health problem could be serious, who perceive that a potential health behavior will prove beneficial, who have a high level of self-efficacy, and who lack barriers to undertaking a health behavior

health disparities   another term for health inequalities

health inequalities   differences in the quality of health based on social class, race and ethnicity, gender, age, and/or sexual orientation and gender identity

health lifestyle   a general pattern of high or low involvement in promotive health behaviors

health   from the World Health Organization, a state of complete physical, mental, and social well-being and not merely the absence of disease or infirmity

heavy drinking   having five or more drinks on the same occasion on each of 5 or more days in the past 30 days

help-seeking behavior   a visit for needed care to a physician or other health care professional

heterosexual privilege   the everyday advantages straight people enjoy because of their sexual orientation and gender identity

hispanic paradox   another term for the Latino paradox

home health care   health care that occurs in the home of a chronically ill patient or in the home of the patient's caregiver

homophily   the tendency of people to have relationships with other people with similar backgrounds, beliefs, interests, and other traits

hospice care   medical and other care for terminally ill people who are expected to live for no longer than six months.

hospital   an institution with at least six beds that provides medical treatment and nursing care for people who are sick or injured

humoral theory   the view that illness stems from an imbalance in a person's four humors: blood, phlegm, yellow bile, and black bile

illness   a person's perceptions of and reactions to perceived medical symptoms and a diagnosis of disease, and to similar perceptions and reactions by other people about that person's symptoms and diagnosis

illness behavior   the health care activities that people with perceived medical symptoms choose to practice or not practice

illness experience   the ways in which people perceive and react to medical symptoms

incidence   in epidemiology, the number of cases of illness in a given location in relation to the population size of the location

independent variable   a variable that affects a dependent variable

individual mandate   The requirement under the Affordable Care Act that every American have health insurance or else pay a tax penalty.

July effect   the idea that errors occur more often in July in teaching hospitals because that is when new medical residents begin working in hospitals after their academic training has ended

Latino paradox   the idea that Latinos have better health overall than would be expected from their lower socioeconomic status

licensed practical nurses   nurses typically have a high-school degree and take a one-year state-approved program of classroom and clinical instruction; they provide very basic nursing care under the supervision of physicians and registered nurses.

life chances   people's ability to live a happy, fulfilling life and to improve their station in life

lifestyles   how people live their lives, including the choices they make about what products to purchase and about which activities to pursue

locus of control   the extent to which individuals feel they have control over their own lives

mainstream health care   health care that is based on the biomedical model and that is widely regarded as normal and conventional

male privilege   the everyday advantages enjoyed by men simply because they are male

Medicaid   the combined federal/state program that provides core medical services (with some copayments) for some low-income children and parents, pregnant women, seniors, and people with disabilities

medical malpractice   negligent treatment by a health care professional that harms a patient

medical sociology   the study of the social causes of health and illness and of the operation of the health care system

medical student burnout   the mental, emotional, and physical stress and exhaustion that many medical students experience during their preclinical and clinical years and during their residencies

medicalization   a process by which nonmedical problems become defined and treated as medical problems, usually in terms of illness and disorders

Medicare   federal program that provides basic medical services for everyone aged 65 and older; it also serves some younger disabled people and dialysis patients

Medicare for all   a proposal for national health insurance for all Americans

midwife   a lay woman who assists pregnant women during their pregnancy and childbirth

modernization theory   the assumption that the wealthy nations of Western Europe became wealthy because several centuries ago they developed certain beliefs and values that helped them become wealthy

monopolizing knowledge   as a common goal of professions, the idea that professions try to control who can enter the profession and who can perform the duties associated with the profession

morbidity

multihospital chain   two or more hospitals owned and operated by a central organization

national health insurance model   a health care system in which physicians and nurses are primarily private employees and government pays for most or all of health care

nursing home   a facility that provides extensive, long-term medical care and practical support for its residents

osteopathic hospital   a hospital that reflects osteopathic principles

out-of-pocket model   a health care system in which most health care is privately provided and citizens pay for most of their health care themselves.

paternalistic model   the traditional, hierarchical model of the physician-patient relationship in which the physician is the "boss" and the patient is the passive, obedient "follower."

physician density   the number of all physicians compared to population size

placebo effect   the idea that people might feel healthier from trying a new health approach or from taking a new medication simply because they expect the new approach or medication to make them feel better.

prevalence   in epidemiology, the number of people with an illness in a given location in relation to the population size of the location

primary health care   health care delivered by primary care physicians such as family physicians and general practitioners

primary prevention   in public health, efforts to distinguish and improve aspects of the social and physical environments that cause health problems

private for-profit hospital   a hospital owned and operated by private investors, who may be individuals, partnerships, or corporations

private nonprofit hospital   a hospital owned and operated by a private group, secular or religious, that is considered a charity and that does not pay taxes to the local, state, or federal governments

profession   an occupation that is highly skilled and that requires prolonged training

professional culture   the distinctive language (jargon), lifestyles, values, and behavior that typify members of professions.

proprietary schools   independent, for-profit medical schools that were established in many cities around the United States during the first half of the 1800s

prospective payment system   Reimbursement by Medicare to hospitals of a fixed amount per inpatient regardless of how long the patient stays in the hospital and regardless of how many tests, procedures, and other services are performed.

public health   all organized measures (whether public or private) to prevent disease, promote health, and prolong life among the population as a whole

public hospital   a hospital owned and managed by local governments (city or county), state governments, or the federal government

rate   another way of expressing a percentage

registered nurses   nurses who often have a four-year college degree in nursing and who perform a variety of complex patient-care duties

reproductive injustice   the fact that women who are poor and /or African American, Latino, or Native American are more likely to experience reproductive problems

retail store clinic   a health care setting found in a big box store or pharmacy chain store that is typically staffed by a nurse practitioner or physician assistant

scientific medicine   the use of science to understand the causes and treatment of, and possible cures for, disease and illness

secondary prevention   in public health, efforts to distinguish and change behaviors and situations that put specific individuals at risk for a health problem

selectivity   in regard to the Latino paradox, the idea that this paradox is partly explained by the fact that healthier Mexicans enter the United States and less healthy Mexicans return to Mexico

self-care   a patient's use of medication or other measures in attempt to relieve one's medical symptoms

sick role   the expectations for behavior of someone who has been designated as ill by society, usually by a medical practitioner

social construction   a concept that does not have objective reality but that exists because people decide it exist

social constructionism   the view that certain social realities exist only because people decide they exist, and that these realities therefore have no objective basis

social control   the regulation of behavior by the various components of society

social environment   Aspects of people's social backgrounds, including gender, social class, race and ethnicity, age, religion, and social networks, and aspects of their place of residence

social epidemiology   the study of the social causes and social distribution of disease, illness, and other health problems

social inequality   the unequal distribution of wealth and other important resources valued by a society

social institutions   socially organized systems of behavior that help a society satisfy its basic needs

social integration   strong, extensive social bonds and the shared norms and values stemming from the social bonds

social relationships   our social ties to other individuals such as spouses, romantic partners, family, and friends

socialization   the learning of a culture's norms, values, and attitudes

sociological imagination   the ability to recognize that public issues often lie at the root of personal troubles

sociological perspective   the view that the social environment influences individuals' behaviors, attitudes, and life outcomes

specialized knowledge   a profession's complex body of facts and theories that is difficult for nonprofessionals to master; medicine's specialized knowledge includes the facts and principles from the medical sciences and the techniques that physicians and other medical professionals use to diagnose and treat patients.

specialty hospital   a hospital that treats patients with specific medical conditions.

stress buffers

stress proliferation   the idea that one stressor may lead to additional stressors

stress   emotional and mental tension resulting from very adverse circumstances or situations

successful aging   living a long and healthy life free or relatively free of health problems

surgicenter   a freestanding ambulatory surgery center that is independent of a hospital

symbolic interactionism   a theory that emphasizes how individuals act with other individuals and how they interpret this social interaction

teaching hospital   a hospital affiliated with a medical school

tertiary prevention   in public health, efforts to minimize or prevent short- and long-term consequences of a health problem

theory of fundamental causes   the idea that a social condition underlies multiple diseases for multiple reasons, that addressing any one reason for disease still permits the condition to induce other diseases, and that when a new disease arises or returns, the social condition will make vulnerable the same kind of people it makes vulnerable for other diseases

theory of help-seeking behavior   David Mechanic's outline and explanation of the factors that make it more or less likely that someone with perceived medical symptoms will seek professional medical care

tolerance of uncertainty   medical students' acceptance of the fact that that their own knowledge of medicine will be uncertain because they cannot know everything known to scientific medicine and because scientific medicine does not know everything about the causes and cures of disease and illness.

toxic stress   childhood stress that is frequent, severe, and prolonged

trepanning   the drilling of holes in the skull of an ill individual to release the evil spirits who had taken over the person's body.

U.S. health disadvantage   the fact that U.S. residents have worse health overall than the residents of other wealthy democracies

underinsurance   a situation in which people are insured but still must pay high deductibles and/or high copayments and thus experience significant out-of-pocket health care costs

universal coverage   a situation in which 99%–100% of a nation's population have all or most of their core health care costs covered by insurance

upstream factors   the factors in the social environment that influence health and illness

urgent-care center   a relatively small health care facility that provides a wide range of minor medical services, with or without an appointment

waste   needless health care spending, including spending on unnecessary or ineffective health care services, spending on medical care to treat complications from ineffective or uncoordinated care or from medical errors, excessive spending arising from administrative complexity, higher prices stemming from a lack of competitive markets, and fraudulent billing for medical services.

References

Abelson, Reed and Julie Creswell. 2012. "Hospital Chain Inquiry Cited Unnecessary Cardiac Work." *The New York Times* August 7:A1.

Abelson, Reed. 2013. "The Face of Future Health Care." *The New York Times* March 21:B1.

Abrams, Melinda K., Rachel Nuzum, Mark A. Zezza, Jamie Ryan, Jordan Kiszla, and Stuart Guterman. 2015. *The Affordable Care Act's Payment and Delivery System Reforms: A Progress Report at Five Years.* New York, NY: The Commonwealth Fund.

Abrams, Melinda K., Rachel Nuzum, Mark A. Zezza, Jamie Ryan, Jordan Kiszla, and Stuart Guterman. 2015. *The Affordable Care Act's Payment and Delivery System Reforms: A Progress Report at Five Years.* New York, NY: The Commonwealth Fund.

Addis, M. E., and J. R. Mahalik. 2003. "Men, Masculinity, and the Contexts of Help Seeking." *American Psychologist* 58:5–14.

Adler, Paul S. 2012. "The Sociological Ambivalence of Bureaucracy: From Weber via Gouldner to Marx." *Organization Science* 23:244–266.

AFL-CIO. 2014. *Death on the Job: The Toll of Neglect.* Washington, DC: AFL-CIO.

Agency for Healthcare Research and Quality. 2014. *2013 National Healthcare Disparities Report.* Rockville, MD: U.S. Department of Health and Human Services.

Agency for Healthcare Research and Quality. 2015. *2014 Healthcare Quality and Disparities Report.* Rockville, MD: Agency for Healthcare Research and Quality, U.S. Department of Health and Human Services.

Aizer, Ayal A., Ming-Hui Chen, Ellen P. McCarthy, Mallika L. Mendu, Sophia Koo, Tyler J. Wilhite, Powell L. Graham, Toni K. Choueiri, Karen E. Hoffman, Neil E. Martin, Jim C. Hu and Paul L. Nguyen. 2013. "Marital Status and Survival in Patients with Cancer." *Journal of Clinical Oncology* 31:3869–3876.

Allen, James. 2013. *Health Law and Medical Ethics.* Upper Saddle River, NJ: Pearson.

Allen, Marshall. 2013. "How Many Die From Medical Mistakes in U.S. Hospitals?" *ProPublica* September 19:http://www.propublica.org/article/how-many-die-from-medical-mistakes-in-us-hospitals.

———. 2014. "One Third of Skilled Nursing Patients Harmed in Treatment." *ProPublica* March 3:http://www.propublica.org/article/one-third-of-skilled-nursing-patients-harmed-in-treatment.

Altman, Lawrence K. 2014. "A Patient's-Eye-View of Nurses." *The New York Times* February 10:http://well.blogs.nytimes.com/2014/02/10/a-patients-eye-view-of-nurses/.

Ambulatory Surgery Center Association. 2013. "ASCs: A Positive Trend in Health Care." http://www.ascassociation.org/AdvancingSurgicalCare/aboutascs/industryoverview/apositivetrendinhealthcare/.

American Association of Colleges of Nursing. 2014a. "Fact Sheet: Enhancing Diversity in the Nursing Workforce." http://www.aacn.nche.edu/media-relations/fact-sheets/enhancing-diversity.

———. 2014b. "Nursing Shortage Fact Sheet." http://www.aacn.nche.edu/media-relations/fact-sheets/nursing-shortage.

American Heart Association. 2014. "Air Pollution and Heart Disease, Stroke." http://www.heart.org/HEARTORG/Conditions/More/MyHeartandStrokeNews/Air-Pollution-and-Heart-Disease-Stroke_UCM_442923_Article.jsp.

American Hospital Association. 2015a. "Fact Facts on US Hospitals." http://www.aha.org/research/rc/stat-studies/fast-facts.shtml.

———. 2015b. "Rural Health Care." http://www.aha.org/advocacy-issues/rural/index.shtml.

American Lung Association. 2014. *State of the Air.* Chicago, IL: American Lung Association.

American Medical Association. 2015. *Physician Characteristics and Distribution in the United States, 2015.* Chicago, IL: American Medical Association.

American Nurses Association. 2011. "2011 ANA Health & Safety Survey: Hazards of the RN Work Environment." http://www.nursingworld.org/MainMenuCategories/WorkplaceSafety/Healthy-Work-Environment/SafeNeedles/2011-HealthSafetySurvey.html.

———. 2015. "Higher Number of Nurses with Baccalaureate Degrees: Linked to Lower Rates of Mortality." http://www.nursingworld.org/MainMenuCategories/ThePracticeofProfessionalNursing/Improving-Your-Practice/One-Strong-Voice-Clinically-Speaking/Higher-Number-of-Nurses-with-Baccalaureate-Degrees-Linked-to-Lower-Rates-of-Mortality.html.

American Osteopathic Association. 2014. *2014 Osteopathic Medical Profession Report*. Chicago, IL: American Osteopathic Association.

Anderson, Kathryn Freeman. 2013. "Diagnosing Discrimination: Stress from Perceived Racism and the Mental and Physical Health Effects." *Sociological Inquiry* 83(1):55–81. doi: http://dx.doi.org/10.1111/j.1475-682X.2012.00433.x.

Angier, Natalie. 2014. "Leprosy, Still Claiming Victims." *The New York Times* July 1:D1.

Ansell, David A., and Edwin K. McDonald. 2015. "Bias, Black Lives, and Academic Medicine." *New England Journal of Medicine* 372:1087–1089.

Anspach, Renee R. 2010. "Gender and Health Care." Pp. 229–248 in *Handbook of Medical Scoiology*, edited by C.E. Bird, P. Conrad, A.M. Fremont, and S. Timmermans. Nashville, TN: Vanderbilt University Press.

Anspach, Renee R. 2010. "Gender and Health Care." Pp. 229–248 in *Handbook of Medical Scoiology*, edited by C. E. Bird, P. Conrad, A. M. Fremont, and S. Timmermans. Nashville, TN: Vanderbilt University Press.

Ard, Kevin L., and Harvey J. Makadon. 2012. *Improving the Health Care of Lesbian, Gay, Bisexual and Transgender (Lgbt) People: Understanding and Improving Health Disparities*. Boston: The Fenway Institute.

Arthur-Cameselle, Jessyca N, and Paula A Quatromoni. 2014. "Eating Disorders in Collegiate Female Athletes: Factors that Assist Recovery." *Eating Disorders* 22:50–61.

Asai, Atsushi, Yasuhiro Kadooka, and Kuniko Aizawa. 2012. "Arguments Against Promoting Organ Transplants from Brain-Dead Donors, and Views of Contemporary Japanese on Life and Death." *Bioethics* 26:215–223.

Association of American Medical Colleges. 2014. *2014 Physician Specialty Data Book*. Washington, DC: Association of American Medical Colleges.

———. 2015. *The Complexities of Physician Supply and Demand: Projections from 2013 to 2025*. Washington, DC: Association of American Medical Colleges.

———. 2015. *U.S. Medical School Faculty, 2015*. https://www.aamc.org/data/facultyroster/reports/453490/usmsf15.html.

———. 2016. "Facts: Applicants, Matriculants, Enrollment, Graduates, M.D.-Ph.D., and Residency Applicants Data." https://www.aamc.org/data/facts/.

Avendano, Mauricio, Johan P. Mackenbach, M. Maria Glymour, and James Banks. 2009. "Health Disadvantage in US and Adults Aged 50 to 74 years: A Comparison of the Health of Rich and Poor Americans With That of Europeans." *American Journal of Public Health* 99:540–548.

Avison, William R., and Stephanie S. Thomas. 2010. "Stress." Pp. 242–267 in *The New Blackwell Companion to Medical Sociology*, edited by W. C. Cockerham. Malden, MA: Wiley-Blackwell.

Babbie, Earl. 2014. *The Basics of Social Research*. Belmont, CA: Wadsworth.

Baer, Hans A. 2010. "Complementary and Alternative Medicine: Processes of Legitimation, Professionalization, and Cooption." Pp. 373–390 in *The New Blackwell Companion to Medical Sociology*, edited by W.C. Cockerham. Malden, MA: Wiley-Blackwell.

Bailey, Melissa. 2016. "Medican Students Demand Better Training to Tackle Opiod Crisis." *STAT* May 17:https://www.statnews.com/2016/05/17/opioid-addiction-medical-schools/.

Bakalar, Nocholas. 2011. "Researchers Link Deaths to Social Ills." *The New York Times* July D5.

Balotsky, Edward R. 2005. "Is It Resources, Habit or Both: Interpreting Twenty Years of Hospital Strategic Response to Prospective Payment." *Health Care Management Review* 30:337–346.

Barkan, Steven E. 2006. "Religiosity and Premarital Sex During Adulthood." *Journal for the Scientific Study of Religion* 45:407–417.

———. 2015. *Criminology: A Sociological Understanding*. Upper Saddle River, NJ: Pearson.

Barkan, Steven E., and Susan F. Greenwood. 2003. "Religious Attendance and Subjective Well-Being among Older Americans: Evidence from the General Social Survey." *Review of Religious Research* 45(2):116–129.

Barker, Kristin K. 2010. "The Social Construction of Illness: Medicalization and Contested Illness." Pp. 147–162 in *Handbook of Medical Sociology*, edited by C.E. Bird, P. Conrad, A.M. Fremont, and S. Timmermans. Nashville, TN: Vanderbilt University Press.

Barr, Donald A. 2014. *Health Disparities in the United States: Social Class, Race, and Health*. Baltimore, MD: Johns Hopkins University Press.

Barrett, Paul and Robert Langreth. 2015. "Pharma Execs Don't Know Why Anyone Is Upset by a $94,500 Miracle Cure." *Bloomberg Businessweek* June 3:http://www.bloomberg.com/news/articles/2015-06-03/specialty-drug-costs-gilead-s-hepatitis-c-cures-spur-backlash.

Barua, Jason Clemens and Bacchus. 2014. "If Universal Health Care Is The Goal, Don't Copy Canada." *Forbes* June 13:http://www.forbes.com/sites/theapothecary/2014/06/13/if-universal-health-care-is-the-goal-dont-copy-canada/.

Basheka, Benon C. 2011. "Economic and Political Determinants of Public Procurement Corruption in Developing Countries: An Emprical Study from Uganda." *Journal of Public Procurement* 11:33–60.

Batina, N.G., A. Trentham-Dietz, R.E. Gangnon, B.L. Sprague, M.A. Rosenberg, N.K. Stout, D.G. Fryback and O. Alagoz. 2013. "Variation in Tumor Natural History Contributes to Racial Disparities in Breat Cancer Stage at Diagnosis." *Breast Cancer Research and Treatment* 138:519–528.

Beauchamp, Tom L., LeRoy Walters, Jeffrey P. Kahn and Anna C. Mastroianni. 2014. *Contemporary Issues in Biomedical Ethics.* Belmont, CA: Cengage Learning.

Becker, Howard S., Blanche Geer, Everett C. Hughes, and Anselm L. Strauss. 1961. *Boys in White: Student Culture in Medical School.* Chicago, IL: University of Chicago Press.

Becker, Marshall H. 1974. "The Health Belief Model and Personal Health Behavior." San Francisco, CA: Society for Public Health Education, Inc.

Begley, Sharon. 2009. "Don't Blame the Caveman." *Newsweek* June 29:52–62.

Bell, Susan E., and Anne E. Figert. 2010. "Gender and the Medicalization of Health Care." Pp. 107–122 in *Palgrave Handbook of Gender and Healthcare*, edited by E.Kuhlmann and E. Annandale. London: Palgrave Macmillan.

———. 2015. "*Reimagining (Bio)Medicalization, Pharmaceuticals and Genetics: Old Critiques and New Engagements.*" New York, NY: Routledge.

Berger, Peter and Thomas Luckmann. 1963. *The Social Construction of Reality.* New York, NY: Doubleday.

Berkman, Lisa F., and Ichiro Kawachi. 2014. "A Historical Framework for Social Epidemiology: Social Determinants of Population Health." Pp. 1–16 in *Social Epidemiology*, edited by L. F. Berkman, I. Kawachi and M. M. Glymour. New York, NY: Oxford University Press.

Bernard, Tara Siegel. 2012. "Getting Lost in the Labyrinth of Medical Bills." *The New York Times* June 23:B1.

Bevington, Rickey. 2015. "Despite Obamacare, One in Five Adult Georgians Still Uninsured." *GPB News* June 25:http://www.gpb.org/news/2015/06/25/despite-obamacare-one-five-georgians-still-uninsured.

Binder, Leah. 2013. "Stunning News On Preventable Deaths In Hospitals." *Forbes* September 23:http://www.forbes.com/sites/leahbinder/2013/09/23/stunning-news-on-preventable-deaths-in-hospitals/.

Binstock, Robert H., and Linda K. George, eds. 2011. *Handbook of Aging and the Social Sciences.* Burlington, MA: Academic Press.

Bird, Chloe E., Peter Conrad, Allen M. Fremont, and Stefan Timmermans. 2010. "Handbook of Medical Sociology." Nashville, TN: Vanderbilt University Press.

Bishop, Louise M. 2007. *Words, Stones, & Herbs: The Healing Word in Medieval and Early Modern England.* Syracuse, NY: Syracuse University Press.

Black, M.C., K.C Basile, M.J. Breiding, S.G. Smith, M.L. Walters, M.T. Merrick, J. Chen and M.R. Stevens. 2011. *The National Intimate Partner and Sexual Violence Survey (Nisvs): 2010 Summary Report.* Atlanta, GA: Centers for Disease Control and Prevention.

Blackstone, Amy. 2012. "Fighting Sexual Harassment in the Workplace." Scholars Strategy Network:http://www.scholarsstrategynetwork.org/sites/default/files/ssn_basic_facts_blackstone_on_sexual_harassment.pdf.

Blue, Laura and Andrew Fenelon. 2011. "Explaining Low Mortality among U.S. Immigrants Relative to Native-Born Americans: The Role of Smoking." *International Journal of Epidemiology* 40:786–793.

Blumenthal, David, Melinda K. Abrams, and Rachel Nuzum. 2015. "The Affordable Care Act at 5 Years." *New England Journal of Medicine* 372:2451–58.

Boardman, Jason D., Jarron M. Saint Onge, Richard G. Rogers, and Justin T. Denney. 2005. "Race Differentials in Obesity: The Impact of Place." *Journal of Health and Social Behavior* 3:229–243.

Bonner, Thomas N. 1995. *Becoming a Physician: Medical Education in Britain, France, Germany, and the United States, 1750–1945.* New York, NY: Oxford University Press.

Boodman, Eric. 2015. "These Medical Experiments Were Horrible, Unethical--and Useful." *Statnews* November 13:http://www.statnews.com/2015/11/13/medical-experiments-horrible-unethical-also-useful/.

Boone-Heinonen, Janne and Penny Gordon-Larsen. 2011. "Life Stage and Sex Specificity in Relationships Between the Built and Socioeconomic Environments and Physical Activity." *Journal of Epidemiology & Community Health* 65:847–852.

Booth, Alan, Douglas A. Granger, Allan Mazur, and Katie T. Kivlighan. 2006. "Testosterone and Social Behavior." *Social Forces* 85:167–191.

Bornstein, David. 2013. "Protecting Children from Toxic Stress." *The New York Times* November 3:SR4.

Boston Women's Health Book Collective. 1973. *Our Bodies, Ourselves: A Book by and for Women.* New York, NY: Simon and Schuster.

Bourdieu, Pierre. 1984. *Distinction.* Translated by R. Nice. Cambridge, MA: Harvard University Press.

Bowman, Jessica. 2015. "88-Year-Old Doctor Fights to Keep Medical License." *msnewsnow. com* January 13:http://www.msnewsnow.com/ story/27832083/88-year-old-doctor-fights-to-keep-medical-license?clienttype=generic&mobilecgbypass&utm_content=buffer103a8&utm_medium=social&utm_source=twitter. com&utm_campaign=buffer.

Bradby, Hannah and James Y. Nazroo. 2010. "Health, Ethnicity, and Race." Pp. 113–129 in *The New Blackwell Companion to Medical Sociology*, edited by W. C. Cockerham. Malden, MA: Wiley-Blackwell.

Bradley, Laura. 2014. "E-Waste in Developing Countries Endangers Environment, Locals." *U.S. News & World Report* August 1:http://www. usnews.com/news/articles/2014/08/01/e-waste-in-developing-countries-endangers-environment-locals.

Bränström, Richard, Mark L. Hatzenbuehler, John E. Pachankis and Bruce G. Link. 2016. "Sexual Orientation Disparities in Preventable Disease: A Fundamental Cause Perspective." *American Journal of Public Health* 106(6):1109–1115.

Bratter, Jennifer L., and Bridget K. Gorman. 2011. "Is Discrimination an Equal Opportunity Risk? Racial Experiences, Socioeconomic Status, and Health Status among Black and White Adults." *Journal of Health and Social Behavior* 52:365–382.

Breslaw, Elaine G. 2014. *Lotions, Potions, Pills, and Magic: Health Care in Early America.* New York, NY: New York University Press.

Brewer, Lindsay and Douglas Grbic. 2010. "Medical Students' Socioeconomic Background and Their Completion of the First Two Years of Medical School." *Analysis in Brief (newsletter of the Association of American Medical Colleges)* 9(11):1–2.

Brill, Steven. 2013. "Bitter Pill: Why Medical Bills are Killing Us." *Time* April 4:http://time. com/198/bitter-pill-why-medical-bills-are-killing-us/.

———. 2015. *America's Bitter Pill: Money, Politics, Back-Room Deals, and the Fight to Fix Our Broken Healthcare System.* New York, NY: Random House.

Brody, Gene H., Man-Kit Lei, David H. Chae, Tianyi Yu, Steven M. Kogan and Steven R. H. Beach. 2014. "Perceived Discrimination among African American Adolescents and Allostatic Load: A Longitudinal Analysis with Buffering Effects." *Child Development* 85:989–1002.

Brody, Jane E. 2014a. "Caring for the Alzheimer's Caregiver." *The New York Times* February 17:http://well.blogs.nytimes. com/2014/02/17/caring-for-the-alzheimers-caregiver/?hp.

———. 2014b. "The Perils of Toughing It Out." *The New York Times* March 4:D7.

Brown, Phil, Crystal Adams, Rachel Morello-Frosch, Laura Senier, and Ruth Simpson. 2010. "Health Social Movements: History, Current Work, and Future Directions." Pp. 380–394 in *Handbook of Medical Sociology*, edited by C.E. Bird, PeterConrad, A.M. Fremont, and S. Timmermans. Nashville, TN: Vanderbilt University Press.

Brown, Theresa. 2012. "Don't Get Sick in July." *The New York Times* July 14:http://opinionator.blogs.nytimes.com/2012/07/14/dont-get-sick-in-july/?_r=0.

———. 2013. "Healing the Hospital Hierarchy." *The New York Times* March 17:SR5.

Budden, Jill S., Elizabeth H. Zhong, Patricia Moulton, and Jeannie P. Cimiotti. 2013. "Highlights of the National Workforce Survey of Registered Nurses." *Journal of Nursing Regulation* 4:5–14.

Budrys, Grace. 2012. *Our Unsystematic Health Care System.* Lanham, MD: Rowman & Littlefield.

Bureau of Labor Statistics. 2015. "Occupational Outlook Handbook: Healthcare Occupations." http://www.bls.gov/ooh/healthcare/.

Burrows, Elizabeth, Ryung Suh, and Danielle Hamann. 2012. *Health Care Workforce Distribution and Shortage Issues in Rural America.* Leawood, KS: National Rural Health Association.

Burtless, Gary and Sveta Milusheva. 2013. "Effects of Employer-Sponsored Health Insurance Costs on Social Security Taxable Wages." *Social Security Bulletin* 73(1):http://www.ssa.gov/policy/ docs/ssb/v73n1/v73n1p83.html.

Bury, Mike. 1982. "Chronic Illness as Biographical Disruption." *Sociolog of Health and Illness* 4:167–182.

Buss, David. 2015. *Evolutionary Psychology: The New Science of the Mind.* Upper Saddle River, NJ: Pearson.

Bynum, William F. 2008. *The History of Medicine: A Very Short Introduction.* New York, NY: Oxford University Press.

Byrne, Joseph P. 2004. *The Black Death.* Westport, CT: Greenwood Press.

Cabieses, Baltica, Kate E. Pickett and Richard G. Wilkinson. 2016. "The Impact of

Socioeconomic Inequality on Children's Health and Well-Being." Pp. 244–265 in *The Oxford Handbook of Economics and Human Biology*, edited by J. Komlols and I. R. Kelley. New York: Oxford University Press.

Cabral, Patricia, Hilary B. Meyer, and Donna Ames. 2011. "Effectiveness of Yoga Therapy as a Complementary Treatment for Major Psychiatric Disorders: A Meta-Analysis." *The Primary Care Companion for CNS Disorders* 13:doi: 10.4088/PCC.10r01068.

Cacioppo, John T., and Stephanie Cacioppo. 2014. "Social Relationships and Health: The Toxic Effects of Perceived Social Isolation." *Social & Personality Psychology Compass* 8:58–72.

Caiazzo, Fabio, Akshay Ashok, Ian A. Waitz, Steve H.L. Yim and Steven R.H. Barrett. 2013. "Air Pollution and Early Deaths in the United States. Part I: Quantifying the Impact of Major Sectors in 2005." *Atmospheric Environment* 79:198–208.

Callahan, Daniel. 1973. "The WHO Definition of 'Health'." *The Hastings Center Studies* 1:77–87.

Campbell, Eric G., Susan Regan, Russell L. Gruen, Timothy G. Ferris, Sowmya R. Rao, Paul D. Cleary, and David Blumenthal. 2007. "Professionalism in Medicine: Results of a National Survey of Physicians." *Annals of Internal Medicine* 147:795–802.

Cancian, Maria and Sheldon H. Danziger, eds. 2009. *Changing Poverty, Changing Policies*. New York, NY: Russell Sage Foundation.

Carr, Debora. 2014. *Worried Sick: How Stress Hurts Us and How to Bounce Back*. New Brunswick, NJ: Rutgers University Press.

Carr, Phyllis L., Arlene S. Ash, Robert H. Friedman, Laura Szalacha, Rosalind C. Barnett, Anita Palepu, and Mark M. Moskowitz. 2000. "Faculty Perceptions of Gender Discrimination and Sexual Harassment in Academic Medicine." *Annals of Internal Medicine* 132:889–896.

Carroll, Aaron E. 2012. "5 Myths About Canada's Health Care System." *AARP Newsletter* April 16:http://www.pnhp.org/news/2012/june/5-myths-about-canada's-health-care-system.

Cassell, Joan. 2008. "The Gender of Care." Pp. 490–502 in *Perspectives in Medical Sociology*, edited by P. Brown. Long Grove, IL: Waveland Press.

Castle, Stephen. 2015. "Britain's National Health Service, Creaking but Revered, Looms Over Elections." *The New York Times* April 26:A8.

Center for Medicaid & CHIP Services. 2014. "State Medicaid and Chip Income Eligibility Standards." http://www.medicaid.gov/medicaid-chip-program-information/program-information/medicaid-and-chip-eligibility-levels/medicaid-chip-eligibility-levels.html.

Center for Reproductive Rights. 2014. *Reproductive Injustice: Racial and Gender Discrimination in U.S. Health Care*. New York, NY: Center for Reproductive Rights.

———. 2014. *Reproductive Injustice: Racial and Gender Discrimination in U.S. Health Care*. New York, NY: Center for Reproductive Rights.

Centers for Disease Control and Prevention. 2011. "Four Specific Health Behaviors Contribute to a Longer life." http://www.cdc.gov/features/livelonger/.

———. 2012. *Preventing Tobacco Use Among Youth and Young Adults: A Report of the Surgeon General*. Atlanta: Centers for Disease Control and Prevention.

Centers for Disease Control and Prevention. 2013. "Breast Cancer Statistics." http://www.cdc.gov/cancer/breast/statistics/index.htm.

———. 2013. "Genomics and Health." http://www.cdc.gov/genomics/resources/diseases/obesity/index.htm.

———. 2013. *Antibiotic Resistant Threats in the United States, 2013*. Atlanta, GA: Centers for Disease Control and Prevention.

———. 2014a. "About the National Health Interview Survey."

———. 2014a. "Alcohol Deaths." http://www.cdc.gov/features/alcohol-deaths/.

———. 2014b. "BRFSS Today: Facts and Highlights."

———. 2014b. "Economic Facts About U.S. Tobacco Production and Use." http://www.cdc.gov/tobacco/data_statistics/fact_sheets/economics/econ_facts/index.htm#costs.

———. 2014c. "Smoking & Tobacco Use: Fast Facts." http://www.cdc.gov/tobacco/data_statistics/fact_sheets/fast_facts/.

Centers for Medicare & Medicaid Services. 2013a. "National Health Expenditures 2013 Highlights." www.cms.gov/...and.../National-HealthExpendData/.../highlights.pdf.

———. 2014. "National Health Expenditures 2013 Highlights." *https://www.cms.gov/research-statistics-data-and-systems/statistics-trends-and-reports/nationalhealthexpenddata/downloads/highlights.pdf.*

———. 2016. *Nursing Home Data Compendium 2015 Edition*. Washington, DC: U.S. Department of Health & Human Services.

Chambliss, Daniel. 2008. "Nurses' Role: Caring, Professionalism, Subordination." Pp. 503–515 in *Perspectives in Medical Sociology*, edited by P. Brown. Long Grove, IL: Waveland Press.

Champion, Victoria L., and Celette Sugg Skinner. 2008. "The Health Belief Model." Pp. 45–66 in *Health Behavior and Health Education: Theory, Research, and Practice*, edited by K. Glanz, B.K. Rimer, and K. Viswanath. San Francisco, CA: Wiley.

Charmaz, Kathy and Dana Rosenfeld. 2010. "Chronic Illness." in *The New Blackwell Companion to Medical Sociology*, edited by W.C. Cockerham. Malden, MA: Wiley-Blackwell.

Chatham-Stephens, Kevin, Jack Caravanos, Bret Ericson, Jennifer Sunga-Amparo, Budi Susilorini, Promila Sharma, Philip J. Landrigan, and Richard Fuller. 2013. "Burden of Disease from Toxic Waste Sites in India, Indonesia, and the Philippines in 2010." *Environmental Health Perspectives* 121:791–796.

Chen, Lena M., Farwell R. Wildon, and Ashish K. Jha. 2009. "Primary Care Visit Duration and Quality: Does Good Care Take Longer?" *Archives of Internal Medicine* 1y9:1866–1872.

Chen, Pauline W. 2011. "When Hospital Overcrowding Becomes Personal." *The New York Times* July 14:http://well.blogs.nytimes.com/2011/07/14/when-hospital-overcrowding-becomes-personal/.

———. 2012a. "The Bullying Culture of Medical School." *The New York Times* August 9:http://well.blogs.nytimes.com/2012/08/09/the-bullying-culture-of-medical-school/.

———. 2012b. "Sharing the Pain of Women in Medicine." *The New York Times* December 4:D7.

———. "The Changing Face of Medical School Admissions." *The New York Times* May 2:http://well.blogs.nytimes.com/2013/05/02/the-changing-face-of-medical-school-admissions/?hp.

———. 2013. "The Gulf Between Doctors and Nurse Practitioners." *The New York Times* June 27:http://well.blogs.nytimes.com/2013/06/27/the-gulf-between-doctors-and-nurse-practitioners/.

———. 2014. "Emergency Rooms Are No Place for the Elderly." *The New York Times* March 13:http://well.blogs.nytimes.com/2014/03/13/emergency-rooms-are-no-place-for-the-elderly/.

Christakis, Nicholas A., and James H. Fowler. 2007. "The Spread of Obesity in a Large Social Network over 32 Years." *New England Journal of Medicine* 357(4):370–379. doi: 10.1056/NEJMsa066082.

Chu, Paula., Rinske A. Gotink, Gloria Y. Yeh, Sue J. Goldie, and MG Myriam Hunink. 2014. "The Effectiveness of Yoga in Modifying Risk Factors for Cardiovascular Disease and Metabolic Syndrome: A Systematic Review and Meta-analysis of Randomized Controlled Trials." *European Journal of Preventive Cardiology* doi: 10.1177/2047487314562741.

Clark, Bryan. 2016. "Pharma and Medical Device Companies Paid Idaho Doctors $24 Million." *Times-News (Twin Falls, ID)* May 8:http://magicvalley.com/news/local/pharma-and-medical-device-companies-paid-idaho-doctors-million/article_3916d3a3-b537-50a5-8972-cfb3f529fd63.html.

Clarke, Laura Hurd and Erica V. Bennett. 2013. "Constructing the Moral Body: Self-Care Among Older Adults with Multiple Chronic Conditions." *Health* 17:211–228.

Clarke, Tainya C., Lindsey I. Black, Barbara J. Stussman, Patricia M. Barnes, and Richard L. Nahin. 2015. *Trends in the Use of Complementary Health Approaches among Adults: United States, 2002–2012*. Hyattsville, MD: National Center for Health Statistics.

Clodfelter, Tammatha A., Michael G. Turner, Jennifer L. Hartman and Joseph B. Kuhns. 2010. "Sexual Harassment Victimization During Emerging Adulthood." *Crime & Delinquency* 56(3):455–481.

Cockerham, William C. 2010. "Health Lifestyles: Bringing Structure Back." Pp. 159–183 in *The New Blackwell Companion to Medical Sociology*, edited by W. C. Cockerham. Oxford: Wiley-Blackwell.

———. 2013a. "The Rise of Theory in Medical Sociology." Pp. 1–10 in *Medical Sociology on the Move: New Directions in Theory*, edited by W. C. Cockerham. New York, NY: Springer.

———. 2013b. *Social Causes of Health and Disease*. Malden, MA: Polity Press.

Cohen, Deborah A., Richard A. Scribner, and Thomas A. Farley. 2000. "A Structural Model of Health Behavior: A Pragmatic Approach to Explain and Influence Health Behaviors at the Population Level." *Preventive Medicine* 30:146–154.

Cohen, Robin A., and Michael E. Martinez. 2015. *Health Insurance Coverage: Early Release of Estimates From the National Health Interview Survey, 2015*. Washington, DC: National Center for Health Statistics.

Cohen, Thomas H. 2004. *Medical Malpractice Trials and Verdicts in Large Counties, 2001*. Washington, DC: Bureau of Justice Statistics, U.S. Department of Justice.

Coleman, James William. 2006. *The Criminal Elite: Understanding White-Collar Crime*. New York, NY: Worth Publishers.

Collett, Jessica L., and Omar Lizardo. 2009. "A Power-Control Theory of Gender and Religiosity." *Journal for the Scientific Study of Religion* 48:213–231.

Collins, Sara R., Munira Gunja, Michelle M. Doty, and Sophie Beutel. 2015a. *How High Is America's Health Care Cost Burden? Findings from the Commonwealth Fund Health Care Affordability Tracking Survey, July–August 2015.* New York, NY: The Commonwealth Fund.

Collins, Sara R., Petra W. Rasmussen, Sophie Beutel, and Michelle M. Doty. 2015b. *The Problem of Underinsurance and How Rising Deductibles Will Make It Worse—Findings from the Commonwealth Fund Biennial Health Insurance Survey.* New York, NY: The Commonwealth Fund.

Comondore, Vikram R., P. J. Devereaux, Zhou Qi, Samuel B. Stone, Jason W. Busse, Nikila C. Ravindran, Karen E. Burns, Ted Haines, Bernadette Stringer, Deborah J. Cook, Stephen D. Walter, Terrence Sullivan, Otavio Berwanger, Mohit Bhandari, Sarfaraz Banglawala, Johh N. Lavis, Brad Petrisor, Holger Schuneemann, Katie Walsh, and Neera Bhatnagar. 2009. "Quality of Care in For-profit and Not-for-profit Nursing Homes: Systematic Review and Meta-analysis." *BMJ: British Medical Journal (Overseas & Retired Doctors Edition)* 339:381–384.

Conger, Krista. 2014. "Dermatologists with Access to Sample Drugs Write Costlier Prescriptions, Study Finds." *Stanford Medical School* April 16:http://med.stanford.edu/news/all-news/2014/04/dermatologists-with-access-to-sample-drugs-write-costlier-prescriptions-study-finds.html.

Conley, Dalton, Kate W. Strully, and Neil G. Bennett. 2003. *The Starting Gate: Birth Weight and Life Chances.* Berkeley, CA: University of California Press.

Conlon, Kendra. 2015. "Patient Applauds Decision Upholding Obamacare." *wtsp.com* June 25:http://www.wtsp.com/story/news/health/2015/06/25/local-patient-applauds-courts decision-to-uphold-obamacare/29313433/.

Conrad, Peter and Cheryl Stults. 2010. "The Internet and the Experience of Illness." Pp. 179–191 in *Handbook of Medical Sociology*, edited by C.E. Bird, P. Conrad, A.M. Fremont, and S. Timmermans. Nashville, TN: Vanderbilt University Press.

Conrad, Peter and Kristin K. Barker. 2010. "The Social Construction of Illness: Key Insights and Policy Implications." *Journal of Health and Social Behavior* 51(S):S67–S79.

Conrad, Peter and Mike Bury. 1997. "Anselm Strauss and the Sociological Study of Chronic Illness: A Reflection and Appreciation." *Sociology of Health & Illness* 19:373–376.

Conrad, Peter and Valterie Leiter. 2013. "The Social Nature of Disease." Pp. 7–9 in *The Sociology of Health & Illness: Critical Perspectivew*, edited by P. Conrad and V. Leiter. New York, NY: Worth Publishers.

Conrad, Peter. 1975. "The Discovery of Hyperkinesis." *Social Problems* 23:12–21.

———. 2008. *The Medicalization of Society: On the Transformation of Human Conditions into Treatable Disorders.* Baltimore, MD: Johns Hopkins University Press.

———. 2013. "The Shifting Engines of Medicalization." Pp. 507–518 in *The Sociology of Health & Illness*, edited by P. Conrad and V. Leiter. New York, NY: Worth Publishers.

Consumer Reports. 2010. "The Dangers of Dietary and Nutritional Supplements Investigated." *Consumer Reports* September:http://www.consumerreports.org/cro/2012/05/dangerous-supplements/index.htm.

———. 2012. "Many Common Medical Tests and Treatments Are Unnecessary." *June* http://www.consumerreports.org/cro/magazine/2012/06/many-common-medical-tests-and-treatments-are-unnecessary/index.htm?loginMethod=auto.

———. 2013. "The Nurse Practitioner Will See You Now." *Consumer Reports* August:http://www.consumerreports.org/cro/magazine/2013/08/the-nurse-practitioner-will-see-you-now/index.htm?loginMethod=auto.

———. 2014. "Why Is Health Care So Expensive?". http://www.consumerreports.org/cro/magazine/2014/11/it-is-time-to-get-mad-about-the-outrageous-cost-of-health-care/index.htm?loginMethod=auto.

———. 2015. "The Rise of Superbugs." August:20–26.

Consumers Union. 2012. "Medicare Study Shows Most Medical Errors Go Unreported (press release)." http://safepatientproject.org/press_release/medicare-study-shows-most-medical-errors-go-unreported.

Cook, Philip J., and Kristin A. Goss. 2014. *The Gun Debate: What Everyone Needs to Know.* New York, NY: Oxford University Press.

Coontz, Stephanie. 2014. "Women Have Come a Long Way, But Still Have Far to Go." *The Courier-Journal* March 16:http://www.courier-journal.com/story/opinion/contributors/2014/03/16/stephanie-coontz-women-have-come-a-long-way-but-still-have-far-to-go/6425971/.

Courtenay, Will H. 2000. "Constructions of Masculinity and Their Influence on Men's Well-being: A Theory of Gender and Health." *Social Science & Medicine* 50:1385–1401.

Creatore, Maria I., Richard H. Glazier, Rahim Moineddin, Ghazal S. Fazli, Ashley Johns, Peter Gozdyra, Flora I. Matheson, Vered Kaufman-Shriqui, Laura C. Rosella, Doug G. Manuel and Gillian L. Booth. 2016. "Association of Neighborhood Walkability with Change in Overweight, Obesity, and Diabetes." *JAMA* 315(20):2211–2220.

Creswell, Julie and Reed Abelson. 2012a. "A Giant Hospital Chain Is Blazing a Profit Trail." *The New York Times* August 15:A1.

———. 2012b. "A Hospital War Reflects a Bind for Doctors in the U.S." December 1:A1.

———. 2014. "Hospital Chain Said to Scheme to Inflate Bills." *The New York Times* January 24:A1.

Creswell, Julie. 2014. "Race Is On to Profit From Rise of Urgent Care." *The New York Times* July 9.

Cruz, Marcio, James Foster, Bryce Quillin and Philip Schellekens. 2015. "Ending Extreme Poverty and Sharing Prosperity: Progress and Policies." http://pubdocs.worldbank.org/pubdocs/publicdoc/2015/10/109701443800596288/PRN03-Oct2015-TwinGoals.pdf.

Cubanski, Juliette, Christina Swoope, Cristina Boccut, Gretchen Jacobson, Giselle Casillas, Shannon Griffin, and Tricia Neuman. 2015. *A Primer on Medicare: Key Facts About the Medicare Program and the People It Covers.* Menlo Park, CA: Kaiser Family Foundation.

Cubbins, Lisa A., and Tom Buchanan. 2009. "Racial/Ethnic Disparities in Health: The Role of Lifestyle, Education, Income, and Wealth." *Sociological Focus* 42:172–191.

Cullen, Francis T., William J. Maakestad and Gray Cavender. 2006. *Corporate Crime under Attack: The Fight to Criminalize Business Violence.* Cincinnati, OH: Anderson Publishing Company.

Cunningham, Andrew and Roger French, eds. 2006. *The Medical Enlightenment of the Eighteenth Century.* Cambridge: Cambridge University Press.

Cunningham, Solveig A., Elizabeth Vaquera, Claire C. Maturo and K. M. Venkat Narayan. 2012. "Is There Evidence That Friends Influence Body Weight? A Systematic Review of Empirical Research." *Social Science & Medicine* 75(7):1175–1183. doi: 10.1016/j.socscimed.2012.05.024.

Cutler, David, Elizabeth Wikler, and Peter Basch. 2012. "Reducing Administrative Costs and Improving the Health Care System." *New England Journal of Medicine* 367:1875–78.

Cutler, David. 2013. "Why Does Health Care Cost So Much in America? Ask Harvard's David Cutler." *PBS Newshour* November 19:http://www.pbs.org/newshour/making-sense/why-does-health-care-cost-so-m/.

D'Antonio, Patricia. 2010. *American Nursing: A History Of Knowledge, Authority, And The Meaning Of Work / Patricia D'Antonio.* Baltimore, MD: Johns Hopkins University Press.

Datz, Todd and Marge Dwyer. 2014. *Risk of Obesity from Fried Foods May Depend on Genetic Makeup.* Harvard School of Public Health: http://www.hsph.harvard.edu/news/press-releases/obesity-risk-from-fried-foods-may-depend-on-genetic-makeup/.

Davis, Karen, Cathy Schoen, and Farhan Bandeali. 2015. *Medicare: 50 Years of Ensuring Coverage and Care.* Washington, DC: The Commonwealth Fund.

Davis, Karen, Kristof Stremikis, David Squires, and Cathy Schoen. 2014. *Mirror, Mirror on the Wall: How the U.S. Health Care System Compares Internationally.* New York, NY: The Commonwealth Fund.

Demos, John. 2009. *The Enemy Within: 2,000 Years of Witch-Hunting in the Western World.* New York, NY: Penguin Books.

DiBlasio, Natalie. 2014. "'Underestimated' Ebola Outbreak Spreads." *USA Today* August 23:http://www.usatoday.com/story/news/world/2014/08/23/ebola-spreads-in-nigeria-liberia-has-1000-cases/14489251/.

Diez Roux, Ana V. 2016. "Neighborhoods and Health: What Do We Know? What Should We Do?" Pp. 430–431 in *American Journal of Public Health*, Vol. 106: American Public Health Association.

Dingwall, Robert and Philip Lewis. 2014. "The Sociology of the Professions: Lawyers, Doctors and Others." New Orleans, LA: Quid Pro Books.

Doane, Michael and Marta Elliott. 2016. "Religiosity and Self-Rated Health: A Longitudinal Examination of Their Reciprocal Effects." *Journal of Religion & Health* 55(3):844–855. doi: 10.1007/s10943-015-0056-z.

Does the Quantity, Timing, and Type of Adversity Matter?". *Journal of Aging and Health* 27(8):1311–1338.

Doja, Albert. 2005. "Rethinking the *Couvade*." *Anthropological Quarterly* 78:917–950.

DPE Research Department. 2014. *The U.S. Health Care System: An International Perspective.* Washington, DC: AFL-CIO.

Draeger, Reid W., and Peter J. Stern. 2014. "Patient-Centered Care in Medicine and Surgery: Guidelines for Achieving Patient-Centered Subspecialty Care." *Hand Clinics* 30:353–359.

Dreier, Peter and Donald Cohen. 2013. "The Texas Fertilizer Plant Explosion Wasn't an Accident." *The Huffington Post* June 4:http://www.huffingtonpost.com/peter-dreier/texas-fertilizer-plant-explosion_b_3384739.html.

Drew Altman. 2016. "The Affordable Care Act after Six Years." *The Wall Street Journal* March 23:http://blogs.wsj.com/washwire/2016/03/23/the-affordable-care-act-after-six-years/.

Dubowitz, Tamara, Lisa M. Bates and Delores Acevedo-Garcia. 2010. "The Latino Health Paradox: Looking at the Intersection of Sociology and Health." Pp. 106–123 in *Handbook of Medical Sociology*, edited by C. E. Bird, P. Conrad, A. M. Fremont and S. Timmermans. Nashville, TN: Vanderbilt University Press.

Dubowitz, Tamara, Melonie Heron, Ricardo Basurto-Davila, Chloe E. Bird, Nicole Lurie, and José J. Escarce. 2011. "Racial/Ethnic Differences in US Health Behaviors: A Decomposition Analysis." *American Journal of Health Behavior* 35:290–304.

Duffin, Jacalyn. 2010. *History of Medicine: A Scandalously Short Introduction*. Toronto, ON: University of Toronto Press.

Duffy, Thomas P. 2011. "The Flexner Report--100 Years Later." *Yale Journal of Biology and Medicine* 84:269–276.

Duran-Pinedoa, Ana E., and Jorge Frias-Lopez. 2015. "Beyond Microbial Community Composition: Functional Activities of the Oral Microbiome in Health and Disease." *Microbes and Infection* doi:10.1016/j.micinf.2015.03.014.

Durisin, Megan and Max Nisen. 2013. "Medical School Student Debt Is Skyrocketing." *Business Insider* April 12:http://www.businessinsider.com/medical-students-burdened-with-staggering-debt-2013-4.

Durkheim, Emile. 1947(1915). *The Elementary Forms of Religious Life*. Translated by J. Swain. Glencoe, IL: Free Press.

———. 1952 (1897). *Suicide*. Translated by J. Spaulding and G. Simpson. New York, NY: Free Press.

Durso, Laura E., Kellan Baker, and Andrew Cray. 2013. *LGBT Communities and the Affordable Care Actfindings from a National Surve*. Washington, DC: Center for American Progress.

Dwyer, Marge. 2013. *Colonoscopy Screening Every Ten Years Could Prevent 40% of Colorectal Cancers*. http://www.hsph.harvard.edu/news/press-releases/colonoscopy-screening-every-ten-years-could-prevent-40-of-colorectal-cancers/.

Dyrbye, Liselotte N., Matthew R. Thomas, F. Stanford Massie, David V. Power, Anne Eacker, William Harper, Steven Durning, Christine Moutier, Daniel W. Szydlo, Paul J. Novotny, Jeff A. Sloan, and Tait D. Shanafelt. 2008. "Burnout and Suicidal Ideation among U.S. Medical Students." *Annals of Internal Medicine* 149(5):334–341.

Ehrenreich, Barbara and Deirdre English. 2005. *For Her Own Good: Two Centuries of the Experts' Advice to Women*. New York, NY: Anchor Books.

Eisenberg, Leon. 1977. "Disease and Illness: Distinctions between Profesional and Popular Ideas of Sickness." *Culture, Medicine and Psychiatry* 1:9–23.

Eisler, Peter and Barbara Hansen. 2013. "Doctors Perform Thousands of Unnecessary Surgeries." *USA Today* June 20:http://www.usatoday.com/story/news/nation/2013/06/18/unnecessary-surgery-usa-today-investigation/2435009/.

———. 2013. "Thousands of Doctors Practicing Despite Errors, Misconduct." *USA Today* August 20:http://www.usatoday.com/story/news/nation/2013/08/20/doctors-licenses-medical-boards/2655513/.

Eitzen, D. Stanley, ed. 2010. *Solutions to Social Problems: Lessons from Other Societies*. Upper Saddle River, NJ: Pearson.

Elhauge, Einer. 2013. "The Best Way to Reform Health Care—and Cut the Deficit." *The Daily Beast* January 6:http://www.thedailybeast.com/articles/2013/01/06/the-best-way-to-reform-health-care-and-cut-the-deficit.html.

Ellison, Christopher G., and Robert A. Hummer, eds. 2010. *Religion, Families, and Health: Population-Based Research in the United States*. New Brunswick, NJ: Rutgers University Press.

Elo, Irma T. 2009. "Social Class Differentials in Health and Mortality: Patterns and Explanations in Comparative Perspective." *Annual Review of Sociology* 35:553–572.

———. 2009. "Social Class Differentials in Health and Mortality: Patterns and Explanations in Comparative Perspective." *Annual Review of Sociology* 35:553–572.

Elwyn, Glyn, Christine Dehlendorf, Ronald M. Epstein, Katy Marrin, James White, and Dominick L. Frosch. 2014. "Shared Decision Making and Motivational Interviewing: Achieving Patient-Centered Care Across the Spectrum of Health Care Problems." *Annals of Family Medicine* 12:270–275.

Emerson, Joan P. 1970. "Behavior in Private Places: Sustaining Definitions of Reality in

Gynecological Examinations." Pp. 74–97 in *Recent Sociology*, Vol. 2, edited by H. P. Dreitzel. New York, NY: Collier.

Enoch, Lindsey, John T. Chibnall, Debra L. Schindler, and Stuart J. Slavin. 2013. "Association of Medical Student Burnout with Residency Specialty Choice." *Medical Education* 47(2):173–181. doi: 10.1111/medu.12083.

Enstrom, James E., and Lester Breslow. 2008. "Lifestyle and Reduced Mortality among Active California Mormons, 1980–2004." *Preventive Medicine* 46(2):133–136. doi: 10.1016/j.ypmed.2007.07.030.

Escarce, José J., Leo S. Morales and Rubén G. Rumbaut. 2006. "The Health Status and Health Behaviors of Hispanics." Pp. 362–409 in *Hispanics and the Future of America*, edited by M. Tienda and F. Mitchell. Washington, DC: National Academies Press.

Evans, Gary W., Jeanne Brooks-Gunn and Pamela Kato Klebanov. 2011. "Stressing out the Poor: Chronic Physiological Stress and the Income-Achievement Gap." *Pathways: A Magazine on Poverty, Inequality, and Social Policy* Winter:16–21.

Faienza, Maria Felicia, David Q. H. Wang, Gema Frühbeck, Gabriella Garruti and Piero Portincasa. 2016. "The Dangerous Link between Childhood and Adulthood Predictors of Obesity and Metabolic Syndrome." *Internal and Emergency Medicine* 11:175–182.

Federal Bureau of Investigation. 2012. "Financial Crimes Report to the Public: Fiscal Years 2010–2011." https://www.fbi.gov/stats-services/publications/financial-crimes-report-2010-2011.

Federal Bureau of Investigation. 2015. *Crime in the United States, 2014*. Washington, DC: Federal Bureau of Investigation.

Federal Trade Commission. 2014. *Self-Regulation in the Alcohol Industry*. Washington, DC: Federal Trade Commission.

Figaro, M. Kathleen, Rhonda BeLue and Bettina M. Beech. 2010. "Obesity." Pp. 179–212 in *Handbook of African American Health*, edited by R. L. Hampton, T. P. Gullotta and R. L. Crowel. New York, NY: Springer.

Finch, Brian K., D. Phuong Do, Melonie Heron, Chloe Bird, Teresa Seeman and Nicole Lurie. 2010. "Neighborhood Effects on Health: Concentrated Advantage and Disadvantage." *Health & Place* 16(5):1058–1060. doi: 10.1016/j.healthplace.2010.05.009.

Fisher, Emily L., and Eugene Borgida. 2012. "Intergroup Disparities and Implicit Bias: A Commentary." *Journal of Social Issues* 68:385–398.

Fletcher, Jason M. 2011. "Peer Effects and Obesity." Pp. 303–312 in *The Oxford Handbook of the Social Science of Obesity*, edited by J. Cawley. New York, NY: Oxford University Press.

Flexner, Abraham. 1910. *Medical Education in the United Sates and Canada*. Washington, DC: Science and Health Publications, Inc.

Fodeman, Jason. 2011. "Medical Residents Shouldn't Be Working 28-Hour Shifts." *The Daily Caller* October 30:http://dailycaller.com/2011/10/30/medical-residents-shouldnt-be-working-28-hour-shifts/.

Ford, Earl S., Guixiang Zhao, James Tsai, and Chaoyang Li. 2011. "Low-Risk Lifestyle Behaviors and All-Cause Mortality: Findings From the National Health and Nutrition Examination Survey III Mortality Study." *American Journal of Public Health* 101:1922–1929.

Fox, Renée C. 1957. "Training for Uncertainty." Pp. 207–241 in *The Student-Physician*, edited by R. K. Merton, G.G. Reader and P. Kendall. Cambridge, MA: Harvard Univeristy Press.

Frank, Reanne. 2007. "What to Make of It? The (Re)Emergence of a Biological Conceptualization of Race in Health Disparities Research." *Social Science & Medicine* 64(10):1977–1983.

Frank, Robert H. 2013. "What Sweden Can Tell Us About Obamacare." *The New York Times* June 16:BU6.

Freidson, Eliot. 1988. *Profession of Medicine: A Study of the Sociology of Applied Knowledge*. Chicago, IL: University of Chicago Press.

———. 1988. *Profession of Medicine: A Study of the Sociology of Applied Knowledge*. Chicago, IL: University of Chicago Press.

Freyer, Felice J. 2015. "State Braces for Measles after Outbreak at Disneyland." *The Boston Globe* February 7:http://www.bostonglobe.com/metro/2015/02/07/mass-readies-for-measles-disneyland-outbreak-spreads/pnUbhZI-SoukyvRUGtRi3CN/story.html.

Fried, Joyce M., Michelle Vermillion, Neil H. Parker, and Sebastian Uijtdehaage. 2012. "Eradicating Medical Student Mistreatment: A Longitudinal Study of One Institution's Efforts." *Academic Medicine* 87:1191–1198.

Friedman, Alexi. 2014. "NJ Biotech Firm Develops 'Female Viagra' for Women with Low Sexual Desire." *The Star-Ledger* April 21:http://www.nj.com/business/index.ssf/2014/04/nj_biotech_firm_moves_ahead_with_its_female_viagara_drug.html.

Friedman, Esther M., Jennifer Karas Montez, Connor McDevitt Sheehan, Tara L. Guenewald and Teresa E. Seeman. 2015. "Childhood Adversities and Adult Cardiometabolic Health: Fuertes,

Jairo N., Prachi Anand, Greg Haggerty, Michael Kestenbaum, and Gary C. Rosenblum. 2015. "The Physician-Patient Working Alliance and Patient Psychological Attachment, Adherence, Outcome Expectations, and Satisfaction in a Sample of Rheumatology Patients." *Behavioral Medicine* 41:60–68.

Friedman, Richard A. 2016. "What Drug Ads Don't Say." *The New York Times* April 24:SR5.

Gabe, Jonathan. 2013. "Medicalization." Pp. 49–53 in *Key Concepts in Medical Sociology*, edited by J. Gabe and L.F. Monaghan. London: Sage Publications.

Galea, Sandro, Melissa Tracy, Katherine J. Hoggatt, Charles DiMaggio and Adam Karpati. 2011. "Estimated Deaths Attributable to Social Factors in the United States." *American Journal of Public Health* 101:1456–1465.

Galewitz, Phil. 2015. "When Hospitals Move, Who Gets Left Behind?" *The Atlantic* April:http://www.theatlantic.com/health/archive/2015/04/when-hospitals-move-who-gets-left-behind/391412/.

Garcia, Lorena, Lihong Qi, Marianne Rasor, Cari Jo Clark, Joyce Bromberger and Ellen B. Gold. 2014. "The Relationship of Violence and Traumatic Stress to Changes in Weight and Waist Circumference: Longitudinal Analyses from the Study of Women's Health across the Nation." *Journal of Interpersonal Violence* 29(8):1459–1476. doi: http://dx.doi.org/10.1177/0886260513507132.

Garrett, Bridgette E., Shanta R. Dube, Cherie Winder, and Ralph S. Caraballo. 2013. "Cigarette Smoking—United States, 2006–2008 and 2009–2010." *Morbidity and Mortality Weekly Report* 62:81–84.

Gaynes, Robert P. 2011. *Germ Theory: Medical Pioneers in Infectious Diseases*. Washington, DC: ASM Press.

Gaynor, Martin and Robert Town. 2012. *The Impact of Hospital Consolidation*. Princeton, NJ: Robert Wood Johnson Foundation.

Genworth. 2015. *Genworth 2015 Cost of Care Survey*. Richmond, VA: Genworth Life Insurance Company.

Gibbs, Lois Marie. 2011. *Love Canal and the Birth of the Environmental Movement*. Washington, DC: Island Press.

Glatter, Robert. 2013. "Medical Malpractice: Broken Beyond Repair?" *Forbes* February 6:http://www.forbes.com/sites/robertglatter/2013/02/06/medical-malpractice-broken-beyond-repair/.

Glick, Thomas, Steven J. Livesey and Faith Wallis, eds. 2005. *Medieval Science, Technology, and Medicine: An Encyclopedia*. New York, NY: Routledge.

Goetz, Thomas. 2014. *The Remedy: Robert Koch, Arthur Conan Doyle, and the Quest to Cure Tuberculosis*. New York, NY: Gotham.

Goldacre, Ben. 2014. *Big Pharma: How Drug Companies Mislead Doctors and Harm Patients*. New York, NY: Faber and Faber.

Gonzales, Gilbert. 2015. "Association of the New York State Marriage Equality Act with Changes in Health Insurance Coverage." *JAMA* doi:10.1001/jama.2015.7950.

Goodman, Deannne. 2015. "Marin General Hospital Penalized For Making Life Threatening Errors." *Novato Patch* May 21:http://patch.com/california/novato/marin-general-hospital-penalized-making-life-threatening-errors-0.

Gordon, Colin. 2004. *Dead on Arrival: The Politics of Health Care in Twentieth-Century America*. Princeton: Princeton University Press.

Gottschalk, Marie. 2008. "'Show Me the Money': Labor and the Bottom Line of National Health Insurance." *Dissent* Spring:http://www.dissentmagazine.org/article/show-me-the-money-labor-and-the-bottom-line-of-national-health-insurance.

Gould, Stephen Jay. 1981. *The Mismeasure of Man*. New York, NY: W.W. Norton.

Gower, Jeremy. 2015. "2015 Medical Payout Analysis." http://www.diederichhealthcare.com/the-standard/2015-medical-malpractice-payout-analysis/.

Goyal, Madhav, Sonal Singh, Erica M. S. Sibinga, Neda F. Gould, Anastasia Rowland-Seymour, Ritu Sharma, Zackary Berger, Dana Sleicher, David D. Maron, Hasan M. Shihab, Padmini D. Ranasinghe, Shauna Linn, Shonali Saha, Eric B. Bass, and Jennifer A. Haythornthwaite. 2014. "Meditation Programs for Psychological Stress and Well-being A Systematic Review and Meta-analysis" *JAMA Internal Medicine* 174:357–368.

Grady, Denise. 2015. "Report Shows Widespread Mistreatment by Health Workers During Childbirth." *The New York Times* July 1:A12.

Grady, Denise. 2013. "Hospitals Profit From Surgical Errors, Study Finds." *The New York Times* April 17:A15.

Grady, Denise. 2013. "Study of Hormone Use in Menopause Reaffirms Complex Mix of Risks and Benefits." *The New York Times* October 2:A10.

Gray-Tofta, Pamela and James G. Andersonb. 2002. "Stress among Hospital Nursing Staff: Its Causes and Effects." *Social Science & Medicine* 15:639–647.

Grbic, Douglas, David J. Jones, and Steven T. Case. 2013. "Effective Practices for Using the Aamc

Socioeconomic Status Indicators in Medical School Admissions." Vol. https://www.aamc.org/download/330166/data/seseffectivepractices.pdf. Washington, DC: Association of American Medical Colleges.

———. 2015. "The Role of Socioeconomic Status in Medical School Admissions: Validation of a Socioeconomic Indicator for Use in Medical School Admissions." *Academic Medicine* 90(7):953-60.

Griffin, Donald J. 2012. *Hospitals: What They are and How They Work*. Burlington, MA: Jones & Bartlett.

Grusky, David and Christopher Wimer. 2011. "Editors' Note." *Pathways: A Magazine on Poverty, Inequality, and Social Policy* Winter:2.

Gugliotta, Guy. 2015. "Rural Hospitals, Best by Financial Problems, Struggle to Survive." *The Washington Post* March 15:http://www.washingtonpost.com/national/health-science/rural-hospitals-beset-by-financial-problems-struggle-to-survive/2015/03/15/d81af3ac-c9b2-11e4-b2a1-bed1aaea2816_story.html.

Gutkind, Lee. 2013. "I Wasn't Strong Like This When I Started Out: True Stories of Becoming a Nurse." Pittsburgh: InFact Books.

Guttman, Monika. 1999. "Why More Men Are Finally Going to the Doctor." *USA Weekend* June 11–13:10.

Haas, Steven A., Maria Glymour and Lisa F. Berkman. 2011. "Childhood Health and Labor Market Inequality over the Life Course." *Journal of Health and Social Behavior* 52:298–313.

Hackett, Rhonda. 2009. "Debunking Canadian Health Care Myths." *The Denver Post* June 7:http://www.denverpost.com/opinion/ci_12523427.

Haelle, Tara. 2014. "Measles Cases Are Spreadingn Despite High Vaccination Rates. What's Going On?". *The Washington Post* June 23:http://www.washingtonpost.com/national/health-science/measles-cases-are-spreading-despite-high-vaccination-rates-whats-going-on/2014/06/23/38c86884-ea97-11e3-93d2-edd4be1f5d9e_story.html.

Halonen, Jaana I., Jussi Vahtera, Mika Kivimäki, Jaana Pentti, Kawachi Ichiro and S. V. Subramanian. 2014. "Adverse Experiences in Childhood, Adulthood Neighbourhood Disadvantage and Health Behaviours." *Journal of Epidemiology & Community Health* 68(8):741–746. doi: 10.1136/jech-2013-203441.

Halpern, Jodi. 2011. *From Detached Concern to Empathy: Humanizing Medical Practice*. New York, NY: Oxford University Press.

Halstead, Richard. 2015. "State Fines Marin General Hospital $100,000 for Leaving Object in Patient's Skull." *San Jose Mercury News* May 21:http://www.mercurynews.com/crime-courts/ci_28163048/state-fines-marin-general-hospital-100-000-leaving.

Haltom, William and Michael McCann. 2004. *Distorting the Law: Politics, Media, and the Litigation Crisis*. Chicago, IL: University of Chicago Press.

Hammaker, Donna K., and Thomas M. Knadig. 2017. *Health Care Ethics and the Law*. Burlington, MA: Jones & Bartlett.

Hansen, Melinda. 2015. "Health Insurers' Request for Higher Rates (Letter to the Editor)." *The New York Post* July 9:A26.

Hanson, Ann. 2010. "Roman Medicine." Pp. 492–523 in *A Companion to the Roman Empire*, edited by D. S. Potter. Malden, MA: Wiley-Blackwell.

Harrell, Eben. 2009. "Is Britain's Health-Care System Really That Bad?" *Time*:http://content.time.com/time/health/article/0,8599,1916570,00.html.

Harris, Gardiner. 2014. "Malnutrition in Well-Fed Children Is Linked to Poor Sanitation." *The New York Times* July 15:A1.

Harrison, Joel A. 2015. "International Resources." http://www.pnhp.org/resources/international-resources.

Hart, Jaime E., Robin C. Puett, Kathryn M. Rexrode, Christine M. Albert and Francine Laden. 2015. "Effect Modification of Long-Term Air Pollution Exposures and the Risk of Incident Cardiovascular Disease in Us Women." *Journal of the American Heart Association* doi: 10.1161/JAHA.115.002301.

Hartley, David. 2004. "Rural Health Disparities, Population Health, and Rural Culture." *American Journal of Public Health* 94:1675–1678.

Hartocollis, Anemona. 2013. "With Money at Risk, Hospitals Push Staff to Wash Hands." *The New York Times*:A18.

Harvey, Vicki L., and Teresa Heinz Housel, eds. 2014. *Health Care Disparities and the Lgbt Population*. Lanham, MD: Lexington Books.

Hatch, Stephani L., and Bruce P. Dohrenwend. 2007. "Distribution of Traumatic and Other Stressful Events by Race/Ethnicity, Gender, Ses, and Age: A Review of the Research." *American Journal of Community Psychology* 40:313–332.

Hayden, Michael Edison. 2014a. "Rural Health Care Blamed for Infant Deaths in Kolkata." *The New York Times* April 1:http://india.blogs.nytimes.com/2014/04/01/rural-health-care-blamed-for-infant-deaths-in-kolkata/.

———. 2014b. "To Be Poor and Sick in India." *The New York Times* March 31:http://india.blogs.nytimes.com/2014/03/31/to-be-poor-and-sick-in-india/?_php=true&_type=blogs&_r=0.

Hayward, Mark D., and Bridget K. Gorman. 2004. "The Long Arm of Childhood: The Influence of Early-Life Social Conditions on Men's Mortality." *Demography* 41(1):87–107.

Heuch, Ivar, Bjarne K. Jacobsen and Gary E. Fraser. 2005. "A Cohort Study Found That Earlier and Longer Seventh-Day Adventist Church Membership Was Associated with Reduced Male Mortality." *Journal of Clinical Epidemiology* 58(1):83–91. doi: 10.1016/j.jclinepi.2004.04.014.

Hill, Terrence D., Catherine E. Ross and Ronald J. Angel. 2005. "Neighborhood Disorder, Psychophysiologicla Distress, and Health." *Journal of Health and Social Behavior* 46:170–186.

Hill, Terrence D., Christopher G. Ellison, Amy M. Burdette, and Marc A. Musick. 2007. "Religious Involvement and Healthy Lifestyles: Evidence from a Survey of Texas Adults." *Annals of Behavioral Medicine* 34:217–222.

Hill, Terrence D., Megan Reid and Corinne Reczek. 2013. "Marriage and the Mental Health of Low-Income Urban Women with Children." *Journal of Family Issues* 34(9):1238–1261. doi: http://dx.doi.org/10.1177/0192513X12441347.

Hillier, Susan M., and Georgia M. Barrow. 2015. *Aging, the Individual, and Society.* Belmont, CA: Cengage.

Hodson, Randy and Teresa A. Sullivan. 2012. *The Social Organization of Work.* Belmont, CA: Wadsworth.

Hoffman, Beatrix. 2003. *The Wages of Sickness: The Politics of Health Insurance in Progressive America.* Chapel Hill, NC: University of North Carolina Press.

Hoffman, Beatrix. 2010. "The Challenge of Universal Health Care: Social Movements, Presidential Leadership, and Private Power."" Pp. 39–49 in *Social Movements and the Transformation of American Health Care,* edited by J. C. Banaszak-Holl, S. R. Levitsky and M. N. Z. (Editor). New York, NY: Oxford University Press.

Hoffman, Catherine. 2009. *National Health Insurance: A Brief History of Reform Efforts in the U.S.* Menlo Park, CA: Kaiser Family Foundation.

Hoffman, Kelly M., Sophie Trawalter, Jordan R. Axt and M. Norman Oliver. 2016. "Racial Bias in Pain Assessment and Treatment Recommendations, and False Beliefs About Biological Differences between Blacks and Whites."

Proceedings Of The National Academy Of Sciences Of The United States Of America 113(16):4296-301. doi: 10.1073/pnas.1516047113.

Holley, Peter. 2015. "This 88-Year-Old Doctor Treats the Poor Out of His Toyota Camry. Mississippi Wants to Punish Him for It." *The Washington Post* January 14:http://www.washingtonpost.com/news/morning-mix/wp/2015/01/14/this-88-year-old-doctor-treats-the-poor-out-of-his-toyota-camry-mississippi-wants-to-punish-him-for-it/.

Holt, Cheryl L., Eddie M. Clark, Katrina J. Debnam and David L. Roth. 2014. "Religion and Health in African Americans: The Role of Religious Coping." *American Journal of Health Behavior* 38(2):190–199. doi: 10.5993/ajhb.38.2.4.

Horn, Erin E., Yishan Xu, Christopher R. Beam, Eric Turkheimer and Robert E. Emery. 2013. "Accounting for the Physical and Mental Health Benefits of Entry into Marriage: A Genetically Informed Study of Selection and Causation." *Journal of Family Psychology* 27(1):30–41. doi: http://dx.doi.org/10.1037/a0029803.

Hoyt, Crystal L., and Jeni L. Burnette. 2014. "Should Obesity Be a 'Disease'?" *The New York Times* February 23:SR12.

Hughes, Mary Elizabeth and Linda J. Waite. 2009. "Marital Biography and Health at Mid-Life." *Journal of Health and Social Behavior* 50(3):344–358.

Hurst, Charles E. 2015. *Social Inequality: Forms, Causes, and Consequences.* New York, NY: Routledge.

Idler, Ellen L. 2010. "Health and Religion." in *The New Blackwell Companion to Medical Sociology,* edited by W. C. cockerham. Oxford: Wiley-Blackwell.

Innes, Stephanie. 2015. "Pay Upfront or No Surgery, Cancer Patient Is Told." *Arizona Daily Star* June 20.

Institute of Medicine. 2000. *To Err is Human: Building a Safer Health System.* Washington, DC: National Academy Press.

———. 2011. *The Future of Nursing: Leading Change, Advancing Health.* Washington, DC: National Academies Press.

———. 2011. *The Health of Lesbian, Gay, Bisexual, and Transgender People: Building a Foundation for Better Understanding.* Washington, DC: National Academies Press.

International Federation of Health Plans. 2013. *2013 Comparative Price Report: Variation in Medical and Hospital Prices by Country.* London: International Federation of Health Plans.

IsHak, Waguih, Rose Nikravesh, Sara Lederer, Robert Perry, Dotun Ogunyemi, and Carol

Bernstein. 2013. "Burnout in Medical Students: A Systematic Review." *Clinical Teacher* 10(4):242–245. doi: 10.1111/tct.12014.

Jacobson, Louis. 2010. "Feinstein Says U.S. is Only Nation to Rely Heavily on For-Profit Insurers for Basic Health Care." *Tampa Bay Times* March 11:http://www.politifact.com/truth-o-meter/statements/2010/mar/11/dianne-feinstein/feinstein-says-us-only-nation-rely-heavily-profit-/.

Jalali, S., Z. Sharafi-Avarzaman, H. Rahmandad and A. S. Ammerman. 2016. "Social Influence in Childhood Obesity Interventions: A Systematic Review." *Obesity Reviews* DOI: 10.1111/obr.12420.

James, John T. 2013. "A New, Evidence-based Estimate of Patient Harms Associated with Hospital Care." *Journal of Patient Safety* 9:122–128.

Janowski, Konrad, Donata Kurpas, Joanna Kusz, Bozena Mroczek, and Tomasz Jedynak. 2013. "Health-Related Behavior, Profile of Health Locus of Control and Acceptance of Illness in Patients Suffering from Chronic Somatic Diseases." *PLOS One* http://www.plosone.org/article/info%3Adoi%2F10.1371%2Fjournal.pone.0063920.

Johnson, David W., and Nancy M. Kane. 2010. "The U.S. Health Care System: A Product of American History and Values." Pp. 323–42 in *The Fragmentation of U.S. Health Care: Causes and Solutions*, edited by E. Elhauge. New York, NY: Oxford University Press.

Joynt, Karen E., John Orav, and Ashish K. Jha. 2014. "Association Between Hospital Conversions to For-Profit Status and Clinical and Economic Outcomes." *JAMA* 312:1644–1652.

Judd, Deborah and Kathleen Sitzman. 2014. *A History of American Nursing: Trends and Eras.* Burlington, MA: Jones & Bartlett Learning.

Kaiman, Jonathan. 2014. "China's Toxic Air Pollution Resembles Nuclear Winter, Say Scientists." *The Guardian* February 25:http://www.theguardian.com/world/2014/feb/25/china-toxic-air-pollution-nuclear-winter-scientists.

Kaiser Family Foundation. 2015. "Total Number of Professionally Active Registered Nurses." http://kff.org/other/state-indicator/total-registered-nurses/.

Kaplan, George A. 2009. *The Poor Pay More: Poverty's High Cost to Health.* Princeton, NJ: Robert Wood Johnson Foundation.

Karnieli-Millera, Orit and Zvi Eisikovitsb. 2009. "Physician as Partner or Salesman? Shared Decision-making in Real-time Encounters." *Social Science & Medicine* 69:1–8.

Kellerman., Arthur L., Grant Somes, Frederick P. Rivara, Roberta K. Lee and MS Joyce G. Banton.

1998. "Injuries and Deaths Due to Firearms in the Home." *Journal of Trauma* 45(2):263–267.

Kelli, Heval Mohamed, Hina Ahmed, Muhammad Hammadah, Matthew Topel, Salim Hayek, Mosaab Awad, Keyur Patel, Brandon Gray, Kareem Mohammed, Yi-An Ko, Laurence Sperling, Tene T. Lewis, Greg Martin, Gary Gibbons and Arshed Quyyumi. 2016. "The Association of Living in Food Deserts with Cardiovascular Risk Factors and Subclinical Vascular Disease." *JACC: Journal of the American College of Cardiology* 67:1883.

Kennedy, Michael. 2004. *A Brief History of Disease, Science, and Medicine: From the Ice Age to the Genome Projec.* Cranston, RI: Writers' Collective.

Kershaw, Sarah. 2004. "Suffering Effects of 50's a-Bomb Tests." *The New York Times* September 5:A1.

Keyi, Sheng. 2014. "China's Poisonous Waterways." *The New York Times* April 6:SR4.

Khaw, Kay-Tee, Nicholas Wareham, Sheila Bingham, Ailsa Welch, Robert Luben, and Nicholas Day. 2008. "Combined Impact of Health Behaviours and Mortality in Men and Women: The EPIC-Norfolk Prospective Population Study." *PLOS Medicine* 5:e70. doi: 10.1371/journal.pmed.0050070.

Khazan, Olga. 2014. "What American Healthcare Can Learn From Germany." *The Atlantic* April 9:http://www.theatlantic.com/health/archive/2014/04/what-american-healthcare-can-learn-from-germany/360133/.

Kheirbek, Iyad, Kazuhiko Ito, Richard Neitzel, Jung Kim, Sarah Johnson, Zev Ross, Holger Eisl and Thomas Matte. 2014. "Spatial Variation in Environmental Noise and Air Pollution in New York City." *Journal of Urban Health* 91(3):415–431. doi: 10.1007/s11524-013-9857-0.

Kilbourne, Jean. 2011. "Deadly Persuasion: 7 Myths Alcohol Advertisers Want You to Believe." *Center for Media Literacy* http://www.medialit.org/reading-room/deadly-persuasion-7-myths-alcohol-advertisers-want-you-believe.

Killalea, Debra. 2014. "Beijing to Close Coal-Burning Power Stations to Clean Up Air Pollution." *News.com.au* August 5:http://www.news.com.au/technology/environment/beijing-to-close-coalburning-power-stations-to-clean-up-air-pollution/story-e6frflp0-1227014059863.

King, Leslie and Deborah McCarthy Auriffeille, eds. 2014. *Environmental Sociology: From Analysis to Action.* Lanham, MD: Rowman & Littlefield Publishers.

Kirk, Chris Michael and Rhonda K. Lewis. 2013. "The Impact of Religious Behaviours on the Health and Well-Being of Emerging Adults." *Mental Health, Religion & Culture* 16:1030–1043.

Klass, Perri. 2013. "Poverty as a Childhood Disease." *The New York Times* May 14:D4.

Klein, Ezra. 2013a. "21 Graphs That Show America's Health-Care Prices Are Ludicrous." *The Washington Post* March 26:http://www.washingtonpost.com/blogs/wonkblog/wp/2013/03/26/21-graphs-that-show-americas-health-care-prices-are-ludicrous/.

———. 2013b. "Why an Mri Costs $1,080 in America and $280 in France." *The Washington Post* March 15:http://www.washingtonpost.com/blogs/wonkblog/wp/2013/03/15/why-an-mri-costs-1080-in-america-and-280-in-france/.

Kleinke, J.D. 2012. "The Conservative Case for Obamacare." *The New York Times* September 30:SR4.

Kliff, Sarah and Dan Keating. 2013. "One Hospital Charges $8,000--Another, $38,000." *The Washington Post* May 8:http://www.washingtonpost.com/blogs/wonkblog/wp/2013/05/08/one-hospital-charges-8000-another-38000/.

Kliff, Sarah. 2012. "Everything You Ever Wanted to Know About Canadian Health Care in One Post." *The Washington Post* July 1:http://www.washingtonpost.com/blogs/ezra-klein/wp/2012/07/01/everything-you-ever-wanted-to-know-about-canadian-health-care-in-one-post/.

———. 2012a. "Everything You Ever Wanted to Know About Canadian Health Care in One Post." *The Washington Post* July 1:http://www.washingtonpost.com/blogs/ezra-klein/wp/2012/07/01/everything-you-ever-wanted-to-know-about-canadian-health-care-in-one-post/.

———. 2012b. "What Canada Can Teach Us about Fixing Medicare." *The Washington Post* October 30:http://www.washingtonpost.com/blogs/wonkblog/wp/2012/10/30/what-canada-can-teach-us-about-fixing-medicare/.

———. 2013. "When Your Surgery Goes Wrong, Hospitals Profit." *The Washington Post* April 16:http://www.washingtonpost.com/blogs/wonkblog/wp/2013/04/16/when-your-surgery-goes-wrong-hospitals-profit/?hpid=z4.

———. 2013. "You're Spending Way More on Your Health Care Benefits Than You Think." *The Washington Post* August 30:http://www.washingtonpost.com/blogs/wonkblog/wp/2013/08/30/youre-spending-way-more-on-your-health-benefits-than-you-think/.

Kluger, Jeffrey. 2013. "Women Make Better Doctors Than Men." *Time* October 17:http://healthland.time.com/2013/10/17/women-make-better-doctors-than-men/.

Koenig, Harold G., Dana E. King and Verna Benner Carson, eds. 2012. *Handbook of Religion and Health*. New York, NY: Oxford University Press.

Kollipaka, R., B. Arounassalame, and S. Lakshminarayanan. 2013. "Does Psychosocial Stress Influence Menstrual Abnormalities in Medical Students?". *Journal of Obstetrics & Gynaecology* 33(5):489–493. doi: 10.3109/01443615.2013.782272.

Komaromy, Miriam, Andrew B. Bindman, Richard J. Haber, and Merle A. Sande. 1993. "Sexual Harassment in Medical Training." *New England Journal of Medicine* 328(5):322326.

Kotar, S. L., and J. E. Gessler. 2013. *Smallpox: A History*. Jefferson, NC: McFarland & Company.

Kowalczyk, Liz. 2013. "Doctors Firing Back at Patients' Online Critiques." *The Boston Globe* March 31.

———. 2013a. "Married Medical Residents Juggle Grueling Schedules, Try Not to Miss Key Family Moments." *The Boston Globe* February 18:http://www.boston.com/lifestyle/health/2013/02/18/married-medical-residents-juggle-grueling-schedules-try-not-miss-key-family-moments/LcfBp9jd117YqKMypwXF6H/story.html.

Kowalczyk, Liz. 2013b. "Empathy Gap in Medical Students." *The Boston Globe* March 25:http://www.bostonglobe.com/lifestyle/health-wellness/2013/03/24/medical-students-empathy-drops-just-they-start-caring-for-patients/rWqFiVVsr9oze6EWRLwzwN/story.html.

Krause, Elliott A. 1977. *Power & Illness: The Political Sociology of Health and Medical Care*. New York, NY: Elsevier.

Kristof, Nicholas. 2015. "Polluting Our Bodies ". *The New York Times* November 29:SR 9.

Krueger, Patrick M., Jarron M. Saint Onge, and Virginia W. Chang. 2011. "Race/ethnic Differences in Adult Mortality: The Role of Perceived Stress and Health Behaviors." *Social Science & Medicine* 73:1312–1322.

Kulkarni, Karmeen D. 2004. "Food, Culture, and Diabetes in the United States." *Clinical Diabetes* 22:190–192.

Labaton, Stephen. 2005. "Senate Approves Measure to Curb Big Class Actions." *The New York Times* February 11:A1.

Lallemand, Nicole Cafarella. 2012. "Reducing Waste in Health Care." *Health Affairs* http://www.healthaffairs.org/healthpolicybriefs/brief.php?brief_id=82.

Landivar, Liana Christin. 2013. "Men in Nursing Occupations: American Community Survey

Highlight Report." Washington, DC: U.S. Census Bureau (http://www.census.gov/people/io/publications/reports.html).

Landry, Laura J., and Andrea E. Mercurio. 2009. "Discrimination and Women's Mental Health: The Mediating Role of Control." *Sex Roles: A Journal of Research* 61:3–4.

LaVeist, Thomas A., Darrell J. Gaskin and Patrick Richard. 2009. *The Economic Burden of Health Inequalities in the United States*. Washington, DC: Joint Center for Political and Economic Studies.

Lavelle, Bridget, Frederick O. Lorenz and K. A. S. Wickrama. 2012. "What Explains Divorced Women's Poorer Health? The Mediating Role of Health Insurance and Access to Health Care in a Rural Iowan Sample." *Rural Sociology* 77:601–625.

Lazar, Kay. 2015. "Doctors Key to Whether Patients Choose Hospice,Study Finds.""*The Boston Globe* June 9:A1.

Leape, Lucian L., Miles F. Shore, Jules L. Dienstag, Robert J. Mayer, RSusan Edgman-Levitan, Gregg S. Meyer, and Gerald B. Healy. 2012. "Perspective: A Culture of Respect, Part I: The Nature and Causes of Disrespectful Behavior by Physicians." *Academic Medicine* 87:845–852.

Lee, Gary A. 1995. "U.S. Energy Agency Radiation Tests Involved 9,000, Study Says." *The Washington Post* February 10:A13.

Lee, Min-Ah and Kenneth F. Ferraro. 2009. "Perceived Discrimination and Health among Puerto Rican and Mexican Americans: Buffering Effect of the Lazo Matrimonial?". *Social Science & Medicine* 68:1966–1974.

Lehmann, Joan B., Wehner P. Christopher, U. Lehmann, and Linda M. Savory. 1996. "Gender Bias in the Evaluation of Chest Pain in the Emergency Department." *American Journal of Cardiology* 77(8):641–644.Leibert, Michael. 2010. "Performance of State Medical Boards: Implications For Hospitals and Health Systems." *Hospital Topics* 88:107–115.

Leonard, Kimberly. 2014. "Health Officials: No Ebola Outbreak in U.S., but We're Prepping Anyway." *U.S. News & World Report* July 31:http://www.usnews.com/news/articles/2014/07/31/health-officials-no-ebola-outbreak-in-us-but-were-prepping-anyway.

Leshner, Alan I., Bruce M. Altevogt, Arlene F. Lee, Margaret A. McCoy and Patrick W. Kelley. 2013. *Priorities for Research to Reduce the Threat of Firearm-Related Violence*. Washington, DC: The National Academies Press.

Levine, Sol and Martin A. Kozoloff. 1978. "The Sick Role: Assessment and Overview." *Annual Review of Sociology* 4:317–343.

Levinson, Wendy, Cara S. Lesser, and Ronald M. Epstein. 2010. "Developing Physician Communication Skills For Patient-Centered Care." *Health Affairs* 29:1310–1318.

Lewis, Tené T., Courtney D. Cogburn and David R. Williams. 2015. "Self-Reported Experiences of Discrimination and Health: Scientific Advances, Ongoing Controversies, and Emerging Issues." *Annual Review of Clinical Psychology* 11:407–440.

Lieberman, Trudy. 2014. "Comparing U.S., Canadian Health Care Systems." http://healthjournalism.org/blog/2014/01/comparing-u-s-canadian-health-care-systems/.

Lindsey, Linda L. 2015. *Gender Roles: A Sociological Perspective*. Upper Saddle River, NJ: Prentice Hall.

Link, Bruce and Jo C. Phelan. 2002. "Mckeown and the Idea That Social Conditions Are Fundamental Causes of Disease." *American Journal of Public Health* 92:730–32.

———. 2010. "Social Conditions as Fundamental Causes of Health Inequalities." Pp. 3–17 in *Handbook of Medical Sociology*, edited by C. E. Bird, P. Conrad, A. M. Fremont and S. Timmermans. Nashville, TN: Vanderbilt University Press.

Link, Bruce G., and Jo Phelan. 1995. "Social Conditions as Fundamental Causes of Disease." *Journal of Health and Social Behavior* 35(Extra Issue):80–94.

Llamas, Michelle. 2014. "Big Pharma Cashes in on Americans Paying (Higher) Prices for Prescription Drugs." *drugwatch.com* October 15:http://www.drugwatch.com/2014/10/15/americans-pay-higher-prices-prescription-drugs/.

Lopez, German. 2014. *5 Disease Outbreaks Happening Right Now That Vaccines Could Have Prevented*. Vox Media: http://www.vox.com/2014/4/14/5604318/six-disease-outbreaks-that-vaccines-could-have-prevented.

Lorber, Judith and Lisa Jean Moore. 2002. *Gender and the Social Construction of Illness*. Lanham, MD: Rowman & Littlefield.

Lovell, Brenda L., Raymond T. Lee, and Celeste M. Brotheridge. 2010. "Physician Communication: Barriers to Achieving Shared Understanding and Shared Decision Making with Patients." *Journal of Participatory Medicine* 2:http://www.jopm.org/evidence/research/2010/10/13/physician-communication-barriers-to-achieving-shared-understanding-and-shared-decision-making-with-patients/.

Ludman, Evette J., Do Peterson, Wayne J. Katon, Elizabeth H. B. Lin, Michael Von Korff, Paul Ciechanowski, Bessie Young, and Jochen Gensichen. 2013. "Improving Confidence for Self

Care in Patients with Depression and Chronic Illnesses." *Behavioral Medicine* 39:1–6.

Ludmerer, Kenneth M. 2010. "Understanding the Flexner Report." *Academic Medicine* 85(2):193–196.

Lutfey, Karen and Jeremy Freese. 2005. "Toward Some Fundamentals of Fundamental Causality: Socioeconomic Status and Health in the Routine Clinic Visit for Diabetes." *American Journal of Sociology* 110(5):1326–1372.

MacIntyre, Sally and Anne Ellaway. 2003. "Neighborhoods and Health: An Overview." Pp. 20–44 in *Neighborhoods and Health*, edited by I. Kawachi and L. F. Berkman. New York, NY: Oxford University Press.

MacIntyre, Sally and Anne Ellaway. 2003. "Neighborhoods and Health: An Overview." Pp. 20–44 in *Neighborhoods and Health*, edited by I. Kawachi and L. F. Berkman. New York, NY: Oxford University Press.

Magner, Lois N. 2005. *A History of Medicine.* Boca Raton, FL: Taylor & Francis.

Maioni, Antonia. 2014. "Obamacare Vs. Canada: Five Key Differences." *The Globe and Mail* January 1:http://www.theglobeandmail.com/globe-debate/obamacare-vs-canada-five-key-differences/article14657740/.

Makary, Martin and Michael Daniel. 2016. "Medical Error–the Third Leading Cause of Death in the Us." *BMJ: British Medical Journal (Overseas & Retired Doctors Edition)* 353:i2139.

Malacrida, Claudia. 2003. *Cold Comfort: Mothers, Professionals, and Attention Deficit Disorder.* Toronto, ON: University of Toronto Press.

Mangan, Dan. 2013. "Medical Bills Are the Biggest Cause of Us Bankruptcies: Study." *CNBC* June 25:http://www.cnbc.com/id/100840148.

March of Dimes. 2014. "Low Birthweight." http://www.marchofdimes.com/baby/low-birthweight.aspx.

Markides, Kyriacos S., and Karl Eschbach. 2005. "Aging, Migration, and Mortality: Current Status of Research on the Hispanic Paradox." *Journals of Gerontology: Series B* 60B:68–75.

Marr, Chuck and Chye-Ching Huang. 2014. *Higher Tobacco Taxes Can Improve Health And Raise Revenue.* Washington, DC: Center on Budget and Priority Policies.

Martinez, Michael E., and Robin A. Cohen. 2015. *Health Insurance Coverage: Early Release of Estimates from the National Health Interview Survey, January–June 2015.* Washington, DC: National Center for Health Statistics.

Marusak, Joe. 2014. "McClintock Middle School to Celebrate the Life of Late Teacher." *The Charlotte Observer* May 30:http://www.charlotteobserver.com/2014/05/30/4943772/mcclintock-middle-school-to-celebrate.html#.U43yCZRdV2s.

Mata, Douglas A., Marco A. Ramos, Narinder Bansal, Rida Khan, Constance Guille, Emanuele Di Angelantonio, and Srijan Sen. 2015. "Prevalence of Depression and Depressive Symptoms among Resident Physicians a Systematic Review and Meta-Analysis." *JAMA* 314(22):2373–2383.

Mavis, Brian, Aron Sousa, Wanda Lipscomb, and Marsha D. Rappley. 2014. "Learning About Medical Student Mistreatment from Responses to the Medical School Graduation Questionnaire." *Academic Medicine* 89(5):705–711.

Mazurkiewicz, Rebecca, Deborah Korenstein, Robert Fallar, and Jonathan Ripp. 2012. "The Prevalence and Correlations of Medical Student Burnout in the Pre-Clinical Years: A Cross-Sectional Study." *Psychology, Health & Medicine* 17(2):188–195. doi: 10.1080/13548506.2011.597770.

McCanne, Don. 2009. "Uwe Reinhardt on Comparing U.S. To Canada." *Physicians for a National Health Program* January 28:http://pnhp.org/blog/2009/01/28/uwe-reinhardt-on-comparing-us-to-canada/.

McIntosh, Peggy. 2007. "White Privilege and Male Privilege: A Personal Account of Coming to See Correspondence through Work in Women's Studies." in *Race, Class, and Gender: An Anthology*, edited by M. L. Andersen and P. H. Collins. Belmont, CA: Wadsworth.

McKinlay, John B. 2013. "A Case for Refocusing Upstream: The Political Economy of illness." Pp. 583–596 in *The Sociology of Health & Illness*, edited by P. Conrad. New York, NY: Worth Publishers.

McKinlay, John B., and Lisa D. Marceau. 2002. "The End of the Golden Age of Doctoring." *International Journal of Health Services* 32:379–416.

McKinlay, John B., and Sonja M. McKinlay. 2013. "Medical Measures and the Decline of Mortality." Pp. 10–23 in *The Sociology of Health & Illness*, edited by P. Conrad and V. Leiter. New York, NY: Worth Publishers.

McLeod, Jane D. 2013. "Social Stratification and Inequality." Pp. 229–254 in *Handbook of the Sociology of Mental Health*, edited by C. S. Aneshensel, J. C. Phelan and A. Bierman. New York, NY: Springer.

McNeil, Donald G., Jr. 2014. "Polio's Return after near Eradication Prompts a Global Health Warning." *The New York Times* May 6:A8.

———. 2016. " Newly Opening Door to Tropical Diseases." *The New York Times* January 5:D3.

Mechanic, David. 1978. *Medical Sociology.* New York, NY: The Free Press.

Medicare Payment Advisory Commission. 2012. *Report to the Congress: Medicare Payment Policy.* Washington, DC: Medicare Payment Advisory Commission.

Mehrotra, Ateev, Hangsheng Liu, John L. Adams, Margaret C. Wang, Judith Lave, N. Marcus Thygeson, Leif I. Solberg, and Elizabeth A. McGlynn. 2009. "Comparing Costs and Quality of Care at Retail Clinics with That of Other Medical Settings for 3 Common Illnesses." *Annals of Internal Medicine* 151:321–328.

Meier, Barry. 2007. "Narcotic Maker Guilty of Deceit over Marketing." *The New York Times* May 10:A1.

Mello, Michelle M., Amitabh Chandra, Atul A. Gawande, and David M. Studdert. 2010. "National Costs of The Medical Liability System." *Health Affairs* 29:1569–1577.

Melnick, Meredith. 2011. "CDC: Why Gay and Bisexual Teens Are More Likely to Risk Their Health." *Time* June 6:http://healthland.time.com/2011/06/06/cdc-gay-and-bisexual-teens-are-more-likely-to-risk-their-health/.

Merton, Robert K., George G. Reader, and Patricia Kendall, eds. 1957. *The Student-Physician.* Cambridge, MA: Harvard University Press.

Meyer, Vicki F. 2001. "The Medicalization of Menopause: Critique and Consequences." *International Journal of Health Sciences* 24:769–792.

Miller, Matthew, David Hemenway and Deborah Azrael. 2007. "State-Level Homicide Victimization Rates in the Us in Relation to Survey Measures of Household Firearm Ownership, 2001–2003." *Social Science and Medicine* 64:656–664.

Mills, C. Wright. 1959. *The Sociological Imagination.* London: Oxford University Press.

Mirowsky, John and Catherine E. Ross. 2003. *Education, Social Status and Health.* Hawthorne, New York, NY: Aldine De Gruyter.

Monaghan, Lee F. 2013. "Illness and Health-Related Behaviour." Pp. 53–58 in *Key Concepts in Medical Sociology*, edited by J. Gabe and L. F. Monaghan. London: Sage Publications.

Moniz, Cynthia and Stephen Gorin. 2014. *Health Care Policy and Practice: A Biopsychosocial Perspective.* New York, NY: Routledge.

Monk, Ellis P., Jr,. 2015. "The Cost of Color: Skin Color, Discrimination, and Health among African-Americans." *American Journal of Sociology* 121(2):396–444.

Monnat, Shannon M., and Raeven Faye Chandler. 2015. "Long-Term Physical Health Consequences of Adverse Childhood Experiences." *The Sociological Quarterly* doi: 10.1111/tsq.12107.

Moody, Heather, Joe T. Darden and Bruce Wm. Pigozzi. 2016. "The Racial Gap in Childhood Blood Lead Levels Related to Socioeconomic Position of Residence in Metropolitan Detroit." *Sociology of Race and Ethnicity* 2(2):200–218.

Mooney, Linda A., David Knox, and Caroline Schacht. 2015. *Understanding Social Problems.* Belmont, CA: Cengage Learning.

Morris, Nathaniel P. 2013. "Beautiful Pathologies." *The New York Times* August 15:A23.

Mossialos, Elias, Martin Wenzl, Robin Osborn, and Chloe Anderson. 2015. *International Profiles of Health Care Systems, 2014: Australia, Canada, Denmark, England, France, Germany, Italy, Japan, The Netherlands, New Zealand, Norway, Singapore, Sweden, Switzerland, and the United States.* New York, NY: The Commonwealth Fund.

Muench, Ulrike, Jody Sindelar, Susan H. Busch, and Peter I. Buerhaus. 2015. "Salary Differences Between Male and Female Registered Nurses in the United States." *JAMA* 313:1266–1267.

Mullin, Emily. 2013. "How to Pay for Nursing Home Costs." *U.S. News & World Report* February 26:http://health.usnews.com/health-news/best-nursing-homes/articles/2013/02/26/how-to-pay-for-nursing-home-costs.

Munnich, Elizabeth L., and Stephen T. Parente. 2014. "Procedures Take Less Time At Ambulatory Surgery Centers, Keeping Costs Down And Ability To Meet Demand Up." *Health Affairs* 33:764–769.

Musumeci, MaryBeth. 2012. *A Guide to the Supreme Court's Decision on the Aca's Medicaid Expansion.* Menlo Park, CA: Kaiser Family Foundation.

Nack, Adina. 2008. *Damaged Goods? Women Living With Incurable Sexually Transmitted Diseases.* Philadelphia, PA: Temple University Press.

Nader, Ralph. 2013. "21 Ways Canada's Single-Payer System Beats Obamacare." *AlterNet* November 22:http://www.alternet.org/news-amp-politics/21-ways-canadas-single-payer-system-beats-obamacare?akid=11202.128059.A6ktfC&rd=1&src=newsletter930687&t=17.

National Cancer Institute. 2014. "Surveillance, Epidemiology, and End Results Program." http://seer.cancer.gov/.

National Center for Complementary and Integrative Health. 2015. "Spotlighted Research Results—Meditation." *https://nccih.nih.gov/health/223/research.*

National Center for Health Statistics. 2012. *Health, United States, 2011.* Hyattsville, MD: Centers for Disease Control and Prevention.

———. 2014. *Health, United States, 2013.* Hyattsville, MD: Centers for Disease Control and Prevention.

———. 2015. *Health, United States, 2014.* Hyattsville, MD: Centers for Disease Control and Prevention.

National Center for Health Workforce Analysis. 2013. *The U.S. Nursing Workforce: Trends in Supply and Education.* Washington, DC: Health Resources and Services Administration.

National Hospice and Palliative Care Organization. 2014. *NHPCO Facts and Figures: Hospice Care in America.* Alexandria, VA: National Hospice and Palliative Care Organization.

———. 2015. *Nhpco Facts and Figures: Hospice Care in America.* Alexandria, VA: National Hospice and Palliative Care Organization.

Nolte, Ellen and Martin McKee. 2011. "Variations in Amenable Mortality—Trends in 16 High-Income Nations." *Health Policy* 103:47–52.

Nora, Lois M., Margaret A. McLaughlin, Sue E. Fosson, S.K. Jacob, J.L. Schmidt, and Don Witzke. 1996. "Does Exposure to Gender Discrimination and Sexual Harassment Impact Medical Students' Specialty Choices and Residency Program Selections?". *Academic Medicine* 71(10):S22–S24.

Nordrum, Amy. 2015. "Why Are Prescription Drugs So Expensive? Big Pharma Points to the Cost of Research and Development, Critics Say That's No Excuse." *International Business Times* May 19:http://www.ibtimes.com/why-are-prescription-drugs-so-expensive-big-pharma-points-cost-research-development-1928263.

Nossiter, Adam and Alan Cowell. 2014. "Ebola Virus Is Outpacing Efforts to Control It, World Health Body Warns." *The New York Times* August 2:A4.

Nossiter, Adam. 2014. "Lax Quarantine Undercuts Ebola Fight in Africa." *The New York Times* August 5:A1.

Novak, Diana. 2015. "UIC Nurse's Research Helps Moms Bond with Preemies." *Chicago Sun-Times* April 10:http://chicago.sun-times.com/news-chicago/7/71/514365/uic-nurses-research-helps-moms-bond-preemies.

Nutton, Vivian. 2013. *Ancient Medicine.* New York, NY: Routledge.

O'Connor, Anahad. 2015a. "Many Probiotics Taken for Celiac Disease Contain Gluten." *The New York Times* May 20.

———. 2015b. "Study Warns of Diet Supplement Dangers Kept Quiet by F.D.A." *The New York Times* April 8.

O'Donnell, Jayne and Laura Ungar. 2014. "Rural Hospitals in Critical Condition." *USA Today* 2014:http://www.usatoday.com/story/news/nation/2014/11/12/rural-hospital-closings-federal-reimbursement-medicaid-aca/18532471/.

O'Donnell, Jayne. 2000. "Suffering in Silence." *USA Today* April 3:1A.

Oberlander, Jonathan. 2005. "Health Care Reform's Failure: The Song Remains the Same." *Health Affairs* 24(1679–1680).

OECD. 2013. *Health at a Glance 2013: OECD Indicators.* Paris: OECD Publishing.

Ogden, Cynthia L., Molly M. Lamb, Margaret D. Carroll, and Katherine M. Flegal. 2010. *Obesity and Socioeconomic Status in Adults: United States, 2005–2008.* Hyattsville, MD: Centers for Disease Control and Prevention.

Ogden, Cynthia L., Margaret D. Carroll, Brian K. Kit and Katherine M. Flegal. 2014. "Prevalence of Childhood and Adult Obesity in the United States, 2011-2012." *JAMA* 311:806–814.

Olinto, Pedro, Kathleen Beegle, Carlos Sobrado, and Hiroki Uematsu. 2013. "The State of the Poor: Where Are The Poor, Where Is Extreme Poverty Harder to End, and What Is the Current Profile of the World's Poor?" http://siteresources.worldbank.org/EXTPREMNET/Resources/EP125.pdf.

Olshansky, S. Jay and A. Brian Ault. 1986. "The Fourth Stage of the Epidemiologic Transition: The Age of Delayed Degenerative Diseases." *The Milbank Quarterly* 64(3):355–391. doi: 10.2307/3350025.

Omran, Abdel R. 2005. "The Epidemiologic Transition: A Theory of the Epidemiology of Population Change." *Milbank Quarterly* 83(4):731–757. doi: 10.1111/j.1468-0009.2005.00398.x.

Ornstein, Charles, Eric Sagara and Ryann Grochowski Jones. 2014. "Drug Makers Spending Less on Md Speakers." *The Boston Globe* March 14:http://www.bostonglobe.com/business/2014/03/04/some-drug-companies-have-slashed-payments-doctors-for-promotional-talks/JLMSJg3Z9ba3hEk56fWC6O/story.html.

Ornstein, Charles. 2012. "The 10 Most Common Nursing Home Violations." *ProPublica* November 16:http://www.propublica.org/article/the-10-most-common-nursing-home-violations.

Pagnin, Daniel, Valéria De Queiroz, Márcio Amaral De Oliveira Filho, Naira Vanessa Anomal Gonzalez, Ana Emília Teófilo Salgado, Bernardo Cordeiro E. Oliveira, Caio Silva Lodi and Raquel Muniz Da Silva Melo. 2013. "Burnout and Career Choice Motivation in Medical Students." *Medical Teacher* 35(5):388–394. doi: 10.3109/0142159x.2013.769673.

Pais, Jeremy, Kyle Crowder and Liam Downey. 2014. "Unequal Trajectories: Racial and Class Differences in Residential Exposure to Industrial Hazard." *Social Forces* 92:1189–1215.

Palmer, Karen S. 1999. *A Brief History: Universal Health Care Efforts in the Us*. Chicago: Physicians for a National Health Program http://www.pnhp.org/facts/a-brief-history-universal-health-care-efforts-in-the-us.

Pampel, Fred C., Patrick M. Krueger and Justin T. Denney. 2010. "Socioeconomic Disparities in Health Behaviors." *Annual Review of Sociology* 36:349–370.

Park, Crystal L., Shane J. Sacco and Donald Edmondson. 2012. "Expanding Coping Goodness-of-Fit: Religious Coping, Health Locus of Control, and Depressed Affect in Heart Failure Patients." *Anxiety, Stress & Coping* 25(2):137–153. doi: 10.1080/10615806.2011.586030.

Parsons, Talcott. 1951. *The Social System*. New York, NY: Free Press.

———. 1975. "The Sick Role and Role of the Physician Reconsidered." *Milbank Memorial Fund Quarterly* 53:257–278.

Patzer, Rachel E, Jennie Perryman, Justin D Schrager, Stephen Pastan, Sandra Amaral, J.A. Gazmararian, M. Klein, N. Kutner, and W.M' McClellan. 2012. "The Role of Race and Poverty on Steps to Kidney Transplantation in the Southeastern United States." *American Journal of Transplantation* 12:358–368.

Pear, Robert, Margot Sanger-Katz, and Reed Abelson. 2015. "Insurance Subsidies Remain, but So Do Health Law Questions." *The New York Times* June 26:A1.

Pear, Robert. 2015. "Many Say High Deductibles Make Their Health Law Insurance All but Useless." *The New York Times* November 15:A22.

Pearlin, Leonard I. 1999. "The Stress Process Revisited: Reflections on Concepts and Their Interrelatinships." Pp. 395–415 in *Handbook of the Sociology of Mental Health*, edited by C. S. Anehensel and J. C. Phelan. New York, NY: Kluwer Academic/Plenum.

Pearlin, Leond I., Scott Shierman, Elena M. Fazio and Steven C. Meersman. 2005. "Stress, Health, and the Life Course: Some Conceptual Perspectives." *Journal of Health and Social Behavior* 46:205–219.

Peet, Richard and Elaine Hartwick. 2015. *Theories of Development: Contentions, Arguments, Alternatives*. New York, NY: Guilford Press.

Pendrick, Daniel. 2013. "Accupuncture is Worth a Try for Chronic Pain." *Harvard Health Blog* http://www.health.harvard.edu/blog/acupuncture-is-worth-a-try-for-chronic-pain-201304016042.

Penn, Nolan E., Joyce Kramer, John F. Skinner, Roberto J. Velasquez, Barbara W.K. Yee, Letticia M. Arellano and Joyce P. Williams. 2000. "Health Practices and Health-Care Systems among Cultural Groups." Pp. 101–132 in *Handbook of Gender, Culture, and Health*, edited by R. M. Eisler and M. Hersen. New York, NY: Routledge.

Pérez-Escamilla, Rafael. 2009. "Dietary Quality among Latinos: Is Acculturation Making Us Sick?". *Journal Of The American Dietetic Association* 109(6):988–991.

Perry, Brea L., Kathi L. H. Harp and Carrie B. Oser. 2013. "Racial and Gender Discrimination in the Stress Process: Implications for African American Women's Health and Well-Being." *Sociological Perspectives* 56(1):25–48. doi: http://dx.doi.org/10.1525/sop.2012.56.1.25.

Pescosolido, Bernice A. 2011. "Taking 'The Promise' Seriously: Medical Sociology's Role in Health, Illness and Healing in a Time of Social Change." Pp. 3–20 in *Handbook of the Sociology of Health, Illness, and Healing: A Blueprint for the 21st Century*, edited by B.A. Pescosolido, J.K. Martin, J.D. McLeod, and A.Rogers. New York, NY: Springer.

Petterson, Srephen M., Robert L. Phillips, Andrew W. Bazemore, and Gerald T. Konis. 2013. "Unequal Distribution of the U.S. Primary Care Workforce." *American Family Physician* 87:1.

Phelan, Jo C., and Bruce G. Link. 2015. "Is Racism a Fundamental Cause of Health of Inequalities in Health?". *Annual Review of Sociology* 41:doi: 10.1146/annurev-soc-073014-112305.

Phelan, Jo C., Bruce G. Link and Parisa Tehranifar. 2010. "Social Conditions as Fundamental Causes of Health Inequalities: Theory, Evidence, and Policy Implications." *Journal of Health and Social Behavior* 51(S):28–40.

Phillips, Robert L., Jr., Martey S. Dodoo, Stephen Petterson, Imam Xierali, Andrew Bazemore, Bridget Teevan, Keisa Bennett, Cindy Legagneur, JoAnn Rudd, and Julie Phillips. 2009. *Specialty and Geographic Distribution of the Physician Workforce: What Influences Medical Student & Resident Choices?* Washington, DC: The Robert Graham Center.

Pierret, Janine. 2003. "The Illness Experience: State of Knowledge and Perspectives for Research." *Sociology of Health & Illness* 25(3):4–22.

Pollack, Andrew. 2013. "A.M.A. Recognizes Obesity as a Disease." *The New York Times* June 19:B1.

Pololi, Linda H., Janet T. Civian, Robert T. Brennan, Andrea L. Dottolo, and Edward Krupat. 2013. "Experiencing the Culture of Academic Medicine: Gender Matters, a National Study." *Journal of General Internal Medicine* 28:201–207.

Polsky, Daniel, Michael Richards, Simon Basseyn, Douglas Wissoker, Genevieve M. Kenney,

Stephen Zuckerman, and Karin V. Rhodes. 2015. "Appointment Availability after Increases in Medicaid Payments for Primary Care." *New England Journal of Medicine* 372:537–545.

Pope, C. Arden, III, R.T. Burnett, G.D. Thurston, M.J. Thun, E.E. Calle, D. Krewski and J.J. Godleski. 2004. "Cardiovascular Mortality and Long-Term Exposure to Particulate Air Pollution: Epidemiological Evidence of General Pathophysiological Pathways of Disease." *Circulation* 109(January 6):71–77.

Porter, Sam. 2001. "Women in a Women's Job: The Gendered Experience of Nurses." Pp. 307–319 in *Readings in Medical Sociology*, edited by W. C. Cockerham and M. Glasser. Upper Saddle River, NJ: Pearson.

Price, Polly J. 2014. "If Tuberculosis Spreads . . ." *The New York Times* July 9:A25.

Quadagno, Jill. 2006. *One Nation, Uninsured: Why the United States Has No National Health Insurance.* New York, NY: Oxford University Press.

Quah, Stella. 2010. "Health and Culture." in *The New Blackwell Companion to Medical Sociology*, vol. 27–46, edited by W.C. Cockerham. Malden, MA: Wiley-Blackwell.

Qualls, Sara Honn. 2014. "What Social Relationships Can Do for Health." *Generations* 38(1):8–14.

Queenan, Emily S. 2015. "Why This U.S. Doctor Is Moving to Canada." *The Toronto Star* April 28.

Ramirez, José, Jr. 2009. *Squint: My Journey with Leprosy.* Jackson, MS: University Press of Mississippi.

Ranji, Usha, Adara Beamesderfer, Jennifer Kates, and Alina Salganicoff. 2015. *Health and Access to Care and Coverage for Lesbian, Gay, Bisexual, and Transgender Individuals in the U.S.* Menlo Park, CA: Kaiser Family Foundation.

Rau, Jordon. 2015. "After the Favorable Ruling, Obamacare Still Faces Struggles." *Newsweek* June 25:http://www.newsweek.com/after-favorable-ruling-obamacare-still-faces-struggles-346950.

Read, Jen'nan G., and Bridget M. Gorman. 2010. "Gender and Health Inequality." *Annual Review of Sociology* 36:371–386.

Reid, T.R. 2010. *The Healing of America: A Global Quest for Better, Cheaper, and Fairer Health Care.* New York, NY: Penguin Press.

Reverby, Susan. 2013. "A Caring Dilemma: Womanhood and Nursing in Historical Perspective." Pp. 272–282 in *The Sociology of Health & Illness*, edited by P. Conrad and V. Leiter. New York, NY: Worth Publishers.

Ricker, Patricia P., and Choe E. Bird. 2005. "Rethinking Gender Differences in Health: Why We Need to Integrate Social and Biological Perspectives." *Journals of Gerontology Series B* 60:S40–S47.

Rieker, Patricia P., Chloe E. Bird and Matha E. Lang. 2010. "Understanding Gender and Health: Old Patterns, New Trends, and Future Directions." Pp. 52–74 in *Handbook of Medical Sociology*, edited by C. E. Bird, P. Conrad, A. M. Fremont and S. Timmermans. Nashville, TN: Vanderbilt University Press.

Rier, David A. 2010. "The Patient's Experience of Illness." Pp. 163–178 in *Handbook of Medical Sociology*, edited by C.E. Bird, P. Conrad, A.M. Fremont, and S. Timmermans. Nashville, TN: Vanderbilt University Press.

Riosmena, Fernando, Rebeca Wong and Alberto Palloni. 2013. "Migration Selection, Protection, and Acculturation in Health: A Binational Perspective on Older Adults." *Demography* 50:1039–1064.

Riska, Elianne. 2010. "Health Professions and Occupations." Pp. 337–354 in *The New Blackwell Companion to Medical Sociology*, edited by W. C. Cockerham. Malden, MA: Wiley-Blackwell.

Risse, Guenter B. 1999. *Mending Bodies, Saving Souls: A History of Hospitals.* New York, NY: Oxford University Press.

Rivara, Frederick P., Richard Sattin, Andrea Gielen and Debra Houry. 2013. "The Role of Research in Addressing the Public Health Problem of Gun Violence." *Injury Prevention* 19(3):224–24.

Robbins, Alexandra. 2015. "We Need More Nurses." *The New York Times* May 28:A25.

———. 2015. *The Nurses: A Year of Secrets, Drama, and Miracles with the Heroes of the Hospital.* New York, NY: Workman Publishing.

Robert, Stephanie A., Kathleen A. Cagney and Margaret M. Weden. 2010. "A Life-Course Apporach to the Study of Neighborhoods and Health." Pp. 124–143 in *Handbook of Medical Sociology*, edited by C. E. Bird, PeterConrad, A. M. Fremont and S. Timmermans. Nashville, TN: Vanderbilt University Press.

Roberts, Chris. 2014. "Old Housing May Have Rampant Lead Violations." *San Francisco Examiner* July 13:http://www.sfexaminer.com/sanfrancisco/old-housing-may-have-rampant-lead-violations/Content?oid=2846946.

Robinson, James C., and Kelly Miller. 2014. "Total Expenditures per Patient in Hospital-Owned and Physician-Owned Physician Organizations in California." *JAMA* 312:1663–1669.

Rodberg, Leonard. 2013. "Profit-Driven Health Care (Letter to the Editor)." *The New York Times* January 21:http://www.nytimes.

com/2013/01/22/opinion/profit-driven-health-care.html?ref=opinion&_r=0.

Rodriguez, Nancy. 2013. "Concentrated Disadvantage and the Incarceration of Youth: Examining How Context Affects Juvenile Justice." *Journal of Research in Crime and Delinquency* 50:189–215.

Rogers, Richard G., Bethany G. Everett, Jarron M. Saint Onge and Patrick M. Krueger. 2010. "Social, Behavioral, and Biological Factors, and Sex Difrrences in Mortality." *Demography* 47(3):555–578.

Rosen, Dennis. 2014. *Vital Conversations: Improving Communication between Doctors nad Patients* New York, NY: Columbia University Press.

Rosenberg, Charles E. 1987. *The Care of Strangers: The Rise of America's Hospital System.* New York, NY: Basic Books.

Rosenstock, Irwin. 1966. "Why People Use Health Services." *Milbank Memorial Fund Quarterly* 44:94–127.

Rosenthal, Elisabeth. 2013a. "The $2.7 Trillion Medical Bill: Colonoscopies Explain Why U.S. Leads the World in Health Expenditures." *The New York Times* June 1:A1.

———. 2013b. "As Hospital Prices Soar, a Stitch Tops $500." *The New York Times* December 3:A1.

———. 2015. "Insured, but Not Covered." *The New York Times* February 8:SR1.

Rosoff, Stephen M., Henry N. Pontell and Robert Tillman. 2014. *Profit without Honor: White Collar Crime and the Looting of America.* Upper Saddle River, NJ: Prentice Hall.

Ross, Catherine E. 2000. "Walking, Exercising, and Smoking: Does Neighborhood Matter?" *Social Science & Medicine* 51:265–274.

Ross, Catherine E., and John Mirowsky. 2001. "Neighborhood Disadvantage, Disorder, and Health." *Journal of Health and Social Behavior* 42:258–276.

———. 2010. "Why Education Is the Key to Socioeconomic Differentials in Health." in *Handbook of Medical Sociology*, edited by C. E. Bird, P. Conrad, A. M. Fremont and S. Timmermans. Nashville, TN: Vanderbilt University Press.

Ross, Craig S., Joshua Ostroff, Michael B. Siegel, William DeJong, Timothy S. Naimi, and David H. Jernigan. 2014. "Youth Alcohol Brand Consumption and Exposure to Brand Advertising in Magazines." *Journal of Studies on Alcohol and Drugs* 75:615–622.

Rostow, Walt W. 1990. *The Stages of Economic Growth: A Non-Communist Manifesto.* New York, NY: Cambridge University Press.

Roter, Debra and Judith A. Hall. 2013. "Doctor-Patient Communication: Why and How Communication Contributes to the Quality of Medical Care." Pp. 622–627 in *Encyclopedia of Behavioral Medicine*, edited by M. D. Gellman and J. R. Turner. New York, NY: Springer.

———. 2015. "Women Doctors Don't Get the Credit They Deserve." *JGIM: Journal of General Internal Medicine* 30:273–274.

Roy, Avid. 2011. "How the Heritage Foundation, a Conservative Think Tank, Promoted the Individual Mandate." *Forbes* October 20:http://www.forbes.com/sites/theapothecary/2011/10/20/how-a-conservative-think-tank-invented-the-individual-mandate/.

Rubinstein, Sidney M., Caroline B. Terwee, Willem J.J. Assendelft, Michiel R. de Boer, and Maurits W. van Tulder. 2012. "Spinal Manipulative Therapy for Acute Low-Back Pain." *The Cochrane Library* doi: 10.1002/14651858. CD008880.pub2.

Russell, James W. 2015. *Double Standard: Social Policy in Europe and the United States.* Lanham, MD: Rowman & Littlefield.

Rustgi, Sheila D., Michelle M. Doty, and Sara R. Collins. 2009. *Women at Risk: Why Many Women are Forgoing Needed Medical Care.* New York, NY: The Commonwealth Fund.

Rutkow, Ira M. 2010. *Seeking the Cure: A History of Medicine in America.* New York, NY: Scribner.

Saguy, Abigail C., and Kjerstin Gruys. 2013. "Morality and Health: News Media Constructions of Overweight and Eating Disorders." Pp. 127–145 in *The Sociology of Health & Illness*, edited by P. Conrad and V. Leiter. New York, NY: Worth Publishers.

Saint Louis, Catherine 2015. "Stubborn Pay Gap Is Found in Nursing." *The New York Times* March 25:A20.

Salazar, Christine F. 2013. "Treating the Sick and Wounded." Pp. 294–312 in *The Oxford Handbook of Warfare in the Classical World*, edited by B. Campbell and L. A. Tritle. New York, NY: Oxford University Press.

Samal, Lipika, Stuart R. Lipsitz and LeRoi S. Hicks. 2012. "Impact of Electronic Health Records on Racial and Ethnic Disparities in Blood Pressure Control at Us Primary Care Visits." *Archives of Internal Medicine* 172(1):75–76.

Samuelson, Robert J. 2011. "A Grim Diagnosis for Our Ailing Health Care System." *The Washington Post* November 28:http://www.washingtonpost.com/opinions/a-grim-diagnosis-for-our-ailing-us-health-care-system/2011/11/25/gIQARdgm2N_story.html.

Sanger-Katz, Margot. 2016. "Medical Debt Often Crushing Even for Insured." *The New York Times* January 6:A1.

Sanofi-Aventis. 2015. "2014 Hospitals/Systems Digest." *https://www.managedcaredigest.com/ereader/HospitalsSystemsDigest/files/assets/basic-html/page3.html.*

Save the Children. 2013. *Surviving the First Day: State of the World's Mothers 2013.* London: Save the Children.

Scanlan, Stephen J., J. Craig Jenkins, and Lindsey Peterson. 2010. "The Scarcity Fallacy." *Contexts* 9:34–39.

Schaefer, Richard T. 2015. *Racial and Ethnic Groups.* Upper Saddle River, NJ: Pearson.

Schieber, Anne-Cécile, Cyrille Delpierre, Benoît Lepage, Anissa Afrite, Jean Pascal, Chantal Cases, Pierre Lombrail, Thierry Lang, and Michelle Kelly-Irving. 2014. "Do Gender Differences Affect the Doctor-Patient Interaction during \Consultations inGeneral Practice? Results from the INTERMEDE Study." *Family Practice* 31:706–713.

Schneider, Keith. 1993. "Military Spread Nuclear Fallout in Secret Tests." *The New York Times* December 16:A1.

Schneider, Mary-Jane. 2017. *Introduction to Public Health.* Burlington, MA: Jones and Bartlett.

Schoen, C., S. L. Hayes, D. C. Radley, and S. R. Collins. 2014. *Access to Primary and Preventive Health Care Across States Prior to the Coverage Expansions of the Affordable Care Act.* New York, NY: The Commonwealth Fund.

Schoenborn, Charlotte A., Patricia F. Adams, and Jennifer A. Peregoy. 2013. *Health Behaviors of Adults: United States, 2008–2010.* Hyattsville, MD: Centers for Disease Control and Prevention.

Schulman, Kevin A., Jesse A. Berlin, William Harless, Jon F. Kerner, Shryl Sistrunk, Bernard J. Gersh, Ross Dubé, Christopher K. Taleghani, Jennifer E. Burke, Sankey Williams, John M. Eisenberg, and José J. Escarce. 1999. "The Effect of Race and Sex on Physicians' Recommendations for Cardiac Catheterization." *The New England Journal of Medicine* 340:618–626.

Schwarz, Alan. 2013. "The Selling of Attention Deficit Disorder." *The New York Times* December 15:A1.

Scommegna, Paola. 2013. "Exploring the Paradox of U.S. Hispanics' Longer Life Expectancy." Population Reference Bureau:http://www.prb.org/Publications/Articles/2013/us-hispanics-life-expectancy.aspx.

Scott, Alison. 2013. "Illness Meanings of AIDS Among Women with HIV: Merging Immunology and Life Experience." Pp. 146–158 in *The Sociology of Health & Illness*, edited by P. Conrad and V. Leiter. New York, NY: Worth Publishers.

Seabury, Seth A., Anupam Jena, and Amitabh Chandra. 2013. "Trends in the Earnings of Male and Female Health Care Professionals in the United States, 1987 to 2010." *JAMA Internal Medicine* 173:1748–1750.

Seidman, Laurence. 2015. "The Affordable Care Act Versus Medicare for All." *Journal of Health Politics, Policy and Law* 40(4):909–19.

Shams, Tarek and Ragaa El-Masry. 2015. "Cons and Pros of Female Anesthesiologists: Academic versus Nonacademic." *Journal of Anaesthesiology Clinical Pharmacology* 31:86–91.

Sharkey, Patrick. 2013. *Stuck in Place: Urban Neighborhoods and the End of Progress toward Racial Equality.* Chicago, IL: University of Chicago Press.

Shi, Leiyu and Douglas A. Singh. 2015. *Delivering Health Care in America: A Systems Approach.* Burlington, MA: Jones & Bartlett.

Shu, Leiyu. 2012. "The Impact of Primary Care: A Focused Review." *Scientifica* 2012:http://dx.doi.org/10.6064/2012/432892.

Sierra Hernandez, Carlos A., Christina Han, John L. Oliffe, and John S. Ogrodniczuk. 2014. "Understanding Help-Seeking Among Depressed Men." *Psychology of Men & Masculinity* doi: 10.1037/a0034052.

Sifferlin, Alexandra. 2016. "How the United States Is Bracing for Zika." *Time* April 22:http://time.com/4304851/how-the-united-states-is-bracing-for-zika/.

Singer, Natasha and Duff Wilson. 2009. "Menopause, as Brought to You by Big Pharma." *The New York Times* December 13:BU1.

Smedley, Brian D., Adrienne Y. Stith and Alan R. Nelson. 2003. "Unequal Treatment: Confronting Racial and Ethnic Disparities in Health Care." Washington, DC: National Academies Press.

Smith-Barrow, Delece. 2016. "10 Most Competitive Medical Schools." *U.S. News & World Report* March 17:http://www.usnews.com/education/best-graduate-schools/the-short-list-grad-school/articles/2016-03-17/10-medical-schools-with-the-lowest-acceptance-rates.

Smith, Kirsten P., and Nicholas A. Christakis. 2008. "Social Networks and Health." *Annual Review of Sociology* 34:405–429.

Smith, Mark, Robert Saunders, Leigh Stuckhardt, and J. Michael McGinnis, eds. 2012. *Best Care at Lower Cost: The Path to Continuously Learning Health Care in America.* Washington, DC: The National Academies Press.

Smith, Steve and Pamela Kirkpatrick. 2013. "Use of Solution-focused Brief Therapy to Enhance Therapeutic Communication in Patients with COPD." *Primary Health Care* 23:27–32.

Snow, John. 1855. *On the Mode of Communication of Cholera*. London: John Churchill.

Sohail, Nudrat. 2013. "Stress and Academic Performance among Medical Students." *Journal of The College of Physicians And Surgeons--Pakistan* 23(1):67–71. doi: 01.2013/jcpsp.6771.

Spray, E.C. 2013. "Health and Medicine in the Enlightenment." Pp. 82–99 in *The Oxford Handbook of the History of Medicine*, edited by M. Jackson. Oxford: Oxford University Press.

Squires, David A. 2012. *Explaining High Health Care Spending in the United States: An International Comparison of Supply, Utilization, Prices, and Quality*. New York, NY: The Commonwealth Fund.

Starfield, Barbara, Leiyu Shu, and James Macinko. 2005. "Contribution of Primary Care to Health Systems and Health." *The Milbank Quarterly* 83:457–502.

Starr, Paul. 1982. *The Social Transformation of American Medicine*. New York, NY: Basic Books.

Stein, Sam and Jeffrey Young. 2014. "Cbo: Obamacare Will Cost Less Than Projected, Cover 12 Million Uninsured People This Year." *The Huffington Post* April 14:http://www.huffingtonpost.com/2014/04/14/cbo-obamacare-report_n_5146896.html.

Stempniak, Marty. 2015. "URGENT CARE 2.0." *H&HN: Hospitals & Health Networks* 89:32–35.

Stevens, Carl D., David L. Schriger, Brian Raffetto, Anna C. Davis, David Zingmond and Dylan H. Roby. 2014. "Geographic Clustering of Diabetic Lower-Extremity Amputations in Low-Income Regions of California." *Health Affairs* 33:1383–1390.

Stevens, Fred. 2010. "The Convergence and Divergence of Modern Health Care Systems." Pp. 434–454 in *The New Blackwell Companion to Medical Sociology*, edited by W. C. Cockerham. Malden, MA: Wiley-Blackwell.

Stevens-Watkins, D., and S. Rostosky. 2010. "Binge Drinking in African American Males from Adolescence to Young Adulthood: The Protective Influence of Religiosity, Family Connectedness, and Close Friends' Substance Use." *Substance Use and Misuse* 45:1435–1451.

Strauss, Anselm L., and Barney G. Glaser. 1975. *Chronic Illness and the Quality of Life*. St. Louis, MO: Mosby.

Strully, Kate W., David H. Rehkopf, and Ziming Xuan. 2010. "Effects of Prenatal Poverty on Infant Health: State Earned Income Tax Credits and Birth Weight." *American Sociological Review* 75:534–562.

Su, Dejun and L. Li. 2011. "Trends in the Use of Complementary and Alternative Medicine in the United States: 2002–2007." *Journal of Health Care for the Poor and Underserved* 22:295–309.

Suchman, Edward A. 1966. "Stages of Illness and Medical Care." *Journal of Health and Social Behavior* 6:2–16.

Szalavitz, Maia. 2012. "The Legacy of the Cia's Secret Lsd Experiments on America." *Time* March 23:http://healthland.time.com/2012/03/23/the-legacy-of-the-cias-secret-lsd-experiments-on-america/.

Takeuchi, David T., Emily Walton and ManChui Leung. 2010. "Race Social Contexts, and Health: Examining Geogrpahic Spaces and Places." Pp. 92–105 in *Handbook of Medical Sociology*, edited by C. E. Bird, P. Conrad, A. M. Fremont and S. Timmermans. Nashville, TN: Vanderbilt University Press.

Tausig, Mark. 2013. "The Sociology of Chronic Illness and Self-Care Management." *Research in the Sociology of Health Care* 31:247–272.

Tavernise, Sabrina. 2013. "The Health Toll of Immigration." *The New York Times* May 19:A1.

———. 2015. "Rural Nebraska Offers Stark View of Nursing Autonomy Debate." *The New York Times* May 26:http://www.nytimes.com/2015/05/26/health/rural-nebraska-offers-stark-view-of-nursing-autonomy-debate.html?emc=edit_tnt_20150525&nlid=41663&tntemail0=y&_r=0.

———. 2015a. "After Health Care Act, Sharp Drop in Spending on Birth Control." *The New York Times* July 7:http://www.nytimes.com/2015/07/08/health/after-health-care-act-sharp-drop-in-spending-on-birth-control.html?emc=edit_tnt_20150707&nlid=41663&tntemail0=y.

———. 2015b. "Rise in Early Cancer Detection in Young Women Is Linked to Affordable Care Act." *The New York Times* November 25:A19.

Terrill, Alexandra L., John P. Garofalo, Elizabeth Soliday and Rebecca Craft. 2012. "Multiple Roles and Stress Burden in Women: A Conceptual Model of Heart Disease Risk." *Journal of Applied Biobehavioral Research* 17:4–22.

The Washington Post. 2010. *Landmark: The inside Story of America's New Health-Care Law—the Affordable Care Act—and What It Means for Us All* New York: PublicAffairs.

The World Bank. 2014a. "Poverty." http://www.worldbank.org/en/topic/poverty.

———. 2014b. *World Development Report 2014*. Washington, DC: The World Bank.

Thoits, Peggy A. 2010. "Stress and Health: Major Findings and Policy Implications." *Journal of Health and Social Behavior* 51:S41–S53.

Thomas, Gordon. 1989. *Journey into Madness: The True Story of Secret Cia Mind Control and Medical Abuse.* New York, NY: Bantom Books.

Thomas, Lillian. 2014. "Hospitals, Doctors Moving Out of Poor City Neighborhoods to More Affluent Areas." *Milwaukee Journal Sentinel* June 14:http://www.jsonline.com/news/health/hospitals-doctors-moving-out-of-poor-city-neighborhoods-to-more-affluent-areas-b99284882z1-262899701.html.

Timmermans, Stefan and Hyeyoung Oh. 2010. "The Continued Social Transformation of the Medical Profession." *Journal of Health and Social Behavior* 51:S94–S106.

Travis, Jeremy and Michelle Waul. 2002. *Reflections on the Crime Decline: Lessons for the Future?* Washington, DC: Urban Institute.

Treuhaft, Sarah and Allison Karpyn. 2010. *The Grocery Gap: Who Has Access to Healthy Food and Why It Matters.* Oakland and Philadelhia: PolicyLink and The Food Trust.

Truman, Jennifer L., and Lynn Langton. 2015. *Criminal Victimization 2014.* Washington, DC: Bureau of Justice Statistics, U.S. Department of Justice.

Turner, Heather A., Anne Shattuck, Sherry Hamby and David Finkelhor. 2013. "Community Disorder, Victimization Exposure, and Mental Health in a National Sample of Youth." *Journal of Health and Social Behavior* 54:258–275.

U.S. Department of Health & Human Services. 2005. *Facts About Menopausal Hormone Therapy.* http://www.nhlbi.nih.gov/health/women/pht_facts.pdf.

———. 2012. *Hospital Incident Reporting Systems Do Not Capture Most Patient Harm.* Washington, DC: U.S. Department of Health & Human Services.

———. 2013. *2012 National Survey of Organ Donation Attitudes and Behaviors.* Rockville, MD: U.S.Department of Health and Human Services.

Ulmer, Cheryl, Diane Miller Wolman, and Michael M.E. Johns. 2008a. *Resident Duty Hours: Enhancing Sleep, Supervision, and Safety.* Washington, DC: Institute of Medicine.

———. 2008b. *Resident Duty Hours: Enhancing Sleep, Supervision, and Safety. Report Brief.* Washington, DC: Institute of Medicine.

Ulrich, Beth. 2010. "Gender Diversity and Nurse-Physician Relationships." *AMA Journal of Ethics* 12:41–45.

Umberson, Debra and Jennifer Karas Montez. 2010. "Social Relationships and Health: A Flashpoint for Health Policy." *Journal of Health and Social Behavior* 51(S):S54–S66.

Umberson, Debra, Kristi Williams, Patricia A. Thomas, Hui Liu and Mieke Beth Thomeer. 2014. "Race, Gender, and Chains of Disadvantage: Childhood Adversity, Social Relationships, and Health." *Journal of Health and Social Behavior* 55:20–38.

Umberson, Debra, Robert Crosnoe, and Corinne Reczek. 2010. "Social Relationships and Health Behavior Across the Life Course." *Annual Review of Sociology* 36:139–157.

UN News Centre. 2015. "After Missteps on Ebola, WHO Must Re-establish Itself as 'Guardian of Global Public Health'--Review Panel." July 7:http://www.un.org/apps/news/story.asp?NewsID=51349#.VabetirBzGc.

UNAIDS. 2013. *Global Report: UNAIDS Report on the Global AIDS Epidemic 2013.* New York, NY: Joint United Nations Programme on HIV/AIDS.

Underwood, Anne. 2009. "Health Care Abroad: Germany." *The New York Times* September 29:http://prescriptions.blogs.nytimes.com/2009/09/29/health-care-abroad-germany/.

Ungar, Laura. 2014. "What Ails Appalchia Ails the Nation." *USA Today* August 8:http://www.usatoday.com/story/news/nation/2014/08/07/appalachia-health-cdc-frieden-disease/13643547/.

UNICEF. 2009. *The State of the World's Children: Special Edition.* New York, NY: UNICEF.

UNOCHA. 2014. *Haiti Humanitarian Action Plan 2014.* New York, NY: United Nations Office for the Coordination of Humanitarian Affairs.

van Ryn, Michelle and Jane Burke. 2000. "The Effect of Patient Race and Socio-Economic Status on Physicians' Perceptions of Patients." *Social Science & Medicine* 50:81328.

Vanderminden, Jennifer and Sharyn J. Potter. 2010. "Challenges to the Doctor-Patient Relationship in the Twenty-First Century." Pp. 355–372 in *The New Blackwell Companion to Medical Sociology,* edited by W. C. Cockerham. Malden, MA: Wiley-Blackwell.

Velasquez-Manoff, Moises. 2013. "Status and Stress." *The New York Times* July 28:SR1.

Verlander, Glese. 2004. "Female Physicians: Balancing Career and Family." *Academic Psychiatry* 28:331–336.

Visser, Susanna N., Melissa L. Danielson, Rebecca H. Bitsko, Joseph R. Holbrook, Michael D. Kogan, Reem M. Ghandour, and Ruth Perou. 2014. "Trends in the Parent-Report of Health Care Provider-Diagnosed and Medicated Attention-Deficit/Hyperactivity Disorder: United States, 2003–2011." *Journal of the American*

Academy of Child & Adolescent Psychiatry 53:34–46.

Waddington, Keir. 2011. *An Introduction to the Social History of Medicine : Europe since 1500.* New York, NY: Palgrasve Macmillan.

Waldman, Peter and David Armstrong. 2010. "Doctors Getting Rich with Fusion Surgery Debunked by Studies." *Bloomberg Business* http://www.bloomberg.com/news/articles/2010-12-30/highest-paid-u-s-doctors-get-rich-with-fusion-surgery-debunked-by-studies.

Waldron, Ingrid. 1997. *Changing Gender Roles and Gender Differences in Health Behavior.* New York, NY: Plenum Press.

Walker, K. Odom, R. Ramey, F.L. Nunez, R. Beltran, R.G. Splawn, and A.F. Brown. 2010. "Recruiting and Retaining Primary Care Physicians in Urban Underserved Communities: The Importance of Having a Mission to Serve." *American Journal of Public Health* 100:2168–2175.

Waller, John. 2002. *The Discovery of the Germ: Twenty Years That Transformed the Way We Think About Disease.* New York, NY: Columbia University Press.

Ward, Brian W., James M. Dahlhamer, Adena M. Galinsky and Sarah S. Joestl. 2014. *Sexual Orientation and Health among U.S. Adults: National Health Interview Survey, 2013* Hyattsville, MD: Natonal Center for Health Statistics.

Washington, Harriet A. 2006. *Medical Apartheid: The Dark History of Medical Experimentation on Black Americans from Colonial Times to the Present.* New York, NY: Doubleday.

Wear, Delese, Julie M. Aultman, and Nicole J. Borges. 2007. "Retheorizing Sexual Harassment in Medical Education: Women Students' Perceptions at Five U.S. Medical Schools." *Teaching & Learning in Medicine* 19(1):20–29. doi: 10.1207/s15328015tlm1901_5.

Weber, Max. 1978(1921). *Economy and Society: An Outline of Interpretive Sociology.* Translated by E. b. G. R. a. C. Wittich. Berkeley, CA: University of California Press.

Weber, Zachary A., Jessica Skelley, Gloria Sachdev, Mary Ann Kliethermes, Starlin Haydon-Greatting, Binita Patel, and Samantha Schmidt. 2015. "Integration of Pharmacists into Team-based Ambulatory Care Practice Models." *American Journal of Health-System Pharmacy* 72:745–751.

Welsh, Brandon C., Anthony A. Braga and Christopher J. Sullivan. 2014. "Serious Youth Violence and Innovative Prevention: On the Emerging Link between Public Health and Criminology." *JQ: Justice Quarterly* 31(3):500–523. doi: 10.1080/07418825.2012.690441.

Wertz, Richward W., and Dorothy C. Wertz. 1989. *Lying In: A History of Childbirth in America.* New Haven, CT: Yale University Press.

Weston, Maria J. 2010. "Strategies for Enhancing Autonomy and Control Over Nursing Practice." *OJIN: The Online Journal of Issues in Nursing* 15:http://www.nursingworld.org/MainMenuCategories/ANAMarketplace/ANAPeriodicals/OJIN/TableofContents/Vol152010/No1Jan2010/Enhancing-Autonomy-and-Control-and-Practice.html.

Whooley, Owen. 2013. *Knowledge in the Time of Cholera: The Struggle over American Medicine in the Nineteenth Century.* Chicago: University of Chicago Press.

Wikiquote. 2014, "M*a*S*H (Tv Series)." Retrieved January 2, 2015 from Http://En.Wikiquote.Org/W/Index.Php?Title=M*a*S*H_(Tv_Series)&Oldid=1811290. Retrieved January 2, 2015.

Wilde, Mary H., Donna Z. Bliss, Joanne Booth, Francine M. Cheater, and Cara Tannenbaum. 2014. "Self-Management of Urinary and Fecal Incontinence." *AJN, American Journal of Nursing* 114:38–45.

Wiley, Andrea S., and John S. Allen. 2013. *Medical Anthropology: A Biocultural Approach.* New York, NY: Oxford University Press.

Williams, David R. 2012. "Miles to Go before We Sleep: Racial Inequities in Health." *Journal of Health and Social Behavior* 53:279–295.

Williams, David R., and Chiquita Collins. 2001. "Racial Residential Segregation: A Fundamental Cause of Racial Disparities in Health." *Public Health Reports* 116:404–416.

Williams, David R., and Michelle Sternthal. 2010. "Understanding Racial-Ethnic Disparities in Health: Sociological Contributions." *Journal of Health and Social Behavior* 51(S):S15–S27.

Williams, Stacy L., Laura Pecenco, and Mary Blair-Loy. 2013. *Medical Professions: The Status of Women and Men.* San Diego: Center for Research on Gender in the Professions, University of California-San Diego.

Wilper, Andrew P., Steffie Woolhandler, Karen E. Lasser, Danny McCormick, David H. Bor, and David U. Himmelstein. 2009. "Health Insurance and Mortality in Us Adults." *American Journal of Public Health* 99(12):1–7.

Winnick, Terrie A. 2013. "From Quackery to 'Comlementary' Medicine: The American Medical Profession Confronts Alternative Therapies." Pp. 282–298 in *The Sociology of Health & Illness*, edited by PeterConrad and V. Leiter. New York, NY: Worth Publishers.

WOAI. 2015. "Local Doctors Say Obamacare Physician Rules Are Arbitrary, Restrictive."http://

www.woai.com/articles/woai-local-news-sponsored-by-five-119078/local-doctors-say-obamacare-physician-rules-13729761/.

Wodtke, Geoffrey T., David J. Harding and Felix Elwert. 2011. "Neighborhood Effects in Temporal Perspective: The Impact of Long-Term Exposure to Concentrated Disadvantage on High School Graduation." *American Sociological Review* 76(5):713–736. doi: 10.1177/0003122411420816.

Wong, Edward. 2014. "Most Chinese Cities Fail Minimum Air Quality Standards, Study Says." *The New York Times* March 28:A8.

Wood, Skip. 2014. "Wayne Curry, former Prince George's County Executive, dead at 63." http://www.wjla.com/articles/2014/07/wayne-curry-former-prince-george-s-county-executive-dead-at-63-104704.html#ixzz37N-jQbR00.Woods, L. M., B. Rachet and M. P. Coleman. 2006. "Origins of Socio-Economic Inequalities in Cancer Survival: A Review." *Annals of Oncology* 17:5–19.

Woolf, Steven H., and Laudan Aron. 2013. "U.S. Health in International Perspective: Shorter Lives, Poorer Health." Washington, DC: National Academies Press.

World Health Organization. 2013. "Lead Poisoning and Health." http://www.who.int/mediacentre/factsheets/fs379/en/.

———. 2014, "Public Health". Available: Http://Www.Who.Int/Trade/Glossary/Story076/En/.

———. 2014. "Ambient (Outdoor) Air Quality and Health." http://www.who.int/mediacentre/factsheets/fs313/en/.

———. 2014a. "Children's Environmental Health." http://www.who.int/features/factfiles/children_environmental_health/en/index.html.

———. 2014b. "Environment and Health in Developing Nations." http://www.who.int/heli/risks/ehindevcoun/en/.

———. 2014c. *Global Update on the Health Sector Response to HIV, 2014.* Geneva: World Health Organization.

———. 2014d. "HIV/AIDS." http://www.who.int/hiv/en/.

———. 2014e. "Identification of Severe Acute Malnutrition in Children 6–59 Months of Age." http://www.who.int/elena/titles/sam_identification/en/.

Wray, Linda A., A. Regula Herzog, Robert J. Willis, and Robert B. Wallace. 1998. "The Impact of Education and Heart Attack on Smoking Cessation Among Middle-Aged Adults." *Journal of Health and Social Behavior* 39:271–294.

Wright, Thomas. 2013. *William Harvey: A Life in Circulation.* New York, NY: Oxford University Press.

Yanga, Yang Claire, Courtney Boena, Karen Gerkena, Ting Lid, Kristen Schorppa and Kathleen Mullan Harris. 2016. "Social Relationships and Physiological Determinants of Longevity across the Human Life Span." *PNAS* doi: 10.1073/pnas.1511085112 http://www.pnas.org/content/early/2016/01/02/1511085112.

Yap, Sheau-Fen and Christina Kwai Choi Lee. 2013. "Does Personality Matter in Exercise Participation?" *Journal of Consumer Behavior* 12:401–411.

Yasmin, Seema. 2014. "Decoding the 'Hispanic Paradox'." *The Dallas Morning News* January 23:http://www.dallasnews.com/opinion/sunday-commentary/20140117-decoding-the-hispanic-paradox.ece.

Yonek, Julie, Stephen Hines, and Maulik Joshi. 2010. *A Guide to Achieving High Performance in Multi-Hospital Health Systems.* Chicago, IL: Health Research & Educational Trust.

Yoon, Paula W., Brigham Bastian, Robert N. Anderson, Janet L. Collins, and Harold W. Jaffe. 2014. "Potentially Preventable Deaths from the Five Leading Causes of Death -- United States, 2008-2010." *MMWR: Morbidity & Mortality Weekly Report* 63:369–374.

You, Danzhen, Tessa Wardlaw, Peter Salama, and Gareth Jones. 2010. "Levels and trends in under-5 mortality, 1990-2008." *Lancet* 375:100–103.

Young, J. T. 2004. "Illness Behaviour: A Selective Review and Synthesis." *Sociology of Health & Illness* 26:1–31.

Young, John Q., Sumant R. Ranji, Robert M. Wachter, Connie M. Lee, Brian Niehaus, and Andrew D. Auerbach. 2011. "'July Effect': Impact of the Academic Year-End Changeover on Patient Outcomes: A Systematic Review." *Annals of Internal Medicine* 155:309–315.

Zborowski, Mark. 1952. "Cultural Components in Responses to Pain." *Journal of Social Issues* 8:16–30.

Zhang, Zhenmei, Mark Hayward and Chuntain Lu. 2012. "Is There a Hispanic Epidemiological Paradox in Later Life? A Closer Look at Chronic Morbidity." *Research on Aging* 34:548–571.

Ziguras, Christopher. 2004. *Self-Care: Embodiment, Personal Autonomy and the Shaping of Health Consciousness.* New York, NY: Routledge.

Zimring, Franklin E., and Gordon Hawkins. 1997. *Crime Is Not the Problem: Lethal Violence in America.* New York, NY: Oxford University Press.

Index